Fodor's

MOSCOW &
ST. PETERSBURG

8th Edition

Where to Stay and Eat
for All Budgets

Must-See Sights
and Local Secrets

Ratings You Can Trust

Fodor's Travel Publications   New York, Toronto, London, Sydney, Auckland
www.fodors.com

FODOR'S MOSCOW & ST. PETERSBURG

Editor: Salwa Jabado

Editorial Production: Linda Schmidt
Editorial Contributors: Matt Brown, Ira Iosebashvili, Anna Malpas, Kevin O'Flynn, Irina Titova, Oksana Yablokova
Maps & Illustrations: David Lindroth, *cartographer*; Bob Blake, Rebecca Baer, and William Wu *map editors*
Design: Fabrizio LaRocca, *creative director*; Guido Caroti, Siobhan O'Hare, *art directors*; Tina Malaney, Chie Ushio, Ann McBride, *designers*; Melanie Marin, *senior picture editor*; Moon Sun Kim, *cover designer*
Cover Photo (The Assumption Cathedral, Kremlin, Moscow): Andrew McConnell/Alamy
Production/Manufacturing: Matthew Struble

8th Edition

ISBN 978–1–4000–0717–2

ISSN 1538–6082

SPECIAL SALES

This book is available at special discounts for bulk purchases for sales promotions or premiums. Special editions, including personalized covers, excerpts of existing books, and corporate imprints, can be created in large quantities for special needs. For more information, write to Special Markets/Premium Sales, 1745 Broadway, MD 6-2, New York, New York 10019, or e-mail specialmarkets@randomhouse.com.

AN IMPORTANT TIP & AN INVITATION

Although all prices, opening times, and other details in this book are based on information supplied to us at press time, changes occur all the time in the travel world, and Fodor's cannot accept responsibility for facts that become outdated or for inadvertent errors or omissions. So **always confirm information when it matters,** especially if you're making a detour to visit a specific place. Your experiences—positive and negative— matter to us. If we have missed or misstated something, **please write to us.** We follow up on all suggestions. Contact the Moscow & St. Petersburg editor at editors@fodors.com or c/o Fodor's at 1745 Broadway, New York, NY 10019.

PRINTED IN THE UNITED STATES OF AMERICA
10 9 8 7 6 5 4 3 2 1

Be a Fodor's Correspondent

Your opinion matters. It matters to us. It matters to your fellow Fodor's travelers, too. And we'd like to hear it. In fact, we need to hear it.

When you share your experiences and opinions, you become an active member of the Fodor's community. That means we'll not only use your feedback to make our books better, but we'll publish your names and comments whenever possible. Throughout our guides, look for "Word of Mouth," excerpts of your unvarnished feedback.

Here's how you can help improve Fodor's for all of us.

Tell us when we're right. We rely on local writers to give you an insider's perspective. But our writers and staff editors—who are the best in the business—depend on you. Your positive feedback is a vote to renew our recommendations for the next edition.

Tell us when we're wrong. We're proud that we update most of our guides every year. But we're not perfect. Things change. Hotels cut services. Museums change hours. Charming cafés lose charm. If our writer didn't quite capture the essence of a place, tell us how you'd do it differently. If any of our descriptions are inaccurate or inadequate, we'll incorporate your changes in the next edition and will correct factual errors at fodors.com immediately.

Tell us what to include. You probably have had fantastic travel experiences that aren't yet in Fodor's. Why not share them with a community of like-minded travelers? Maybe you chanced upon a beach or bistro or B&B that you don't want to keep to yourself. Tell us why we should include it. And share your discoveries and experiences with everyone directly at fodors.com. Your input may lead us to add a new listing or highlight a place we cover with a "Highly Recommended" star or with our highest rating, "Fodor's Choice."

Give us your opinion instantly at our feedback center at www.fodors.com/feedback. You may also e-mail editors@fodors.com with the subject line "Moscow & St. Petersburg Editor." Or send your nominations, comments, and complaints by mail to Moscow & St. Petersburg Editor, Fodor's, 1745 Broadway, New York, NY 10019.

You and travelers like you are the heart of the Fodor's community. Make our community richer by sharing your experiences. Be a Fodor's correspondent.

Happy Traveling!

Tim Jarrell, Publisher

CONTENTS

ABOUT THIS BOOK

Our Ratings

Sometimes you find terrific travel experiences and sometimes they just find you. But usually the burden is on you to select the right combination of experiences. That's where our ratings come in.

As travelers we've all discovered a place so wonderful that its worthiness is obvious. And sometimes that place is so unique that superlatives don't do it justice: you just have to be there to know. These sights, properties, and experiences get our highest rating, **Fodor's Choice**, indicated by orange stars throughout this book.

Black stars highlight sights and properties we deem **Highly Recommended**, places that our writers, editors, and readers praise again and again for consistency and excellence.

By default, there's another category: any place we include in this book is by definition worth your time, unless we say otherwise. And we will.

Disagree with any of our choices? Care to nominate a place or suggest that we rate one more highly? Visit our feedback center at www.fodors.com/feedback.

Budget Well

Hotel and restaurant price categories from ¢ to $$$$ are defined in the opening pages of each chapter. For attractions, we always give standard adult admission fees; reductions are usually available for children, students, and senior citizens. Want to pay with plastic? **AE, D, DC, MC, V** following restaurant and hotel listings indicate whether American Express, Discover, Diners Club, MasterCard, and Visa are accepted.

Restaurants

Unless we state otherwise, restaurants are open for lunch and dinner daily. We mention dress only when there's a specific requirement and reservations only when they're essential or not accepted—it's always best to book ahead.

Hotels

Hotels have private bath, phone, TV, and air-conditioning and operate on the European Plan (aka EP, without meals), unless we specify that they use the Continental Plan (CP, with a Continental breakfast), Breakfast Plan (BP, with a full breakfast), or Modified American Plan (MAP, with breakfast and dinner) or are all-inclusive (AI, including all meals

and most activities). We always list facilities but not whether you'll be charged to use them.

Many Listings

★	Fodor's Choice
★	Highly recommended
⊠	Physical address
✛	Directions
⌖	Mailing address
☎	Telephone
🖷	Fax
⊕	On the Web
✆	E-mail
🖃	Admission fee
☉	Open/closed times
Ⓜ	Metro stations
⊟	Credit cards

Hotels & Restaurants

🏠	Hotel
⌖	Number of rooms
⚭	Facilities
⦿|	Meal plans
✕	Restaurant
⌂	Reservations
⌇	Smoking
🄱🄿	BYOB
✕🏠	Hotel with restaurant that warrants a visit

Outdoors

⚐	Golf
⛺	Camping

Other

☾	Family-friendly
⇨	See also
⊠	Branch address
☞	Take note

WHAT'S WHERE

MOSCOW	Cosmopolitan in flavor, Moscow exudes prosperity and vigor, at least in the center. In the Russian capital things tend to be done on the grand scale. In contrast to reserved and self-contained St. Petersburg (often referred to as the country's "cultural capital"), Moscow seeks to capture rather than captivate, to welcome with a rough bear hug. There's a festive spirit about the ornate churches with shiny golden cupolas, as well as the no-nonsense ambition of the six-lane highways and monumental Stalinist architecture. Even the metro stations are carved in marble. All shades of human nightlife are here—from trendy raves to large-scale popular entertainment. Russian provincials liken the city to Babylon, denouncing its crowded streets, its galloping break-neck pace, its refusal to sleep, and its unfortunate penchant for going over the top. A merchant capital by birth, Moscow was fashioned for big spenders, and money always made the wheels go 'round here. In postcommunist times, it has easily won a place among the world's most expensive cities. The only possible limit is the size of your wallet.
MOSCOW ENVIRONS & THE GOLDEN RING	The Golden Ring is a chain of medieval Russian towns northeast of Moscow. In the 12th to 14th centuries, they were the most important political, religious, and commercial centers in Russia until Moscow usurped all power. Nowadays these ancient enclaves, with no political clout and minimal commercial activity apart from tourism, are great destinations for rolling back the centuries. Their medieval convents, churches, gates, trade chambers, and kremlins form a living encyclopedia of Russian culture. These provincial towns are largely populated by the elderly. Although in Vladimir there are some modern five-story concrete apartment buildings, in the smaller Golden Ring towns like Suzdal many people still live in wooden houses. These are called *izba,* and their interiors and the lifestyle of their occupants differ little from that of their 19th-century ancestors.
ST. PETERSBURG	Serenity and reflection reign in this city. Tsars don't rush—it would be undignified. St. Petersburg was founded as the new capital of the Russian Empire in 1703 by Peter the Great and still carries itself with austere regal grace. So much so that energetic and impatient Muscovite visitors pull faces at the slow and—to them at least—sleepy pace of life.

Many 18th-century European critics mocked Peter the Great for imitating Western cities, suggesting that "the artificial city" would never become the real thing. Now, it attracts more tourists than anywhere else in Russia. A brilliant fusion created by Italian and French architects, St. Petersburg invites comparisons with Amsterdam, Venice, and Stockholm. And yet compared with them it makes surprisingly little use of its abundant waterways. The compact historical center is best explored on foot or from the water and it enthralls with a decadent, aristocratic flair. The delicate classical center has been preserved in its original form, with no ugly modern blocks intruding.

The big attractions here are the pastimes of the nobility—classical concerts, ballet, fine dining, and idyllic promenading in the 19th-century landscape.

SUMMER PALACES & HISTORIC ISLANDS

A sense of St. Petersburg's Imperial history is greatly enhanced by a visit to one of the city's outlying summer residences. Though all enjoy the same aristocratic origins, the fortunes of these places, which are the size of small towns, varied enormously after the Bolshevik revolution. As a result, there are great differences in their appearance and state of repair.

Peterhof (Petrodvorets) and Pushkin (Tsarskoye Selo) have become much-visited museums with impressive promotion budgets. Peterhof's park is Russia's answer to Versailles. The most sumptuous country seat of all is Pushkin's Catherine Palace, housing the legendary Amber Room.

Although it is a UNESCO World Heritage Site, the former royal estate of Lomonosov (Oranienbaum) has attracted little attention from tourists and little care from authorities. The headquarters of a Soviet defense center until 1983, the marvelous palaces were off limits to visitors and crumbled into ruins but are now undergoing restoration. Konstantine Palace languished in a similar state of neglect until Russian businesspeople sponsored its reconstruction, turning the building into a venue for international conferences and major events.

WHEN TO GO

The climate in Russia changes dramatically with the seasons. Both Moscow and St. Petersburg are best visited in late spring or early autumn, just before and after the peak tourist season. The weather is always unpredictable, but you are most apt to encounter pleasantly warm and sunny days in late May and late August. In Moscow, summers tend to be hot, and thunderstorms and heavy rainfall are common in July and August. In St. Petersburg, on the other hand, it rarely gets very hot, even at the height of summer, though you'll likely need an umbrella. If this maritime city is your only destination, try to visit St. Petersburg during the White Nights (June to early July), when the northern day is virtually endless.

In winter months both cities are covered in an attractive blanket of snow, but only the hardiest tourists should visit between late November and early February, when the days are short and dark—extremely so in St. Petersburg—and the weather is often bitterly cold. St. Petersburg is flooded with tourists in the summer months but a foreign language is barely heard in town in winter. The city's most famous cultural institutions have teamed up with leading hotels to offer discounted arts packages under the brand "White Days," a campaign whose success is yet to be determined, to encourage tourism in the winter. New art festivals are launched in winter in an effort to show that St. Petersburg is not a deserted place totally obscured by snow.

Moscow

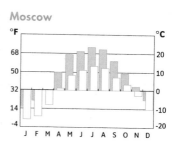

Climate

Forecasts **Weather Channel Connection** (☎900/932-8437, 95¢ per minute ⊕www.weather.com).

QUINTESSENTIAL MOSCOW & ST. PETERSBURG

Festivals

Rio and Venice may have their colorful carnivals, but Russians have something no less amazing up their sleeves—Maslenitsa, or Shrovetide, celebrated on the last week before Lent on the Julian calendar.

Today Shrovetide is a rambunctious outdoor spring festival where Russians indulge in dressing up and wild singing and dancing. Russian *blini* (pancakes), golden and round to symbolize the sun, are served in virtually every eatery across the nation during this week.

The White Nights Festival takes place in St. Petersburg at the end of June. Named in honor of the remarkably long days around the summer solstice, the festival features performances by Russia's top ballet, opera, and musical ensembles, as well as a massive fireworks display once the sun finally does set.

Epic Food

In Russian folk tales, amorous admirers ply their sweethearts with *pryaniki pechatnie* (printed gingerbreads). This ancient Russian culinary delight is a baked sweet pastry filled with honey or jam and flavored with spices; try it at any bakery.

While gingerbread might have done the trick in the olden days, caviar is one of the preferred methods of impressing your darling in modern Russia. It's sold everywhere, from grocery stores to local markets called *rynoks*. The best caviar comes from the beluga variety of sturgeon. It is silvery gray, uniform in size and shape, and tastes like a million bucks.

Another favorite is *kvas,* a refreshing nonalcoholic drink. Kvas, which literally translates as "sour drink," is made with fermented rye bread and is a renowned hangover remedy.

Experience Russia with all your senses and discover what "Russianness" means. We guide you through some of the most exciting pursuits, basic rituals, and beloved symbols of this country.

Vodka

Social lubricant and vice of choice for centuries, the national drink is produced by hundreds of brands and comes in many flavor varieties. A few of the best labels are Flagman, Russky Standart, Beluga, and Beloye Zoloto. If straight shots aren't your thing, flavored vodkas can help take the edge off. *Limonnaya*, slightly sweet lemon-flavor vodka, is particularly tasty, as is spicy *pertsovka*, infused with peppercorns and chilies.

At the bar, toasts such as *Vashe zdorovie!* (To your health!) and clinking glasses accompany every shot as do *zakuski (appetizers)* chasers, which vary from humble pickles to fine caviar. For reasons shrouded in the mists of time, empty bottles are considered bad luck and are immediately discarded or put on the floor, so watch your step and mind your manners.

Banya

Sweaty people whipping themselves with wet bundles of birch twigs in a room full of steam may sound like purgatory or sadomasochism. But for Russians the *banya* experience is the way to nirvana and longevity. Most people in Russia believe the excruciating wet heat of the banya makes you shed toxins ultrafast, through heavy sweating, and that it rejuvenates the internal organs. If you're willing to give it a try, Moscow's ornate Sandunovskiye bani is the gold standard.

The banya also appears in an ancient Russian legend. In the year 945, Olga, widow of Kievan prince Igor, lured his murderers—the elite corps of an East Slavic tribe of Drevlyane—into a banya and set the bathhouse on fire. Meet Russia's first saint.

IF YOU LIKE

Palaces and Estates

Lovers of all things beautiful and luxurious should not miss Russia's imperial estates and palaces. Far from frugal, the tsars truly went all out when it came to their residences. Hiring the world's best architects and using literally tons of gold, marble, and semiprecious stones was only the beginning—these palaces and estates are truly Russian in size as well. Most were built close to Moscow and St. Petersburg as the tsars' summer residences and are therefore just a day trip away from the major cities.

Peterhof (Petrodvorets). Nicknamed the "Russian Versailles," the elaborate interiors, formal gardens, and beautiful fountains of Peter the Great's summer palace live up to their moniker. This is St. Petersburg's most famous imperial residence, located in the suburbs about 40 minutes away.

Pushkin (Tsarskoye Selo). This St. Petersburg palace, with its richly decorated baroque facade, was the favorite residence of the last Russian tsar, Nicholas II. It's main draw is the turquoise and gold Catherine Palace, home to the sumptuous Amber Room.

Romanov Palace Chambers in Zaryadye. Located in Moscow's historic Kitai Gorod neighborhood, this palace-museum gives a taste of the luxurious boyar lifestyle, including period costume, furniture, and household items.

Kuskovo. Pastel pink and neoclassical in style, this estate just outside of Moscow was once the summer residence of the Sheremetyevs, one of Russia's wealthiest and most distinguished families. It also houses the celebrated Kuskovo State Ceramics museum.

Ballet

Classical ballet is the only art form that never really went dissident in Russia. Russia's last tsar, Nicholas II, fell for the charms of ballerina Matilda Kshessinskaya, and from then on, through the Communist era and into the Putin years, ballet and especially ballerinas have been beyond criticism and free from oppression. As ballet has continued to thrive under state sponsorship, it has become an essential part of any official visit, as much a part of protocol as a trip to the war memorials.

Russian ballet is known for its exquisite blend of expressiveness, technique, and ethereal flair. Visiting ballet professionals envy both coordination and torso, the two strongest elements of Russian ballet training. Russian classical ballet, with its antique poetic charm, has preserved its precious legacy without becoming old-fashioned. New stars, such as the amazing Nikolai Tsiskaridze, inject new life into one of Russia's oldest and most respected arts.

Swan Lake. See this signature ballet at the Bolshoi (Moscow) or Mariinsky (St. Petersburg) theaters.

Sleeping Beauty. This marvel of 19th-century choreography has been meticulously restored in its original form at the Mariinsky Theatre in St. Petersburg.

The Nutcracker. The Bolshoi, Mariinsky, and other companies perform this Christmas classic year-round.

Vaganova Ballet Academy in St. Petersburg. Russia's most prestigious classical ballet academy is alma mater to Anna Pavlova, George Balanchine, and Mikhail Baryshnikov. It has a wonderful museum.

Exploring the Communist Legacy

Since the downfall of the Soviet empire, Russia has been struggling to get over its totalitarian past—or so the Western pundits would have you believe. In reality, attitudes toward Soviet times are much more complex, with many people of all ages regarding them as "the good old days." Soviet themes and symbols are everywhere, from old monuments and inscriptions on buildings to the red star, which is still the symbol of the Russian armed forces. There are a handful of Soviet-style bars and clubs as well, although the recent nostalgia for Soviet-era cuisine has, thankfully, come and gone.

KGB Museum, Moscow. Housed in the infamous Lubyanka Square building that served as KGB headquarters since the days of Felix Dzerzhinsky (aka "Iron Felix"), who founded its first incarnation, the CHEKA, in 1917, the KGB museum is a chilling reminder of Russia's often repressive past.

Lenin's Mausoleum, Moscow. Vladimir Lenin has lain in state here since his death in 1924. Though there are no longer endless lines of Russians waiting to view Lenin's body, it is still a pilgrimage site for diehard Communists.

The Seven Sisters, Moscow. The seven legendary skyscrapers which dominate Moscow's skyline were constructed just after World War II by Stalin and intended as a symbol of Soviet power at the beginning of the Cold War.

Russian Political History Museum, St. Petersburg. The only gallery of its kind documents all aspects of the Communist past, from Soviet realism to the paraphernalia of spying to propaganda.

Porcelain and Folk Art

When Catherine the Great ordered her elaborate dinner service from the renowned Imperial Porcelain Manufacturer, porcelain was the exclusive preserve of aristocrats. But since then it has become almost every Russian's favorite gift.

In addition to porcelain, Russia also has a large number of other folk handicrafts, such as Gzhel ceramics, Palekh boxes, and of course, the ubiquitous *matryoshka* doll.

Lomonosov Porcelain Factory. Arguably the most famous porcelain manufacturer in Russia, this St. Petersburg gem was founded in 1744 and owned for a time by the Romanovs. Its patented and instantly recognizable cobalt-blue pattern lends a distinctly Russian flavor to any event.

Palekh Boxes. These beautiful hand-painted lacquer boxes are handicrafts of the Golden Ring towns. They require about two months to create and the finer details are drawn using a special brush made from a squirrel's tail.

Gzhel Ceramics. First manufactured in the village of Gzhel outside of Moscow in the 6th century, this famous white-and-blue pottery may be Russia's oldest folk art.

Matryoshka. Dating from 1890, these nesting dolls are a relatively new Russian handicraft. The largest wooden doll opens to reveal ever-smaller wooden figures inside. They usually depict red-cheeked, brightly dressed peasant women, although matryoshkas can be purchased featuring everyone from Soviet leaders to Star Wars characters.

GREAT ITINERARIES

Russia may span 11 time zones and two continents, but it's still possible to take in the sights of two major cities and a bit of countryside in just six days.

Day 1: The Kremlin, Moscow

Devote this day to exploration of the Kremlin museums and cathedrals. Stroll through Red Square, St. Basil's Cathedral, and the shopping arcades of GUM. Admire the crowns of the Russian tsars at the Armory Palace. If you're into treasures, don't miss the notorious 190-carat Orlov Diamond at the Diamond Fund. Lenin's Mausoleum is entirely optional. Take a ride on the world's most opulent and ornate metro, with its marble columns, mosaic panoramas, elaborate chandeliers, and quirky Soviet-era monuments. If you have any energy left, spend the evening at the Bolshoi Theatre.

Logistics: The most fascinating metro stations are on the brown circle line (#5). Mayakovskaya and Ploshchad Revolutsii are also exciting. The Armory is closed on Thursday, and the Mausoleum, open Tuesday through Sunday, closes at 1 PM.

Day 2: Old Moscow

Discover old Moscow: wander through the winding narrow streets and visit the ancient churches of Kitai Gorod and pass through the cheerful Old Arbat. Make a pilgrimage to the sad and stately 1524 New Maiden's Convent, a refuge for exiled noble women in the tsarist era. Be sure to see the Romanov Palace Chambers in Zaryadye, the impressive 16th-century palace of the Romanov boyars, and the home of the Romanov family before they made it to the throne. End your day with a steam at a banya—the palatial, venerable Sandunovskiye bani has been considered the best in Russia since the 19th century.

Logistics: The Romanov palace is open to groups with reservations during the week and Saturday; Sunday is the best day for individual visitors. It costs from 800 to 1,000 rubles per person to visit Sandunovskiye bani.

Day 3: Tretyakov Gallery & Cathedral of Christ Our Savior

Spend the morning at the Tretyakov Gallery, which has one of the finest collections of Russian art. To feel the vigor of the new Moscow, head to the resurrected Cathedral of Christ Our Savior, demolished in 1931 and rebuilt from scratch. Travel to St. Petersburg on the stylish Nikolayevsky Express, fashioned to resemble an early-20th-century train and named after Russia's last tsar, Nicholas II.

Logistics: Nikolayevsky Express leaves from Moscow daily at 11:30 PM, and gets to St. Petersburg at 7:40 AM. A second train departs from St. Petersburg at 11:30 PM and arrives in Moscow at 7:40 AM.

Day 4: St. Petersburg from Above & the Hermitage

For an invigorating start, climb the 260 steps to the colonnade of St. Isaac's Cathedral for a fabulous all-around panorama of the historical center. Then head to the State Hermitage Museum. But don't try to rush through this huge place all in one go. Make a list of your favorite things and return when you can. In the evening attend a performance at the Mariinsky Theatre, and take a short detour before the start of the show to visit the magnificent 18th-century St. Nicholas (patron saint of sailors) Cathedral.

Logistics: The Hermitage is free on the first Thursday of every month.

Day 5: Icons, Onion Domes & Peter and Paul Fortress

Culture vultures should begin the day at the State Museum of Russian Art, home to the world's largest collection of Russian art, from icons to avant-garde to socialist realism. The brightly colored onion domes of the Church of the Savior on Spilled Blood are just around the corner. In good weather, spend an hour observing the city from the water on one of the many boat trips. Visit the Peter and Paul Fortress in the late afternoon. Sightseeing can be continued even during a meal. The Bessonnitsa ("Insomnia") restaurant next to the fortress overlooks the Hermitage, Admiralty, and the Strelka.

Logistics: The quickest way to get to the Peter and Paul Fortress from Nevsky Prospect is to travel one stop by metro and get off at Gorkovskaya. When you get out of the station, turn right and walk through a little park until you reach the fortress.

Day 6: A Palace Visit

Devote the day to a trip to one of the former royal residences. Choose Pushkin (Tsarskoye Selo) in winter and Peterhof (Petrodvorets) in summer.

Logistics: It takes 30 minutes to get to Peterhof by hydrofoils departing from several quays along Dvortsovaya embankment, near the Hermitage and the Bronze Horseman.

TIPS

■ All top tourist sights and central metro stations in both cities are notorious for pickpockets. Be extra careful.

■ To save time and money, buy tickets for Moscow's Bolshoi and St. Petersburg's Mariinsky theaters online at ⊕ www.bolshoi.ru and ⊕ www.mariinsky.ru.

■ To prepare best for the Russian banya, go to the Sandunovskiye bani's Web site (⊕ www.sanduny.ru) and read the expertly written "secrets" section (available in English).

■ Be sure to bring an umbrella. According to the latest research, St. Petersburg boasts a pathetic 30–40 cloudless days a year.

■ Consider staying in one of St. Petersburg's more than 200 mini-hotels—small, 8–10 room guesthouses that offer an intimate alternative to the city's major hotels. Most are centrally located, reasonably priced, and if you travel in a group, you could have the property all to yourselves.

■ Alcohol counterfeiting, which can lead to alcohol poisoning, is a problem, so try to purchase vodka from a reputable-looking store or, if buying from a kiosk, check to see that the seal has not been broken.

■ In some museums, galleries, and palaces, such as the Tretyakov Gallery, you may be asked to put on plastic booties, similar to the kind surgeons wear, over your shoes before entering the gallery. When entering a Russian home, always remove your shoes at the entryway.

ON THE CALENDAR

	With the demise of the Soviet Union and the accompanying religious revival, church holy days are now more widely celebrated than traditional political holidays. These days, November 7, the anniversary of the Bolshevik Revolution, merits only a rally of the Communist supporters. But within St. Petersburg, November 7 is now celebrated as the anniversary of the city's renaming from Leningrad back to St. Petersburg. Listed below are major holidays celebrated in Russia.
WINTER Dec.	**December Nights** is a monthlong festival of music, dance, theater, and art held in Moscow.
	New Year's Eve is a favorite holiday marked by merrymaking and family gatherings. Friends and family exchange small gifts, putting them under a New Year's tree (the Russian version of a Christmas tree), a tradition that began when Christmas and other religious holidays were not tolerated by the Soviet authorities.
Dec.–Jan.	The **International Arts Square Festival** is a classical music festival at the St. Petersburg Philharmonic.
Jan.	New Year's Eve is celebrated twice—first on December 31, with the rest of the world, and then again on January 13, **"Old" New Year's Eve** (according to the Julian calendar used in Russia until the revolution).
	Russian Orthodox Christmas has become an increasingly important holiday and is celebrated on January 7 with lights, *yolkas* (fir trees), and modest gifts under the tree.
Feb.	February 23, **Defenders of the Fatherland Day** *(formerly Soviet Army and Navy Day)*, is somewhat similar to Father's Day in the United States. Even though not every man ends up in the army, the holiday traditionally honors all men, not just members of the military. The day ends with fireworks in the evening.
Feb.–Mar.	**Shrovetide (Maslenitsa)** *(Butter Week)* is a Slavic version of Carnival that takes place the week before Lent. It's largely a celebration of the sun and spring—hence the round, sunshape *blini* (pancakes) that are consumed in massive amounts this week.
	St. Petersburg Tennis Cup, Russia's second-largest tennis tournament, is held in the waning days of winter.

Mar.	March 8, **International Women's Day,** is a popular holiday similar to Mother's Day, but honoring all women, especially wives. Giving a gift of flowers or a torte to female friends is de rigueur for men.
SPRING Mar.–Apr.	**Orthodox Easter,** which generally falls a few weeks after Easter in the West, is a major national holiday in Russia. Festive church services begin at midnight and run through the night.
Apr.	St. Petersburg's **Spring Jazz Festival** brings together the finest jazz performers from across Russia.
May	**Prazdnik Vesny** *(Spring Holiday)* on May 1, is a celebration of spring; in Soviet times this holiday was observed as International Labor Day.
	May 9, **Victory Day,** is one of the country's most important holidays; World War II veterans appear on the streets decked out in their medals and are honored throughout the day at open-air festivals and parades.
	The Mariinsky's Valery Gergiev started the **Easter Festival** in Moscow. The program, played by top classical musicians, devotes special attention to spiritual–religious music (orthodox chants and bell-ringing concerts).
	St. Petersburg City Day is May 27.
	May 30, the **Day of Kostroma,** celebrates the anniversary of this city northeast of Moscow; the celebration usually stretches for three days.
	Yaroslavl celebrates its founding on May 31, the **Day of Yaroslavl.**
SUMMER June	The first Sunday of June is the **Festival of Pushkin's Poetry,** celebrated in the poet's hometown of Pskov.
	June 12 is **Russian Independence Day.**
	The International Moscow Film Festival is an annual event showcasing both international and Russian film offerings.
	Ivan Kupala Day (June 24) is based on a pagan celebration of the summer solstice that has had Christian tones superimposed on it.

	In St. Petersburg, the **White Nights Music Festival**—with jazz, fine arts, and film events—is held during the whole of June.
July	The last Sunday in July in St. Petersburg is **Fleet Day,** with wonderful naval parades and celebrations at the mouth of the Neva.
Late Aug.–early Sept.	Moscow's **International Chekhov Theater Festival** highlights but is not limited to plays by Chekhov.
FALL Sept.	Thousands of Muscovites take to the streets the first weekend of September to celebrate **Moscow City Day,** with parades, performances, competitions, and sports events. Local motorists rue the day the capital was founded, since City Day events close most of the main thoroughfares. September 12, **Alexander Nevsky Day,** which is centered on St. Petersburg's Alexander Nevsky Square, is an annual festival with a typically Russian flavor, featuring brass bands and choruses. Alexander Nevsky was a medieval ruler who defended the country from German invaders. The **New Drama Festival** in Moscow showcases cutting-edge Russian plays staged by prominent Moscow companies.
Oct.	The **Kremlin Cup,** Russia's biggest tennis tournament, is held every October at Moscow's Olympisky Sports Complex.
Nov.	November 7, **Day of Reconciliation and Agreement,** formerly celebrated as the anniversary of the Bolshevik Revolution, is mainly now an excuse for a day off, and for pro- and anti-Communist demonstrations.
Nov.–Dec.	**The Cup of Russia,** an international ice-skating competition and part of the ISU Grand Prix of Figure Skating, is held in St. Petersburg.

MOSCOW

WORD OF MOUTH

"Moscow is huge, busy and fascinating. It is like New York in terms of crowds, traffic, and pace. If you enjoy the hustle and bustle of the world's largest cities consider Moscow. . . . It is the heart of Russia, everything important in Russia happens there."

—John_R

"Don't miss the Metro in Moscow. On certain runs we saw art that is in no museum we've ever visited. Bronze, mosaics, frescos . . . absolutely amazing."

—Katherinemaepardee

Updated
by Ira
Iosebashvili,
Anna Malpas,
Kevin O'Flynn,
and Oksana
Yablokova

IT MAY BE DIFFICULT FOR Westerners to appreciate what an important place Moscow holds in the Russian imagination as a symbol of spiritual and political power. Throughout much of its history the city was known as Holy Moscow, and was valued as a point of pilgrimage not unlike Jerusalem, Mecca, or Rome. Founded in the 12th century as the center of one of several competing minor principalities, Moscow eventually emerged as the heart of a unified Russian state in the 15th century. One hundred years later it had grown into the capital of a strong and prosperous realm, one of the largest in the world. Although civil war and Polish invasion ravaged the city in the early 17th century, a new era of stability and development began with the establishment of the Romanov dynasty in 1613.

The true test for Moscow came under Peter the Great (1672–1725). Profoundly influenced by his exposure to the West, Peter deliberately turned his back on the old traditions and established his own capital— St. Petersburg—on the shores of the Baltic Sea. Yet Western-looking St. Petersburg never succeeded in replacing Moscow as the heart and soul of the Russian nation. Moscow continued to thrive as an economic and cultural center, despite its demotion. More than 200 years later, within a year of the Bolshevik Revolution in 1917, the young Soviet government restored Moscow's status as the nation's capital. In a move just as deliberate as Peter the Great's, the new Communist rulers transferred the seat of government back to the Russian heartland, away from the besieged frontier and Russia's imperial past.

Moscow thus became the political and ideological center of the vast Soviet empire. And even though it has been nearly two decades since that empire broke apart, the city retains its political, industrial, and cultural sway as Russia's capital. With a population of more than 10 million, Moscow is Russia's largest city and the site of some of the country's most renowned cultural institutions, theaters, and film studios. It's also the country's most important transportation hub—even today most flights to the former Soviet republics are routed through Moscow's airports. To salvage and propel Russia's giant economy, the government and business communities of Moscow are actively pursuing outside investments and setting their own economic plans and agendas. For visitors this translates into a modern, fast-paced city with increased availability of Western-style services and products. Even as Moscow becomes a hub of international business activity, however, the metropolis is determinedly holding onto its Russian roots.

As Russia enters the 21st century, development and reconstruction are at an all-time high. Parts of the city, especially within the Boulevard Ring (Bulvarnoye Koltso), are now sparkling clean and well kept. Although the Russians are protecting some of their architectural heritage, they're also creating a new, often controversial legacy, in the form of skyscrapers, shopping malls, and churches. Many of these buildings are designed to be harmonious with the ancient Russian style, but there's a growing number of shockingly modern steel-and-glass office towers, particularly in central Moscow. The 21st century promises growth, excitement, and hurdles to overcome. Moscow is ready.

TOP REASONS TO GO

Red Square at Night: The heart of Russia is transformed at night by the glowing red stars atop the Kremlin towers and the lit-up fairy-tale onion domes of St. Basil's Cathedral.

Chekhov to Tchaikovsky: Tapping into the thriving arts scene in Moscow is easy; choosing from among your many options is the hard part. Be it a play at the Moscow Art Theater, opera or ballet at the Bolshoi Theatre, or classical music at the Conservatory, you won't leave Moscow without a bit of culture.

Hidden City: If you can conquer your fear of getting lost, wandering through the intricate side streets can be a rewarding experience. You may accidentally bump into architectural wonders, like the Melnikov House,

hidden away on Krivoarbatsky pereulok, or find a quiet square or pond such as Patriarch's Pond.

Eating Well: Whether sharing drinks and zakuski (appetizers) with friends, grabbing a blini on the run, or sitting down to a warming bowl of borscht and pelmeni (meat dumplings), dining in Moscow is a truly unique experience.

Church Choirs: Although you can often hear a choir sing in the three cathedrals of the Kremlin, don't let that stop you from visiting the dozens of churches in the city center, such as the Church of the Resurrection on Bryusov pereulok, which can be an oasis of serenity in the bustling city.

EXPLORING MOSCOW

Moscow is an in-your-face metropolis that can often overwhelm with monstrous-size avenues, unbearable traffic jams, and a 24-hour lifestyle à la New York or London that seems to exclude any peace and harmony. But behind that brash facade is a city that has been built up and knocked down and built up again for centuries and where, with a little guidance, a visitor can find those quiet moments of serenity and beauty.

Muscovites often find themselves in new corners of the city that they have never before seen. Don't be afraid to wander off the beaten track, for the city, despite its disorganized and chaotic edge, is organized in a clear manner. Russians often call Moscow a *bolshaya derevnya,* or "big village" and the center itself is a more compact and vital place than many other world capitals.

GETTING ORIENTED

The best way to orient yourself in Moscow is via the city's efficient and highly ornate metro system. Most of the sights in this chapter are located on or within the metro's brown line (#5) which circles the old historic center. Learning the Cyrillic alphabet will prove infinitely useful in helping you to distinguish between metro stops. ◾TIP➔ **When asking locals for directions, it's often more fruitful to discuss locations by the nearest metro stop than by neighborhood names.**

Moscow is laid out in a series of concentric circles that emanate from its heart—the Kremlin/Red Square area. This epicenter, encircled by

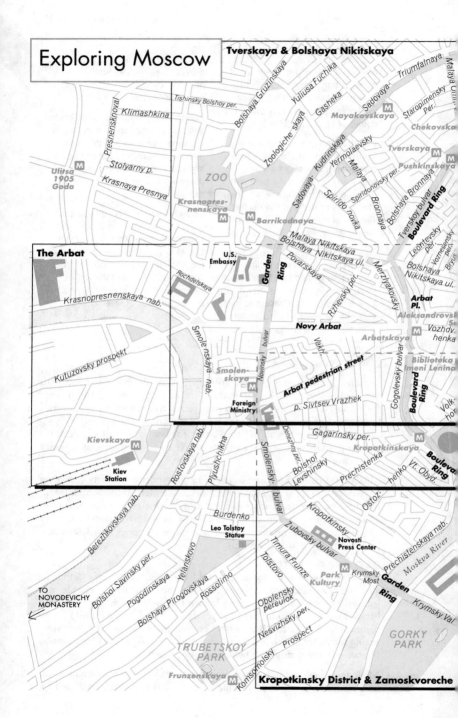

Exploring Moscow

Tverskaya & Bolshaya Nikitskaya

The Arbat

Kropotkinsky District & Zamoskvoreche

TO NOVODEVICHY MONASTERY

Tishinsky Bolshoy per.
Klimashkina
Presnenskova
Ulitsa 1905 Goda
Stolyarny p.
Krasnaya Presnya
ZOO
Krasnopresnenskaya
Barrikadnaya
Bolshaya Gruzinskaya
Yuliusa Fuchika
Gasheka
Mayakovskaya
Sadovaya-
Triumfalnaya
Staropimensky Per.
Malaya Utita
Chekovska
Tverskaya
Pushkinskaya
Zoologicheskaya
Yermolaevsky
Sadovaya- Kudrinskaya
Malaya Bronnaya
Spiridonovsky per.
Bolshaya Bronnaya
Tverskoy bulvar
Boulevard Ring
Spirido novka
Malaya Nikitskaya
Bolshaya Nikitskaya ul.
Povarskaya
Leontevsky per.
Voznesensky per.
Bryus
U.S. Embassy
Garden Ring
Rzhevsky per.
Merzlyakovsky
Bolshaya Nikitskaya ul.
Arbat Pl.
Aleksandrovsk Sa
Rochdelskaya
Krasnopresnenskaya nab.
Novy Arbat
Arbatskaya
Vozhd henka
Kutuzovsky prospekt
Smolenskaya nab.
Novinsky bulvar
Smolenskaya
Vakht.
Arbat pedestrian street
p. Sivtsev Vrazhek
Gogolevsky bulvar
Biblioteka imeni Lenina
Boulevard Ring
Volk hor
Foreign Ministry
Denezhny per.
Gagarinsky per.
Kropotkinskaya
Kievskaya
Kiev Station
Rostovskaya nab.
Plyushchikha
Smolensky-
Bolshoi Levshinsky
Prechistenka
Vt. Obyd.
henko
Ostoz
Bouleva Ring
Berezhkovskaya nab.
Bolshoi Savinsky per.
Pogodinskaya
Yelanskovo
Burdenko
Leo Tolstoy Statue
Kropotkinsky
Zubovsky bulvar
Novosti Press Center
Timura Frunze
Park Kultury
Krymsky Most
Moskva River
Prechistenskaya nab.
Garden Ring
Krymsky Val
Bolshaya Pirogovskaya
Rossolimo
Tolstovo
Obolensky pereulok
Nesvizhsky per.
GORKY PARK
TRUBETSKOY PARK
Frunzenskaya
Komsomolsky Prospect

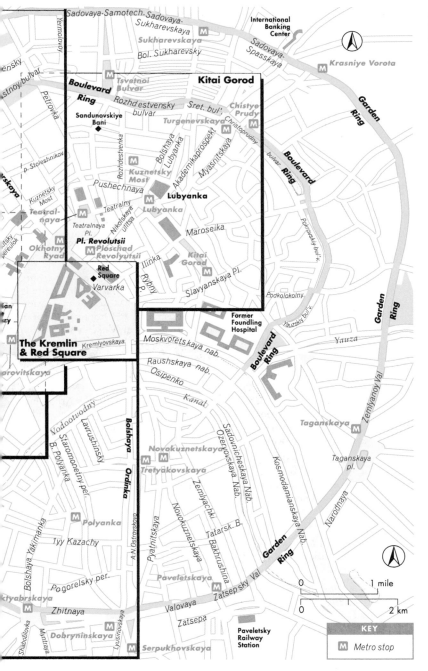

the tree-lined Boulevard Ring (*Bulvarnoye Koltso*), is rich with palaces and churches. Although the individual streets that make up the Boulevard Ring have different names, most of them have the word for boulevard, *bulvar* in their names. The Boulevard Ring passes by stations Arbatskaya, Pushkinskaya, and Chistye Prudy on its way around the city. Much of your time may be spent near metro stop Pushkinskaya, located a few hundred yards up ulitsa Tverskaya, the city's main street which goes north directly from the Kremlin.

Marking the outer edge of the city center is the Garden Ring (*Sadovoe Koltso*), a wide boulevard which sadly has lost all the trees it was once famous for. The metro's brown number 5 line almost follows the route of the Garden Ring. Metro stations Smolenskaya, Barrikadnaya, Mayakovskaya, Sukharevskaya, Krasniye Vorota, Taganskaya, Paveletskaya, Oktyabrskaya, and Park Kultury are all located on the Garden Ring road.

Northeast of the Kremlin/Red Square area and within the Boulevard Ring is Kitai Gorod. This neighborhood began as an outgrowth of the Kremlin and contains sights such as the Bolshoi Theatre, Sandunovskiye Bani, and numerous cathedrals.

North of the Kremlin is the famous northern road to St. Petersburg, Tverskaya ulitsa, which extends from the Kremlin through the Boulevard Ring and out to the Garden Ring. This is Moscow's main shopping street. The Museum of the Contemporary History of Russia on Tverskaya ulitsa provides an interesting look at Moscow's evolution. Farther west is Bolshaya Nikitskaya ulitsa, another main thoroughfare and home to the Tchaikovsky Conservatory.

The next two main streets radiating out of the Kremlin to the west, are the Stary Arbat (Old Arbat) and the Novy Arbat (New Arbat). The Stary Arbat is referred to by Russians simply as "the Arbat" and is a cobblestone pedestrian street with cafés, street performers, and all manner of souvenir shops. Novy Arbat is a modern thoroughfare with casinos and upscale restaurants.

Southwest of the Kremlin, the Kropotkinsky District is home to the Pushkin Museum of Fine Arts and the Tolstoy Memorial Museum. South of the Moskva River, the main area of interest is Zamoskvoreche neighborhood located around the Tretyakovskaya and Polyanka metro stations. Among other sights here are the Tretyakov Gallery and several beautiful churches.

Most of Moscow's major sights, hotels, and restaurants can be found within the above-mentioned neighborhoods. There are a few, however, which lie in the outskirts of the city.

Numbers in the text correspond to numbers in the margin and on the Kremlin & Red Square; Kitai Gorod; Tverskaya & Bolshaya Nikitskaya; The Arbat; and Kropotkinsky District & Zamoskvoreche maps.

GREAT ITINERARIES

You can get a nice introduction to the capitol city in just a few days, leaving time to travel to St. Petersburg.

IF YOU HAVE 3 DAYS

Start with a stroll across Red Square, a tour of St. Basil's Cathedral, the shopping arcades of GUM, and, if you're a devoted student of Soviet history and/or embalming techniques, the Lenin Mausoleum. Then walk through Alexander Garden to reach the tourist entrance to the Kremlin. Plan on spending the better part of your first day exploring the churches, monuments, and exhibits within the grounds of this most famous of Russian fortresses. On the second day, spend the morning sightseeing and shopping on Tverskaya ulitsa. In the afternoon, head to Kitai Gorod; this neighborhood has churches and historic buildings on Varvarka ulitsa, which extends from the eastern edge of Red Square, just behind St. Basil's. Try also, toward the end of the day, to squeeze in a stroll across Teatralnaya Ploshchad to see the Bolshoi and Maly theaters. Devote the third morning to the Tretyakov

Gallery, which has the finest collection of Russian art in the country. In the afternoon stroll down the Arbat, where you can find plenty of options for haggling over Russian souvenirs.

IF YOU HAVE 7 DAYS

Follow the three-day itinerary above. On the fourth day explore Bolshaya Nikitskaya ulitsa, with its enchanting mansions. Devote the fifth day to the Pushkin Museum of Fine Arts and an exploration of some of the streets in the surrounding Kropotkinsky District. Come back the next day and walk from the Russian State Library to the Kropotkinsky District. Be sure to include the Pushkin Memorial Museum and a walk along the Kremlyovskaya naberezhnaya (the embankment of the Moskva River) in the late afternoon for the spectacular views of the cupolas and towers of the Kremlin. Depending on whether your interests tend toward the religious or the secular, you could spend your last day visiting either the New Maiden's Convent and the adjoining cemetery or Gorky Park and the Tolstoy House Estate Museum, where Tolstoy once lived.

HEART OF RUSSIA: THE KREMLIN & RED SQUARE КРЕМЛЬ & КРАСНАЯ ПЛОЩАДЬ

Fodor'sChoice ★ Few places in the world possess the historic resonance of the **Kremlin**, the walled ancient heart of Moscow and the oldest part of the city. The first wooden structure was erected on this site sometime in the 12th century. As Moscow grew, the city followed the traditional pattern of Russian cities, developing in concentric circles around the elevated fortress at its center (*kreml* means "citadel" or "fortress"). After Moscow emerged as the center of a vast empire in the late 15th century, the Kremlin came to symbolize the mystery and power of Russia, as it has ever since. Before the black-suited men of the Bolshevik Revolution took over, tsars were ceremoniously crowned and buried here. In the 20th century the Kremlin became synonymous with the Soviet government, and "Kremlinologists," Western specialists who studied the movements of the politicians in and around the fortress, made careers out of trying to decipher Soviet Russian policies. Much has changed since the Soviet Union broke up, but the Kremlin itself remains mysteriously alluring. A visit to the ancient Kremlin grounds reveals many signs of the old—and new—Russian enigma.

You can buy tickets for the Kremlin grounds and cathedrals at the two kiosks on either side of the Kutafya Tower. Tickets, which cost 300R, grant you access to all the churches and temporary exhibits within the Kremlin. Tickets to the Armory Palace (Oruzheynaya Palata) and Diamond Fund (Almazny Fond) cost extra (350R each); you can buy them at the kiosks or at the entrances to these buildings. Tickets for the Diamond Fund are limited in number and are sold 1½ hours before the four showings each day. Between April and October tickets are also available for a changing-of-the-guard ceremony, which takes place on Saturday at noon. Tickets cost 1,000R and include entry to all the churches and temporary exhibits. Ignore scalpers selling tickets. Keep in mind that you need to buy a 50R ticket if you wish to take pictures with your camera, and that video cameras are not allowed. All heavy bags must be checked for about 60R at the *kamera khraneniya,* which is in Aleksandrovsky Sad (Alexander Garden), to the right down and behind the stairs from the ticket kiosks.

■ TIP→ **The best way to get to the Kremlin/Red Square area is to take the metro to one of the following stations: Ploschad Revolyutsii, Alexsandrovsky Sad, Borovitskaya, or Teatralnaya.**

TIMING Plan to spend a half day, at the very least, touring the Kremlin; budget a full day or more if you want to linger at the museums. The Kremlin grounds and cathedrals are open 10 to 5 every day except Thursday. The Armory Palace and Diamond Fund are also closed on Thursday. Note that the Kremlin occasionally closes on other days for official functions. Check with your hotel concierge.

If you don't want to tackle all of this solo, you should consider a tour of the Kremlin grounds, which includes the Armory Palace, available from virtually any tour service in Moscow. A tour is particularly helpful because there are no signs, in any language, explaining the displays.

Plan to come back in the evening, when Red Square and its surrounding buildings are beautifully illuminated.

MAIN ATTRACTIONS

🄯 **Annunciation Cathedral** *(Blagoveshchensky Sobor,* Благовещенский Собор*).* This remarkable monument of Russian architecture, linking three centuries of art and religion, was the private chapel of the royal family. Its foundations were laid in the 14th century, and in the 15th century a triangular brick church in the early Moscow style was erected on the site. Partially destroyed by fire, it was rebuilt in the 16th century during the reign of Ivan the Terrible, when six gilded cupolas were added. Tsar Ivan would enter the church by the southeast-side porch entrance, built especially for him. He was married three times too many

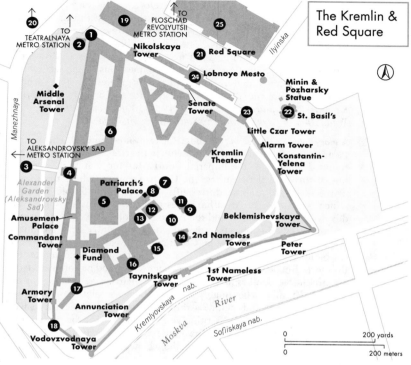

(for a total of six wives) and was therefore, under the bylaws of the Orthodox religion, not allowed to enter the church through its main entrance. The interior is decorated by brilliant frescoes painted in 1508 by the Russian artist Feodosy. The polished tiles of agate jasper covering the floor are said to be a gift from the Shah of Persia. Most striking of all is the chapel's iconostasis. The fine icons of the second and third tiers were painted by some of Russia's greatest masters—Andrei Rublyov, Theophanes the Greek, and Prokhor of Gorodets. ⊠*Kremlin, Kremlin/Red Square* ☎*495/203–0349* ⬚*300R Kremlin ticket* ☉*Fri.– Wed. 10–5* Ⓜ*Aleksandrovsky Sad or Borovitskaya.*

❼ Armory Palace *(Oruzheynaya Palata,* Оружейная Палата*).* The Armory Palace is the oldest and richest museum in the Kremlin. It was originally founded in 1806 as the Imperial Court Museum, which was created out of three royal treasuries: the Court Treasury, where the regalia of the tsars and ambassadorial gifts were kept; the Stable Treasury, which contained the royal harnesses and carriages used by the tsars during state ceremonies; and the Armory, a collection of arms, armor, and other valuable objects gathered from the country's chief armories and storehouses. The Imperial Court Museum was moved to the present building in 1851. It was further enhanced and expanded after the Bolshevik Revolution with valuables confiscated and nationalized from wealthy noble families as well as from the Patriarchal Sacristy of the Moscow Kremlin. The roughly 4,000 artifacts here date from the 12th century to 1917, and include a rare collection of 17th-century silver. The museum tour (at this writing you could only visit the museum by taking one of these tours) begins on the second floor. Halls (*zal*) VI–IX are on the first floor, Halls I–V on the second.

Fodor'sChoice
★

Hall I displays the works of goldsmiths and silversmiths of the 12th through 19th centuries, and **Hall II** contains a collection of 18th- to 20th-century jewelry. One of the most astounding exhibits is the collection of Fabergé eggs on display in Hall II (Case 23). Among them is a silver egg whose surface is engraved with a map of the Trans-Siberian Railway. The "surprise" inside the egg, which is also on display, was a golden clockwork model of a train with a platinum engine, windows of crystal, and a headlight made of a tiny ruby. ■TIP➡ **Feeling overwhelmed by everything to see at the Armory Palace? If nothing else, be sure to see the Fabergé eggs. If the weather is too good to spend all day indoors, check out the splendor of the Cathedral Square and come back to see the Armory another day.**

Hall III contains Asian and Western European arms and armor, including heavy Western European suits of armor from the 15th to 17th centuries; pistols; and firearms.

Hall IV showcases a large collection of Russian arms and armor from the 12th to early 17th centuries, with a striking display of helmets. The earliest helmet here dates from the 13th century. Here, too, is the helmet of Prince Ivan, the son of Ivan the Terrible. The prince was killed by his father at the age of 28, an accidental victim of the tsar's unpredictable rage. The tragic event has been memorialized in a famous painting by Ilya Repin now in the Tretyakov Gallery, showing the frightened tsar holding his mortally wounded son.

Hall V is filled with foreign gold and silver objects, mostly ambassadorial presents to the tsars. Among the displays is the "Olympic Service" of china presented to Alexander I by Napoléon after the signing of the Treaty of Tilsit in 1807.

Hall VI holds vestments of silk, velvet, and brocade, embroidered with gold and encrusted with jewels and pearls.

Hall VII contains regalia and the imperial thrones. The oldest throne, veneered with carved ivory, belonged to Ivan the Terrible. The throne of the first years of Peter the Great's reign, when he shared power with his older brother Ivan, has two seats in front and one hidden in the back. The boys' older sister, Sophia (1657–1704), who ruled as regent from 1682 to 1689, sat in the back, prompting the young rulers to give the right answers to the queries of ambassadors and others. Among the crowns, the oldest is the sable-trimmed Cap of Monomakh, which dates to the 13th century. Also on display in this section are several coronation dresses, including the one Catherine the Great wore in 1762.

Hall VIII contains dress harnesses of the 16th through 18th centuries.

Hall IX has a marvelous collection of court carriages. Here you'll find the Winter Coach that carried Elizaveta Petrovna (daughter of Peter the Great and someone who clearly liked her carriages; 1709–62) from St. Petersburg to Moscow for her coronation. ✉ *Kremlin, Kremlin/Red Square* ☎ *495/202–4631* 💵 *350R, tickets sold one hour before each tour* ⏱ *Fri.–Wed. tours at 10, 12:30, 2:30, and 4:30* Ⓜ *Aleksandrovsky Sad.*

⑫ Assumption Cathedral *(Uspensky Sobor,* Успенский Собор*).* The dominating structure of Cathedral Square is one of the oldest edifices of the Kremlin. Designed after the Uspensky Sobor of Vladimir, it was built in 1475–79 by the Italian architect Aristotle Fiorovanti, who had spent many years in Russia studying traditional Russian architecture. Topped by five gilded domes, the cathedral is both austere and solemn. The ceremonial entrance faces Cathedral Square; the visitor entrance is on the west side (to the left). After visiting the Archangel and Annunciation cathedrals, you may be struck by the spacious interior here, unusual for a medieval church. Light pours in through two rows of narrow

---

FABERGÉ EGGS

Intricate, playful, and exuberantly luxurious, Fabergé eggs were created by the 19th-century jeweler Carl Fabergé for the tsarist family. Alexander III began the tradition by ordering a bejeweled egg as an Easter present for his wife. Sixty-eight eggs in all were created before the Bolshevik Revolution; each one is unique and contains an Easter surprise inside. On display in the Armory Palace are two eggs, one with a train dedicated to the Trans-Siberian Railway, the other with a cruiser ship to commemorate a sea journey made by the Royal Family in 1890.

windows. The cathedral contains rare ancient paintings, including the icon of the Virgin of Vladimir (the work of an 11th-century Byzantine artist), the 12th-century icon of St. George, and the 14th-century Trinity icon. The carved throne in the right-hand corner belonged to Ivan the Terrible, and the gilt wood throne to the far left was the seat of the tsarina. Between the two is the patriarch's throne. Until the 1917 revolution, Uspensky Sobor was Russia's principal church. This is where the crowning ceremonies of the tsars took place, a tradition that continued even after the capital was transferred to St. Petersburg. Patriarchs and metropolitans were enthroned and buried here. After the revolution the church was turned into a museum, but in 1989 religious services were resumed here on major church holidays. ⊠ *Kremlin, Kremlin/Red Square* ☎ *495/203–0349* 🎟 *300R Kremlin ticket* ⊗ *Fri.–Wed. 10–5* Ⓜ *Aleksandrovsky Sad.*

⓮ **Cathedral of the Archangel** (*Arkhangelsky Sobor,* **Архангельский Собор**). This five-dome cathedral was commissioned by Ivan the Great (1440–1505), whose reign witnessed much new construction in Moscow and in the Kremlin in particular. The cathedral was built in 1505–09 to replace an earlier church of the same name. The architect was the Italian Aleviso Novi, who came to Moscow at the invitation of the tsar; note the distinct elements of the Italian Renaissance in the cathedral's ornate decoration, particularly in the scallop-shaped gables on its facade. Until 1712, when the Russian capital was moved to St. Petersburg, the cathedral was the burial place of Russian princes and tsars. Inside there are 46 tombs, including that of Ivan Kalita (Ivan "Moneybags"; circa 1304–40), who was buried in the earlier cathedral in 1340. The tomb of Ivan the Terrible (1530–84) is hidden behind the altar; that of his young son, Dmitry, is under the stone canopy to your right as you enter the cathedral. Dmitry's death at the age of seven is one of the many unsolved mysteries in Russian history. He was the last descendant of Ivan the Terrible, and many believe he was murdered because he posed a threat to the ill-fated Boris Godunov (circa 1551–1605), who at the time ruled as regent. A government commission set up to investigate Dmitry's death concluded that he was playing with a knife and "accidentally" slit his own throat. The only tsar to be buried here after 1712 was Peter II (Peter the Great's grandson; 1715–30), who died of smallpox while visiting Moscow.

The walls and pillars of the cathedral are covered in frescoes that tell the story of ancient Russian history. The original frescoes, painted right after the church was built, were repainted in the 17th century by a team of more than 50 leading artists from several Russian towns. Restoration work in the 1950s uncovered some of the original medieval frescoes, fragments of which can be seen in the altar area. The pillars are decorated with figures of warriors; Byzantine emperors; the early princes of Kievan Rus' (the early predecessor of modern-day Russia and Ukraine), Vladimir and Novgorod; as well as the princes of Moscow, including Vasily III, the son of Ivan the Great. The frescoes on the walls depict religious scenes, including the deeds of Archangel Michael. The carved baroque iconostasis is 43 feet high and dates from the

19th century. The icons themselves are mostly 17th century, although the revered icon of Archangel Michael is believed to date to the 14th century. ⊠*Kremlin, Kremlin/Red Square* ☎495/203–0349 ⊡*300R Kremlin ticket* ⊙*Fri.–Wed. 10–5* Ⓜ*Aleksandrovsky Sad.*

NEED A BREAK? **There are plenty of outdoor cafés along the side of the Manezh closest to the Kremlin, but if it's sunny, head up to 5 Kamergersky ulitsa, the second street on your right as you go up ulitsa Tverskaya and grab a bite from the sandwich shop Prime Star. You can sit outside here or return to Aleksandrovsky Sad and picnic on the lawn.**

❿ Cathedral Square (*Sobornaya Ploshchad,* Соборная Площадь). This paved square, the ancient center of the Kremlin complex, is framed by three large cathedrals in the old Russian style, the imposing Ivan the Great Bell Tower, and the Palace of Facets. A changing-of-the-guard ceremony takes place in the square every Saturday at noon in the summer months. ⊠*Kremlin, Kremlin/Red Square* ☎*No phone* Ⓜ*Aleksandrovsky Sad.*

★ Diamond Fund (*Almazny Fond,* Алмазный Фонд). In 1922 the fledgling Soviet government established this amazing collection of diamonds, jewelry, and precious minerals. The items on display within the Armory Palace date from the 18th century to the present. Highlights of the collection are the Orlov Diamond, a present from Count Orlov to his mistress, Catherine the Great (1729–96); and the Shah Diamond, which was given to Tsar Nicholas I (1796–1855) by the Shah of Persia as a gesture of condolence after the assassination in 1829 of Alexander Griboyedov, the Russian ambassador to Persia and a well-known poet. ⊠*Armory Palace, Kremlin/Red Square* ☎495/229–2036 ⊡*350R, tickets are limited in number and sold 1 ½ hours before the four showings each day* ⊙*Fri.–Wed. 10–5* Ⓜ*Aleksandrovsky Sad.*

⓰ Great Kremlin Palace (*Bolshoi Kremlyovsky Dvorets,* Большой Кремлевский Дворец). The palace actually consists of a group of buildings. The main section is the newest, built between 1838 and 1849. Its 375-foot-long facade faces south, overlooking the Moskva River. This was for centuries the site of the palace of the grand dukes and tsars, but the immediate predecessor of the present building was badly damaged in the 1812 conflagration. It's currently closed to the general public.

The other buildings of the Great Kremlin Palace include the 17th-century **Terem** (Tower Chamber), where the tsarina received visitors, and the 15th-century **Granovitaya Palata** (Palace of Facets). Both of these buildings are also closed to the public. ⊠*Kremlin, Kremlin/Red Square* ☎495/203–0349 Ⓜ*Aleksandrovsky Sad.*

㉕ GUM (ГУМ). Pronounced "goom," the initials are short for Gosudarstvenny Universalny Magazin, or State Department Store. This staggeringly enormous emporium, formerly called the Upper Trading Rows, was built in 1889–93 and has long been one of the more famous sights of Moscow. Three long passages with three stories of shops run the length of the building. A glass roof covers each passage, and there are balconies and bridges on the second and third tiers. Another series of passages runs perpendicular to the three main lines, creating a maze-like mall. In feel, it resembles a cavernous turn-of-the-20th-century European train station. There are shops (both Western and Russian) aplenty here now, and a saunter down at least one of the halls is enjoyable. The elegant Bosco restaurant on the ground floor has a small summer terrace that looks out onto Red Square. ⊠*3 Red Sq., Kremlin/Red Square* ☎*495/929–3470* ◷*Mon.–Sat. 9–9, Sun. 10–8* Ⓜ*Ploshchad Revolutsii.*

⑲ **Historical Museum** *(Istorichesky Muzey,* **Исторический Музей***).* This redbrick museum was built in 1874–83 in the pseudo-Russian style, which combined a variety of architectural styles. You may recognize the building's twin towers if you've ever caught clips of Soviet military parades on television. Against the backdrop of the towers' pointed spires, the tanks and missiles rolling through Red Square seemed to acquire even more potency. The museum's extensive archaeological and historical collections and interesting temporary exhibits outline the development of Russia. Also here are a rich collection of Russian arms and weaponry and a restaurant called Krasnaya Ploshchad that uses 200-year-old recipes, including dishes from tsars' coronation menus. ⊠*1/2 Red Sq., Kremlin/Red Square* ☎*495/692–4019* 💳*150R* ◷*Wed.–Sat. 10–6, Sun. 11–8* Ⓜ*Ploshchad Revolutsii.*

⑪ **Ivan the Great Bell Tower** *(Kolokolnya Ivana Velikovo,* **Колокольня Ивана Великого***).* The octagonal main tower of this, the tallest structure in the Kremlin, rises 263 feet. According to a tradition established by Boris Godunov no building in Moscow is allowed to rise higher than the bell tower. The first bell tower was erected on this site in 1329. It was replaced in the early 16th century, during the reign of Ivan the Great (hence the bell tower's name). But it was during the reign of Boris Godunov that the tower received its present appearance. In 1600 the main tower was rebuilt, crowned by an onion-shaped dome and covered with gilded copper. For many years it served as a watchtower; Moscow and its environs could be observed for a radius of 32 km (20 mi). Altogether, the towers have 52 bells, the largest weighing 70 tons. The annex of the bell tower is used for temporary exhibits of items from the Kremlin collection; tickets may be purchased at the entrance. ⊠*Kremlin, Kremlin/Red Square* ☎*495/203–0349* 💳*300R Kremlin ticket* ◷*Fri.–Wed. 10–5* Ⓜ*Aleksandrovsky Sad.*

❸ **Kutafya Tower** *(Kutafya Bashnya,* **Кутафья Башня***).* This white bastion, erected in 1516, once defended the approach to the drawbridge that linked Aleksandrovsky Sad to the Kremlin. In Old Slavonic, *kutafya* means "clumsy" or "confused"; this adjective was applied to the tower because it so differs in shape and size from the other towers of the Kremlin. Kutafya Tower marks the main public entrance to the Kremlin, which opens promptly at 10 AM every day except Thursday. You can buy tickets to the Kremlin grounds and cathedrals at the kiosks on either side of the tower. The guards may ask where you're from and check inside your bags; there's a small security checkpoint to walk through, similar to those at airports. ⊠ *Manezhnaya ul., Kremlin/ Red Square* ☏ *No phone* 💲 *300R Kremlin ticket* ⊗ *Fri.–Wed. 10–5* Ⓜ *Aleksandrovsky Sad.*

㉔ **Lenin Mausoleum** *(Mavzolei Lenina,* **Мавзолей Ленина***).* Except for a brief interval during World War II, when his body was evacuated to the Urals, Vladimir Ilyich Lenin (1870–1924) has lain in state here since his death in 1924. His body is said to be immersed in a chemical bath of glycerol and potassium acetate every 18 months to preserve it. Whether it's really Lenin or a wax

look-alike is probably one of those Russian mysteries that will go down in history unanswered. From 1924 to 1930 there was a temporary wooden mausoleum, which has been replaced by the pyramid-shaped mausoleum you see now. It's made of red, black, and gray granite, with a strip of black granite near the top level symbolizing a band of mourning. Both versions of the mausoleum were designed by one of Russia's most prominent architects, Alexei Shchusev, who also designed the grand Kazansky train station near Komsomolskaya metro station.

In the Soviet past, there were notoriously endless lines of people waiting to view Lenin's body, but this is now rarely the case, although if a large tourist group has just encamped the wait may be long. Now only the curious tourist or the ardent Communist among Russians visits the mausoleum. A visit to the mausoleum, however, is still treated as a serious affair. The surrounding area is cordoned off during visiting hours, and all those entering are observed by uniformed police officers. It's forbidden to carry a camera or any large bag. Inside the mausoleum it's cold and dark. It's considered disrespectful to put your hands inside your pockets (the same applies when you visit an Orthodox church).

Outside the mausoleum you can look at the Kremlin's burial grounds. When Stalin died in 1953, he was placed inside the mausoleum alongside Lenin, but in the early 1960s, during Khrushchev's tenure, the body was removed and buried here, some say encased in heavy concrete. There has been talk of finally burying Lenin, but even in today's Russia this would be a very controversial move, so he is likely to remain in Red Square for some time. Also buried here are such Communist leaders as Zhdanov, Dzerzhinsky, Brezhnev, Chernenko, and Andropov. The American journalist John Reed, friend of Lenin and author of *Ten Days That Shook the World,* an account of the October revolution, is buried alongside the Kremlin wall. Urns set inside the wall contain ashes of the Soviet writer Maxim Gorky; Lenin's wife and collaborator, Nadezhda Krupskaya; Sergei Kirov, the Leningrad Party leader whose assassination in 1934 (believed to have been arranged by Stalin) was followed by enormous purges; the first Soviet cosmonaut,

Yury Gagarin; and other Soviet eminences. ⊠ *Red Sq., Kremlin/Red Square* ☎ *495/923–5527* 🎟 *Free* ⏰ *Tues.–Thurs. and weekends 10–1* Ⓜ *Ploshchad Revolutsii.*

Lobnoye Mesto (Лобное Место). The name of the strange, round, white-stone dais in front of St. Basil's Cathedral literally means "place of the brow," but it has come to mean "execution site," for it is next to the spot where public executions were once carried out. Built in 1534, the dais was used by the tsars as a podium for public speeches and the proclamation of imperial *ukazy* (decrees). When the heir apparent reached the age of 16, he was presented to the people from this platform. ⊠ *Red Sq., Kremlin/Red Square* Ⓜ *Ploshchad Revolutsii.*

Minin and Pozharsky statue (Памятник Минину и Пожарскому). In 1818 sculptor Ivan Martos built this statue, which honors Kuzma Minin (a wealthy Nizhni-Novgorod butcher) and Prince Dmitry Pozharsky, who drove Polish invaders out of Moscow in 1612 during the Time of Troubles. This period of internal strife and foreign intervention began in approximately 1598 with the death of Tsar Fyodor I and lasted until 1613, when the first Romanov was elected to the throne. This was the first monument of patriotism funded by the public. The inscription on the pedestal reads, "To citizen Minin and Prince Pozharsky from a thankful Russia 1818." The statue originally stood in the center of the square, but was later moved to its current spot in front of St. Basil's. In 2005, November 4 was named a new public holiday in honor of Minin and Pozharsky, replacing the old Communist November 7 holiday, which celebrated the anniversary of the Bolshevik Revolution. ⊠ *Red Sq., Kremlin/Red Square* Ⓜ *Ploshchad Revolutsii.*

㉑ **Red Square** *(Krasnaya Ploshchad,* **Красная Площадь***).* World famous for the grand military parades staged here during the Soviet era, this was originally called the Torg, the Slavonic word for marketplace. Many suppose that the name "Red Square" has something to do with Communism or the Bolshevik Revolution. In fact, however, the name dates to the 17th century. The adjective *krasny* originally meant "beautiful," but over the centuries the meaning of the word changed to "red," hence the square's present name. The square is most beautiful and impressive at night, when it's entirely illuminated by floodlights, with the ruby-red stars atop the Kremlin towers glowing against the dark sky. There are five stars in all, one for each of the tallest towers. They made their appearance in 1937 to replace the double-headed eagle, a tsarist symbol that is again an emblem of Russia. The glass stars, which are lighted from inside and designed to turn with the wind, are far from dainty: the smallest weighs a ton. ⊠ *Red Sq., Kremlin/Red Square* ☎ *No phone* Ⓜ *Ploshchad Revolutsii.*

Fodor's Choice
★

㉓ **Resurrection Gates** *(Voskresenskiye Vorota,* **Воскресенские Ворота***).* These gates, which formed part of the Kitai Gorod defensive wall, were named for the icon of the Resurrection of Christ that hangs above them. However, the gates are truly "resurrection" gates; they have been reconstructed many times since they were first built in 1534. In 1680 the gates were rebuilt and a chapel honoring the Iberian Virgin Mary was added. In 1931 they were destroyed by the Soviets. Stalin ordered their demolition partly so that tanks could easily make their way onto Red Square during parades. They were most recently rebuilt in 1994–95. Today the red-brick gates with the bright-green-and-blue chapel dedicated to the Iberian Virgin are truly a magnificent sight and a fitting entrance to Red Square. The bronze compass inlaid in the ground in front of the chapel marks Kilometer Zero on the Russian highway system.

> ## HISTORY OF THE ONION DOME
>
> Historians argue over the origin of the onion dome commonly associated with Russian churches. One theory for the dome shape is that it was simply a way to ensure the snow slid off the church in the winter. Others say that the style was borrowed from the Mongols who enslaved Russia. St. Basil's Cathedral is home to the most famous onion domes in the world.

⊠ *Red Sq., Kremlin/Red Square* 🕾 *No phone* 🕙 *Chapel daily 8* AM–*10* PM Ⓜ *Ploshchad Revolutsii.*

㉒ **St. Basil's Cathedral** (*Pokrovsky Sobor,* **Покровский Собор**). Although Fodor'sChoice it's popularly known as St. Basil's Cathedral, the proper name of this ★ whimsical structure is Church of the Intercession. It was commissioned by Ivan the Terrible to celebrate his conquest of the Tatar city of Kazan on October 1, 1552, the day of the feast of the Intercession. The central chapel, which rises 107 feet, is surrounded by eight towerlike chapels linked by an elevated gallery. Each chapel is topped by an onion dome carved with its own distinct pattern and dedicated to a saint on whose day the Russian army won battles against the Tatars. The cathedral was built between 1555 and 1560 on the site of the earlier Trinity Church, where the Holy Fool Vasily (Basil) had been buried in 1552. Basil was an adversary of the tsar, publicly reprimanding Ivan the Terrible for his cruel and bloodthirsty ways. He was protected, however, from the tsar by his status as a Holy Fool, for he was considered by the Church to be an emissary of God. Ironically, Ivan the Terrible's greatest creation has come to be known by the name of his greatest adversary. In 1558 an additional chapel was built in the northeast corner over Basil's remains, and from that time on the cathedral has been called St. Basil's.

Very little is known about the architect who built the cathedral. It may have been the work of two men—Barma and Postnik—but now it seems more likely that there was just one architect, Postnik Yakovlyev, who went by the nickname Barma. Legend has it that upon completion of the cathedral, the mad tsar had the architect blinded to ensure that he would never create such a masterpiece again.

After the Bolshevik Revolution, the cathedral was closed and in 1929 turned into a museum dedicated to the Russian conquest of Kazan. Although services are held here on Sunday at 10 AM, the museum is still open. The antechamber houses displays outlining the various stages of the Russian conquest of Kazan as well as examples of 16th-century Russian and Tatar weaponry. Another section details the history of the cathedral's construction, with displays of the building materials used. After viewing the museum exhibits, you're free to wander through the cathedral. Compared with the exotic exterior, the dark and simple interiors are somewhat disappointing. The brick walls are decorated with faded flower frescoes. The most interesting chapel is the main one, which contains a 19th-century baroque iconostasis. ⊠ *Red Sq., Kremlin/Red Square* ☎ *495/298–3304* 🎫 *100R* ⊙ *Daily 11–6. Closed 1st Mon. of month* Ⓜ *Ploshchad Revolutsii.*

> **WORD OF MOUTH**
>
> "Saint Basil's in the snow looks like a fairytale."
>
> –katya_NY

❷ Tomb of the Unknown Soldier *(Mogila Neizvestnovo Soldata,* **Могила Неизвестного Солдата***).* Dedicated on May 9, 1967, the 22nd anniversary of the Russian victory over Germany in World War II, this red-granite monument within Alexander Garden contains the body of an unidentified Soviet soldier, one of those who, in autumn 1941, stopped the German attack at the village of Kryukovo, just outside Moscow. To the right of the grave there are six urns holding soil from the six "heroic cities" that so stubbornly resisted the German onslaught: Odessa, Sevastopol, Stalingrad, Kiev, Brest, and Leningrad (St. Petersburg). Very likely, no matter what time of year you are visiting, you'll see at least one wedding party. The young couple in full wedding regalia, along with friends and family, customarily stops here after getting married, leaving behind flowers and snapping photographs along the way. The gray obelisk just beyond the Tomb of the Unknown Soldier was erected in 1918 to commemorate the Marxist theoreticians who contributed to the Bolshevik Revolution. It was created out of an obelisk that had been put up three years earlier, in honor of the 300th anniversary of the Romanov dynasty. ⊠ *Manezhnaya ul. Kremlin/Red Square* ☎ *No phone* Ⓜ *Ploshchad Revolutsii.*

❾ Tsar Bell *(Tsar Kolokol,* **Царь-Колокол***).* The world's largest bell is also the world's most silent: it has never rung once. Commissioned in the 1730s, the bell was damaged when it was still in its cast. It weighs more than 200 tons and is 20 feet high. The bas-reliefs on the outside show Tsar Alexei Mikhailovich and Tsarina Anna Ivanovna. ⊠ *Kremlin, Kremlin/Red Square* ☎ *No phone* Ⓜ *Aleksandrovsky Sad.*

❼ Tsar Cannon *(Tsar Pushka,* **Царь-Пушка***).* This huge piece of artillery *(pushka)* has the largest caliber of any gun in the world, but like the Tsar Bell that has never been rung, it has never fired a single shot. Cast in bronze in 1586 by Andrei Chokhov, it weighs 40 tons and is 17½ feet long. Its present carriage was cast in 1835, purely for display purposes. ⊠ *Kremlin, Kremlin/Red Square* ☎ *No phone* Ⓜ *Aleksandrovsky Sad.*

ALSO WORTH SEEING

Alexander Garden *(Aleksandrovsky Sad,* **Александровский Сад***).* Laid out in the 19th century by the Russian architect Osip Bove, this garden named after Alexander I stretches along the northwest wall of the Kremlin, where the Neglinnaya River once flowed. The river now runs beneath the garden, through an underground pipe. Bove added the classical columns topped with an arc of chipped bricks; in the 19th century such "romantic" imitation ruins were popular in gardens. Today this mock ruin is blocked by a gate, but in eras past it was a famous place for winter sledding. A few pleasant outdoor cafés opened opposite the garden on the side of the Manezh building providing a nice place to rest after a tour of the Kremlin. ✉*Manezhnaya ul., Kremlin/Red Square* ☎*No phone* 🕙*Fri.–Wed. 10–5* Ⓜ*Aleksandrovsky Sad.*

Amusement Palace (*Poteshny Dvorets*, **Потешный Дворец**). Behind the State Kremlin Palace stands the Amusement Palace—so called because it was used by *boyarin* (nobleman) Alexei in the 17th century as a venue for theatrical productions. Later, both Stalin and Trotsky had apartments here. ✉*Kremlin, Kremlin/Red Square* ☎*495/203–0349* 📷*300R Kremlin ticket* 🕙*Fri.–Wed. 10–5* Ⓜ*Aleksandrovsky Sad.*

❻ Arsenal (**Арсенал**). Commissioned in 1701 by Peter the Great, the weapons arsenal was partially destroyed by the fire that greeted Napoléon as he stormed the city in 1812 (some say the Russian army set fire to the city intentionally). Its present form dates from the early 19th century, when it was given its yellow color and simple, but impressive form by Osip Bove (the same architect who designed the Alexander Garden). Today it houses government offices and is closed to the public. ✉*Kremlin, Kremlin/Red Square* ☎*495/203–0349* Ⓜ*Aleksandrovsky Sad.*

⓲ Borovitskaya Tower (*Borovitskaya Bashnya*, **Боровицкая Башня**). The main entrance to the Kremlin rises to more than 150 feet. At its base a gate pierces its thick walls, and you can still see the slits for the chains of the former drawbridge. Formerly black Volgas and, now, top-of-the-line Mercedes and BMWs whiz through the vehicular entrance, carrying government employees to work. ✉*Manezhnaya ul., Kremlin/Red Square* ☎*No phone* Ⓜ*Borovitskaya.*

❽ Cathedral of the Twelve Apostles (*Sobor Dvenadtsati Apostolov*, **Собор Двенадцати Апостолов**). Built in 1655–56 by Patriarch Nikon, this was used as his private church. An exhibit here displays icons removed from other Kremlin churches destroyed by the Soviets. The silver containers and stoves were used to make holy oil. Next door to the church is the Patriarch's Palace. ✉*Kremlin, Kremlin/Red Square* ☎*495/203–0349* 📷*300R Kremlin ticket* 🕙*Fri.–Wed. 10–5* Ⓜ*Aleksandrovsky Sad.*

⓭ Church of the Deposition of the Virgin's Robe (*Tserkov Rizopolozheniya*, **Церковь Ризоположения**). This single-dome church was built in 1484–86 by masters from Pskov. It was rebuilt several times and restored to its 15th-century appearance by Soviet experts in the 1950s. Brilliant frescoes dating to the mid-17th century cover the church's walls, pillars, and vaults. The most precious treasure is the iconostasis by Nazary Istomin. On display inside the church is an exhibit of ancient Russian wooden sculpture from the Kremlin collection. ✉*Kremlin, Kremlin/Red Square* ☎*495/203–0349* 📷*300R Kremlin ticket* 🕙*Fri.–Wed. 10–5* Ⓜ*Aleksandrovsky Sad.*

Patriarch's Palace *(Patriarshy Dvorets,* Патриарший Дворец*)*. Adjoining the Cathedral of the Twelve Apostles, the Patriarch's Palace has housed the **Museum of 17th-Century Applied Art** since 1963. The exhibits here were taken from the surplus of the Armory Palace and include books, tableware, clothing, and household linen. ⊠*Kremlin, Kremlin/Red Square* ☎*495/921–4720, 495/203–8817, or 495/202–0347* ☜*300R Kremlin ticket* ☉*Fri.–Wed. 10–5* Ⓜ*Aleksandrovsky Sad or Borovitskaya.*

❶ **Sobakina Tower** *(Sobakina Bashnya,* Собакина Башня*)*. More than 180 feet high, the Sobakina (formerly Arsenal) Tower at the northernmost part of the thick battlements that encircle the Kremlin was an important part of the Kremlin's defenses. It was built in 1492 and its thick walls concealed a secret well, which was of vital importance during times of siege. It isn't open for touring. ⊠*Manezhnaya ul., Kremlin/Red Square* ☎*No phone* ☜*300R Kremlin ticket* Ⓜ*Ploshchad Revolutsii.*

❺ **State Kremlin Palace** *(Gosudarstvenny Kremlyovsky Dvorets,* Государственный Кремлевский Дворец*)*. In 1961 this rectangular structure of glass and aluminum was built as the Dvorets Syezdov (Palace of Congresses) to accommodate meetings of Communist Party delegates from across the Soviet Union. Today it's affiliated with the Bolshoi Theater and is used for concerts, fashion shows, and ballets. Big names such as Tom Jones, Elton John, and Rod Stewart have played here. A sizable portion of the palace is underground: the architect designed the structure this way so that it wouldn't be higher than any of the other Kremlin buildings. Apart from attending a concert, the building is of no real interest. ⊠*Kremlin, Kremlin/Red Square* ☎*495/917–2396* Ⓜ*Aleksandrovsky Sad.*

㉓ **Tower of the Savior** *(Spasskaya Bashnya,* Спасская Башня*)*. Until Boris Yeltsin's presidency (1991–99) this 1491 tower served as the main entrance to the Kremlin. Indeed, in the centuries before Communist rule, all who passed through it were required to doff their hats and bow before the icon of the Savior that hung on the front of the tower. The icon was removed, but you can see the outline of where it was. The embellished roof and the first clock were added in 1625. President Vladimir Putin uncharacteristically used the Spasskaya Tower exit in May 2003 when hurrying to the Paul McCartney concert on Red Square. ⊠*Red Sq., Kremlin/Red Square* ☎*495/203–0349* Ⓜ*Ploshchad Revolutsii.*

❹ **Troitskaya Tower** *(Troitskaya Bashnya,* Троицкая Башня*)*. Rising 240 feet above the garden, this is the tallest *bashnya* (tower) in the Kremlin wall and is the passage to the Kremlin territory. This tower is linked to the Kutafya Tower by a bridge that once spanned a moat. Its deep, subterranean chambers were once used as prison cells. Napoléon supposedly lost his hat when he entered the Kremlin through this gate in 1812. ⊠*Aleksandrovsky Sad, Kremlin/Red Square* ☎*495/203–0349* ☜*300R Kremlin ticket* ☉*Fri.–Wed. 10–5* Ⓜ*Aleksandrovsky Sad.*

KITAI GOROD КИТАЙ-ГОРОД

Kitai Gorod, with its twisting and winding streets, is the oldest section of Moscow outside the Kremlin. The literal translation of Kitai Gorod is "Chinatown," but there has never been a Chinese settlement here. The origin of the word *kitai* is disputed; it may come from the Tatar word for fortress, but most likely it derives from the Russian word *kita,* in reference to the bundles of twigs that were used to reinforce the earthen wall that once surrounded the area.

Kitai Gorod begins where Red Square ends. Settlement of this area began in the 12th century, around the time that the fortified city of Moscow was founded on Borovitsky Hill (the site of the present-day Kremlin). By the 14th century Kitai Gorod was a thriving trade district, full of shops and markets. At that time it was surrounded by earthen ramparts, which were replaced in the 16th century by a fortified wall, remnants of which still remain. As Moscow grew, so did Kitai Gorod. At the time of the Bolshevik Revolution it was the city's most important financial and commercial district, with major banks, warehouses, and trading companies concentrated here. These days the multitude of shops, restaurants, and banks demonstrates the area's reasserted role as an energized commercial center.

■TIP▶ Kitai Gorod is served by the Kitai Gorod, Lubyanka, Kuznetsky Most, Turgenevskaya, Chistye Prudy, and Tsvetnoi Bulvar metro stations.

TIMING   Taken at a leisurely pace, with stops at least to glance at the interiors of the many churches in this neighborhood, you can easily spend a day in the area exploring. If you intend to take a quick look at the exhibits in the museums along the way in addition to the churches, you'll need half a day more.

MAIN ATTRACTIONS

19 **Bolshoi Theatre** (Большой Театр). Moscow's "big" (*bolshoi* means "big") and oldest theater, formerly known as the Great Imperial Theater, was

Fodor'sChoice ★ completely rebuilt after a fire in 1854. Its main building is closed for a renovation and is expected to reopen partly in 2008 with complete renovation finished in 2010. You can still see performances at the Novaya Tsena (New Stage) to the left of it. The building itself is remarkable: its monumental colonnade is topped by a statue of bronze horses pulling the chariot of Apollo, patron of music. Its crimson-and-gold interior is similarly grand. All of this splendor is matched by the quality of the resident opera and ballet troupes—two of the most famous performing-arts companies in the world. If you want to have the pleasure of seeing a performance at the Bolshoi, be sure to book one of its 2,155 seats as far as possible in advance on their Web site, because performances can sell out quickly. An interesting footnote in the theater's and the Soviet Union's history: Lenin made his last public speech here, in 1922. Also to the left of the Bolshoi is the **RAMT** (Russian Academic Youth Theater), which puts on performances with a talented group of young actors. This is where you'll find the Bolshoi's main ticket office. The plaza, with fountains and fine wooden benches, is a nice spot

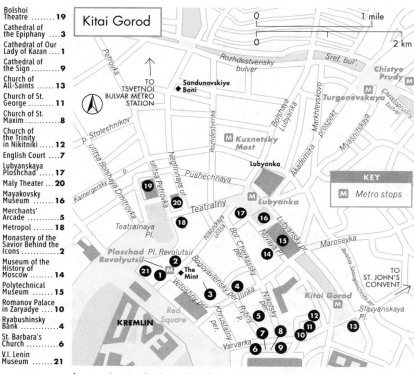

for a relaxing look at the theater. ⊠*1 Teatralnaya Pl., Kitai Gorod* ☎*495/250–7317 tickets* ⊕*www.bolshoi.ru* Ⓜ*Teatralnaya.*

NEED A BREAK?

The small café-bar at the Metropol (⊠*4 Teatralny proyezd, Kitai Gorod* ☎*495/927–6010* Ⓜ*Teatralnaya*) is a sophisticated spot for tea, coffee, and a selection of delicious cakes and pastries. In this busy part of town its expense is worth the calming effect of comfy, padded seats and intimate service. The hotel also has a famous (and even pricier) restaurant with an enormous dining hall in art nouveau style. The entrance to the café is on the right-hand side of the hotel. Coffeemania (⊠*6/9 Rozhdestvenka ul., Kitai Gorod* ☎*495/624–0075* Ⓜ*Kuznetsky Most*) is just around the corner from the Bolshoi Theater. Good coffee and food make it a favorite spot with theatergoers.

❶ Cathedral of Our Lady of Kazan (*Kazansky Sobor*, Казанский Собор). Built between 1633 and 1636 to commemorate Russia's liberation from Polish occupation during the Time of Troubles, this church was purposely blown up in 1936, and then rebuilt and fully restored in 1993. Its salmon-and-cream–painted brick and gleaming gold cupolas are now a colorful magnet at the northeast corner of Red Square, between the Historical Museum and GUM. Inside and outside hang icons of Our Lady of Kazan. Many worshippers visit throughout the day. ✉ *8 Nikolskaya ul., at Red Sq., Kitai Gorod* ✆ *Free* ☉ *Daily 8–7, except Mon., when it closes at end of 5* PM *vespers service. Sun. services at 7 and 10* AM Ⓜ *Ploshchad Revolutsii.*

❼ **English Court** *(Anglisky Dvor,* **Английский Двор***).* Built in the mid-16th century, this white-stone building with a steep shingled roof and narrow windows became known as the English Court because Ivan the Terrible—wanting to encourage foreign trade—presented it to English merchants trading in Moscow. In 1994 Queen Elizabeth II presided over the opening of the building as a branch of the Museum of the History of Moscow. Its displays about Russian–British trade relations over the centuries may be particularly interesting to visitors from the United Kingdom. Phone ahead for information on tours in English. ✉ *4 Varvarka ul., Kitai Gorod* ✆ *495/698–3952* ✆ *50R* ☉ *Tues., Thurs., and weekends 10–5:30, Wed. and Fri. 11–6* Ⓜ *Ploshchad Revolutsii or Kitai Gorod.*

⓱ **Lubyanskaya Ploshchad** (**Лубянская Площадь**). Now called by its prerevolutionary name again, this circular "square" had been renamed Dzerzhinsky Square in 1926 in honor of Felix Dzerzhinsky, a Soviet revolutionary and founder of the infamous CHEKA, the forerunner of the KGB. His statue once stood in the center of the square but was toppled in August 1991, along with the old regime. A slab of stone now stands in the middle of the square as a tribute to those who were repressed by the Soviet government. The stone comes from the Solovetsky Islands, once home to a famous prison camp. The large yellow building facing the square, with bars on the ground-floor windows, was once the notorious Lubyanka Prison and KGB headquarters. The **KGB Museum** is in an annex of this building and is accessible only by prearranged guided tour. It chronicles the history of espionage in Russia and includes spy gadgets. ✉ *Kitai Gorod* Ⓜ *Lubyanka.*

⓰ **Mayakovsky Museum** *(Muzey Mayakovskovo,* **Музей Маяковского***).* The museum for one of Russia's great revolutionary poets is suitably among the most imaginative and revolutionary installations in the city. The museum, which is housed in the building the poet inhabited opposite the headquarters of the KGB, relies on symbols to explain Vladimir Mayakovsky's (1893–1930) life. The entrance gate is shaped like a rib cage. Emblems of the life and loves of the poet hang everywhere inside, tracing his early revolutionary activities, complicated love affairs, and death. The collection includes archival documents, photos, manuscripts, paintings, and posters of and by the poet, including his handwritten suicide note. ✉ *3/6 Lyubansky proyezd, Kitai Gorod* ✆ *495/928–2569* ✆ *100R* ☉ *Tues. and Fri.–Sun. 10–5, Thurs. 1–8* Ⓜ *Lubyanka.*

❺ **Merchants' Arcade** *(Gostinny Dvor,* **Гостиный Двор***).* This market, which takes up an entire block between ulitsa Ilinka and Varvarka ulitsa, just east of Red Square, is made up of two imposing buildings. Running the length of Khrustalny pereulok is the Old Merchant Arcade, erected by the Italian architect Quarenghi between 1791 and 1805; on the other side of the block, bordering Rybny pereulok, is the New Merchant Arcade, built between 1838 and 1840 on the site of the old fish market. The entire complex has been renovated and is now an expo center complete with a number of restaurants and shops. ✉ *Ul. Ilinka, Kitai Gorod* Ⓜ*Ploshchad Revolutsii or Kitai Gorod.*

> **WORD ON THE STREET**
>
> The following Russian words are useful to know when finding addresses in Moscow:
>
> ▪ *pereulok* (per.)–lane
> ▪ *ulitsa* (ul.)–street
> ▪ *prospekt* (pr.)–avenue
> ▪ *Ploshchad* (Pl.)–square

⓲ Metropol (**Метрополь**). Built at the turn of the 20th century in preparation for the celebrations commemorating 300 years of the Romanov dynasty, the Metropol underwent reconstruction in the late 1980s to restore its brilliant art nouveau facade to its original colorful guise. The ceramic mosaics are especially arresting as the sun bounces off the tiles. Look for the Princess "Greza" panel made by Mikhail Vrubel, as inspired by the plays of Edmond Rostand. On the main facade of the building is a mosaic depicting the four seasons. The hotel was the focus of heavy fighting during the revolution, and it was also the venue of many historic speeches, including a few by Lenin. For some time the Central Committee of the Russian Soviet Federal Republic met here under its first chairman, Yakov Sverdlov. ✉ *1/4 Teatralny proyezd, Kitai Gorod* ☎*499/501–7800* Ⓜ*Ploshchad Revolutsii or Teatralnaya.*

❷ Monastery of the Savior Behind the Icons *(Zaikonospassky Monastyr,* **Заиконоспасский Монастырь***).* The monastery was founded at the beginning of the 17th century by Boris Godunov. Russia's first institution of higher learning, the Slavonic-Greco-Latin Academy, was opened in this building in 1687. Many an illustrious scholar studied here, including scientist and poet Mikhail Lomonosov (1711–65) from 1731 to 1735. Hidden inside the courtyard is the monastery's cathedral, **Spassky Sobor,** built in 1600–61 in the Moscow baroque style. Although the church is currently under ongoing renovation, services are held here daily. ✉ *7 Nikolskaya ul., Kitai Gorod* ☎*No phone* Ⓜ*Ploshchad Revolutsii.*

⓮ Museum of the History of Moscow *(Muzey Istorii Goroda Moskvy,* **Музей Истории Города Москвы***).* This small, manageable museum, housed in the former Church of St. John the Baptist (1825), presents Moscow's architectural history through paintings and artifacts. It's worth stopping in for a brief visit to get a fuller view of the Moscow history only hinted at in older neighborhoods. ✉ *12 Novaya Pl., Kitai Gorod* ☎*495/924–8490* ⊕*www.museum-city-moscow.ru* ✑*50R* ☉*Tues., Thurs., and weekends 10–6, Wed. and Fri. 11–7. Closed last Friday of month* Ⓜ*Lubyanka.*

St. John's Convent *(Ivanovsky Monastyr,* **Ивановский Монастырь***).* This convent, which was built in the 16th century and restored in the 19th century, was used as a prison in the Stalinist era and was in shambles for many years after that. The convent is open for services. Among the noblewomen who were forced to take the veil here were Empress Elizabeth's illegitimate daughter, Princess Augusta Tarakanova, and the mad serf owner Dariya Saltykova, who was imprisoned here after she murdered 138 of her serfs, most of them young women. ⊠*Zabelina ul. and Maly Ivanovsky per., Kitai Gorod* ☎*495/624–7521* 🆓*Free* ⊙*Services weekdays at 7* AM *and 5* PM*, weekends at 8:30* AM *and 5* PM Ⓜ*Kitai Gorod.*

Fodor'sChoice
★
Sandunovskiye Bani (Сандуновские Бани). Dating to the late 1800s, this impeccably clean banya, known to locals simply as "Sanduny," is probably the city's most elegant bathhouse, with a lavish interior. Prices depend on your gender and which section you visit, but range from 800R to 1,000R. On-site facilities include a beauty parlor and, of course, massage. ⊠*14 Neglinniy per., Kitai Gorod* ☎*495/625–4631* ⊕*www.sanduny.ru* 🆓*800R–1,000R* ⊙*Daily 8* AM*–10* PM Ⓜ*Kuznetsky Most.*

㉑ V. I. Lenin Museum (*Muzey V. I. Lenina*, Музей В.И. Ленина). Although during the time of Soviet Russia this was a solemn and sacred place, the museum is now closed. The magnificent redbrick exterior is well worth a look, however. Former disciples of Lenin usually congregate outside the museum selling pamphlets, books, and old badges, and arguing the wrongs of the world away. ⊠*Ploshchad Revolutsii, Kitai Gorod* Ⓜ*Teatralnaya.*

ALSO WORTH SEEING

❸ Cathedral of the Epiphany (*Bogoyavlensky Sobor*, Богоявленский Собор). This church is all that remains of the monastery that was founded on this site in the 13th century by Prince Daniil of Moscow. A good example of the Moscow baroque style, the late-17th-century cathedral is undergoing a long-overdue and very slow renovation. It is, however, open for services. ⊠*2/4 Bogoyavlensky per., Kitai Gorod* ☎*495/298–3771* 🆓*Free* ⊙*Daily 8–8* Ⓜ*Ploshchad Revolutsii.*

❾ Cathedral of the Sign (*Znamensky Sobor*, Знаменский Собор). This was part of the monastery of the same name, built on the estate of the Romanovs in the 16th century, right after the establishment of the Romanov dynasty. After the death of the last heir to Ivan the Terrible, a dark period set in, marked by internal strife and foreign intervention. That period, commonly known as the Time of Troubles, ended in 1613, when the Boyar Council elected the young Mikhail Romanov tsar. ⊠*8a Varvarka ul., Kitai Gorod* ☎*495/298–0490* ⊙*Daily 8–8. Services daily at 8* AM *and 5* PM Ⓜ*Kitai Gorod.*

⓭ Church of All-Saints in Kulishki (*Tserkov Vsekh Svyatykh na Kulishkakh*, Церковь Всех Святых на Кулишках). A fine example of 17th-century religious architecture, this graceful church is one of the few survivors of the Soviet reconstruction of the area. It's open for services. ⊠*2 Slavyansky Pl., Kitai Gorod* ☎*No phone* Ⓜ*Kitai Gorod.*

⓫ Church of St. George on Pskov Hill *(Tserkov Georgiya na Pskovskoy Gorke,* Церковь Георгия на Псковской Горке*).* This graceful five-dome church with blue cupolas studded by gold stars, built in 1657 by merchants from Pskov, stands right next to the Romanov Palace Chambers in Zaryadye. The bell tower is an addition from the 19th century. The interior of the church is mostly bare, though an art boutique on the premises is open daily 11–7. ✉ *12 Varvarka ul., Kitai Gorod* ☎ *No phone* Ⓜ *Kitai Gorod.*

❽ Church of St. Maxim the Blessed *(Tserkov Maksima Blazhennovo,* Церковь Максима Блаженного*).* In 1698 this white-stone church was built on the site where the Holy Fool Maxim was buried. It's between St. Barbara's and the Cathedral of the Sign (in front of the northern side of the Rossiya). An art boutique here is open daily 11–6. ✉ *6 Varvarka ul., Kitai Gorod* ☎ *No phone* Ⓜ *Kitai Gorod.*

⓬ Church of the Trinity in Nikitniki *(Tserkov Troitsy v Nikitnikakh,* Церковь Троицы в Никитниках*).* Painted with white trim and topped by five green cupolas, this lovely redbrick creation—one of the most striking churches in the city—mixes baroque decoration with the principles of ancient Russian church architecture. The church was built between 1628 and 1634 for the merchant Grigory Nikitnikov; the private chapel on the south side was the family vault. The murals and iconostasis were the work of Simon Ushakov, a famous icon painter whose workshop was nearby in the brick building across the courtyard. Although surrounded with barriers and still under reconstruction, it's a working church. Services are at 8:30 AM on Sunday and 5 PM on Saturday. Times of masses are also posted on the barriers. ✉ *3 Nikitnikov per., Kitai Gorod* ☎ *495/298–5018* Ⓜ *Kitai Gorod.*

⓴ Maly Theater (Малый Театр). Writer Maxim Gorky (1868–1936), known as the father of Soviet socialist realism, once called this theater famous for its productions of Russian classics "the Russian people's university." It opened in 1824 and was originally known as the Little Imperial Theater (*maly* means "little"). Out front stands a statue of a beloved and prolific playwright whose works are often performed here, the 19th-century satirist Alexander Ostrovsky. ✉ *1/6 Teatralnaya Pl., Kitai Gorod* ☎ *495/623–2621* Ⓜ *Teatralnaya.*

The Mint *(Monetny Dvor,* Монетный Двор*).* Built in 1697, the former mint, near the Cathedral of Our Lady of Kazan, is an excellent example of old baroque architecture. Its facade can be seen through the courtyard of an 18th-century building immediately next to the cathedral. ✉ *Nikolskaya ul. at Red Sq., Kitai Gorod* ☎ *No phone* Ⓜ *Ploshchad Revolutsii.*

⓯ Polytechnical Museum *(Politekhnichesky Muzey,* Политехнический Музей*).* The achievements of science and technology, including an awesome collection of old Russian cars, fill an entire Moscow block. When this museum opened in 1872 it was originally called the Museum of Applied Knowledge. There are many good temporary exhibits. ✉ *3/4 Novaya Pl., Kitai Gorod* ☎ *495/623–0756* ⊕ *www.polymus.ru* 💴 *200R* ☉ *Tues.–Sun. 10–6. Closed last Fri. of month* Ⓜ *Lubyanka.*

❿ Romanov Palace Chambers in Zaryadye (*Palaty Romanovykh v Zaryadye,* **Палаты Романовых в Зарядье**). It's believed that Mikhail Romanov (1596–1645), the first tsar of the Romanov dynasty, was born in this house. Today the mansion houses a lovely museum devoted to the boyar lifestyle of the 16th and 17th centuries. Period clothing, furniture, and household items furnish the rooms, illustrating how the boyars lived. During the week the museum is generally open only to groups with advance reservations, but if you ask, you may be allowed to join a group. On Sunday the museum is open to the general public; as during the rest of the week, you can only visit in groups, but after a short wait, enough individuals will gather here to form a tour. Tours are available in English, but you must make reservations. The entrance is downstairs. ⊠ *10 Varvarka ul., Kitai Gorod* ☎ *495/698–3706* ⊡ *150R* ⊗ *Mon. and Wed.–Sat. 10–6, Sun. 11–5* Ⓜ *Kitai Gorod.*

❹ Ryabushinsky Bank (**Рябушинский Банк**). Fyodor Shekhtel designed this turn-of-the-20th-century art nouveau masterpiece for the rich merchant Ryabushinsky. The pale-orange building on the opposite side of the street, built in the classical style at the end of the 19th century, is the former Birzha (Stock Exchange); it now houses the Russia Chamber of Commerce and Industry. ⊠ *Birzhevaya Pl. at ul. Ilinka, Kitai Gorod* ☎ *No phone* Ⓜ *Ploshchad Revolutsii.*

❻ St. Barbara's Church (*Tserkov Velikomuchenitsy Varvary,* **Церковь Великомученицы Варвары**). This peach-and-white church, built in the classical style at the end of the 18th century, lends its name to the street. ⊠ *Varvarka ul. off Red Sq., Kitai Gorod* ☎ *No phone* ⊗ *Services daily at 5* PM Ⓜ *Ploshchad Revolutsii.*

TVERSKAYA ULITSA: MOSCOW'S FIFTH AVENUE ТВЕРСКАЯ УЛИЦА

As the line of the road that led from the northern tip of the Kremlin to the ancient town of Tver, Tverskaya ulitsa had been an important route for centuries. Later that road was extended all the way to the new capital on the Baltic Sea, St. Petersburg. Tverskaya ulitsa is Moscow's main shopping artery, attracting shoppers hungry for the latest trends. The lovely, wide boulevard is lined with perfumeries, banks and exchanges, eateries, and bookshops. Some of the city's best and biggest stores are on the ground floors of massive apartment buildings, some quite attractive and graced by a fine art nouveau style. On a sunny day, Tverskaya is an especially pleasant walk. Keep an eye out for plaques (in Russian) etched in stone on building walls. These will tell you about the famous people, usually artists, politicians, or academicians, who lived or worked here.

■ TIP→ The area around Tverskaya ulitsa can be reached through the Tver-skaya, Pushkinskaya, Chekhovskaya, Mayakovskaya, and Okhotny Ryad metro stations.

TIMING   If you stay in Moscow for more than a few days you will always end up on or near Tverskaya ulitsa. Consider spending half a day if you'd like to visit the museums in this neighborhood.

MAIN ATTRACTIONS

② **Central Telegraph** *(Tsentralny Telegraf,* Центральный Телеграф*).* The striking semicircular entrance is adorned with a large, illuminated, and constantly revolving globe and a huge digital clock. Inside, you can buy stamps, send a fax home, make a phone call abroad, or use the Internet. There are also currency-exchange counters and ATMs in the lobby, plus the main post office. ✉ *7 Tverskaya ul., Tverskaya* ☎ *495/504–4444* ◷ *Daily 9–8* Ⓜ *Okhotny Ryad.*

④ **Church of the Resurrection** *(Tserkov Voskreseniya,* Церковь Воскресения*).* Built in 1629, this is one of the few lucky churches to have stayed open throughout the years of Soviet rule. As a survivor, the church was the recipient of many priceless icons from less fortunate churches destroyed or closed by the Soviets. Services are still held here daily. Be sure to look at the beautiful frescoes on the ceilings in the chapels on either side of you as you enter. Two famous icons, depicting the Coronation of the Virgin Mary and the Assumption of the Blessed Virgin Mary, hang in the vaults on either side of the vestibule. ✉ *2 Bryusov per., Tverskaya* ☎ *495/229–6616* Ⓜ *Tverskaya.*

③ **Moscow Art Theater** *(MKhAT,* Московский Художественный Театр*).* One of Moscow's most historically important theaters, this perfor-mance space is renowned for its productions of the Russian classics, especially those of Anton Chekhov (1860–1904). Founded in 1898 by the celebrated actor and director Konstantin Stanislavsky (1863–1938) and playwright and producer Vladimir Nemirovich-Danchenko (1858–1943), the theater staged the first productions of Chekhov's and Maxim Gorky's (1868–1936) plays. It was here that Stanislavsky devel-oped the Stanislavsky Method, based on the realism in traditional Rus-sian theater. After the successful production of Chekhov's *The Seagull* (the first staging in St. Petersburg had bombed), the bird was chosen as the theater's emblem. An affiliated, more modern theater, with a seat-ing capacity of 2,000, also confusingly called the Moscow Art Theater, was opened in 1972 on Tverskoi bulvar, near Stanislavsky's home. The mural opposite the old theater depicts Anton Chekhov, as does the statue at the start of Kamergersky pereulok. ✉ *3 Kamergersky per., Tverskaya* ☎ *495/692–6748* ⊕ *www.art.theatre.ru* Ⓜ *Okhotny Ryad.*

⑤ **Moscow City Council** *(Mossoviet,* Моссовет*).* This impressive structure was built at the end of the 18th century by Matvey Kazakov for the Moscow governor-general. During the reconstruction of Tverskaya ulitsa in the 1930s, the building was moved back about 45 feet in order to widen the street. The top two stories—a mirror image of the mansion's original two stories—were added at that time. ✉ *22 Tver-skaya ul., Tverskaya* Ⓜ *Tverskaya.*

Tverskaya & Bolshaya Nikitskaya

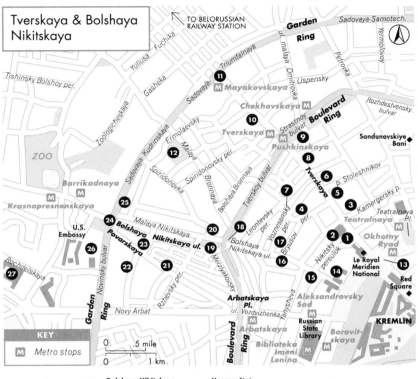

TO BELORUSSIAN RAILWAY STATION

KEY

Ⓜ *Metro stops*

0   .5 mile

0   1 km

Tverskaya Ulitsa ▼

Central Telegraph **2**

Church of the Resurrection **4**

Moscow Art Theater **3**

Moscow City Council **5**

Museum of the Contemporary History of Russia **10**

Patriarch's Pond **12**

Pushkin Square **9**

Stanislavsky Museum **7**

Triumphal Square **11**

Tverskaya Square **6**

Yeliseyevsky's **8**

Yermolova Theater **1**

Bolshaya Nikitskaya Ulitsa ▼

Bely Dom **27**

CDL: Central House of Writers **23**

Chaliapin House Museum **26**

Chekhov House Museum **25**

Church of the Great Ascension **19**

Episcopal Church **17**

Gorky Literary Museum **21**

Kudrinskaya Ploshchad **24**

Manezhnaya Ploshchad **13**

Moscow State University **14**

Nikitskiye Vorota **18**

Oriental Art Museum **28**

Ryabushinsky Mansion **20**

Tchaikovsky Conservatory **16**

Tsvetaeva House Museum **22**

Zoological Museum **15**

Dostoyevsky Memorial Apartment *(Muzey-Kvartira Dostoevskovo,* Музей-квартира Достоевского*).* This museum is devoted to the great Russian novelist. It's on the grounds of the hospital where he was born and where his father, Mikhail Andreevich, resided and worked as a doctor. Fyodor Dostoyevsky (1821–81) lived here until he was 16. The museum has kept things much as they were, from family pictures to the neat, middle-class furniture. ✉*2 ul. Dostoevskovo, Northern Outskirts* ☎*495/681–1085* ⛁*40R* ☉ *Wed. and Fri. 2–7, Thurs. and weekends 11–6. Closed last day of month* Ⓜ*Novoslobodskaya.*

⑩ **Museum of the Contemporary History of Russia** *(Muzey Sovremennoi Istorii Rossii,* Музей Современной Истории России*).* The onetime social center of the Moscow aristocracy has an entrance flanked by two smirking lions. Originally built by Giliardi in 1787, the mansion was rebuilt in the classical style after the Moscow Fire of 1812. The building housed the Museum of the Revolution from 1926 to the late 20th century, at which time the museum was converted to its present purpose. Although it retains many of its former exhibits—heavily imbued with Soviet propaganda—the museum has been updated to reflect the changing political climate in Russia and exhibits cover events up to 2000. The permanent exhibit, on the second floor, begins with a review of the first workers' organizations in the 19th century. The exhibits outlining the 1905 and 1917 revolutions include the horse-drawn machine-gun cart of the First Cavalry Army, the texts of the first decrees of the Soviet government on peace and land, dioramas and paintings portraying revolutionary battles, and thousands of other relics. The next rooms outline the history of Soviet rule, with extensive material devoted to Stalin's rise to power before whizzing through the short post-Soviet history.

With a huge archive and the country's best collection of political posters and medals, the museum has a reputation for hosting excellent temporary exhibits. Explanations are only in Russian, but you can arrange a tour in English by calling ahead. The fine gift shop sells Russian souvenirs (including some beautiful amber) and great vintage items like flags and political-rally posters. ✉*21 Tverskaya ul., Tverskaya* ☎*495/699–6724* ⊕*www.sovr.ru* ⛁*150R* ☉ *Tues.–Sun. 10–6. Closed last Fri. of month* Ⓜ*Tverskaya.*

⑫ **Patriarch's Pond** *(Patriarshy Prudy,* Патриаршие Пруды*).* The beginning of Russian satirist and novelist Mikhail Bulgakov's (1891–1940) novel *The Master and Margarita* is set in this small park. Bulgakov is most famous for this novel and his satirical novel *Heart of a Dog.* The park and pond were named after the patriarch of the Orthodox Church, who once owned the area. Shaded by trees and with plenty of benches, it's a nice spot for a break, and there are several good restaurants nearby. In winter the pond is used as a skating rink. Cafe Margarita is nearby at 28 Malaya Bronnaya, and its lively musical performers and Bulgakov mural make it worth a visit, especially if you've read any Bulgakov. ✉*ul. Malaya Bronnaya, Tverskaya* ☎*No phone* Ⓜ*Mayakovskaya.*

1

9 Pushkin Square (*Pushkinskaya Ploshchad*, **Пушкинская Площадь**). Pushkin Square is the favorite spot of lovers and the most popular meeting place in town. Every evening in good weather you will see dozens of people waiting by the bronze statue of Alexander Pushkin (1799–1837), which stands at the top of a small park. It's the work of Alexander Opekushin and was erected by public subscription in 1880. It is impossible to underestimate Russia's love for the poet who is credited with founding modern Russian literature. One of his most famous lines, from his novel in verse *Eugene Onegin* (1823) is about Moscow: "Moscow. how many strains are fusing / in that one sound, for Russian hearts! / what store of riches it imparts!" Summer and winter, fresh flowers on the pedestal prove that the poet's admirers are still ardent and numerous. The city's first McDonald's—once the busiest in the world is also at this site—where the Boulevard Ring crosses Tverskaya ulitsa. ✉*Junction between Tverskaya and Boulevard Ring, Tverskaya* ☏*No phone* Ⓜ*Pushkinskaya.*

Le Royal Meridien National (**Гостиница Националь**). The ornate art nouveau splendor of the National, built in 1903, belies its revolutionary function as the pre-Kremlin residence for Lenin, and subsequent home for Communist Party operatives and fellow travelers, such as author John Reed. Beautiful mosaics adorn the hotel facade; inside, the luxurious rooms and restaurants conjure up the National's prerevolutionary dominance in elegance. ✉*15/1 Mokhovaya ul., Tverskaya* ☏*495/258–7000* 🌐*www.national.ru* Ⓜ*Okhotny Ryad.*

7 Stanislavsky Museum (*Muzey Stanislavskovo*, **Музей Станиславского**). Konstantin Stanislavsky was a Russian actor, director, and producer, as well as the founder of the Stanislavsky Method, the catalyst for method acting. He was also one of the founders of the Moscow Art Theater. Stanislavsky lived and worked in this house during the last 17 years of his life. The house, which has been kept as it was while he lived here, showcases photos and theater memorabilia. ✉*6 Leontyevsky per., Tverskaya* ☏*495/629–2442 or 495/229–2855* 🎟*100R* ⏰ *Wed.–Sun. 12–7. Closed Mon. and Tues, and last Thurs. of month* Ⓜ*Pushkinskaya.*

11 Triumphal Square (*Triumfalnaya Ploshchad*, **Триумфальная Площадь**). This major intersection is where the grand boulevard of Moscow, the Garden Ring, crosses Tverskaya ulitsa. Traffic here also passes through a tunnel running below Tverskaya ulitsa, and there's an underpass for pedestrians. A statue of the revolutionary poet Vladimir Mayakovsky (1893–1930) stands in the center of the square. It's generally believed that Mayakovsky committed suicide out of disillusionment with the revolution he had so passionately supported.

METRO 2

Moscow's metro is one of the deepest in the world but below it, if you believe the Soviet legend, is a second even deeper metro system, Metro 2. This metro was purportedly built for Stalin as a private line for top party officials. One of the lines supposedly led from the Kremin to the Lubyanka, the home of the feared KGB.

The square is a center of Moscow's cultural life. The **Tchaikovsky Concert Hall,** opened in 1940, stands on the corner nearest you. In its foyer are various food outlets, where you can get anything from pizza at Pizza Hut to croissants and coffee at the dependable Brioche. The **Satire Theater** is right next door, on the Garden Ring. On the far side of the square stands the **Moskva Cinema;** the popular **Mossoviet Theater** is also nearby, at 16 Bolshaya Sadovaya. To your far left is the multitiered tower of the imposing **Peking Hotel,** opened in 1956 as a mark of Sino-Soviet friendship. Looking to your right, you'll see the **American Bar and Grill** and **City Grill,** popular with Russians as well as the foreign community.

While you're here, it's worth riding the escalator down for a peek at the spectacular interior of the **Mayakovskaya metro station,** which like many early stations, lies deep underground (it doubled as a bomb shelter during World War II). Stalin made a famous speech here on the 24th anniversary of the Bolshevik Revolution, at the height of the Siege of Moscow. Colorful, pastel mosaics depicting Soviet achievements in outer space decorate the ceiling. ⊠ *Junction between Tverskaya and the Garden Ring, Tverskaya* Ⓜ *Mayakovskaya.*

❽ **Yeliseyevsky's** (**Елисеевский**). Of all the stores and boutiques on Tverskaya ulitsa, this grocery store at No. 14, in a Matvei Kazakov–designed, late-18th-century, classical mansion, has the most dazzling interior, with chandeliers, stained glass, and gilt wall decorations. Under Communist administration, the store had the official, generic title Gastronom No. 1, but it once again carries the name that most people continued to call it even then—Yeliseyevsky's, after the rich merchant from St. Petersburg who owned the store before the revolution. The large alcohol section in the back room includes a number of vodkas, some in bottles shaped as bears or, for one brand, Pushkin's head. Coffee beans, caviar, and candy are other items you can buy here. One of the few food stores in the city center, and open 24 hours, it's a good place to stock up on items. ⊠ *14 Tverskaya ul., Tverskaya* ☎ *495/209–0760* ⊗ *Daily, 24 hrs* Ⓜ *Tverskaya or Pushkinskaya.*

ALSO WORTH SEEING

❻ **Tverskaya Square** *(Tverskaya Ploshchad,* **Тверская Площадь***).* This square, which dates to 1792, was named for the street, but in 1918 it was renamed Sovetskaya (Soviet) Ploshchad. In 1994 its historical name, Tverskaya, was reinstated. In the small park here stands a statue of Prince Yuri Dolgoruky, the founder of Moscow in 1147. The equestrian statue was erected in 1954, shortly after the celebrations marking Moscow's 800th anniversary. ⊠ *Tverskaya* ☎ *No phone* Ⓜ *Tverskaya.*

Tverskaya-Yamskaya ulitsa (**Тверская-Ямская улица**). This last section of Tverskaya ulitsa leads to the Belorussian railway station, which also has two interconnecting metro stations. The station is where trains roll in from Western Europe. A statue of Maxim Gorky, erected in the 1950s, stands in a small park outside the station. It's near the site of the former Triumphal Gates, built in the 19th century by the architect Osip

Moscow's Magnificent Metro

Even if you don't plan on using the metro to get around Moscow, it's still worth taking a peek at this wonder of the urban world. The first line opened in 1935 and the earliest stations—in the city center and along the ring line—were built as public palaces. Many of the millions of commuters using the system each day bustle past chandeliers, sculptures, stained-glass windows, beautiful mosaics, and pink, white, and black marble. With its rich collection of decorative materials, the metro has often been called a museum; it's even been said that no geological museum in the world has such a peculiar stone library.

Mayakovskaya station, opened in 1938, may well be the jewel in the crown of the Moscow metro. The vaulted ceiling of the grand central hall has 33 mosaic panels, based on the theme "One Day of Soviet Skies," by Russian artist Alexander Deineka.

Novoslobodskaya, opened in 1952, sparkles, thanks to its light-backed stained glass. With their Soviet-inspired designs, several other stations—such as **Ploshchad Revolutsii,** with its bronze figures from the socialist world order (farmers, soliders, and such)—are tourist attractions in their own right.

In the past, Moscow's metro architects won international architecture awards for their designs. Designs of new stations, however, have departed somewhat from these grand old stations; they lack brass sculptures and intricate stained glass, for example. But with indirect lighting, exquisite marble, and an open, airy feeling, these new stations reflect modern life in a way that the monumental Soviet displays of past glories do not. Moscow's metro is in the top three most heavily used metro system in the world.

Bove to commemorate the Russian victory in the war with Napoléon. The gates were demolished in a typical fit of destruction in the 1930s. Fragments can be found on the grounds of the Donskoy Monastery. A replica of the original gates was erected in 1968 near Poklonnaya Hill, at the end of Kutuzovsky prospekt. ⊠ *Tverskaya* ☎ *No phone* Ⓜ *Mayakovskaya.*

❶ **Yermolova Theater** *(Teatr imeni Yermolovoi,* **Театр имени Ермоловой***).* The theater housed in this short building with an arched entrance was founded in 1937 and named after the Russian actress Maria Yermolova (1853–1928). ⊠ *5 Tverskaya ul., Tverskaya* ☎ *495/629–0031* Ⓜ *Okhotny Ryad.*

THE OLD MOSCOW OF BOLSHAYA NIKITSKAYA ULITSA БОЛЬШАЯ НИКИТСКАЯ УЛИЦА

Bolshaya Nikitskaya ulitsa is one of the many old streets radiating from the Kremlin, spokelike as Tverskaya ulitsa to the northeast and Novy Arbat to the southwest. The street was laid out along the former road to Novgorod, an ancient town northwest of Moscow, and is divided into two sections. The first part is lined with 18th- and 19th-century mansions; it begins at Manezhnaya Ploshchad, across from the fortification walls of the Kremlin. The second section, notable for its enchanting art nouveau mansions, starts at Nikitskiye Vorota Square, where Bolshaya Nikitskaya ulitsa intersects with Bulvarnoye Koltso (the Boulevard Ring).

■TIP→ **Bolshaya Nikitskaya is served by the Krasnopresnenskaya, Barrikadnaya, Okhotny Ryad, and Arbatskaya metro stations.**

TIMING   This neighborhood is spread over quite a bit of territory and includes detours down crooked streets, so it's best to allow a full day to see everything at a leisurely pace. If you start out at the Okhotny Ryad metro station and walk through the sights to end at the Barrikadnaya station, you'll have walked roughly 3 km (2 mi).

MAIN ATTRACTIONS

㉗ Bely Dom *(White House,* **Белый Дом***)* . This large, white, modern building perched along the riverbank, across the river from the Ukraina hotel, is one of the seven "Stalin Gothic" skyscrapers built in Moscow in the mid-20th century. Before the August 1991 coup, the White House was the headquarters of the Russian Republic of the USSR. You may have first seen the building on television when it was shelled in October 1993 in response to the rioting and near-coup by Vice President Alexander Rutskoi and parliamentarians. They had barricaded themselves in the White House after Yeltsin's decision to dissolve parliament and hold new elections. Today the building houses the prime minister's and the Russian government's offices and is called the Dom Pravitelstvo, or Government House. ⊠*2 Krasnopresnenskaya nab., Bolshaya Nikitskaya* ☎*495/205–5735* Ⓜ*Krasnopresnenskaya.*

㉓ CDL: Central House of Writers *(Tsentralny Dom Literatorov,* **Центральный Дом Литераторов***).* The CDL is an exclusive club for members of the Writers' Union. The club (at 53 Bolshaya Nikitskaya; it's the same building, but the club entrance is on another street) is off-limits, but the dining room is open to the public and is now one of the city's very best restaurants. There's also an art-house cinema on the floor above the restaurant. Next door (No. 52) is a large mansion, enclosed by a courtyard, that houses the administrative offices of the Writers' Union. It's commonly believed that Leo Tolstoy (1828–1910) used this mansion as a model for his description of the Rostov home in *War and Peace.* A statue of Tolstoy stands in the courtyard. Mikhail Bulgakov (1891–1940) set part of his wonderful satire of Soviet life, *The Master and Margarita,* here. ⊠*50 Povarskaya ul., Bolshaya Nikitskaya* ☎*495/291–1515* Ⓜ*Barrikadnaya.*

㉖ Chaliapin House Museum *(Dom-muzey Chaliapina,* **Дом-музей Шаляпина***).* Fyodor Chaliapin (1873–1938), one of the world's greatest opera singers, lived in this beautifully restored manor house from 1910 to 1922. Chaliapin was stripped of his Soviet citizenship while on tour in France in 1922; he never returned to Russia again. The Soviets turned his home into an apartment building, and until restorations in the 1980s, the building contained 60 communal apartments. With help from Chaliapin's family in France, the rooms have again

CLOSE UP

The Seven Gothic Sisters

1

With their spookily lit cornices dominating the skyline since the mid-20th century, the "Seven Sisters" (also known as the "Stalin Gothics") are as much a part of the Moscow experience as the Empire State Building is in New York. The neo-Gothic buildings are often called "wedding cake" skyscrapers because their tiered construction creates a sense of upward movement and grandeur, like a rocket on standby.

The seven buildings—the White House (Bely Dom) at the end of the Arbat; the Ukraina and Leningradskaya hotels; the residential buildings at Kudrinskaya Ploshchad (Kudrinsky Square), Kotelnicheskaya naberezhnaya (Kotelnicheskaya Embankment), and Krasniye Vorota; and the imposing Moscow State University on Sparrow Hills—were constructed when the country lay in ruins, just after World War II, intended as a symbol of Soviet power at the beginning of the Cold War. Stalin ordered the skyscrapers to be built in 1947, on the 800th anniversary of Moscow's founding. German prisoners of war were forced to work on several of the buildings.

An eighth skyscraper was planned (before the others were started) but never built: the grandiose Palace of Soviets, which was meant to replace the Kremlin as the seat of government power. It was intended to be the tallest building in the world, with a height of 1,378 feet topped by a 300-foot statue of Lenin. The site of the Cathedral of Christ Our Savior on the Moskva River was chosen, and the church was demolished in 1931. Only later did builders realize that the ground was too wet to support such an enormous structure. The plans were abandoned, and the area was turned into a swimming pool until the cathedral was rebuilt in 1997.

According to the Soviet propaganda of the time, most of the new buildings were part of the government's drive to replace slums with better housing. In truth, residents were mainly party members, actors, writers, and other members of the elite. With few ordinary people living in or having access to the buildings, legendary stories developed around the Seven Sisters. The Ukraina's spire was said to hide a nuclear-rocket launcher, while Moscow State University was rumored to have a secret tunnel leading to Stalin's dacha. The university was also said to run as deep underground as it did above, concealing secret study centers and a metro connection. The building at Kudrinskaya Ploshchad overlooks the U.S. embassy. It was said that KGB spies kept an eye on the embassy compound from certain windows.

Today you can easily visit most of the skyscrapers, particularly the Ukraina and Leningradskaya hotels.

been arranged and furnished as they were when the singer lived here. The walls are covered with works of art given to Chaliapin by talented friends, such as the artists Mikhail Vrubel and Isaac Levitan. Also on display are Chaliapin's colorful costumes, which were donated to the museum by his son. When you reach the piano room, you're treated to original recordings of Chaliapin singing his favorite roles. Entrance is from inside the courtyard. English-language tours are available and should be reserved ahead of time. ✉25–27 Novinsky bulvar, Bol-

shaya Nikitskaya ☎495/252–2530 💲*100R* ⏰*Tues. and Sat. 10–6,*
Wed. and Thurs. 11:30–6:30, Sun. 10–4. Closed last day of month
Ⓜ*Barrikadnaya.*

㉕ Chekhov House Museum *(Dom-muzey Chekhova,* **Дом-музей Чехова***).*
The sign DR. CHEKHOV still hangs from the door of this home where
Chekhov resided from 1886 to 1890. The rooms are arranged as they
were when he lived here, and his manuscripts, letters, photographs,
and personal effects are exhibited. ✉*6 Sadovaya-Kudrinskaya ul., Bol-*
shaya Nikitskaya ☎*495/291–6154 or 495/291–3837* 💲*40R* ⏰*Wed.–*
Fri. 2–6, weekends 11–4 Ⓜ*Barrikadnaya.*

⑲ Church of the Great Ascension *(Tserkov Bolshovo Vozneseniya,*
Церковь Большого Вознесения*).* Like Moscow State University, this
classical church was designed by Matvei Kazakov and built in the
1820s. For years it stood empty and abandoned, but after major repair,
religious services have resumed here. The church is most famous as the
site where the Russian poet Alexander Pushkin married the younger
Natalya Goncharova; Pushkin died outside St. Petersburg six years
after their wedding, in a duel defending her honor. There is a much
despised (for its kitschyness) statue of the couple on the square outside
the church. (History has judged Natalya harshly; she was probably
not guilty of adultery, although she did enjoy flirting.) The statue in
the park to the left of the church as you face it is of Alexey Tolstoy, a
relative of Leo's and a well-known Soviet writer of historical novels.
A house museum dedicated to him is next to the Ryabushinsky Mansion. ✉*36 Malaya Nikitskaya ul., Bolshaya Nikitskaya* ☎*No phone*
Ⓜ*Arbatskaya.*

㉔ Kudrinskaya Ploshchad *(Kudrinsky Square,* **Кудринская Площадь***).*
Along one side of this square, cars race along the Garden Ring, the
major circular road surrounding Moscow. If you approach the ring
from Bolshaya Nikitskaya ulitsa or Povarskaya ulitsa, the first thing to
catch your eye will be the 22-story skyscraper directly across Novinsky bulvar. One of the seven Stalin Gothics, this one is 525 feet high.
The ground floor is taken up by shops and the rest of the building
contains apartments. This area saw heavy fighting during the uprisings
of 1905 and 1917 (the plaza was previously called Ploshchad Vosstaniya, or Insurrection Square). The Barrikadnaya (Barricade) metro
station is very close by. Cross the ulitsa Barrikadnaya and bear right
and down the hill; you'll see people streaming into the station to your
right. ✉*Bolshaya Nikitskaya* ☎*No phone* Ⓜ*Barrikadnaya.*

⑬ Manezhnaya Ploshchad *(Manezh Square,* **Манежная Площадь***).* When
the Soviets razed this square in 1938, many of the area's old buildings
were lost. The plan, which never came to pass, was to build a superhigh-
way through the area. In 1967 the square was renamed "50th Anniversary of the October Revolution Square." In the 1990s the square
reverted to its original name and construction of an underground shopping mall was begun. Construction was halted in 1993 to let archaeolo-
gists excavate the area. The team found a plethora of artifacts dating as
far back as the 13th century. In 1997 the Manezh shopping mall was

finally opened, much to the chagrin of most Muscovites, who saw it as an eyesore. The present (and prerevolutionary) name comes from the Imperial Riding School, or Manezh, that stands on the opposite side of the square from the Moskva Hotel. The 1817 structure was gutted by a fire in early 2004, but has since been restored.

Opened in 1935, the **Moskva Hotel** was one of the first buildings erected as part of Stalin's reconstruction plan for Moscow. Despite protests, the hotel that's featured on Stolichnaya vodka labels was demolished in late 2003 to make way for a new Moskva, which is planned to exactly replicate the facade of the original structure; the new hotel is still under construction at this writing.

18 **Nikitskiye Vorota** (**Никитские Ворота**). This square was named after the *vorota* (gates) of the white-stone fortification walls that once stood here. On one side of the square is a modern building with square windows; this is the office of ITAR-TASS, once the official news agency of the Soviet Union and the mouthpiece of the Kremlin. In the park in the center of the square stands a monument to Kliment Timiryazev, a famous botanist.

The busy road intersecting Bolshaya Nikitskaya ulitsa is the **Bulvarnoye Koltso** (Boulevard Ring), which forms a semicircle around the city center. It begins at the banks of the Moskva River, just south of the Kremlin, running in a northeastern direction. After curving eastward, and then south, it finally reaches the riverbank again after several miles, near the mouth of the Yauza River, northeast of the Kremlin. Its path follows the lines of the 16th-century white-stone fortification wall that gave Moscow the name "White City." The privilege of living within its walls was reserved for the court nobility and craftsmen serving the tsar. The wall was torn down in 1775, on orders from Catherine the Great, and was replaced by the current Boulevard Ring. The perfect way to get a good view of the inner city is to slowly walk along the ring—this is best done on the weekend or late at night to avoid traffic on the boulevard. Running along its center is a broad strip of trees and flowers, dotted with playgrounds and benches. Summer brings out a burst of outdoor cafés, ice-cream vendors, and strolling lovers along the boulevard. ⊠ *Bolshaya Nikitskaya* Ⓜ *Arbatskaya*.

Cook Street (*Povarskaya ulitsa,* **Поварская улица**). This is where the tsars' cooks lived. After the revolution the street was renamed Vorovskovo, in honor of a Soviet diplomat who was assassinated by a Russian, but it has returned to its prerevolutionary name. Povarskaya ulitsa is an important center of the Moscow artistic community, with the film actors' studio, the Russian Academy of Music (the Gnesin Institute), and the Tsentralny Dom Literatorov (Central House of Writers) all located here. Many of the old mansions have been preserved, and the street retains its prerevolutionary tranquillity and charm. In the first flush days of summer your walk is likely to be accompanied by a rousing drum set or tinkling piano sonata issuing from the open windows of the music school. ⊠ *Bolshaya Nikitskaya* Ⓜ *Arbatskaya*.

⑳ Ryabushinsky Mansion *(Dom Ryabushinskovo,* Дом Рябушинского*).* This marvelous example of Moscow art nouveau was built in 1901 for a wealthy banker and designed by the architect Fyodor Shektel. (If you arrived in Moscow by train, you may have noticed the fanciful Yaroslav station, another of his masterpieces, just opposite the Leningrad railway station.) The building has been wonderfully preserved. This was thanks in part to the fact that Maxim Gorky lived here from 1931 until his death in 1936. Although Gorky was a champion of the proletariat, his home was rather lavish. Gorky himself apparently hated the *style moderne,* as art nouveau was termed back then. Those who don't, however, are charmed by this building of ecru brick and stone painted pink and mauve atop gray foundations. On the exterior, a beautiful mosaic of irises forms a border around the top of most of the house, and a strangely fanciful yet utilitarian iron fence matches the unusual design of the window frames. The spectacular interior is replete with a stained-glass roof and a twisting marble staircase that looks like a wave of gushing water. Tours in English are available; call ahead for more information. ✉ *6/2 Malaya Nikitskaya ul., Bolshaya Nikitskaya* ☎ *495/290–0535* 🎫 *Free* ☉ *Wed.–Fri. and Sun. 11–6, Sat. 10–5. Closed last Thurs. of month* Ⓜ *Arbatskaya.*

⑯ Tchaikovsky Conservatory *(Konservatoriya imeni Chaykovskovo,* Консерватория имени Чайковского*).* The famous Tchaikovsky Music Competition takes place every four years in this conservatory's magnificent concert hall (the next one is scheduled for 2010). The conservatory was founded in 1866 and moved to its current location in 1870. Rachmaninoff, Scriabin, and Tchaikovsky are among the famous composers who worked here. There's a statue of Tchaikovsky in the semicircular park outside the main entrance. It was designed by Vera Mukhina, a famous Soviet sculptor. You can buy reasonably priced tickets to excellent concerts of classical music in the lobby ticket office in the main building. You can also just sit back with a coffee and listen to rehearsals and concerts from the summer garden of the Coffeemania here, near the Tchaikovsky statue. ✉ *13 Bolshaya Nikitskaya ul., Bolshaya Nikitskaya* ☎ *495/629–9401 or 495/629–8745* ⊕ *www. mosconsv.ru* Ⓜ *Okhotny Ryad or Arbatskaya.*

㉒ Tsvetaeva House Museum *(Dom-muzey Tsvetaevoy,* Дом-музей Цветаевой*).* Marina Tsvetaeva (1892–1941), the renowned poet, lived in an apartment on the second floor of this building from 1914 to 1922. Today the building houses not only a museum dedicated to her but also a cultural center that arranges international literary evenings, musical events, and annual conferences covering the Silver Age (1890s–1917) and Tsvetaeva. You must ring the bell to enter the museum, which begins on the second floor. Although the rooms are decorated in the style of the early 1900s, they are not as they were when Tsvetaeva lived here. The poetry written on the wall in her bedroom has been re-created. The children's room has some stuffed animals in place of the real animals—a dog, a squirrel, and a turtle, to name a few—Tsvetaeva kept in her home. This place is well worth a visit even if you're not familiar with Tsvetaeva's work, because the staff is enthusiastic and the apartment is well representative of the period. Tours can be arranged in English if you call ahead. ⊠ *6 per. Borisoglebski, Bolshaya Nikitskaya* ☎ *495/202–3543* 🖭 *Free* 🕓 *Daily noon–5* Ⓜ *Arbatskaya.*

ALSO WORTH SEEING

🈧 **Episcopal Church** *(Episcopalnaya tserkov,* Епископальная Церковь*).* Moscow's only Episcopal church is inside this attractive red-sandstone building. Built in 1884, it served the British-expatriate community for more than 40 years, including a mass for Queen Victoria after her death in 1901. No bells were rung then, however, because only Orthodox churches were allowed to have them in the city. Instead the tower was used as a strong room for the rich British merchant community. The 1917 revolution ended spiritual and secular functions, however, and the church was closed. The pews are believed to have been subsequently burned in the harsh winters of the early 1920s, and the stained glass was replaced when the building was converted into a recording studio. Today the English have reacquired the property, and it's again a working church and gathering place for the community. ⊠ *8 Voznesensky per., Bolshaya Nikitskaya* ☎ *No phone* Ⓜ *Okhotny Ryad.*

🈩 **Gorky Literary Museum** *(Literaturny Muzey Gorkovo,* Литературный Музей Горького*).* For Gorky buffs only, this museum is packed with the letters, manuscripts, and pictures of the great proletarian writer. There are also portraits of him by Nesterov and Serov. Gorky never lived here, but there is a red wooden reproduction of his childhood home, complete with village yard and outbuildings. You probably won't be able to leave without the kindly but fierce matrons who protect this place compelling you to sign the guest book. Phone ahead for individual or group tours in English. ⊠ *25a Povarskaya ul., Bolshaya Nikitskaya* ☎ *495/290–5130* 🖭 *Free* 🕓 *Mon., Tues., and Thurs. 10–5, Wed. and Fri. noon–6. Closed 1st Thurs. of month* Ⓜ *Barrikadnaya.*

🈛 **Moscow State University** *(Moskovsky Gosudarstvenny Universitet,* Московский Государственный Университет*).* Russia's oldest university was founded in 1755 by the father of Russian science, Mikhail Lomonosov. The neoclassical buildings here were originally designed by Matvei Kazakov in 1786–93. They were rebuilt and embellished in the mid-19th century, after the 1812 fire. The law and journalism schools are still housed in these quarters. The university's main campus is on Sparrow Hills (formerly Lenin Hills), southwest of the city center, in the largest of the so-called Stalin Gothic skyscrapers. ⊠ *19 Mokhovaya ul., Bolshaya Nikitskaya* Ⓜ *Okhotny Ryad.*

🈰 **Oriental Art Museum** *(Muzey Iskusstva Narodov Vostoka,* Музей Искусства Народов Востока*).* Glass cases filled to capacity with artwork and clothing from the Central Asian republics, China, Japan, and Korea make up the museum's large permanent collection. The museum itself is a cool and calm place to take a leisurely look at the magnificent holdings. Most of the placards in the museum are in Russian, but there are a few annotations in English. ⊠ *12a Nikitsky bulvar, Bolshaya Nikitskaya* ☎ *495/291–0212* 🖭 *100R* 🕓 *Tues.–Sun. 11–8* Ⓜ *Arbatskaya.*

☾ **Zoo** *(Zoopark,* **Зоопарк***).* Zurab Tsereteli, Moscow's most ubiquitous sculptor, designed the statues and gates of Moscow's small zoo. Some people appreciate the whimsical design, which looks as if it came out of a fairy-tale land envisioned by Walt Disney. Others consider it yet another one of Tsereteli's outrageous creations. Visit on a weekday to avoid the large crowds on weekends. ✉ *1 Bolshaya Gruzinskaya ul., Bolshaya Nikitskaya* ☎ *495/255–5375* ⊕ *www.zoo.ru* ☜ *150R* ☾ *Apr.–Sept., Tues.–Sun. 10–8; Oct.–Mar., Tues.–Sun. 10–5* Ⓜ *Barrikadnaya.*

⓯ **Zoological Museum** *(Zoologichesky Muzey,* **Зоологический Музей***).*
☾ This museum, founded in 1902, is always swarming with schoolchildren, who take a special delight in its huge collection of stuffed mammals, birds, amphibians, and reptiles. The museum also has a collection of more than 1 million insects, including more than 100,000 butterflies donated by a Moscow resident. ✉ *6 Bolshaya Nikitskaya ul., Bolshaya Nikitskaya* ☎ *495/203–8923* ⊕ *www.zoo.ru* ☜ *30R* ☾ *Tues.–Sun. 10–5. Closed last Tues. of month* Ⓜ *Okhotny Ryad.*

THE ARBAT, OLD & NEW АРБАТ

Two of downtown Moscow's most interesting and important avenues are the Arbat (also known as the Stary Arbat, or Old Arbat) and Novy Arbat (New Arbat), which are two more spokelike routes leading away from the Kremlin. Stary Arbat is closed to all traffic and revered by Muscovites, who usually refer to it simply as "the Arbat." The area is an attractive, cobbled pedestrian precinct with many gift shops, cafés, and kiosks selling all manner of souvenirs. It's a carnival of portrait artists, poets, and musicians, as well as the enthusiastic admirers of their work. One of the oldest sections of Moscow, the Arbat dates from the 16th century, when it was the beginning of the road that led from the Kremlin to the city of Smolensk. At that time it was also the quarter where court artisans lived, and several of the surrounding streets still recall this in such names as Plotnikov (Carpenter), Serebryany (Silversmith), and Kalashny (Pastry Cook). Early in the 19th century the Arbat became a favorite district of the aristocracy, and a century later it became a favorite shopping street.

Novy Arbat has both a different history and spirit. For almost 30 years it was named Kalinin prospekt, in honor of Mikhail Kalinin, an old Bolshevik whose prestige plummeted after 1991. The stretch from the Kremlin to Arbatskaya Ploshchad has been given back its prerevolutionary name of ulitsa Vozdvizhenka. The second section—which begins where Vozdvizhenka ends and runs west for about a mile to the Moskva River—is now called Novy Arbat. In contrast to ulitsa Vozdvizhenka, which has retained some of its prerevolutionary charm, and the Arbat, which is actively re-creating the look of its past, Novy Arbat is a modern thoroughfare. It is now something of an entertainment area, with flashy casinos and lots of decent restaurants.

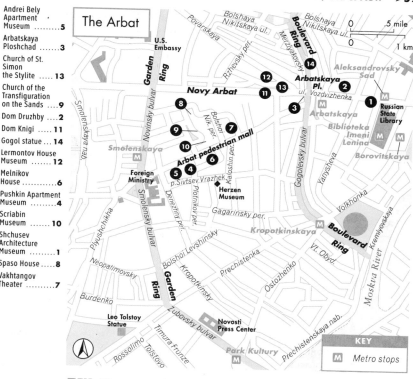

■ **TIP→ You can reach the Arbat via the Arbatskaya, Smolenskaya, and Biblioteka Imeni Lenina metro stations.**

TIMING You can easily spend a whole day exploring this neighborhood especially if you go souvenir shopping at the shops and street kiosks you'll see along the way. There are the numerous charming side streets just off the Old Arbat and plenty of cafés to stop off for a break. If you want to avoid crowds, check this neighborhood out on a weekday; the pedestrian zone on the Old Arbat, in particular, draws big crowds on the weekends. The museums in this neighborhood are all fairly small; you'll need no more than an hour for each of them.

MAIN ATTRACTIONS

❺ **Andrei Bely Apartment Museum** (*Muzey-kvartira Andreya Belovo,* **Музей-квартира Андрея Белого**). On display are artifacts from the life of the writer Andrei Bely (1880–1934), considered to be one of the great Russian Symbolists and most famous for his novel *Petersburg.* The "Lines of Life" drawing on the wall of the first room shows the "energy" of Bely's life (the blue line in the middle) marked by dates and names of people he knew during specific times. The keepers of the museum offer exhaustive tours of the apartment in Russian. The general entrance to the museum is through the souvenir shop. ✉ *55 Arbat, Arbat* ☎ *495/241–7702* 🎫 *60R* ☉ *Wed.–Sun. 10–6* Ⓜ *Smolenskaya.*

❸ **Arbatskaya Ploshchad** *(Arbat Square, Арбатская Площадь)*. At this busy intersection, ulitsa Vozdvizhenka crosses the Boulevard Ring. The pedestrian underpass here has become a bustling marketplace (before you head underground take a look behind you at one of Russia's oldest movie theaters, the Kinoteatr Khudozhestvenny, which was opened in 1912). In the underpass itself, artists set up their easels, trying to entice passersby into having their portraits painted. And in spring and summer you'll find lots of impromptu flower vendors with the season's latest blooms (usually homegrown) for sale. Later in the evening musicians gather to play pretty good rock, foreign, and Russian music, in the underpass. When you emerge from the dizzying minimarket, you will be in front of the Praga restaurant, a three-story neoclassical building. ⊠*Arbat* ☎*No phone* Ⓜ*Arbatskaya.*

NEED A BREAK? Among the numerous cafés along the Arbat where you can take a break and have a drink is **Zhiguli** (⊠*11/1 Novy Arbat, off Arbatsky per., Arbat* ☎*495/291–4144* Ⓜ*Arbatskaya*), which feeds on a new wave of nostalgia for the Soviet Union. Fortunately the service and the food are better than they were in the old days. The café is not very far from the brightly tiled **Stena Mira** (Peace Wall) near the eastern end of the Arbat. Carolyna Marks created the first World Wall for Peace in Berkeley, California, in 1988. A Russian woman then set about bringing Marks to Moscow. Marks worked with thousands of Russian teens to build this one in 1990.

⑬ **Church of St. Simon the Stylite** *(Tserkov Simeona Stolpnika, Церковь Симеона Столпника)*. This 17th-century church stands out in stark contrast to the modern architecture dominating the area. During the reconstruction of Novy Arbat in the 1960s, many old churches and buildings were destroyed, but this one was left purposely standing as a "souvenir" of the past. For years it housed a conservation museum, but now it's been returned to the Orthodox Church and is active. Nothing remains, however, of the original interiors. ⊠*4 ul. Novy Arbat, Arbat* ☎*No phone* Ⓜ*Arbatskaya.*

❾ **Church of the Transfiguration on the Sands** *(Khram Spasa Preobrazheniya na Peskakh, Храм Спаса Преображения на Песках)*. Built in the 17th century, this elegant church was closed after the 1917 revolution and turned into a cartoon-production studio. Like many churches throughout Russia, however, it has been returned to its original purpose. The church is depicted in Vasily Polenov's well-known canvas *Moskovsky Dvornik (Moscow Courtyard)*, which now hangs in the Tretyakov Gallery. Services are at 10 on Sunday. ⊠*4 Spasopeskovsky per., Arbat* ☎*495/241–6203* ⌸*Free* ☉*Daily 8–8* Ⓜ*Smolenskaya.*

❷ **Dom Druzhby** *(Friendship House, Дом Дружбы)*. One of Moscow's most interesting buildings—it looks like a Moorish castle—was built in the late 19th century by the architect V. A. Mazyrin for the wealthy (and eccentric) industrialist Savva Morozov (Tolstoy mentions this home in his novel *Resurrection*). The building's name is a holdover from the Soviet days, when Russians and foreigners were supposed to meet only in officially sanctioned places. Today its more popular name is Dom Evropy, because the Federation Internationale Maisons de l'Europe is headquartered here. The interior is a veritable anthology of decorative styles, ranging from imitation Tudor to classical Greek and baroque, but, unfortunately, the building is not open to the public. ✉ *16 Vozdvizhenka ul., Arbat* ☎ *No phone* Ⓜ *Arbatskaya.*

⓫ **Dom Knigi** *(House of Books,* **Дом Книги***).* The country's largest bookstore has an English-language section on the second floor, and there's also often a good selection at the individual vendors' stalls outside the store. ✉ *26 Novy Arbat, Arbat* ☎ *495/789–3591* ⊙ *Weekdays 9 AM–11 PM, Sat. 10 AM–11 PM* Ⓜ *Arbatskaya.*

Herzen Museum *(Muzey Gertsena,* **Музей Герцена***).* Here you can learn not only about the writer, philosopher, and revolutionary Alexander Herzen (1812–70), but also about life in the 1840s in Russia and the Decembrists who rebelled against tsarist rule in 1825. Herzen himself may be most famous for his novel *Who Is to Blame?* as well as his short stories *Magpie the Thief* and *Dr. Krupov.* Explanations in English are available. You'll have to ring the bell to enter the museum, and you'll be given slippers to wear inside. ✉ *27 Sivtsev Vrazhek, Arbat* ☎ *495/241–5859* 🎫 *40R* ⊙ *Tues., Thurs., and Sat. 11–6, Wed. and Fri. 1–6. Closed last day of month* Ⓜ *Arbatskaya.*

⓬ **Lermontov House Museum** *(Dom-muzey Lermontova,* **Дом-музей Лермонтова***).* The Romantic poet and novelist Mikhail Lermontov (1814–41) lived in this house with his grandparents from 1830 to 1832. Several rooms are on display, including a small salon where Lermontov wrote poetry and drew pictures of his love interest. You can see these artifacts on the writing desk here. In the big salon in which the family entertained guests, there are family portraits and four small friezes depicting the War of 1812 hanging on the walls. Another room displays remarkably good pen-and-ink drawings by Lermontov. A steep staircase leads up to Lermontov's bedroom, complete with a guitar on the bed, a sketch on an easel, and portraits of Pushkin and others he admired. ✉ *2 Malaya Molchanovka ul., Arbat* ☎ *495/291–5298* 🎫 *40R* ⊙ *Thurs. and Sat. 11–5, Wed. and Fri. 2–5* Ⓜ *Arbatskaya.*

❻ **Melnikov House** *(Dom Melnikova,* **Дом Мельникова***).* This cylindrical concrete building was designed by the famous Constructivist architect Konstantin Melnikov in the late 1920s. The house is as remarkable outside with its wall-length windows as it is inside with its spiral staircases linking the three floors. Plans to open it as a museum have been in motion for years but look nowhere near completion. The architect's granddaughter lives in the house. ✉ *10 Krivoarbatsky per., Arbat* ☎ *No phone* Ⓜ *Smolenskaya.*

❹ **Pushkin Apartment Museum** *(Muzey-kvartira Pushkina,* **Музей-квартира Пушкина***).* The poet Alexander Pushkin lived here with his bride, Natalya Goncharova, for several months in 1831, right after they were married. Experts have re-created the original layout of the rooms and interior decoration. The first floor presents various trinkets and poems, plus information on Pushkin's relationship with Moscow; the second floor is a reconstruction of a typical early-19th-century room.

✉ *53 Arbat, Arbat* ☎ *495/241–9295* 💳 *60R* ⊙ *Wed.–Sun. 11–7* Ⓜ *Smolenskaya.*

⓾ **Scriabin Museum** *(Muzey Scriabina,* **Музей Скрябина***)*. This charming, dusty house-museum is in the composer Alexander Scriabin's (1872–1915) last apartment, where he died of blood poisoning in 1915. Visitors are scarce because foreign tourist groups are not usually brought here. The rooms are arranged and furnished just as they were when Scriabin lived here. Downstairs there's a concert hall where accomplished young musicians perform his music, usually on Tuesday and Wednesday evenings. Call for more information. ✉ *11 Bolshoi Nikolopeskovsky per., Arbat* ☎ *495/241–1901* 💳 *150R* ⊙ *Thurs. and weekends 10–5, Wed. and Fri. noon–6. Closed last Fri. of month* Ⓜ *Smolenskaya.*

❶ **Shchusev Architecture Museum** *(Muzey Arkhitektury imeni Shchuseva,* **Музей Архитектуры имени Щусева***)*. This museum, in an 18th-century neoclassical mansion, has a good reputation for displaying works by some of the best and most controversial architects in Russia and from around the world. The temporary exhibits cover Moscow architecture from ancient through contemporary times. ✉ *5 Vozdvizhenka ul., Arbat* ☎ *495/291–2109* ⊕ *www.muar.ru* 💳 *50R* ⊙ *Weekdays 11–6, weekends 11–4* Ⓜ *Biblioteka Imeni Lenina.*

ALSO WORTH SEEING

⓮ **Gogol statue** (Pamyatnik Gogolyu, **Памятник Гоголю**). This statue of a melancholy Nikolai Gogol (1809–52) originally stood at the start of Gogolevsky bulvar but was replaced by a more "upbeat" Gogol. The statue now stands inside a courtyard near the apartment building where the writer spent the last months of his life. The statue actually captures Gogol's sad disposition perfectly. He gazes downward, with his long, flowing cape draped over his shoulder, protecting him from the world. Gogol is perhaps best known in the West for his satirical drama *Revizor* (*The Inspector General*), about the unannounced visit of a government official to a provincial town. Characters from this and other Gogol works are engraved on the pedestal. ✉ *7 Nikitsky bulvar, Arbat* ☎ *No phone* Ⓜ *Arbatskaya.*

❽ **Spaso House** (**Спасо-Хаус**). The yellow neoclassical mansion behind the iron gate is the residence of the American ambassador. It was built in the early 20th century for a wealthy merchant. From Nikolopeskovsky pereulok, what you first see of this mansion is actually the back side of the building; it's much more impressive from the front. To get there, bear right at the small park, which is usually filled with neighborhood kids and their grandmothers. It's a pleasant place to take a break. ✉ *Spasopeskovskaya Pl., Arbat* Ⓜ *Smolenskaya.*

❼ **Vakhtangov Theater** *(Teatr imeni Vakhtangova,* **Театр имени Вахтангова***)*. An excellent traditional theater is housed within this impressive structure named after Stanislavsky's pupil Evgeny Vakhtangov (1883–1922). The gold statue of Princess Turandot and stone fountain to the right of the theater were created in honor of the 850th anniversary of Moscow in 1997; they are loved and hated by an equal proportion of Muscovites. ✉ *26 Arbat, Arbat* ☎ *495/241–1679* Ⓜ *Arbatskaya.*

THE KROPOTKINSKY DISTRICT
РАЙОН КРОПОТКИНСКОЙ

This picturesque old neighborhood is known as the Kropotkinsky District after the famous Russian anarchist Prince Pyotr Kropotkin. Head for the metro, which is also named in honor of him, that leads to the area's main street ulitsa Prechistenka. It's yet another ancient section of Moscow whose history dates back nearly to the foundation of the city itself. Almost none of its earliest architecture has survived, but this time the Soviets are not entirely to blame. The area suffered badly during the 1812 conflagration of Moscow, so most of its current buildings date to the postwar period of reconstruction, when neoclassicism and the so-called Moscow Empire style were in vogue. Before the revolution, the area was the favored residence of Moscow's old nobility, and it's along its thoroughfares that you'll find many of their mansions and homes, often called "nests of the gentry." It was also the heart of the literary and artistic community, and there were several famous literary salons here. Prince Kropotkin compared it to the Saint-Germain quarter of Paris.

■ TIP→ The Kropotkinsky District is served by the Kropotkinskaya, Borovitskaya, Biblioteka Imeni Lenina, and Park Kultury metro stations.

TIMING Taken at a leisurely pace, you could cover the neighborhood in three to four hours but the area is worth spending at least half a day on and, with stops at any of the various museums here, your exploration could easily expand to two days (the Pushkin Museum of Fine Arts alone is worth a day). If you're definitely interested in visiting some of the museums in this district, do *not* head out on a Monday, as most of the museums are closed that day.

MAIN ATTRACTIONS

❹ **Cathedral of Christ Our Savior** (*Khram Khrista Spasitelya,* **Храм Христа Спасителя**). This cathedral carries an amazing tale of destruction and reconstruction. Built between 1839 and 1883 as a memorial to the Russian troops who fell fighting Napoléon's forces in 1812, the cathedral was the largest single structure in Moscow and dominated the city's skyline. It had taken almost 50 years to build what only a few hours would destroy. On December 5, 1931, the cathedral was blown up. Under Stalin, the site had been designated for a mammoth new "Palace of Soviets," intended to replace the Kremlin as the seat of the Soviet government. Plans called for topping the 1,378-foot structure with a 300-foot statue of Lenin, who, had the plans ever materialized, would have spent more time above the clouds than in plain view. World War II delayed construction, and the entire project was scrapped when it was discovered that the land along the embankment was too damp to support such a heavy structure.

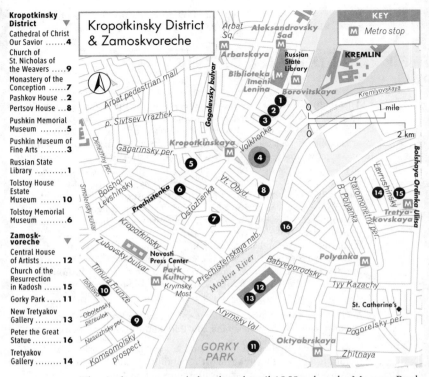

The site lay empty and abandoned until 1958, when the Moscow Pool, one of the world's largest outdoor swimming pools, was built. Divided into several sections, for training, competition, diving, and public swimming, it was heated and kept open all year long, even in the coldest days of winter. The pool was connected to the locker rooms by covered tunnels, and you could reach it by swimming through them. The pool was dismantled in 1994. Then—in perhaps one of architectural history's stranger twists—the cathedral was resurrected in 1997 from the ruins at a cost of more than $150 million. Today the giant cathedral is complete, with a stunning interior. ⊠*15–17 ul. Volkhonka, on the bank of the Moskva river, Kropotkinsky District* ☎*No phone* ⊕*www.xxc.ru* Ⓜ*Kropotkinskaya.*

❼ **Monastery of the Conception** (*Zachatievsky Monastyr,* **Зачатьевский Монастырь**). Founded in the 16th century, this working monastery is the oldest complex in the district, though nothing remains of the original buildings. Only the 17th-century redbrick Gate Church survives, and even that has been carefully renovated. It was built by the last surviving son of Ivan the Terrible, in what amounted to a plea to God for an heir (hence the monastery's name). He and his wife failed to have a son, however, and Boris Godunov became the next Russian leader. ⊠*Zachatievsky per., Kropotkinsky District* Ⓜ*Kropotkinskaya.*

2 **Pashkov House** *(Dom Pashkova,* **Дом Пашкова***).* Designed by Vasily Bazhenov, one of Russia's greatest architects, this mansion was erected between 1784 and 1786 for the wealthy Pashkov family. The central building is topped by a round belvedere and flanked by two service wings. In the 19th century it housed the Rumyantsev collection of art and rare manuscripts. Following the 1917 revolution, the museum was closed and the art collection was transferred to the Hermitage in St. Petersburg and the Pushkin Museum of Fine Art. The manuscripts were donated to the Russian State Library which now owns this building. The building, after twenty years of restoration, is now open to visitors. Exhibitions will go on display in its grand surroundings. ⊠*Mokhovaya ul. and ul. Znamenka, Kropotkinsky District* Ⓜ*Borovitskaya.*

> **THE OLD CATHEDRAL OF CHRIST OUR SAVIOUR**
>
> On your way to the Cathedral of Christ Our Savior, stop in the Kropotkinskaya metro station to see what is left of the original cathedral, which was bombed by the Bolsheviks in 1931. The interior of the station is decorated using marble stripped from the old cathedral before it was destroyed.

8 **Pertsov House** *(Dom Pertsova,* **Дом Перцова***).* One of the finest examples of Moscow art nouveau was built in 1905–07 by the architects Schnaubert and Zhukov. The facade of the steep-roofed and angled building, which is closed to the public, is covered in colorful mosaics. Walk all the way to the end of Soymonovsky pereulok, coming out at the river, and straight across you'll see a large, redbrick compound. This is the **Krasny Oktyabr (Red October) candy factory,** which used to fill the neighborhood with the smell of chocolate early in the morning. To your left, the buildings of the Kremlin line the distance, the golden cupolas of its churches all agleam. To the right you can see the behemoth Peter the Great statue. ⊠*Soymonovsky per. and Kropotkinskaya nab., Kropotkinsky District* ☏*No phone* Ⓜ*Kropotkinskaya.*

3 **Pushkin Museum of Fine Arts** *(Muzey Izobrazitelnykh Iskusstv imeni Pushkina,* **Музей Изобразительных Искусств имени Пушкина***).* One of the finest art museums in Russia, the Pushkin is famous for its Gauguin, Cézanne, and Picasso paintings, among other masterpieces. Founded by Ivan Vladimirovich Tsvetayev (1847–1913) of Moscow State University, father of poet Marina Tsvetaeva, the museum was originally established as a teaching aid for art students, which explains why a large part of its collection is made up of copies. The original building dates from 1895 to 1912 and was first known as the Alexander III Museum. It was renamed for Pushkin in 1937, on the centennial of the Russian poet's death. Next door, the **Musey Chastnykh Kollektsiy** (Museum of Private Collections) hosts some of the museum's most famous works and has separate hours and a small entrance fee.

Fodor'sChoice
★

The first-floor exhibit halls in the original building contain a fine collection of ancient Egyptian art (Hall 1); Greece and Rome are well represented, though mostly by copies (Room 7). The Italian school from the 15th century (Room 5) is represented by Botticelli's *The Annuncia-*

tion, Tomaso's *The Assassination of Caesar,* Guardi's *Alexander the Great at the Body of the Persian King Darius,* and Sano di Pietro's *The Beheading of John the Baptist,* among others. When you reach the Dutch School of the 17th Century (Hall 10), look for Rembrandt's *Portrait of an Old Woman,* whose subject may have been the artist's sister-in-law. Flemish and Spanish art from the 17th century are also well represented, with paintings by Murillo, Rubens, and Van Dyck (Hall 11).

The Museum of Private Collections (☎495/203–1546 ⌨40R ☾ Wed.–Sun. noon–6) houses a stunning assortment of impressionist, postimpressionist, and modern art. There are many fine canvases by Picasso (Hall 17), including several from his "blue" period. The same hall contains fascinating works by Henri Rousseau, including *Jaguar Attacking a Horse.* There are 10 works by Gauguin, mainly in Hall 18, which also houses Cézanne's *Pierrot* and *Harlequin.* The museum owns several works by Matisse (Hall 21), although they're not all on display. In the same hall hangs the poignant *Landscape at Auvers After the Rain* by Vincent van Gogh. The collection ends at Hall 23, which has works by Degas, Renoir, and Monet, including Monet's *Rouen Cathedral at Sunset.* ✉12 and 14 ul. Volkhonka, Kropotkinsky District ☎495/203–7998 or 495/203–9578 ⊕www.museum.ru/gmii ⌨300R ☾Tues.–Sun. 10–7 Ⓜ Kropotinskaya.

❶ Russian State Library *(Rossiyskaya Gosudarstvennaya Biblioteka,* **Российская Государственная Библиотека***)*. Once called Biblioteka Imeni Lenina, or the Lenin Library, this is Russia's largest library, with more than 30 million books and manuscripts. The modern building was built between 1928 and 1940. Bronze busts of famous writers and scientists adorn the main facade. The portico, supported by square black pillars, is approached by a wide ceremonial staircase. A 12-foot statue of the great Dostoyevsky was erected in front of the library in 1997 in honor of the 850th anniversary of Moscow. Dostoyevsky, sculpted by Alexander Rukavishnikov, sits where the Soviets once considered erecting a giant Lenin head. In theory, anyone can visit the library as a day visitor, but you may need some persistence to fill in forms and deal with the bureaucracy (bring your passport). It's worth it, though, to see the grand main hall. ✉3 ul. Vozdvizhenka, Kropotkinsky District ☎495/202–5790 ⊕www.rsl.ru ☾Mon.–Sat. 9–9 Ⓜ Biblioteki Imeni Lenina.

❻ Tolstoy Memorial Museum *(Muzey Tolstovo,* **Музей Толстого***)*. Architect Afanasy Grigoriev designed this mansion, a fine example of the Moscow Empire style (1822–24). The minor poet Lopukhin, a distant relative of Tolstoy's, lived here, and the mansion was converted into a museum in 1920. The exhibit halls contain a rich collection of manuscripts and photographs of Tolstoy and his family, as well as pictures and paintings of Tolstoy's Moscow. Even if you don't know Russian, you can read the writer's life story through the photographs, and in each room there's a typed handout in English to help explain its holdings. Note the picture of 19th-century Moscow in the second hall (on the left-hand wall). The huge cathedral taking up more than half the photograph is the Cathedral of Christ Our Savior—the original 19th-century structure that was subsequently replaced by the Moscow Pool. ✉ *11 ul. Prechistenka, Kropotkinsky District* ☎ *499/766–9328* ⊕ *www.tolstoymuseum.ru* 🖙 *50R* ☉ *Tues.–Sun. 11–5. Closed last Fri. of month* Ⓜ *Kropotkinskaya.*

❿ Tolstoy House Estate Museum *(Muzey-usadba Tolstovo,* **Музей-усадьба Толстого***)*. Tolstoy bought this house in 1882, at the age of 54, and spent nine winters here with his family. In summer he preferred his country estate in Yasnaya Polyana. The years here were not particularly happy ones. By this time Tolstoy had already experienced his "religious conversion," which prompted him to disown his earlier great novels, including *War and Peace* and *Anna Karenina*. His conversion sparked a feud among his own family members, which manifested itself even at the dining table: Tolstoy's wife, Sofia Andreevna, would sit at one end with their sons, while the writer would sit with their daughters at the opposite end.

The ground floor has several of the children's bedrooms and the nursery where Tolstoy's seven-year-old son died of scarlet fever in 1895, a tragedy that haunted the writer for the rest of his life. Also here are the dining rooms and kitchen, as well as the Tolstoys' bedroom, in which you can see the small desk used by his wife to meticulously copy all of her husband's manuscripts by hand.

Upstairs you'll find the Tolstoys' receiving room, where they held small parties and entertained guests, who included most of the leading figures of their day. The grand piano in the corner was played by such greats as Rachmaninoff and Rimsky-Korsakov. When in this room, you should ask the attendant to play the enchanting recording of Tolstoy greeting a group of schoolchildren, followed by a piano composition written and played by him. Also on this floor is an Asian-style den and Tolstoy's study, where he wrote his last novel, *Resurrection*.

Although electric lighting and running water were available at the time to the lesser nobility, Tolstoy chose to forgo both, believing it better to live simply. The museum honors his desire and shows the house as it was when he lived there. Tickets to the museum are sold in the administrative building to the far back left. Inside the museum, each room has signs in English explaining its significance and contents, but you might want to consider a guided tour (which must be booked in advance). You can also arrange a tour of the museum's attractive gardens, which include a number of trees from Tolstoy's time. ✉ *9 ul. Lva Tolstovo, Kropotkinsky District* ☎ *495/246–9444* 🖙 *200R* ☉ *Tues.–Sun. 10–5. Closed last Fri. of month* Ⓜ *Park Kultury.*

NEED A BREAK?

Good Mexican food can be found at Hemingway's (✉ *13 Komsomolsky pr., Kropotkinsky District* ☎ *495/246-5726* ⊕ *www.hemingways.su* Ⓜ *Park Kultury***), a new favorite of expats for its friendly atmosphere.**

ALSO WORTH SEEING

⑨ Church of St. Nicholas of the Weavers *(Tserkov Nikoly v Khamovnikakh,* **Церковь Николы в Хамовниках***)*. This church, which was built between 1679 and 1682 and remained open throughout the years of Communist rule, has been wonderfully preserved and its elegant bell tower is particularly impressive. Five gilded domes top the church, and the saucy colorfulness of the orange and green trim against a perfectly white facade makes it look like a frosted gingerbread house. In fact, the design was meant to suggest a festive piece of woven cloth, for it was the weavers, who settled in considerable numbers in this quarter in the 17th century, who commissioned the building of this church. Morning and evening services are held daily, and the church, with its wealth of icons, is as handsome inside as out. ⊠ *Komsomolsky pr. and ul. Lva Tolstovo, Kropotkinsky District* ☎ *No phone* Ⓜ *Park Kultury.*

⑤ Pushkin Memorial Museum *(Muzey Pushkina,* **Музей Пушкина***)*. Aleksandr Pushkin (1799–1837) never lived here and probably never even visited this fine yellow mansion built in the 19th century by architect Afanasy Grigoriev, but don't let that put you off. A redesign in 1999 that coincided with the 200th anniversary of Pushkin's birth made this one of the smartest museums in town and an increasingly popular place for conferences and business bashes. Upon first entering the museum you'll step into a beautiful atrium that floods the building with light. Beyond the atrium are several rooms showcasing Pushkin's sketches, letters, and personal effects. ⊠ *12 ul. Prechistenka, Kropotkinsky District* ☎ *495/201–5674* ⬚ *80R* ☉ *Tues.–Sun. 10–6* Ⓜ *Kropotinskaya.*

ZAMOSKVORECHE ЗАМОСКВОРЕЧЬЕ

Zamoskvoreche means literally "beyond the Moskva River" and applies to the southern area of the old city opposite the Kremlin. Until modern times Zamoskvoreche had a sleepy rural feel—even today the old twisting streets give it a character all but obliterated in other parts of the city. By the 17th century Zamoskvoreche was well settled by a population of artisans serving the Court as well as being the first line of defense against the Tatars. In the 19th century members of the most distinctive of classes, the Moscow merchants, built their homes here. They also sponsored artists and after time created Russia's first art museum, Tretyakov Gallery.

Gorky Park, popularized by Martin Cruz Smith's Cold War novel of the same name, is situated along the right bank of the Moskva River, just beyond Krymsky Most (Crimea Bridge). Aside from the park and the Tretyakov Gallery, Bolshaya Ordinka ulitsa is a draw for its Russian Orthodox churches.

■ TIP→ **Zamoskvoreche is served by the Tretyakovskaya, Polyanka, and Oktyabrskaya metro stations.**

TIMING   There is a lot to see in this area so it might be worth spending a day or even two on the sights. To truly enjoy the Tretyakov Gallery, it's probably best to plan a separate visit. A full exploration of Gorky Park could also easily take an afternoon. Note that many of the sights are closed on Monday.

MAIN ATTRACTIONS

Bolshaya Ordinka ulitsa. Russian Orthodox churches, many recently restored, line this north–south street that runs for more than a mile. Near the Dobrininskaya metro, the white classical-style **St. Catherine's Church** (*Tserkov Ekaterini*, **Церковь Екатерины** ✉*No. 60, Zamoskvoreche* ☎*No phone*) sits on the corner of Pogorelsky pereulok. It was commissioned by Catherine the Great in 1763 and designed by Karl Blank. The interior is in a bad state, but you can still make out some frescoes. Walk farther north to reach **Martha and Mary Convent** (*Marfo-Mariinskaya Obitel*, **Марфо-Мариинская Обитель** ✉*No. 34, Zamoskvoreche* ☎*No phone*), which opened in 1909 and is most noted for its white Church of the Intercession of the Virgin Mary. It has been recently restored and is open for services on Sunday at 8:30 AM. The religious order of the convent is now across the street. A few doors from the convent is **Church of St. Nicholas in Pyzhi** (*Tserkov Nikoly v Pyzhakh*, **Церковь Николы в Пыжах** ✉*No. 27a, Zamoskvoreche* ☎*495/231–3742* ⊙*Mon., Tues., and Thurs. noon–6:30, weekends 10–6:30* Ⓜ*Dobrininskaya*), an ornate, bright-white building with five gold cupolas, dating from 1670. Continue up Bolshaya Ordinka ulitsa and take a right on Klimentovsky pereulok. Push your way through the throngs exiting the metro to the middle of the small alleyway to view the baroque **St. Clement's Church** (*Tservkov Klimenta*, **Церковь Климента** ✉*26 Klimentovsky per., Zamoskvoreche* ☎*No phone* Ⓜ*Tretyakovskaya*). The construction of this church, begun in 1743 and designed by Pietro Antonio Trezzini, took three decades. Today it is set to be restored and its star-studded cupolas and redbrick baroque building are especially impressive. Retrace your steps to Bolshaya Ordinka ulitsa and cross the street and take a right. A few steps away is the yellow **Church of the Virgin of All Sorrows** (*Tserkov Bogomateri Vsekh Skorbyashchikh Radostei* ✉*No. 20, Zamoskvoreche* ☎*No phone* Ⓜ*Tretyakovskaya*). Designed by Osip Bove and built between 1828 and 1835, the neoclassical-era church is an excellent example of the Empire style popular in the early 19th century. It replaced one that had burned down in the fire of 1812. The interior, filled with icons and gold, is nothing earth-shattering, but is good for getting the feel of a typical working church. Sunday services are often at 10 AM, but the church is usually open daily. From here, you're not far from the famous Tretyakov Gallery. ✉*Bolshaya Ordinka ul., Zamoskvoreche* Ⓜ*Oktyabrskaya or Dobrininskaya.*

⑫ **Central House of Artists** (*TsDKh; Tsentralny Dom Khudozhnikov*, **Центральный Дом Художников**). The street entrance of this huge, modern building leads to the exhibit halls of the Artists' Union, where members display their work on three floors. This is a great place to find a sketch or watercolor to take home with you. The building also houses the modern branch of the Tretyakov Gallery. Next door is the **Art Park,** where contemporary sculpture and old statues of Soviet dignitaries stand side by side. It's a pleasant place for a stroll. ✉*10 Krym-*

sky Val, Zamoskvoreche ☎️*495/238–9843 or 495/238–9634* 💳*100R*
🕐*Tues.–Sun. 11–8* Ⓜ️*Park Kultury or Oktyabrskaya.*

⓯ Church of the Resurrection in Kadosh *(Tserkov Voskreseniya v Kadashakh,*
Церковь Воскресения в Кадашах*).* Because a high fence surrounds it,
this colorful church is best viewed from far away. Look for a red-and-
white brick bell tower and a large green-blue onion dome surrounded
by three smaller ones. Built in 1687, the church, which is undergoing
a very slow renovation process, is an excellent example of the Moscow baroque style. ✉️*7 Vtoroi (2nd) Kadshovksy per., Zamoskvoreche*
☎️*No phone* Ⓜ️*Tretyakovskaya.*

⓭ New Tretyakov Gallery *(Novaya Tretyakovskaya Galereya,* **Новая**
Третьяковская Галерея*).* This branch of the Tretyakov Gallery is in
the same building, through a side entrance, as the Tsentralny Dom
Khudozhnikov (Central House of Artists) across from Gorky Park.
Often called the "New Branch," it has a permanent exhibit titled "Art
of the 20th Century" that spans from prerevolutionary work by Cha-
gall, Malevich, and Kandinsky to the Socialist Realist, Modern, and
Postmodern periods. ✉️*10 Krymsky Val, through sculpture-garden side*
entrance, Zamoskvoreche ☎️*495/238–1378 or 495/238–2054* 🌐*www.*
tretyakov.ru 💳*225R* 🕐*Tues.–Sun. 10–7* Ⓜ️*Park Kultury.*

⓮ Tretyakov Gallery *(Tretyakovskaya Galereya,* **Третьяковская Галерея***).*

Fodor'sChoice The Tretyakov Gallery—now often called the "Old Tretyakov" in
★   light of the annex, the New Tretyakov—is the repository of some of
the world's greatest masterpieces of Russian art. Spanning the 11th
through the 20th centuries, the works include sacred icons, stunning
portrait and landscape art, the famous Russian Realists' paintings that
culminated in the Wanderers' Group, and the splendid creations of
Russian Symbolism, impressionism, and art nouveau.

The Tretyakov was officially opened in 1892 as a public state museum,
but its origins predate that time by more than 35 years. In the mid-
1800s, a successful young Moscow industrialist, Pavel Mikhailovich
Tretyakov, was determined to amass a collection of national art that
would be worthy of a museum of fine arts for the entire country. In
pursuit of this high-minded goal, he began to purchase paintings, drawings, and sculpture, adjudged both on high artistic merit and on their
place within the various important canons of their time. For the most
part undeterred by critics' disapproval and arbiters of popular taste, he
became one of the—if not *the*—era's most valued patrons of the arts,
with honor and gratitude conferred upon him still to this day.

Up until six years before his death, Tretyakov maintained his enormous collection as a private one, but allowed virtually unlimited free
access to the public. In 1892 he donated his collection to the Moscow
city government, along with a small inheritance of other fine works
collected by his brother Sergei. The holdings have been continually
increased by subsequent state acquisitions, including the nationaliza-
tion of privately owned pieces after the Communist revolution.

There are no English-language translations on the plaques here, but you can rent an audio guide or buy an English-language guidebook.

It may be the rich collection of works completed after 1850, however, that pleases museumgoers the most, for it comprises a selection of pieces from each of the Russian masters, sometimes of their best works. Hanging in the gallery are paintings by Nikolai Ge (*Peter the Great Interrogating the Tsarevich Alexei*), Vasily Perov (*Portrait of Fyodor Dostoyevsky*), Vasily Polenov (*Grandmother's Garden*), Viktor Vasnetsov (*After Prince Igor's Battle with the Polovtsy*), and many others. Several canvases of the beloved Ivan Shishkin, with their depictions of Russian fields and forests—including *Morning in the Pine Forest*, of three bear cubs cavorting—fill one room. There are also several paintings by the equally popular Ilya Repin, whose most famous painting, *The Volga Boatmen*, also bedecks the walls. Later works, from the end of the 19th century, include an entire room devoted to the Symbolist Mikhail Vrubel (*The Princess Bride, Demon Seated*); Nestorov's glowing *Vision of the Youth Bartholomew*, the boy who would become St. Sergius, founder of the monastery at Sergeyev-Posad; and the magical pieces by Valentin Serov (*Girl with Peaches, Girl in Sunlight*). You'll also see turn-of-the-20th-century paintings by Nikolai Konstantinovich Roerikh (1874–1947), whose New York City home is a museum.

The first floor houses the icon collection. Among the many delights here are icons painted in the late 14th and early 15th centuries by the master Andrei Rublyov, including his celebrated *Holy Trinity*. Also on display are icons of his disciples, Daniel Chorny among them, as well as some of the earliest icons to reach ancient Kievan Rus', such as the 12th-century *Virgin of Vladimir*, brought from Byzantium.

The second floor holds 18th-, 19th-, and 20th-century paintings and sculpture and is where indefatigable Russian art lovers satisfy their aesthetic longings. A series of halls of 18th-century portraits, including particularly fine works by Dmitry Levitsky, acts as a time machine into the country's noble past. Other rooms are filled with works of the 19th century, embodying the burgeoning movements of romanticism and naturalism in such gems of landscape painting as Silvester Shchedrin's *Aqueduct at Tivoli* and Mikhail Lebedev's *Path in Albano* and *In the Park*. Other favorite pieces to look for are Karl Bryullov's *The Last Day of Pompeii*, Alexander Ivanov's *Appearance of Christ to the People*, and Orest Kiprensky's well-known *Portrait of the Poet Alexander Pushkin*.

When you leave the gallery, pause a moment to look back on the fanciful art nouveau building itself, which is quite compelling. Tretyakov's original home, where the first collection was kept, still forms a part of the gallery. As the demands of a growing collection required additional space, the house was continually enlarged, until finally an entire annex was built to function as the gallery. In 1900, when there was no longer a family living in the house, the artist Viktor Vasnetsov undertook to create the wonderful facade the gallery now carries, and more space was later added. Keep in mind that the ticket office closes at 6:30 PM.

✉12 *Lavrushinsky per., Zamoskvoreche* ☎495/951–1362 ⊕*www. tretyakov.ru* 🖃250R ⊙*Tues.–Sun. 10–7:30* Ⓜ*Tretyakovskaya.*

Superb cakes and pastries, an à la carte menu, and alcoholic refreshments await you at Café Kranzler (✉*1 Balchug ul., Zamoskvoreche* ☎*495/230– 6500* Ⓜ*Novokuznetskaya*) **inside the luxurious Balchug hotel. It is not cheap but it's the perfect place to relax after a long walk.**

ALSO WORTH SEEING

⓫ **Gorky Park** (Парк Горького). Muscovites usually refer to this park made famous by Martin Cruz Smith's Cold War novel *Gorky Park* as Park Kultury (Park of Culture); its official title is actually the Central Park of Culture and Leisure. The park was laid out in 1928 and covers an area of 275 acres. It's the city's most popular all-around recreation center, and in summer, especially on weekends, it's crowded with children and adults enjoying its many attractions. A giant Ferris wheel dominates the park's green; if you're brave enough to ride it, you'll be rewarded with great views of the city. The even braver may want to venture onto the roller coaster. Note that the park's admission price does not include individual rides. The park also has a boating pond, a fairground, sports grounds, and numerous cafés. In summer, boats leave from the pier for excursions along the Moskva River, and in winter the ponds are transformed into skating rinks. ✉*9 Krymsky Val, Zamoskvoreche* 🖀*No phone* 🖃*100R in summer, free in winter* ⊙*Daily 10–10* Ⓜ*Oktyabrskaya.*

⓰ **Peter the Great statue** (Памятник Петру Великому). The enormous statue of the tsar stands atop a base made in the form of a miniature ship. He's holding the steering wheel of a ship, symbolizing his role as the founder of the Russian naval force in the 1700s. The statue, measuring 90 feet high, has been a source of controversy since construction started on it in 1996. Most Muscovites agree that the statue, made by Moscow mayor Yuri Luzhkov's favorite sculptor, Zurab Tsereteli, is not only an eyesore but also has no place in Moscow since Peter the Great was the one who moved the capital of Russia from Moscow to St. Petersburg. After citizens complained, a board of art experts was formed to decide if the statue would stay. They decided to keep it. The decision was made mostly in light of the fact that erecting the statue cost $20 million and dismantling it would cost half that amount. When you finally set eyes on the statue you'll probably understand why common nicknames for it are "Cyclops" and "Gulliver." The colossal statue is so tall that a red light had to be put on its head to warn planes. ✉*Krymskaya nab., Zamoskvoreche* Ⓜ*Park Kultury.*

SOUTHERN OUTSKIRTS

Southwest and southeast of the city center are some of Moscow's most notable holy sites. Especially of interest are Donskoy Monastery and New Maiden's Convent in the east and, in the west, the monasteries across the river from the Kremlin built to defend the capital.

DONSKOY MONASTERY & NEW MAIDEN'S CONVENT
ДОНСКОЙ МОНАСТЫРЬ & НОВОДЕВИЧИЙ МОНАСТЫРЬ

The New Maiden's Convent, southwest of the city center, is one of Moscow's finest and best-preserved ensembles of 16th- and 17th-century Russian architecture. It's interesting not only for its impressive cathedral and charming churches but also for the dramatic chapters of Russian history that have been played out within its walls. It stands in a wooded section bordering a small pond, making this a particularly pleasant place for an afternoon stroll. After the Bolshevik Revolution, the convent was made into a museum. One of the convent's churches is open for services. Attached to the convent is a fascinating cemetery where some of Russia's greatest literary, military, and political figures are buried. A few metro stops away is another fabled religious institution, Donskoy Monastery, founded in the 16th century by Boris Godunov, with a cathedral commissioned a century later by the regent Sophia, Peter the Great's half-sister.

■TIP➜These sights can be reached via the Sportivnaya and Shabolovskaya metro stations. Note that it will take you about 45 minutes' travel time each way from downtown Moscow.

Fodor'sChoice **Donskoy Monastery** (*Donskoy Monastyr*, **Донской Монастырь**). The
★ 16th-century Donskoy Monastery, situated in a secluded, wooded area in the southwest section of Moscow, is a fascinating memorial to Russian architecture and art. From 1934 to 1992, a branch of the Shchusev Architecture Museum, keeping architectural details of churches, monasteries, and public buildings destroyed under the Soviets, was located—more or less secretly—inside its walls. Today the monastery is once again functioning as a religious institution. But the bits and pieces of demolished churches and monuments remain, forming a graveyard of destroyed architecture from Russia's past.

The monastery grounds are surrounded by a high defensive wall with 12 towers, the last of the defense fortifications to be built around Moscow. The monastery was built on the site where, in 1591, the Russian army stood waiting for an impending attack from Tatar troops grouped on the opposite side of the river. According to legend, the Russians awoke one morning to find the Tatars gone. Their sudden retreat was considered a miracle, and Boris Godunov ordered a monastery built to commemorate the miraculous victory. Of course, it didn't happen quite like that, but historians confirm that the Tatars did retreat after only minor skirmishes, which is difficult to explain. Never again would they come so close to Moscow. The victory was attributed to the icon of the Virgin of the Don that Prince Dimitry Donskoy had supposedly carried previously, during his campaign in 1380 (in which the Russians won their first decisive victory against the Tatars). The monastery was named in honor of the wonder-working icon.

When you enter the grounds through the western gates, an icon of the Virgin of the Don looks down on you from above the entrance to the imposing **New Cathedral.** The brick cathedral was built in the late 17th century by Peter the Great's half-sister, the regent Sophia. It has been under restoration for decades; services are held in the gallery surrounding the church, where the architectural exhibits were once housed. The smaller **Old Cathedral** stands to the right of the New Cathedral. The attractive red church with white trim was built between 1591 and 1593, during the reign of Boris Godunov. It's open for services.

One of the most fascinating sections of the monastery is its graveyard, with many fine examples of memorial art. After the plague swept through Moscow in 1771, Catherine the Great forbade any more burials in the city center. The Donskoy Monastery, at that time on the city's outskirts, became a fashionable burial place for the well-to-do. The small **Church of the Archangel** built against the fortification wall on the far right was the private chapel and crypt of the prominent Golitsyn family (original owners of the Arkhangelskoye estate). Many leading intellectuals, politicians, and aristocrats were buried here in the 18th, 19th, and 20th centuries. ✉ *1 Donskaya Pl., Southern Outskirts* ☎ *495/952–1646* 🎫 *Free* ⊙ *Daily 7:20–6* Ⓜ *Shabolovskaya.*

Novodevichy cemetery (Новодевичье кладбище). The Novodevichy cemetery (*kladbishche*) contains a fascinating collection of memorial art, but it's difficult for non-Russian speakers to identify the graves. For more than a generation, the cemetery was closed to the general public in large part because the controversial Nikita Khrushchev (1894–1971) is buried here, rather than on Red Square, like other Soviet leaders. Thanks to glasnost, the cemetery was reopened in 1987, and now anyone is welcome to visit its grounds.

Khrushchev's grave is near the rear of the cemetery, at the end of a long tree-lined walkway. If you can't find it, any of the *babushki* (a colloquial term, which means "grandmothers," used throughout Russia to refer to museum caretakers, often hearty grandmothers who wear babushka head coverings of the same name) will point out the way. Krushchev was deposed in 1964 and lived his next and last seven years in disgrace, under virtual house arrest. The memorial consists of a stark black-and-white slab, with a curvilinear border marking the separation of the two colors. The contrast of black and white symbolizes the contradictions of his reign. The memorial caused a great furor of objection among the Soviet hierarchy when it was unveiled. It was designed by the artist Ernst Neizvestny, himself a controversial figure. In the 1960s Khrushchev visited an exhibit of contemporary art that included some of Neizvestny's works. Khrushchev dismissed Neizvestny's contributions as "filth," and asked the name of their artist. When Neizvestny (which means "Unknown") answered, Khrushchev scornfully said that the USSR had no need for artists with such names. To this the artist replied, "In front of my work, I am the premier." Considering the times, it was a brave thing to say to the leader of the Soviet Union. Neizvestny eventually joined the ranks of the émigré artists; he now lives in the United States.

Many of those buried in the cemetery were war casualties in 1941 and 1942. Among the memorials you might want to look for are those to the composers Prokofiev and Scriabin and the writers Chekhov,

1

Gogol, Bulgakov, and Mayakovsky. Chekhov's grave is decorated with the trademark seagull of the Moscow Art Theater, the first to successfully produce his plays. Recent burials include Russia's first president Boris Yeltsin and cellist and conductor Mstislav Rostropovich. You can request a tour in English from the cemetery's excursion bureau; call and reserve ahead as they usually need advance warning. In light of the bountiful history and scant English translations, these tours can be very rewarding. ⊠*Luzhnetsky proyezd, Southern Outskirts* ☎*495/246–6614 or 495/246–7527* ⏍*Free* ⊙*Daily 10–6* Ⓜ*Sportivnaya.*

Fodor'sChoice **New Maiden's Convent** (*Novodevichy Monastyr,* **Новодевичий**
★ **Монастырь**). Enclosed by a crenellated wall with 12 colorful battle towers, the convent comprises several groups of buildings. Tsar Vasily III (1479–1533) founded the convent in 1524 on the road to Smolensk and Lithuania—a strategic way to commemorate Moscow's capture of Smolensk from Lithuania. Due to the tsar's initiative, it enjoyed an elevated position among the many monasteries and convents of Moscow and became a convent primarily for ladies of noble birth. Little remains of the original structure. The convent suffered severely during the Time of Troubles (approximately 1598–1613), concluding when the first Romanov was elected to the throne. Its current appearance dates largely from the 17th century, when the convent was significantly rebuilt and enhanced.

Among the first of the famous women to take the veil here was Irina, wife of the feebleminded Tsar Fyodor and the sister of Boris Godunov, in the 16th century. Opera fans may be familiar with the story of Boris Godunov, the subject of a well-known work by Mussorgsky. Godunov was a powerful nobleman who exerted much influence over the tsar. When Fyodor died, Godunov was the logical successor to the throne, but rather than proclaim himself tsar, he followed his sister to Novodevichy. Biding his time, Godunov waited until the clergy and townspeople begged him to become tsar. His election took place at the convent, inside the Cathedral of Smolensk. But his rule was ill-fated, touching off the Time of Troubles.

In the next century, Novodevichy became the residence of yet another royal: Sophia, the half-sister of Peter the Great, who ruled as his regent from 1682 through 1689, while he was still a boy. She did not wish to give up her position when the time came for Peter's rule and was deposed by him. He then kept her prisoner inside Novodevichy. Even that was not enough to restrain the ambitious sister, and from her cell at the convent she organized a revolt of the *streltsy* (Russian militia). The revolt was summarily put down, and to punish Sophia, Peter had the bodies of the dead streltsy hung up along the walls of the convent and outside Sophia's window. Despite his greatness, Peter had a weakness for the grotesque, especially when it came to punishing his enemies. He left the decaying bodies hanging for more than a year. Yet another of the convent's later "inmates" was Yevdokiya Lopukhina, Peter's first wife. Peter considered her a pest and rid himself of her by sending her to a convent in faraway Suzdal. She outlived him, though, and eventually returned to Moscow. She spent her final years at Novodevichy, where she is buried.

You enter the convent through the arched passageway topped by the **Preobrazhensky Tserkov** (Gate Church of the Transfiguration), widely considered one of the best examples of Moscow baroque. To your left as you enter is the ticket booth, where tickets are sold to the various exhibits housed in the convent. Exhibits include rare and ancient Russian paintings, both ecclesiastical and secular; woodwork and ceramics; and fabrics and embroidery. There's also a large collection of illuminated and illustrated books, decorated with gold, silver, and jewels. The building to your right is the Lophukin House, where Yevdokiya lived from 1727 to 1731. Sophia's prison, now a guardhouse, is to your far right, in a corner of the northern wall.

The predominant structure inside the convent is the huge five-dome **Sobor Smolenskoy Bogomateri** (Cathedral of the Virgin of Smolensk), dedicated in 1525 and built by Alexei Fryazin. It was closely modeled after the Kremlin's Assumption Cathedral. Inside, there's a spectacular iconostasis with 84 wooden columns and icons dating from the 16th and 17th centuries. Simon Ushakov, a leader in 17th-century icon art, was among the outstanding Moscow artists who participated in the creation of the icons. Also here are the tombs of Sophia and Yevdokiya. Yet another historic tale connected to the convent tells how the cathedral was slated for destruction during the War of 1812. Napoléon had ordered the cathedral dynamited, but a brave nun managed to extinguish the fuse just in time, and the cathedral was spared.

To the right of the cathedral is the **Uspensky Tserkov** (Church of the Assumption) and **Refectory,** originally built in 1687 and then rebuilt after a fire in 1796. It was here that the blue-blooded nuns took their meals.

If a convent can have a symbol other than an icon, then Novodevichy's would be the ornate belfry towering above its eastern wall. It rises 236 feet and consists of six ornately decorated tiers. The structure is topped by a gilded dome that can be seen from miles away. ⊠1 *Novodevichy proyezd, Southern Outskirts* ☎495/246–8526 or 495/246–2201 💳150R ☉Museum Thurs.–Tues. 10–5, convent daily 10–7. Closed last Mon. of month Ⓜ Sportivnaya.

NEED A BREAK?

U Pirosmani (⊠*4 Novodevichy proyezd, Southern Outskirts* ☎495/247–1926 Ⓜ*Sportivnaya*), a well-known restaurant specializing in the spicy cuisine of Georgia, is across the pond from the convent. If you're visiting on a weekend, you may want to book ahead.

THE MONASTERIES OF SOUTHEAST MOSCOW
МОНАСТЫРИ ЮГО-ЗАПАДА МОСКВЫ

There are three ancient monasteries along the banks of the Moskva River, in the southeast section of Moscow. Their history dates to Moscow's earliest days, when it was the center of a fledgling principality and constantly under threat of enemy attack. A series of monasteries was built across the river from the Kremlin to form a ring of defense fortifications. Two of the monasteries here were once part of that fortification ring.

Formerly suburban, this area did not fare well as the city grew. Beginning in the 19th century, factories were built along the banks of the river, including the famous Hammer and Sickle metallurgical plant. In the midst of the long-gone industrial center are the quaint monasteries of Moscow's past, being slowly restored.

■ TIP➡ These sights can be reached via the Proletarskaya and Taganskaya metro stations.

Andronik Monastery (*Andronikov Monastyr*, **Андроников Монастырь**). A stroll inside the heavy stone fortifications of this monastery, which is in far better condition than Novospassky Monastyr or Krutitskoye Podvorye, is an excursion into Moscow's past. The loud crowing of birds overhead drowns out the rumble of the city. Even the air seems purer here, perhaps because of the old birch trees growing on the monastery grounds and just outside its walls. The monastery was founded in 1360 by Metropolitan Alexei and named in honor of its first abbot, St. Andronik. The site was chosen not only for its strategic importance—on the steep banks of the Moskva River—but also because, according to legend, it was from this hill that Metropolitan Alexei got his first glimpse of the Kremlin.

The dominating structure on the monastery grounds is the **Spassky Sobor** (Cathedral of the Savior), Moscow's oldest stone structure. Erected in 1420–27 on the site of an earlier, wooden church, it rests on the mass grave of Russian soldiers who fought in the Battle of Kulikovo (1380), the decisive Russian victory that eventually led to the end of Mongol rule in Russia. Unfortunately, the original interiors, which were painted by Andrei Rublyov and another famous icon painter, Danil Chorny, were lost in a fire in 1812. Fragments of their frescoes have been restored, however. The cathedral is open for services at 5:30 PM on Saturday and 9 AM on Sunday.

The building to your immediate left as you enter the monastery is the former abbot's residence. It now houses a permanent exhibit titled "Masterpieces of Ancient Russian Art," with works from the 13th through 16th centuries. The exhibit includes icons from the Novgorod, Tver, Rostov, and Moscow schools. A highlight of the collection is the early-16th-century *St. George Smiting the Dragon*, from the Novgorod School.

The next building, to the left and across the pathway from the Cathedral of the Savior, is the **Refectory**. Like the Novospassky Monastyr, it was built during the reign of Ivan the Great, between 1504 and 1506. Today it houses an exhibit of the monastery's newer acquisitions, primarily icons from the 19th to 20th centuries. Attached to the Refectory is the **Tserkov Archangela Mikhaila** (Church of St. Michael the Archangel), another example of the style known as Moscow baroque.

It was commissioned by the Lopukhin family—relatives of Yevdokiya Lopukhina, the first, unloved wife of Peter the Great—as the family crypt in 1694. But there are no Lopukhins buried here, as Peter had Yevdokiya banished to a monastery in faraway Suzdal before the church was even finished, and her family was exiled to Siberia.

The last exhibit is in the former monks' residence, the redbrick building just beyond the Tserkov Archangela Mikhaila. The exhibit is devoted to 3rd-century saint Nikolai the Miracle Worker, better known in the West as St. Nicholas or Santa Claus and contains icons depicting his life and work. From Ploshchad Ilyicha, follow Sergiya Radonezhskovo until you come out onto a square with tramlines. On your right you will find the monastery. ⊠ *10 Andronevskaya Pl., Southern Outskirts* ☎ *495/678–1467* ☞ *Free* ☉ *Daily 8–8* Ⓜ *Ploshchad Ilyicha.*

Church of St. Martin the Confessor *(Tserkov Svyatitelya Martina Ispovednika,* Церковь Святителя Мартина Исповедника*).* This lovely church dates from the late 18th century and is in need of a restoration, but it remains a working church. Farther down the street, at No. 29, is another building of historic importance: the apartment house where the theater director Stanislavsky was born in 1863. After exiting Taganskaya station, you need to cross the square. On the other side of the square will be two roads leading away from the square. Take the one on the left and you will reach St. Martin. ⊠ *15 Bolshaya Kommunisticheskaya ul., Southern Outskirts* Ⓜ *Taganskaya.*

Krutitskoye Ecclesiastical Residence *(Krutitskoye Podvorye,* Крутицкое Подворье*).* The first cathedral on this hill was erected sometime in the 13th century. Its name comes from the word *kruta,* meaning "hill." This was originally a small monastery, a site of defense in the 14th century against the Tatar-Mongol invaders. At the end of the 16th century the monastery's prestige grew when it became the suburban residence of the Moscow metropolitan. The church and grounds were completely rebuilt, and the current structures date from this period. As monasteries go, Krutitskoye's period of flowering was short-lived; it was closed in 1788 on orders from Catherine the Great, who secularized many church buildings. In the 19th century it was used as army barracks, and it's said that the Russians accused of setting the Moscow fire of 1812 were tortured here by Napoléon's forces. In the 20th century, the Soviets turned the barracks into a military prison. Although the buildings have been returned to the Orthodox Church, the prison, now closed, remains on the monastery grounds.

To your left as you enter the monastery grounds is the five-dome, redbrick **Uspensky Sobor** (Assumption Cathedral), erected at the end of the 16th century on the site of several previous churches. It's a working church, undergoing restoration like many of its counterparts throughout the city. Still very attractive inside, it has an assemblage of icons, lovely frescoes, and an impressive all-white altar and iconostasis. The cathedral is attached to a gallery leading to the **Teremok** (Gate Tower), a splendid example of Moscow baroque. It was built between 1688 and 1694, and its exterior decoration is the work of Osip Startsev.

The gallery and Teremok originally served as the passageway for the metropolitan as he walked from his residence (to the right of the Teremok) to the cathedral. Passing through the gate tower, you will see the military prison, replete with lookout towers, on the opposite side of the Teremok gates. Film crews often come to shoot inside the now-defunct prison.

You should go through the gate tower to take a full walk around the tranquil grounds. From this side, you can enter the bell tower, which dates from 1680. Taking the stairs inside, through the door off its first level, you'll have access to the gallery itself and can walk along the walls. To get here from Proletarskaya station, take only lefts out of the station to emerge on Sarinsky proyezd. With your back to the metro, walk toward Trety (3rd) Krutitsky pereulok, the busy street a short distance ahead. Turn right to reach the older, tree-lined street leading up an incline. This is Chetvyorty (4th) Krutitsky pereulok. Climb to the top of the hill and you'll see the five-dome Uspensky Sobor. ✉ *Pervyi (1st) Kruititsky per., Southern Outskirts* ☎ 495/676–9256 ☉ *Daily 8–8. Closed 1st Mon. of month* Ⓜ *Proletarskaya.*

New Savior Monastery (*Novospassky Monastyr,* **Новоспасский Монастырь**). The monastery was built in 1462, but its history dates to the 13th century. It was originally inside the Kremlin, and it's called the *New* Savior Monastery because its new site on the banks of the Moskva River was a transfer ordered by Ivan III, also known as Ivan the Great, who wanted to free up space in the Kremlin for other construction. Ivan was the first Russian leader to categorically (and successfully) renounce Russia's allegiance to the khan of the Golden Horde. It was during his reign that a unified Russian state was formed under Moscow's rule. This monastery was just one of the numerous churches and monasteries built during the prosperous time of Ivan's reign. None of the monastery's original 15th-century structures has survived. The present fortification wall and most of the churches and residential buildings on the grounds date from the 17th century. In uglier modern history, a site just outside the monastery's walls was one of the mass graves for those executed during Stalin's purges.

You enter the monastery at the nearest entrance to the left of the **Bell Tower Gate**, which was erected in 1786. The first thing you see as you enter the grounds is the massive white **Sobor Spasa Preobrazheniya** (Transfiguration Cathedral). You may notice a resemblance, particularly in the domes, to the Kremlin's Assumption Cathedral, which served as this cathedral's model. The structure was built between 1642 and 1649 by the Romanov family, commissioned by the tsar as the Romanov family crypt. The gallery leading to the central nave is decorated with beautiful frescoes depicting the history of Christianity in Kievan Rus'. It's worth timing your visit with a church service (weekdays at 8 AM and 5 PM, Saturday at 8 AM, Sunday at 7 and 9 AM) to see the interior. Even if the church is closed, the doors may be unlocked. No one will stop you from taking a quick peek at the gallery walls.

In front of the cathedral, on the right-hand side, is the small red **Nad-mogilnaya Chasovnya** (Memorial Chapel), marking the grave of Princess Augusta Tarakanova, the illegitimate daughter of Empress Elizabeth and Count Razumovsky. The princess lived most of her life as a nun in Moscow's St. John's Convent, forced to take the veil by Catherine the Great. During her lifetime her identity was concealed, and she was known only as Sister Dofiya. The chapel over her grave was added in 1900, almost a century after her death. In an odd twist, Princess Tarakanova had an imposter who played a more visible role in Russian history. The imposter princess appeared in Rome in 1775, to the alarm of Catherine, who dispatched Count Alexei Orlov to lure the imposter back to Russia. Orlov was successful, and the imposter Tarakanova was imprisoned in St. Petersburg's Petropavlovskaya Krepost (Peter and Paul Fortress). A mysterious character of European origin, the imposter never revealed her true identity. The false Princess Tarakanova died of consumption in 1775. Her death in her flooded, rat-infested cell was depicted in a famous painting by Konstantin Flavitsky in 1864.

To the right as you face Transfiguration Cathedral stands the tiny **Pokrovsky Tserkov** (Church of the Intercession). Directly behind the cathedral is the **Tserkov Znamenia** (Church of the Sign). Painted in the dark yellow popular in its time, with a four-column facade, the church was built between 1791 and 1808 by the wealthy Sheremetyev family and contains the Sheremetyev crypt. In the rear right-hand corner of the grounds, running along the fortification walls, are the former monks' residences.

Proletarskaya station is the closest metro stop. Take only lefts to get out of the station, and you will emerge on Sarinsky proyezd. With your back to the metro, walk toward Trety (3rd) Krutitsky pereulok, the busy street a short distance ahead. This will take you in the direction of the Moskva River, and as you head to where the streets intersect, the yellow belfry of the monastery gate church will appear in the distance to your right (southwest). When you reach the intersection, use the underground passageway to cross to the other side. From here it's just a short walk up a slight incline to the monastery's entrance. ⊠ *10 Krestyansky Pl., Southern Outskirts* ☎*495/676–9570* ⊡*Free* ⊙*Daily 7–7* Ⓜ*Proletarskaya.*

WHERE TO EAT

The Moscow restaurant world is slowly growing into the dining scene that this metropolis deserves. Restaurants of all classes and styles are opening every week, with imported foreign chefs battling it out for Moscow's upper and middle classes. There's a new breed of restaurants serving Russian fare as the fad for Western food loses some, but by no means all, of its glamour. Ethnic restaurants have arrived as well, and you can sample Tibetan, Indian, Chinese, Latin American, or Turkish any night of the week. Be warned, however, that chef turnover is high in Moscow and that a restaurant can swiftly go downhill or uphill.

Reserve plenty of time for your meal. In Russia dining out is an occasion, and Russians often make an evening (or an afternoon) out of going out to eat, especially at those Moscow showplaces replete with gilded cornices, hard-carved oak, and tinkling crystal. An unhurried splendor is definitely the order of the day.

Prices at top restaurants are higher than what you'd expect to pay in the United States. Almost all the expensive hotel restaurants serve a Sunday brunch, when you can enjoy their haute cuisine and elegant surroundings at greatly reduced prices, usually between 750R–2,250R.

WHAT IT COSTS IN RUSSIAN RUBLES					
	¢	$	$$	$$$	$$$$
AT DINNER	under 250R	250R–450R	451R–650R	651R–850R	over 850R

Prices are per person for a main course at dinner.

KREMLIN/RED SQUARE

CAFÉ

¢　✕**Coffeehouse.** This is one of Moscow's biggest coffee chains, and there seems to be a branch within a coffee bean's throw no matter where you are in the city center. In addition to lattes and cappuccinos, Coffeehouse serves beer, wine, toasted sandwiches, and a huge list of coffee cocktails. This branch is open 24 hours. ⊠*3 Malaya Dmitrovka ul., Kremlin/Red Square* ☎*495/699–9728* ⊟*No credit cards* Ⓜ*Pushkinskaya.*

CONTINENTAL

$$$$　✕**Café des Artistes.** Just off Tverskaya ulitsa and opposite the Moscow Art Theater, this is the perfect spot for a pre- or post-theater dinner. The restaurant, which specializes in French, Swiss, and Italian cuisine, comes into its own in summer with its outdoor café. Entrées might include tiger prawns à la Provençale or risotto with black truffles. The business lunch, at 541R for a three-course meal, is one of the best in the city center. ⊠*5/6 Kamergersky per., Kremlin/Red Square* ☎*495/692–4042* ⊕*www.artistico.ru* ⊟*AE, DC, MC, V* Ⓜ*Okhotny Ryad.*

$$$$　✕**Metropol.** Recalling the splendor of prerevolutionary Russia, the opulent interiors of the Metropol hotel's grand dining hall are a stunning memorial to Russian art nouveau. The nearly three-story-high dining room is replete with stained-glass windows, marble pillars, and a leaded-glass roof. Among the famous guests to come here are George Bernard Shaw, Vladimir Lenin, and Michael Jackson. French and Russian delicacies are served here, such as the popular fried duck with wild-cherry sauce and a baked apple. Cap your meal off with wine from the extensive list and cheese. There is also live music at breakfast and in the evenings. ⊠*1/4 Teatralny proyezd, Kremlin/Red Square109012* ☎*495/927–6061* ⚐*Reservations essential Jacket and tie* ⊟*AE, DC, MC, V* Ⓜ*Ploshchad Revolutsii or Teatralnaya.*

FodorsChoice
★

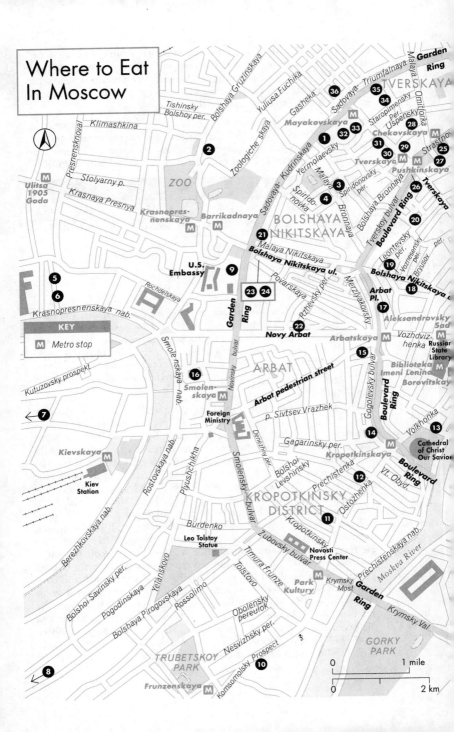

Where to Eat In Moscow

KEY

Ⓜ Metro stop

Map labels:

Sadovaya-Samotech. · Sadovaya-Sukharevskaya · 41
Yermolovoy
40 · Sukharevskaya
Bol. Sukharevsky
Boulevard · Tsvetnoi Bulvar
Ring · Rozhdestvensky bulvar · Sret. bul'.
KITAI · 51 · Turgenevskaya
GOROD · Sandunovskiye Bani
P. Stoleshnikov · 52 · 55 · 53 · 43 · Myasnitskaya
KREMLIN & · 54 · Kuznetsky · Akademikaprospekt
D SQUARE · 56 · Most · Pushechnaya
47 · Lubyanka
57 · Teatralnaya · Teatralny · 45 · 38
58 · 59 · Teatralnaya · Lubyanka · 46
Pl. · 48 · Nikolskaya ulitsa · Maroseika
Okhotny · Pl. Revolyutsii · 39
Ryad · Ploschad · Ilinka · Kitai · 42
Revolyutsii · 50 · Gorod
Red · Square · Rybny P.
Varvarka
Kremlyovskaya · Moskvoretskaya nab.
Raushskaya nab.
Osipenko
Vodootvodny · Kanal
Lavrushinsky · Bolshaya · Ozeryovskaya
Staromonetny · B. Polyanka
60 · Novokuznetskaya
Tretyakovskaya
ZAMOSKVORECHE
Polyanka · Zemlyachki
61 · Novokuznetskaya · Tatarsk.
1yy Kazachy · Ordinka · A.N.Ostrovskovo · Pyatnitskaya · Bakhrushina
Pogorelsky per. · Paveletskaya
ktyabrskaya · Valovaya
Zhitnaya · 62 · Zatsepa
Dobrininskaya · Lyusinovskaya
Serpukhovskaya

1

ECLECTIC

$$$$ ✕ **The Conservatory.** Head to the top floor of the Ararat Park Hyatt to enjoy the view over part of the Kremlin and the Bolshoi Theater with a glass of wine. The balcony, which is very popular with tourists and opens late April to mid-September, stretches around three sides of the hotel for a great panoramic view of the city. The food and service, however, don't always match the quality of the view. Service can be slow and the food—meats and seafood grilled on an outdoor barbecue—is good but unexciting. Drinks, especially cocktails, are pricey. ✉ *4 Neglinnaya ul., Kremlin/Red Square* ☎ *495/783–1234* ▤ *AE, DC, MC, V* Ⓜ *Okhotny Ryad or Teatralnaya.*

$–$$ ✕ **Pyramida.** Despite being housed in a stunningly ugly and vulgar pyramid-shaped building, this is one of the trendiest restaurants in the city. It always seems to be busy (in summer look for the bikers parading their expensive motorbikes and spotlessly clean leather bike wear just outside). Inside, modern, slick lines meet pseudo–ancient Egyptian decor. The food is a mixture of the trendiest items in Moscow: a bit of sushi, some weird fusion concoctions, and lots of salads. ✉ *18a Tverskaya ul., Kremlin/Red Square* ☎ *495/200–3603* ▤ *AE, DC, MC, V* Ⓜ *Pushkinskaya.*

ITALIAN

$$$ ✕ **Bosco Café.** On the first floor of GUM, this Italian restaurant has the enviable advantage of being one the very few places in Moscow with a terrace on Red Square. Bosco charges for the view with very expensive Italian food, but it's tasty, or you can always just order a coffee. The terrace closes once it gets cold. ✉ *3 Red Sq., Kremlin/Red Square* ☎ *495/929–3182* ⊕ *www.bosco.ru/restoration/bosco_cafe* ▤ *AE, DC, MC, V* Ⓜ *Ploshchad Revolutsii.*

RUSSIAN

$ ✕ **Pirogi na Nikolskoy.** Cheap and bohemian, Pirogi na Nikolskoy is part of the O.G.I. (the initials stand for United Humanitarian Publisher who opened a chain of restaurant-café-bar-bookshops in Moscow) chain of inexpensive restaurant-clubs popular among students, the hip, and those who never grow old. The chain is open 24 hours and usually has a small, upmarket bookshop attached. This cellar location is simple but cheerful. Don't expect great service or a smoke-free zone but do expect a good atmosphere, decent food—the beef Stroganoff is worth a try—and a pleasant surprise when you get the bill. The best O.G.I. for location is this one at the end of Tretyakovsky proyezd, a fine juxtaposition as it's one of Moscow's most expensive streets, a few hundred yards from the Kremlin. ✉ *19/21 Nikolskaya ul., Kremlin/Red Square* ☎ *495/621–5827* ▤ *MC, V* Ⓜ *Ploshchad Revolutsii.*

KITAI GOROD

ASIAN

$$$ ✕ **Beloye Solntse Pustyni.** Named after the legendary Soviet film *Beloye Solntse Pustyni* (White Sun of the Desert), this theme restaurant specializes in delicious Uzbek food, which incorporates Russian, Persian, and

Chinese elements. The restaurant's sun-bleached walls instantly sweep you down to Central Asia. Inside, the illusion continues: a diorama with a ship marooned in the desert, waitresses dressed as Uzbek maidens, and intricately carved wooden doors. Make sure you try the salad bar's mouthwatering vegetables. The Dastarkhan, a set meal, overwhelms you with food—unlimited access to the salad bar, a main course such as mutton kebabs and *manty* (large mutton ravioli), *plov* (a Central Asian rice pilaf), and numerous desserts. ⊠*29/14 Neglinnaya ul., Kitai Gorod* ☎*495/623–0585* ⊕*www.bsp-rest.ru* ⌂*Reservations essential* ▭*AE, DC, MC, V* Ⓜ*Kuznetsky Most.*

CAFÉ

$ ✕**Volkonsky.** Moscow has waited years for a place like this to arrive. Volkonsky is a sophisticated French bakery with lines out the door at all three of its Moscow locations. Apart from the mouth water-ing choice of pastries, biscuits, and cakes, it's an ideal place to pick up a sandwich or a freshly prepared salad to go. This branch has a seating area and a range of quiches and pastas for a sit-down lunch. ⊠*4/2 ul. Maroseika, Kitai Gorod* ☎*495/721–1442* ▭*D, MC, V* Ⓜ*Kitai Gorod.*

¢   ✕**Coffee Bean.** This is one of the first and best of the many Seattle-style coffee chains that have opened in Moscow. Giant cappuccinos and some of the best coffee in town are brewed here and served with a smile. There's a sparse selection of sandwiches and lots for dessert, though the latter aren't very good. This is one of the few no-smoking cafés in Moscow. ⊠*18/7 Kuznetsky Most ul., Kitai Gorod* ☎*495/621–4369* ▭*MC, V* Ⓜ*Kuznetsky Most.*

CONTINENTAL

$$$$ ✕**Galereya.** Most nights of the week, large Mercedes, Hummers, and Bentlys are parked outside of Galereya, one of Moscow's hippest res-taurants. Owned by Moscow's restaurant magnate Arkady Novikov, Galereya has sophisticated contemporary food, which rarely hits a false note. The lamb dishes are always tender. People mostly come to Galereya to be seen and to watch the crowds of beautiful people who cram the restaurant. ⊠*27 Petrovka ul., Kitai Gorod* ☎*495/937–4544* ▭*AE, DC, MC, V* Ⓜ*Tsvetnoi Bulvar.*

ECLECTIC

¢   ✕**Propaganda.** Propaganda is one of Moscow's most popular clubs, but before it opens up the dance floor, it lays out the tables for its own hearty food. The club has some of the tastiest food and most reasonable prices in the city center. The cuisine ranges over all the continents from Indian to Thai to Russian, but the dishes are kept simple, and service is quick. ⊠*7 Bolshoi Zlatoustinsky per., Kitai Gorod* ☎*495/623–3665* ⌂*Reservations essential* ▭*No credit cards* Ⓜ*Kitai Gorod.*

JAPANESE

$ ✕**Yakitoria.** This popular restaurant has proved the most reliable of Moscow's many sushi restaurants. The food may not be the most genu-ine article (the real thing goes for bank-breaking prices in Moscow), but the service is quick, most ingredients fresh (though the fish was probably frozen for transport to Moscow), and the menu comprehensive. There are several branches of the restaurant. Lines are common, so reservations are a good idea. ⊠*29 (1st) Tverskaya-Yamskaya ul., Kitai Gorod* ☎*495/250–5385* ☰*DC, MC, V* Ⓜ*Belorusskaya* ⊠*10 Novy Arbat ul., Arbat* ☎*495/290–4311* ☰*DC, MC, V* Ⓜ*Arbatskaya.*

RUSSIAN

$$$ ╳**Vogue Café.** As the name suggests, Vogue is one of the most fashionable restaurants in town but it does it in a distinctly Russian way. The interior is sophisticated and understated, drawing models and the well-heeled. However, the menu is partly a throwback to Soviet times with items such as Russian salami and kefir, a sour-milk drink. It's cool to consume these retro oldies here. The rest of the menu is a mix of Russian, Italian, and French dishes. ⊠*7/9 Kuznetsky Most, Kitai Gorod* ☎*495/623–1701* ☰*AE, DC, MC, V* Ⓜ*Kuznetsky Most.*

$ ╳**Petrovich.** Objets d'art from the Soviet era are scattered around the huge cellar bar-club-restaurant; the menu of filling Russian food is full of insider jokes about life under the old regime; beer is served in old-fashioned mugs; and Soviet pop plays in the background. Try the pelmeni, sturgeon kebabs, or Georgian dishes such as *sulguni* (breaded fried cheese). It turns into a private club in the evening, but if you call ahead you can usually get in. ⊠*24/3 Myasnitskaya ul., head into courtyard behind kiosk at 24 Myasnitskaya ul. and look for metal door on left, Kitai Gorod* ☎*495/623–0082* ⌨*Reservations essential* ☰*No credit cards* Ⓜ*Chistiye Prudy.*

$ ╳**Project O.G.I.** The original O.G.I. (the initials stand for United Humanitarian Publisher), this inexpensive and cheerful hangout has regular concerts, a bookstore, readings, and 24-hour cheap food and drink. It's in a courtyard off one of Moscow's most charming streets. ⊠*8/21 Potapovsky per., Kitai Gorod* ☎*495/627–5366* ☰*AE, DC, MC, V* Ⓜ*Chistiye Prudy.*

¢ ╳**Yaposhka.** Although it looks like just another Japanese restaurant, it's Russified name is a clue to the dual menus—"sushi" and "anti-sushi"—found within. The anti-sushi menu has Russian food and the prices are rock bottom. Better to stick with this menu—the *pelmeni* (meat dumplings) are some of the best in the city and definitely the best value at only 90R. The potato dumplings are even cheaper. Simple wooden tables are packed into a simple interior. Beware, it can get smoky and the music can be annoyingly loud, though the nonstop Tom and Jerry cartoons may serve as an enjoyable distraction. This branch is the easiest place to get a table, and there is free Wi-Fi at all branches. ⊠*26/1 Pokrovka ul., Kitai Gorod* ☎*495/650–5892* ☰*DC, MC, V* Ⓜ*Kitai Gorod.*

¢ ╳**Yolki Palki.** For a gentle introduction to Russian cooking, there is no better value than this, one of the first chain restaurants in Russia. The restaurant, with stuffed chickens and waitresses dressed in national costume, is more kitsch than traditional Russian. Don't miss the salad bar where you can also try numerous types of marinated vegetables. There is a good selection of blini as well as another delicious pancake variety *olady,* which is often made with potatoes. If you overhear "yolki palki" being muttered by a Russian, he's not talking about the restaurant, it's a light curse akin to "fiddlesticks." ⊠*8/10 ul. Neglinnaya, Kitai Gorod* ☎*495/628–5525* ▭*MC, V* Ⓜ*Kuznetsky Most.*

VEGETARIAN

$ ✕**Dzhagannat Express.** This new-age café is one of the few respites for vegetarians in the heavily meat-oriented Moscow restaurant world. Also known as the Center for Healthy Eating and Living, the res-

WORD OF MOUTH

"I like U Pirosmani which is a Georgian restaurant near Novodevichy . . . for cheap eats, there is Shesh Besh, Yolki Palki or Moo Moo which are all chain restaurants."

—Odin

taurant serves Indian-inspired cuisine that is not very spicy. Apart from the curries, the huge salad bar is the best bet, along with the various tofu and dried wheat protein dishes. In keeping with the healthful eating ethos, no alcohol is served, although nonalcoholic beer, wine, and champagne are available. There are also freshly squeezed juices and exotic fruit cocktails. ⊠*11 Kuznetsky Most, Kitai Gorod* ☎*495/628–3580* ▭*No credit cards* Ⓜ*Kuznetsky Most.*

TVERSKAYA ULITSA

AMERICAN

$$$$ ✕**Goodman Steak House.** If you have an urge for steak in Moscow, then Goodman Steak House is a sure-fire bet for high-quality meat and good service. Steaks are of course the specialty, but the lamb shank is not to be spurned. Goodman has two restaurants with the original on Tverskaya winning on atmosphere. At Tverskaya there's a small summer garden that's also open in winter; you'll be provided with coats and hot drinks to ward off the cold. The second location is next to one of the "Stalin Sisters" by the Barrikadnaya metro station. ⊠*23 ul. Tverskaya, Tverskaya* ☎*495/937–5679* ⊕*www.goodman.ru* ▭*AE, DC, MC, V* Ⓜ*Tverskaya.*

$$ ✕**Starlite Diner.** The two branches (at Mayakovskaya and Oktyabrskaya metro stations) of this round-the-clock diner are identical to those back in the United States, with brightly lighted 1950s design, large portions of sandwiches and burgers, and great value for the price. In Moscow these spots are popular with late-night workers, exhausted early-morning partygoers, and old friends getting together for a weekend brunch. It's always full of boisterous first-timers to Russia and expats looking for a taste of home. This location is busier because of its city-center location and its secluded summertime patio, but at the time of writing it was being repaired after a fire inside the restaurant. It is expected to reopen in the near future. Waiters are young and friendly, speak English, and serve fast. ⊠*16 Bolshaya Sadovaya ul., in garden by Mossoviet Theater, Tverskaya* ☎*495/290–9638* ▭*AE, DC, MC, V* Ⓜ*Mayakovskaya.*

$ ✕**American Bar and Grill.** One of the original American bars in Moscow, the Bar and Grill goes for the pseudo–Wild West look that is especially popular with anyone who has never been to the United States.

Buffalo heads hang on walls beside leather saddles and old American road signs. The only really genuine American thing are the huge portions. The 24-hour bar always seems to be busy with clients feeding on its popular chicken wings or downing margaritas. This branch is more popular, but the bigger location near Taganka metro station has a larger summer garden, and bands regularly rock its main room. ⊠*2/1 Pervaya (1st) Tverskaya-Yamskaya ul., Tverskaya* ☎*495/251–7999* ⊟*AE, DC, MC, V* Ⓜ*Mayakovskaya.*

ASIAN

¢ ✕**Barfly.** Moscow does not have a wide variety of cheap Asian places. Barfly is the best option, with a choice of Asian noodles and fillings that won't break the bank. The bar, which is open 24 hours, is in a courtyard near Pushkin Square. Service is quick and efficient. It gets very crowded in evenings so come for lunch, not dinner. ⊠*6 Strastnoi bulvar, Tverskaya* ☎*495/650–2779* ⊟*No credit cards* Ⓜ*Pushkinskaya.*

CAFÉS

$$ ✕**Donna Klara.** Comfy window seats, a laid-back staff, and a selection of sticky cakes make this a cozy place to eat. The wine list may not be very big—and you're better off sticking to the homemade cakes, anyway—but the friendliness of the staff makes this a pleasant family eatery in which to relax the afternoon away. It's always busy, so call ahead, and it's just a few minutes away from Patriarch's Pond. ⊠*21/13 Malaya Bronnaya ul., Tverskaya* ☎*495/290–3848* ⊟*AE, DC, MC, V* Ⓜ*Mayakovskaya.*

$ ✕**Volkonsky.** Volkonsky is a sophisticated French bakery with lines out the door at all three of its Moscow locations. If you're looking for somewhere to eat around Patriarch's Pond, this branch is just a short walk away. *See* the full review *in* the Kitai Gorod neighborhood. ⊠*2/46 Bolshaya Sadovaya ul., Tverskaya* ☎*495/721–1442* ⊟*D, MC, V* Ⓜ*Mayakovskaya.*

¢ ✕**Brioche.** Closeted inside the Tchaikovsky Concert Hall on Triumfalnaya Ploshchad, Brioche is a good pre- or postconcert stop for cake and coffee. There's always a decent selection of sandwiches, the pastries are fresh, and you can buy croissants and baguettes here as well. Ingredients are brought in from France as is, seemingly, the convivial spirit. ⊠*4/31 Triumfalnaya Pl., Tverskaya* ☎*495/699–4284* ⊟*No credit cards* Ⓜ*Mayakovskaya.*

¢ ✕**Coffee Bean.** In a grand 19th-century building, this location is the most convenient location of this coffee chain, one of the first and best of the many Seattle-style coffeehouses that have opened in Moscow. Try to nab a sofa by the window for the best seat. *See* the full review *in* the Kitai Gorod neighborhood. ⊠*10 Tverskaya ul., Tverskaya* ☎*495/788–6357* ⊟*MC, V* Ⓜ*Tverskaya.*

GERMAN

$$ ✕**Bavarius.** Bavarius looks as if it has been transported straight from Munich's Oktoberfest. Oompah music plays in the background, dirndl-clad waitresses carry fistfulls of liter-size beer mugs, and the smell of sauerkraut lingers in the air. Whether you fancy a snack of knockwurst (a mild pork sausage) or just want to sample German and Czech beers,

this is the place. Instead of sitting indoors, head through the arch to the left of the main entrance to reach the quiet courtyard that holds the biggest beer garden in Moscow. Food is served in both areas, but credit cards are accepted only in the restaurant. ⊠*2/30 Sadovaya-Triumfalnaya, Tverskaya* ☎*495/699–4211* ▤*MC, V* Ⓜ*Mayakovskaya.*

PIZZA

$ ✕**Il Patio.** An airy place to find pizza bliss, this branch opposite the statue of Mayakovsky on Triumfalnaya Ploshchad is one of the most popular in the city. The gamut of pizzas have a thin and dusty crust, and daily specials include such dishes as lasagne and cannelloni. There's also a salad bar. A speedy two-course lunch costs 190R and the three-course, 280R. A soft drink is included. Pop music plays softly, and the rooms are always filled with a pleasantly bustling crowd. ⊠*2 (1st) Tverskaya-Yamskaya ul., Tverskaya* ☎*495/930–0815* ▤*AE, DC, MC, V* Ⓜ*Mayakovskaya.*

RUSSIAN

$$$$ ✕**Café Pushkin.** Imagine traveling back in time to when Pushkin strolled
Fodor's Choice the boulevards of 19th-century Moscow. That's what the designers of
★   this high-class Russian restaurant intended when they created a replica mansion not far from the statue of Pushkin. Staff members dress like 19th-century servants; the menu resembles an old newspaper, with letters no longer used in the Russian alphabet; and the food is fit for a tsar. All the favorites can be found here—blini, caviar, pelmeni—and there's a fine wine list. Prices rise with each floor (there are three) of the restaurant. Open daily, 24 hours, Pushkin is popular among the business elite and the golden youth who come for breakfast after a night of clubbing. In summer you can dine on the rooftop patio. ⊠*26a Tverskoi bulvar, Tverskaya 125009* ☎*495/739–0033* ✍*Reservations essential* ▤*AE, DC, MC, V* Ⓜ*Pushkinskaya.*

$$ ✕**Café Margarita.** Set by picturesque Patriarch's Pond, this intimate café is marked by a colorful mural depicting a scene from Mikhail Bulgakov's classic novel *The Master and Margarita,* part of which takes place beside the pond. This has long been a favorite with tourists and locals, but not because of the basic, somewhat overpriced Russian food such as borscht and potato-and-mushroom dumplings. Instead, people come to hear the musicians—some students, some professionals—who play every night, creating a wonderful, sing-along atmosphere with a repertoire of classical music, Russian folk songs, and popular hits. A 100R charge is added to each bill for the music. ⊠*28 Malaya Bronnaya ul., Tverskaya* ☎*495/699–6534* ▤*No credit cards* Ⓜ*Mayakovskaya.*

$ ✕**Ryumka.** Ryumka is the old Russian name for a bar and for the glass that you use to drink vodka. Located just off Moscow's main street, Tverskaya ulitsa, it has become a favorite place for good drinks, good food, and some more good drinks. This one-room bar-restaurant complete with a canary singing in the corner is like being invited into a friend's kitchen for a drink. There is also a splendid choice of more than a dozen different types of vodka. To accompany the alcohol—Russians as a rule always have food with vodka—there is a good selection of Russian dishes, including herring and potatoes, picked vegetables, or caviar. ✉*10/2 Tryokhprudny per., Tverskaya* ☎*495/650–5444* ⊟*AE, MC, V* Ⓜ*Mayakovskaya.*

¢–$ ✕ **Poslednyaya Kaplya.** The Last Drop, which roughly translates as "the last straw" in English, is one of the better bars in the city. Just slip into one of the leather armchairs and order a portion of the excellent pelmeni, some herring, and potatoes, plus the drink of your choice. There's a decent menu of Russian favorites, with a few modern bar snacks thrown in. Be forewarned: if you ask the bartender for a shot, he will ring the ship bell and get you to down the drink in one go. The bar is in a cozy cellar off Pushkinskaya. ✉*4 Strastnoi bulvar, Bldg. 3, Tverskaya* ☎*495/692–7549* ⊟*No credit cards* Ⓜ*Pushkinskaya or Chekhovskaya.*

¢   ✕ **Yaposhka.** Although it looks like just another Japanese restaurant, it's Russified name is a clue to the dual menus—"sushi" and "anti-sushi"—better to stick with the latter menu. This branch is open 24 hours and has free Wi-Fi. *See* the full review *in* the Kitai Gorod neighborhood. ✉*20/1 Tverskaya ul., Tverskaya* ☎*495/984–2817* ⊟*DC, MC, V* Ⓜ*Pushkinskaya.*

SCANDINAVIAN

$$$$ ✕ **Scandinavia.** Cozy and relaxing, this is one of the most serene dining rooms in the city, with comfortable wooden chairs, upholstered benches, and dried-flower arrangements on deep window ledges. The Swedish chef mixes modern European and Scandinavian cooking. If you're out for a purely Scandinavian selection, try the herring with boiled potatoes, which comes with a shot of aquavit. The burgers are the highest ranked in Moscow. Despite being near the bustle of Tverskaya ulitsa, Scandinavia's balcony and summer beer garden are the city's most tranquil and popular places for outdoor dining. There's a slightly cheaper menu for the summer garden. ✉*7 Maly Palashevsky per., Tverskaya* ☎*495/937–5630* ⊕*www.scandinavia.ru* ⊟*AE, DC, MC, V* Ⓜ*Pushkinskaya.*

BOLSHAYA NIKITSKAYA ULITSA

AMERICAN

$$$$ ✕ **Goodman Steak House.** If you have an urge for steak in Moscow, head to this reastaurant next to one of the "Stalin Sisters" by the Barrikadnaya metro station. *See* the full review *in* the Tverskaya ulitsa neighborhood. ✉*31 Novinsky bulvar, Bolshaya Nikitskaya* ☎*495/775–9888* ⊕*www.goodman.ru* ⊟*AE, DC, MC, V* Ⓜ*Barrikadnaya.*

AZERI

¢–$ ✕ **Karetny Dvor.** Popular among the new rich and the new middle class, Karetny Dvor serves an enormous selection of Azeri (from Azerbaijan) and Caucasian dishes. Waiters are good at recommending a selection, but do try the fresh Azeri tomatoes to accompany the dozens of kebabs. Seating is either in a rustic main room or smaller ones that resemble hideaways within an old farmer's barn. In summer there's seating outside. ✉*52 Povarskaya ul., Bolshaya Nikitskaya* ☎*495/291–6376* ⊟*No credit cards* Ⓜ*Barrikadnaya.*

CAFÉS

$$ ✕**Coffeemania.** Tucked into the side of the Tchaikovsky Conservatory, this is the perfect place to come for a snack before or after a concert or just to eavesdrop on the musicians rehearsing during the day. There's a huge indoor area, good coffee, and a decent summer garden overlooking the statue of Tchaikovsky. Apart from the usual coffee assortments, Coffeemania has a large menu with well-prepared Italian, Russian, and Japanese dishes. There is another branch at the end of Bolshaya Nikitskaya. ⊠*13/6 Bolshaya Nikitskaya ul., Bldg. 1, Bolshaya Nikitskaya* ☎*495/229–3901* ⊕*www.coffeemania.ru* ▭*AE, DC, MC, V* Ⓜ*Biblioteka Imeni Lenina* ⊠*46/54 Tchaikovsky Cultural Center, Kudrinsky Pl., Bldg. 1, Bolshaya Nikitskaya* ☎*495/290–0141* ▭*AE, DC, MC, V* Ⓜ*Barrikadnaya.*

ECLECTIC

$ ✕**Kvartira 44.** Hidden away in a courtyard, Kvartira 44 is a relaxed place popular among students. The menu is a reasonable mix of European café fare with the odd Russian dish. Try the borscht or the spinach-and-bacon salad. Books line the shelves and customers are welcome to leave or take a book. Musicians play on the piano upstairs and customers often join in singing Russian songs. It's a smoky atmosphere but there is one small nonsmoking area; there is also free Wi-Fi. ⊠*22/2 Bolshaya Nikitskaya ul., Bolshaya Nikitskaya* ☎*495/291–7503* ▭*DC, MC, V* Ⓜ*Arbatskaya, Pushkinskaya, or Okhotny Ryad.*

ITALIAN

$$ ✕**Correa's.** Originally from the United States, chef Isaac Correa has stood out throughout his long Moscow career. His latest venture is an intimate family restaurant that has become a favorite. Great pizzas and simple, good Italian food with contemporary touches come in large portions and are served by friendly waitstaff. Breakfast for 230R is one of the most civilized in the city. The cozy Bolshaya Gruzinskaya location only has seven tables. ⊠*32 Bolshaya Gruzinskaya ul., Bolshaya Nikitskaya* ☎*495/933–4684* ⊕*www.correas.ru* ▭*AE, DC, MC, V* Ⓜ*Barrikadnaya.*

RUSSIAN

$$$$ ✕**CDL.** Inside this elegant mansion is one of the city's most beautiful
FodorśChoice dining rooms—and one of the best places to sample authentic Russian
★ cuisine. In the 19th century the house served as the headquarters for Moscow's Freemasons; more recently it was a meeting place for members of the Soviet Writers' Union. Crystal chandeliers, rich wood paneling, fireplaces, and antique balustrades place CDL among the warmest and most sumptuous eateries in Moscow. The food is extremely well prepared; try the *ukha* (fish soup) or pelmeni for starters, and move on to the beef Stroganoff. If you're feeling adventurous, cleanse your palate between courses with *kvas* (nonalcoholic bread-beer). There's also a less luxurious Italian restaurant here. ⊠*50 Povarskaya ul., Bolshaya Nikitskaya* ☎*495/291–1515* ▭*AE, DC, MC, V* Ⓜ*Barrikadnaya.*

THE ARBAT

CAFÉ

$ ✕**Volkonsky.** Volkonsky is a sophisticated French bakery with lines out the door at all three of its Moscow locations. This branch has a seating area and a summer garden. *See* the full review *in* the Kitai Gorod neighborhood. ✉*1 ul. Arbat, Arbat* ☎*495/580–9052* ▤*D, MC, V* Ⓜ*Arbatskaya.*

ECLECTIC

$$$ ✕**Tinkoff.** A few yards from the controversial British-embassy building (some think it's a design miracle, others an abomination) is a plain brick building that holds this stylish Russian microbrewery. The series of bars and rooms has a brick-and-glass design. Although there are four cuisines on offer in different areas of the brewery—Japanese, German, Italian, and modern European—people come for the beer, not the food. Ten very different beers are brewed on the premises, with prices starting at less than 179R for a half liter. ✉*11 Protochny per., Arbat* ☎*495/777–3300* ▤*AE, DC, MC, V* Ⓜ*Smolenskaya.*

FRENCH

$$ ✕**Jean Jacques.** You may not be able to smoke in Parisian restaurants anymore, but Jean Jacques, a cheap and cheerful 24-hour French bistro, is a copy of the old smoky Parisian classic. The café is nearly always busy and has one of the best selections of reasonably priced wines by the glass in Moscow. ✉*12 Nikitsky Bulvar, Arbat* ☎*495/290–3886* ▤*MC, V* Ⓜ*Arbatskaya.*

JAPANESE

$ ✕**Yakitoria.** Yakitoria has proved the most reliable of Moscow's many sushi restaurants. *See* the full review *in* the Kitai Gorod neighborhood. ✉*10 Novy Arbat ul., Arbat* ☎*495/290–4311* ▤*DC, MC, V* Ⓜ*Arbatskaya.*

KROPOTKINSKY DISTRICT

CAFÉ

¢ ✕**Coffeehouse.** One of Moscow's biggest coffee chains, this branch is open 24 hours. *See* the full review *in* the Kremlin/Red Square neighborhood. ✉*3/2 Gogolevsky bulvar, Kropotkinsky District* ☎*495/221–8381* ▤*No credit cards* Ⓜ*Kropotkinskaya.*

GEORGIAN

$$ ✕**Genatsvale VIP.** An offshoot of its neighbor Genatsvale, the VIP branch is designed to look like an old Georgian country home. After entering through a tunnel of vine leaves, you're seated at oak tables in a somewhat Disney-esque version of Georgia (the country). The food is genuine, however, and in the evenings you can enjoy an authentic Georgian choir and traditional dancing. If you come in a group, you may want to share the special kebab combination. Complement your food with one of the various Georgian wines served in 1-liter clay bottles. Service can be brusque. ✉*14/2 ul. Ostozhenka, Kropotkinsky District* ☎*495/203–1242* ▤*MC, V* Ⓜ*Kropotkinskaya.*

$–$$ ✕**Tiflis.** Named after the old name for the Georgian capital, Tbilisi, Tiflis is one of the city's oldest Georgian restaurants. Long popular among the expat Georgian community, it's the perfect place on a hot summer evening. One of best balconies in the city sweeps you away to the romantic old town of Tbilisi. The menu has all of the best of Georgian cuisine: piping hot *khachapuris* or cheese pancakes, kebabs cooked over charcoal, and sweet red Georgian wine. ✉ *32 ul. Ostozhenka, Kropotkinsky District* ☎ *495/290–2897* ▭ *MC, V* Ⓜ *Kropotkinskaya.*

PIZZA

$ ✕**Il Patio.** An airy place to find pizza bliss, this cheerful restaurant has a huge back room with a ceiling and walls of glass, letting the sun pour in all day. This original location is a stone's throw from the Pushkin Museum of Fine Arts. *See* the full review *in* the Tverskaya Ulitsa neighborhood. ✉ *13a ul. Volkhonka, Kropotkinsky District* ☎ *495/298–2530* ▭ *AE, DC, MC, V* Ⓜ *Kropotkinskaya.*

SOUTHWESTERN

$ ✕**Hemingway's.** Run by group of long-term expats, this Tex-Mex restaurant located in the basement of a 19th-century mansion lovingly re-creates standards such as nachos, fajitas, and chimichangas. Add to the food the satellite TV's covering home-team sports and you'll understand why it has captured expat hearts. A grand summer terrace is another great draw. Reserve ahead for big sporting events. ✉ *13 Komsomolsky pr., Kropotkinsky District* ☎ *495/246–5726* ⊕ *www.hemingways.su* ▭ *DC, MC, V* Ⓜ *Park Kultury.*

ZAMOSKVORECHE

AMERICAN

$$ ✕**Starlite Diner.** A round-the-clock diner identical to those in the United States, this branch is a hundred yards or so behind the largest Lenin statue left in Moscow. *See* the full review *in* the Tverskaya Ulitsa neighborhood. ✉ *9a Korovy Val, Zamoskvoreche* ☎ *495/959–8919* ▭ *AE, DC, MC, V* Ⓜ *Oktyabrskaya.*

CAFÉ

¢ ✕**Coffee Bean.** This is one of the first and best of the many Seattle-style coffee chains that have opened in Moscow. *See* the full review *in* the Tverskaya Ulitsa neighborhood. ✉ *5 Pyatnitskaya ul., Zamoskvoreche* ☎ *495/953–6726* ▭ *MC, V* Ⓜ *Novokuznetskaya.*

ITALIAN

$$ ✕**Correa's.** A favorite family place, this location is much roomier and more sophisticated than the Bolshaya Nikitskaya ulitsa branch, although it loses some of the charm due to the officelike surroundings. *See* the full review *in* the Bolshaya Nikitskaya Ulitsa neighborhood. ✉ *40 ul. Bolshaya Ordynka, Bldg. 2, Zamoskvoreche* ☎ *495/725–6035* ▭ *AE, DC, MC, V* Ⓜ *Polyanka or Tretyakovskaya.*

NORTHERN OUTSKIRTS

FRENCH

$$$$ ✕**Carré Blanc.** The city's most praised restaurant, Carré Blanc has
★ captured the hearts of Moscow gourmets. A group of expatriates
established the place, which magically melds exquisite French cooking; probably Moscow's best wine collection; and a relaxed, convivial
atmosphere. Try the crème brûlée of foie gras and crepes and, if you
can splurge, go for *pave* (a cold dish made in a rectangular mold) of
veal with morels for a hefty 1,590R. Also here are a bar and a bistro
with somewhat, if not significantly, lower prices. ✉*19/2 Seleznyovs-
kaya ul., Northern Outskirts* ☎*495/258–4403* ⊕*www.carreblanc.ru*
▤*AE, DC, MC, V* Ⓜ*Novoslobodskaya.*

SEAFOOD

$$$$ ✕**Sirena.** There are probably as many live fish as dead denizens of the
deep at this seafood showplace, a longtime favorite of the famous,
including Sting and Liza Minnelli. One room has a glass floor beneath
which huge sturgeon squirm; in another, aquariums surround you with
numerous fish who watch you eat their brethren. Waiters dressed like
sailors greet you as you enter the restaurant via the stern of a ship. The
wide selection of fish main courses, such as the mixed seafood cooked
in parchment, rarely disappoints, but Sirena is still far too expensive.
✉*15 Bolshaya Spasskaya, Northern Outskirts* ☎*495/208–1412*
▤*AE, DC, MC, V* Ⓜ*Sukharevskaya.*

SOUTHERN OUTSKIRTS

GEORGIAN

$ ✕**U Pirosmani.** Whitewashed walls and wood-panel ceilings inside this
popular restaurant named for Georgian artist Niko Pirosmani re-create the aura of an artist's studio. Copies of Pirosmani's naive art decorate the walls. Try to sit by the window in the main hall or on the
balcony so you can enjoy beautiful views of New Maiden's Convent,
across the pond from the restaurant. The menu reads like a Georgian
cookbook. Some complain that the food can be a bit hit or miss but
order the *khachipuri,* or Georgian cheese pies, and some shish kebab
and you can't go wrong. Sadly, there is currently an embargo between
Russia and Georgia and you cannot get the excellent Georgian wine
normally served here. ✉*4 Novodevichy proyezd, Southern Outskirts*
☎*495/247–1926* ▤*MC, V* Ⓜ*Sportivnaya.*

EASTERN OUTSKIRTS

AMERICAN

$ ✕**American Bar and Grill.** One of the original American bars in Moscow,
this location has a large summer garden, and bands regularly rock its
main room. *See* the full review *in* Tverskaya Ulitsa neighborhood. ✉*59
Zemlyanoi Val, Eastern Outskirts* ☎*495/912–3615* ⊕*ambar.rosinter.
com* ▤*AE, DC, MC, V* Ⓜ*Taganskaya.*

CAFÉ

¢ ✕**Coffee Bean.** This is one of the first and best of the many Seattle-style coffee chains that have opened in Moscow. This location is big and has a small summer garden ideal for people-watching. *See* the full review *in* the Tverskaya Ulitsa neighborhood. ⊠*18 Pokrovka, Eastern Outskirts* ☎*495/623–9793* ⊟*MC, V* Ⓜ*Christiye Prudy.*

WESTERN OUTSKIRTS

CONTINENTAL

$$$$ ✕**Krasny Bar.** From the 27th floor of this modern skyscraper you can see the city stretching out in front of you. Nighttime views are particularly fine. Many jokes have been made about the men's bathroom's unique view of the White House, where the government works. The restaurant serves what it calls "modern European" cuisine, which means lots of small salads and fusion. But it's a better bet to just sit with a cocktail and stare out the window. Open until 3 AM, it's perfect for late-night carousing. ⊠*22–24 Kutuzovsky pr., Western Outskirts* ☎*495/730–0808* ⊟*AE, DC, MC, V* Ⓜ*Kievskaya.*

RUSSIAN

$$$$ ✕**Bochka.** One of Moscow's numerous round-the-clock restaurants, Bochka, opposite the Mezhdunarodnaya hotel, is a dependable place for good Russian food, even if the prices are somewhat high. It attracts its fair share of New Russians, businesspeople, and the after-rave set. If you're brave, turn up on Friday, when a giant spit is assembled for the roasting of wild game, including bulls and goats. If that doesn't appeal, the salads are all well worth a try, although the *kholodets,* a portion of meat served wobbling in its own jelly, may inspire doubt. ⊠*2 ul. 1905 Goda, Western Outskirts* ☎*495/252–3041* ⊟*AE, DC, MC, V* Ⓜ*Ulitsa 1905 Goda.*

UKRAINIAN

$$$$ ✕**Shinok.** Half-zoo, half–collective farm, the 24-hour Shinok is a faux-Ukrainian farmyard complete with goats, a cow, hens, and a knitting granny. The enclosure is completely sound- and smell-proof, and the animals don't really impinge on the meal. Ukrainian cuisine doesn't differ that much from Russian, sharing dishes such as borscht, *vareniki* (Ukrainian-style pelmeni stuffed with cottage cheese), and *solyanka* (a spicy, thick stew made with vegetables and meat or fish). For an unusual taste from the Ukraine, try *salo* (thin slices of fat) and the Ukrainian beer Starokiyevskoye. The helpful servers can give advice, although not all speak English. Go on an empty stomach, because the food can be very filling. ⊠*2a ul. 1905 Goda, Western Outskirts* ☎*495/255–0204* ⊟*AE, MC, V* Ⓜ*Ulitsa 1905 Goda.*

WHERE TO STAY

You might think that a world capital with a population of more than 10 million would have a large number of hotels, but this is not yet the case in Moscow. As Russia comes in from the cold, the city's hotel scene is expanding slowly, with on average one new major hotel opening a year. A Ritz-Carlton opened in July 2007 on Tverskaya ulitsa on the site of the former eyesore landmark Intourist hotel, demolished in 2002. Another icon of Moscow, the Moskva hotel featured on the label of Stolichnaya vodka, was torn down in 2003. A deluxe hotel is to rise on the same site with a replica facade of the original in late 2008.

For travelers able and willing to splurge, Moscow's top hotels offer a level of amenities and pampering that was unavailable a decade ago. Fine restaurants, business centers, cafés and cocktail bars, health clubs, and attentive service are now the norm at five-star hotels.

That noted, the city suffers from a dearth of decent mid-range hotels. Some mid-range spots retain their Soviet decor—mouse-brown carpet, tarnished gold-pattern polyester upholstery, and plywood furniture. Some of these hotels also suffer from Soviet-style service, with unhelpful, indifferent, and sometimes even rude staff. Competition among hotels is slowly leading to improvements, but be prepared for a lower level of service than you might expect at home. When reserving, it really pays to ask for a room that has been renovated; the cost is usually the same and the difference can be startling, particularly in the lower-price hotels. If it matters, you should also ask whether your double room has twin beds or one large one; either is possible. ■ TIP→ **To ask for a renovated room in Russian, say:** *Mozhno li poprosit otremontirovanny nomer?* **For a large bed:** *Mozhno li poprosit nomer s bolshoi krovatyu?*

WHAT IT COSTS IN RUSSIAN RUBLES					
	¢	$	$$	$$$	$$$$
FOR 2 PEOPLE	under 2,500R	2,500R–5,000R	5,001R–7,500R	7,501R–10,000R	over 10,000R

Prices are for a standard double room in high season, excluding taxes and service charge.

KREMLIN/RED SQUARE

$$$$ ✕🖼 **Ararat Park Hyatt.** One of the most luxurious of Moscow's hotels combines the traditional and modern. You enter through gigantic stone pillars into a sparkling (occasionally gaudy) interior with glass-and-steel elevators and a dark-wood reception area. Rooms are light and spacious, with elegant beige-fabric furniture, glass tables, and powerful showers in the bathrooms. Café Ararat ($$$), a replica of the landmark café of the same name that stood on this site in the 1940s, serves Armenian cuisine and has design elements based on ancient Armenian culture. The hotel is a short walk from the Bolshoi Theater and the Kremlin. **Pros:** central location; great city view from rooftop café; plush linens; free fruit in rooms every day. **Con:** restaurants are overpriced. ⊠4 *Neglinnaya ul., Kremlin/Red Square* 109012 🕾495/783–1234 ⊕*www.moscow.park.hyatt.com* 📞219 *rooms, 16 suites* ⚇*In-hotel: 2 restaurants, bars, gym, public Wi-Fi* ⊟*DC, MC, V* Ⓜ*Okhotny Ryad or Teatralnaya.*

$$$$
FodorsChoice
★ **Metropol.** Originally built between 1899 and 1903, this first-class hotel has been the stage for some fabled events: Lenin spoke frequently in the assembly hall of the building, and David Lean filmed part of *Doctor Zhivago* in the restaurant. The hotel is one of Moscow's most elegant, with outstanding service and amenities. The lobby and restaurants transport you back a century, and the guest rooms have hardwood floors, Oriental rugs, and modern furnishings. Antiques grace all the suites, and the two presidential suites come with private saunas. The location, opposite the Bolshoi Theater and a five-minute walk from the Kremlin, is top-notch. **Pros:** superb location; beautiful interiors; great buffet breakfast. **Con:** some guest rooms need updating. ⊠ *1/4 Teatralny proyezd, Kremlin/Red Square 103012* ☎ *499/501–7800, 7499/501–7800 outside Russia* ⊕ *www.metropol-moscow.ru* ⤷ *292 rooms, 76 suites* ⌂ *In-hotel: 3 restaurants, room service, bars, gym, public Internet, no-smoking rooms* ☰ *AE, DC, MC, V* Ⓜ *Ploshchad Revolutsii or Teatralnaya.*

$$$$ **Savoy.** The Savoy opened in 1913 in connection with celebrations commemorating the 300th anniversary of the Romanov dynasty. Renovations enlarged guest rooms and made the hotel facade more distinguished. Interiors of gilded chandeliers, ceiling paintings, and polished paneling invoke the spirit of prerevolutionary Russia. The ornate dining room, where a complimentary breakfast is served, exudes romance: a pianist serenades, a fountain blurbles, and painted cherubs seemingly float among clouds. The rooms have new spacious marble bathrooms, some with hydromassage baths. The bedrooms are equipped with king-size beds with orthopedic mattresses and antiallergenic pillows. Views are negligible, owing to the hotel's side-street location, but this gives the advantage of quiet. The hotel is just off Teatralnaya Ploshchad and within walking distance of the Kremlin. **Pros:** great location; beautiful interiors; swimming pool open 24 hours. **Cons:** some rooms are small; English fluency varies among front-desk staff. ⊠ *ul. 3 Rozhdestvenka, Kremlin/Red Square 103012* ☎ *495/620–8500* ⊕ *www.savoy.ru* ⤷ *70 rooms, 17 suites* ⌂ *In-hotel: restaurant, room service, bar, pool* ☰ *AE, DC, MC, V* Ⓜ *Kuznetsky Most.*

KITAI GOROD

$$$$ **Marriott Royal Avrora.** On the corner of ulitsa Petrovka and pedestrianized Stoleshnikov pereulok, the Marriott Royal Avrora is close to the Kremlin, Tverskaya ulitsa, and the Bolshoi Theater, which is only a three-minute walk away. Together with the Marriott Grand on Tverskaya ulitsa, the Marriott Royal, constructed in art nouveau style, symbolizes the Moscow of Mayor Yuri Luzhkov's era and his mid-'90s construction boom. Full butler service for all guests is unique to the city. Each room has three direct telephone lines, individual climate control, and excellent bathroom amenities. **Pros:** perfect location; helpful concierge staff. **Cons:** overpriced Internet access and breakfast. ⊠ *11/20 ul. Petrovka, Kitai Gorod 103050* ☎ *495/937–1000* ⊕ *www.marriotthotels.com* ⤷ *227 rooms, 38 suites* ⌂ *In-room: safe. In-hotel:*

Where to Stay In Moscow

KEY
- Ⓜ Metro stop

0 — 1 mile
0 — 2 km

2 restaurants, bar, pool, gym, public Wi-Fi. ⊟*AE, DC, MC, V* Ⓜ*Okhotny Ryad.*

$$$$ 🏨 **Sretenskaya.** Indulge yourself in the atmosphere of an old Russian fairy tale with massive carved oak furniture, stained-glass windows, and wall paintings depicting popular tales like "Little Scarlet Flower" (the Russian version of "Beauty and the Beast"). The lobby bar is nicely set in the winter garden with rich vegetation. Guest rooms are quite modern, with all amenities. Though centrally located, Sretenskaya is a 25-minute walk from the Red Square. Moscow's famous boulevards and the Garden Ring are only steps away. **Pros:** helpful staff; excellent restaurant. **Cons:** long walk to Red Square; small rooms. ⊠*15 ul. Sretenka, Kitai Gorod 103045* ☎*495/933–5544* ⊕*www.hotel-sretenskaya.ru* ⤳*38 rooms* ⌂*In-hotel: restaurant, bar* ⊟*AE, DC, MC, V* Ⓜ*Sukharevskaya Kitai Gorod.*

$$ 🏨 **Budapest.** Opened in 1876 as a club for noblemen, this city-center hotel later became an accommodation in Soviet days for those visiting Moscow on official business. Now it's a comfortable hotel with a homey old style: high ceilings, Oriental rugs, leather chairs, and small touches such as the wrought-iron mailbox in the lobby. Although the hotel has no restaurant, it serves complimentary Continental breakfast in guest rooms. Just up the block there's a trendy and inexpensive café, Gogol, that serves traditional Russian dishes. **Pro:** great location. **Cons:** Soviet-style service; no restaurant. ⊠*2/18 Petrovsky Linii, Kitai Gorod 103051* ☎*495/923–2356* ⊕*www.hotel-budapest.ru* ⤳*86 rooms, 30 suites* ⌂*In-hotel: bar, no-smoking rooms* ⊟*AE, DC, MC, V* Ⓜ*Kuznetsky Most.*

TVERSKAYA ULITSA

$$$$
Fodor'sChoice
★

🏨 **Golden Apple.** Catching up with the global obsession, this is Moscow's first and only boutique hotel. Cozy, stylish, quirky, and upmarket, Golden Apple embodies the definition of boutique. Shiny metallic panels clash with bright, oddly shaped armchairs in the lobby bar. The enormous golden apple next to the front desk turns out to be a comfortable sofa on closer inspection. Each of the hotel's seven floors is painted a different color. In a reference to the Chekhov play, some rooms have huge propeller-like iron seagulls hanging from the ceiling. **Pro:** fresh fruit and chocolate in guest rooms every day. **Cons:** some rooms are small; bathrooms get flooded after taking a shower; sauna fills fast, it's best to reserve a spot. ⊠*11 ul. Malaya Dmitrovka, Tverskaya 127006* ☎*495/980–7000* ⊕*www.goldenapple.ru* ⤳*92* rooms ⛄In-hotel: restaurant, bar, gym ⊟MC, V Ⓜ Chekhovskaya or Pushkinskaya.

$$$$ 🏨 **Marriott Grand.** Once you step inside, past the renovated turn-of-the-20th-century art nouveau facade, you'll likely feel very much at home—if home is the United States. You'll even find eggs Benedict on the breakfast buffet. The Western-style rooms are spacious, and some overlook a peaceful courtyard. A round central staircase ascends from the lobby's sunny atrium. Service is pleasant. Red Square is 1 km (½ mi) away. **Pros:** beautiful lobby bar area with piano; excellent fitness center. **Con:** overpriced food and drink. ✉26 Tverskaya ul., Tverskaya 103050 ☎495/935–8500, 7502/935–8500 outside Russia ⊕www.marriotthotels.com ⤺377 rooms, 13 suites ⛄In-room: Wi-Fi. In-hotel: 3 restaurants, room service, bars, pool, gym, concierge, no-smoking rooms ⊟AE, DC, MC, V Ⓜ Mayakovskaya or Tverskaya.

$$$$ 🏨 **Ritz-Carlton.** The latest addition to Moscow's luxury hotels, the Ritz-Carlton finally opened its gilded doors on July 1, 2007. Like a phoenix rising from the Soviet rubble, it is located on the spot where eyesore Intourist hotel once stood. Among the most expensive in the chain, walking into the gold and marble foyer you'll quickly understand where the $350 million used to construct the hotel went. Though few can afford to stay, it's worth a trip just to check out the lobby. A night in the five-room presidential suite costs a whopping 420,000R but includes breathtaking views of the Kremlin, a sauna, and a grand piano. **Pros:** prime location; excellent service. **Con:** too expensive for anyone but the über rich. ✉3 Tverskaya ul., Tverskaya 125009 ☎495/225–8888 ⊕www.ritzcarlton.com ⤺334 rooms ⛄In-hotel: 2 restaurants, bars, pool, spa center, sauna ⊟AE, DC, MC, V Ⓜ Okhotny Ryad.

$$$$ Fodor's Choice ★ 🏨 **Le Royal Meridien National.** If you seek luxury and elite service, this 1903 hotel is the place for you. It's the city's most elegant accommodation, right across a plaza from Red Square and at the foot of Tverskaya ulitsa. Inside the stunning landmark art nouveau building are a great marble staircase, elevators topped by silvered twists of ivy, and a Viennese-style café. Most rooms are plush with polished-oak furniture upholstered in silk. Though a bit small, the modern white-tile bathrooms sparkle. For 21,900R a night you can stay in a two-room suite where Lenin lived for a time in 1918. **Pros:** outstanding location; helpful concierge staff. **Cons:** some rooms in the back of the hotel are small; rooms overlook nearby roofs; overpriced restaurant. ✉15/1 Mochovaya ul., Tverskaya 103012 ☎495/258–7000 ⊕www.national.ru ⤺195 rooms, 36 suites ⛄In-hotel: 2 restaurants, room service, bars, pool, gym, public Wi-Fi ⊟AE, DC, MC, V Ⓜ Okhotny Ryad.

$$ 🏨 **Peking.** Occupying a tall 1955 building with a tower, this hotel
★ boasts a superb location and bargain rates. Located on the Garden
Ring across the street from Moscow Conservatory's Tchaikovsky Hall,
the hotel has clean rooms with all the amenities but the rooms vary in
size. It makes sense to ask to see the room before checking in and to
ask for a bigger one if it seems small. If you can, ask for a room on
a higher floor as well, so you can enjoy the view of central Moscow.
Pros: convenient central location; great views from upper floors; several
nice restaurants nearby. **Con:** there is a casino and slot machines on
ground floor where mobster types gather on some nights. ⊠ *5 Bolshaya
Sadovaya ul., Tverskaya 123001* ☎ *495/650–3301* ⊕ *www.hotelpekin.
ru* ⮑ *113 rooms* ⬧ *In-hotel: room service, bar, gym, sauna* ▭ *MC, V*
Ⓜ *Mayakovskaya.*

BOLSHAYA NIKITSKAYA ULITSA & THE ARBAT

$$$$ 🏨 **Courtyard Marriott.** The location of this hotel is probably the best of
★ any hotel in its class. In the heart of the historical center, across from
St. Andrew's Anglican Church and near the Moscow Conservatory, this
hotel consists of three interconnected buildings including a two-story
historical building facing Voznesensky pereulok and a cozy atrium.
The guest rooms, some of which have views of the Kremlin, are spa-
cious, combining comfort and functionality. In addition to high-speed
Internet, the rooms have large desks with conveniently placed lighting
and outlets and ergonomic chairs. Bathrooms are equipped with illu-
minated makeup mirrors. **Pros:** wide selection of restaurants and coffee
shops in the area; great room service breakfast; very comfortable beds.
Con: overpriced Internet access (320R per hour). ⊠ *7 Voznesensky
per., Bolshaya Nikitskaya 125009* ☎ *495/981–3300* ⊕ *www.marriott.
com* ⮑ *218 rooms* ⬧ *In-hotel: 2 restaurants, bar, gym, public Wi-Fi*
▭ *AE, DC, MC, V* Ⓜ *Pushkinskaya or Tverskaya.*

$$$$ 🏨 **Golden Ring.** Although the name refers to the "ring" of ancient Rus-
sian towns northeast of Moscow, there's nothing provincial about this
towering hotel just across the Garden Ring from the Foreign Affairs
Ministry skyscraper. Business travelers check in for the friendly staff,
appealing and spacious guest rooms, and excellent city views, particu-
larly from the hotel's upper floors. The 22nd-floor bar's observation
point is stunning at night, and the Mediterranean restaurant on the top
(23rd floor) has panoramic views. **Pros:** spectacular breakfast room;
close to the Arbat. **Cons:** heavy traffic outside most of the day; some
staff could improve their English. ⊠ *5 Smolenskaya ul., Arbat 119121*
☎ *495/725–0100* ⊕ *www.hotel-goldenring.ru* ⮑ *166 rooms, 81 suites*
⬧ *In-hotel: 2 restaurants, bar, gym, parking (fee)* ▭ *AE, DC, MC, V*
Ⓜ *Smolenskaya.*

$$$$ 🏨 **Marco Polo Presnja.** Opened in 1904 as a residence for English teach-
ers and later the exclusive domain of the Communist Party, this hotel is
an intriguing choice for those interested in the Soviet era. For instance,
the auditorium was once the movie house where Party insiders came
to see Western films unavailable to most Muscovites. The hotel is in a
prestigious residential neighborhood near Patriarch's Pond, and many

rooms have balconies overlooking the quiet green surroundings. In warm months, the inner courtyard is an attractive place to relax. Gray and light-blue walls make the small rooms a bit dark, but multicolor bedspreads add a homey touch. **Pros:** close to Patriarch's Pond with cafés and bars. **Cons:** some unfriendly staff; television reception is bad; guest rooms are small. ⊠ *9 Spiridonevsky per., Bolshaya Nikitskaya 103104* ☎*495/244–3631* ⊕*www.presnja.ru* ⌁*48 rooms, 20 suites* ⌂*In-room: Wi-Fi. In-hotel: restaurant, room service, bar, gym* ⊟*AE, DC, MC, V* Ⓜ*Mayakovskaya or Pushkinskaya.*

KROPOTKINSKY DISTRICT & ZAMOSKVORECHE

$$$$ 🏨 **Baltschug Kempinski.** On the banks of the Moskva River opposite the Kremlin and Red Square, this deluxe hotel has extraordinary views. The building dates to the 19th century, but the sparkling interior is modern. The rooms are stately and well equipped. Rooms with a view cost more but are preferable; request one or you could end up staring at the factory bordering the hotel's eastern side. The hotel is central but not particularly convenient—it's a 15-minute walk from the nearest metro station and the city's main attractions. **Pros:** close to Red Square; best breakfast in town; great swimming pool; kid friendly—they're given sweets upon arrival and there's a kids' menu in the restaurant. **Cons:** overpriced drink and food; far from metro. ⊠ *1 Balchug ul., Zamoskvoreche 113035* ☎*495/230–6500, 7501/230–6500 outside Russia* ⊕*www.kempinski-moscow.com* ⌁*202 rooms, 30 suites* ⌂*In-hotel: 2 restaurants, room service, bars, pool, gym, pubic Wi-Fi, no-smoking rooms* ⊟*AE, DC, MC, V* Ⓜ*Novokuznetskaya, Ploshchad Revolutsii, or Tretyakovskaya.*

$$$$ 🏨 **Katerina–City.** Near the river and Riverside Towers, one of the city's main business centers, this small Swedish-run hotel is popular with European business travelers. The hotel occupies a renovated prerevolutionary mansion and a modern eight-story annex. In the comfortable modern rooms, dark-blue furniture complements the yellow-fabric-covered walls, which are lined with watercolors. The staff is friendly and helpful. Views of the picturesque Moskva River and New Savior Monastery are splendid. Guests who stay on the Privileged Floor can relax in a cozy lounge with a fireplace and cigars. The Stockholm restaurant, serving traditional Scandinavian and Russian cuisine, is a big plus. **Pros:** tasty breakfast; fast and cheap Internet. **Con:** during rush hour, the walk to the metro station and the metro itself may be unpleasantly congested with people. ⊠ *6 Shlyuzovaya nab., Zamoskvoreche 115114* ☎*495/795–2444* ⊕*www.katerina.msk.ru* ⌁*110 rooms, 9 suites* ⌂*In-hotel: restaurant, gym, public Wi-Fi* ⊟*AE, DC, MC, V* Ⓜ*Paveletskaya.*

$$$$ 🏨 **Kebur Palace.** Formerly known as Tiflis, this small, attractive hotel is built in the style of an old Tbilisi town house. It's a little more than a mile south of the Kremlin and close to some of the finest restaurants in town, the Cathedral of Christ Our Savior, and Pushkin Museum of Fine Arts. The rooms with views of a small square and a fountain are big and well lit thanks to floor-to-ceiling windows. Two suites have

Jacuzzis, and one two-story supersuite has a Jacuzzi and sauna. **Pro:** perfect location. **Cons:** some rooms are noisy due to a Georgian restaurant attached to the hotel; the concierge does not have adequate tourist information; better suited to business travelers. ✉ *32 ul. Ostozhenka, Arbat 119034* ☎*495/733–9070* ⊕*www.hoteltiflis.com* ⤷*60 rooms, 7 suites* ⚐*In-room: Wi-Fi. In-hotel: restaurant, room service, bar, pool* ☐*MC, V* Ⓜ*Kropotkinskaya.*

$$$–$$$$ ⚏ **Swissôtel Krasnye Holmy.** Rising 34 stories above the city, this sleek glass and metal cylinder is the tallest member of Moscow's family of luxury hotels, as well as a conspicuous addition to a skyline dominated by Stalin's seven towers. In the heart of a booming business district not far from Paveletsky train station and next to Moscow House of Music, the hotel opened in summer 2005. Guest rooms are among the largest in the city and include espresso coffee machines and electronic safes. Bathrooms are large and modern, with small tiles, glass and chrome, and a heated floor. Swissôtel's greatest attraction: a bar inside an inverted glass bowl on the 34th floor. **Pros:** stunning view of Moscow from top-floor City Space bar; caviar and champagne for breakfast. **Con:** overpriced breakfast. ✉ *52 Kosmodamianskaya nab., Bldg. 6, Zamoskvoreche 115054* ☎*495/787–9800* ⊕*www.swissotel. com* ⤷*235 rooms* ⚐*In-room: Wi-Fi. In-hotel: 2 restaurants, bars, pool, gym, spa* ☐*AE, DC, MC, V* Ⓜ*Paveletskaya or Taganskaya.*

$$ ⚏ **Medea.** If you are looking for privacy and quiet in the very heart
★   of the city, this is the place for you. Although the hotel is small, guest rooms are rather spacious, clean, and functional. The hotel occupies a recently renovated three-story 19th-century pink mansion. A fourth floor was added and houses a two-room suite. **Pros:** very thorough cleaning service; nice gym; bargain room rates. **Cons:** lack of activities and restaurants nearby; small breakfast room. ✉ *4 Pyatnitsky per., Bldg. 1, Zamoskvoreche 113186* ☎*495/777–1938* ⊕*www.medeaho tel.net* ⤷*17 rooms, 4 suites* ⚐*In-room: Internet access. In-hotel: restaurant, room service, bar, gym, sauna* ☐*AE, DC, MC, V* Ⓜ*Tretyakovskaya or Novokuznetskaya.*

NORTHERN OUTSKIRTS

$$$$ ⚏ **ART.** The proprietor of this hotel also owns a gallery in Berlin, and he has covered the hotel walls with contemporary Russian artwork. At the edge of a park and away from the urban crush, this hotel can make you feel as if you're in the country. Some rooms overlook the park and the hotel beer garden, which has live German music and a weekend brunch. Guest rooms are clean and basic, and breakfast is included in the price. Twenty minutes by car from Red Square, Arte is far from public transportation, and necessitates a 20-minute walk or a trolley ride from the metro station. **Pro:** less expensive prices. **Con:** remote location. ✉ *2 Tretya (3rd) Peschannaya ul., Northern Outskirts 125252* ☎*495/725–0905* ⊕*www.arthotel.ru* ⤷*81 rooms, 2 suites* ⚐*In-hotel: restaurant, room service, bar, tennis courts, gym, no-smoking rooms* ☐*AE, DC, MC, V* Ⓜ*Sokol.*

$$$$ **★** 🏠 **Marriott Tverskaya.** After a stroll from Red Square along bustling Tverskaya ulitsa, you may find comfort in the coziness of this eight-story art nouveau building. The small, peaceful lobby is complemented by a four-story atrium, which is overlooked by the alcove booths of the Italian restaurant Gratzi. A sunny guests-only lounge offers coffee and tea in the morning, and drinks at the end of the day. The rooms are understated—ivory, rose, and olive make up the palette, with darker notes provided by wood furniture. Old black-and-white prints of Moscow scenes line the walls on some floors. **Pros:** spacious rooms; comfortable beds; 24-hour health club. **Con:** there have been complaints of unhelpful and even rude staff. ⊠ *Pervaya (1st) Tverskaya-Yamskaya ul., Northern Outskirts 125047* ☎*495/258–3000, 7501/258–3000 outside Russia* ⊕*www.marriotthotels.com* ⇋*115 rooms, 7 suites* ⚒*In-room: Wi-Fi. In-hotel: restaurant, room service, bar, gym, no-smoking rooms* ▤*AE, DC, MC, V* Ⓜ*Belorusskaya.*

$$$$ 🏠 **Renaissance Moscow.** Rooms are large and equipped with every amenity at this hotel, a busy place for conferences and meetings. There's even an English-language movie theater. An executive floor has a lounge for breakfast, butler service, and a separate reception area. The hotel is far from the city center, but it's a good value and convenient to all major arterial roads, and the Prospekt Mira metro stop is a 15-minute walk away. Athletes competing or musicians performing in the nearby Olympic Sports Stadium—used for volleyball, tennis, swimming, and other sporting events, as well as large-scale concerts—often stay here. **Pros:** comfortable beds; shuttle bus service to Pushkin Square every hour after 4 PM. **Cons:** small rooms; no restaurants nearby. ⊠*18/1 Olympisky pr., Northern Outskirts 129110* ☎*495/931–9000* ⊕*www. renaissancehotels.com* ⇋*475 rooms, 13 suites* ⚒*In-room: Wi-Fi. In-hotel: 4 restaurants, room service, bar, pool, gym, no-smoking rooms* ▤*AE, DC, MC, V* Ⓜ*Prospekt Mira.*

$$$$ 🏠 **Sheraton Palace.** The European business community loves this place, thanks to its amenities, which include a chauffeur-driven fleet of cars. However, the rooms are small for the amount and size of furniture put into them. The real winners are those who can afford the duplexes (starting at 14,000R) that are on the Towers Floor, a hotel within a hotel with its own reception and lounge. The hotel's location at the far upper end of Tverskaya ulitsa is excellent, and the soundproof windows keep things quiet. **Pros:** well-organized transportation from airports; delicious breakfast; helpful staff. **Con:** a long walk from the Kremlin. ⊠*19 Pervaya (1st) Tverskaya-Yamskaya ul., Northern Outskirts 125047* ☎*495/931–9700, 7502/256–3000 outside Russia* ⊕*www.starwood.com/sheraton* ⇋*221 rooms, 18 suites* ⚒*In-hotel: 3 restaurants, room service, bars, gym, concierge, public Wi-Fi, parking (no fee), no-smoking rooms* ▤*AE, DC, MC, V* Ⓜ*Belorusskaya.*

$$$ 🏠 **Holiday Inn Lesnaya.** The 12-story hotel opened in 2005 and its big advantage is its conference facilities and central location on Lesnaya ulitsa, near Belorussky station and just steps away from Tverskaya ulitsa. Rooms are spacious with walls stylishly decorated in beige, ivory, and terra-cotta. All standard rooms have Wi-Fi and tea and coffeemakers. The hotel offers guests "a pillow menu" from which to choose various types and sizes of pillows. **Pros:** bargain prices compared to other Moscow hotels; helpful, friendly staff. **Cons:** a long walk to the Kremlin; business conferences can crowd the hotel. ✉*15 Lesnaya ul., Northern Outskirts 123456* ☎*495/101–4105* ⊕*holiday. bookin.ru* ↪*284 rooms, 17 suites* ♿*In-room: ethernet. In-hotel: restaurant, gym* ☰*AE, MC, V* Ⓜ*Belorusskaya.*

$$$ 🏨**Iris Congress.** Iris's dismal views and distant location—in a bleak residential district on the northern outskirts of town, adjacent to the world-famous Fyodorov Eye Institute and about halfway between the city center and the airport—are unfortunate, because this is a fine French-run hotel with spacious, cheery rooms that have lots of closet space, large bathrooms, and balconies. Complimentary shuttle buses run hourly until 11 PM to two central stops. The hotel also provides free narrated English bus tours of the city and excursions to the popular weekend Izmailovsky flea market. **Pros:** large rooms; close to Sheremetyevo airport. **Con:** far from the city center. ✉*10 Korovinskoye shosse, Northern Outskirts 103051* ☎*495/488–8000* ⊕*www.iris-hotel.ru* ↪*155 rooms, 40 suites* ♿*In-hotel: 2 restaurants, room service, bar, pool, gym, no-smoking rooms* ☰*AE, DC, MC, V* Ⓜ*Petrovsko-Razumovskaya.*

$$$ 🏨**Novotel Moscow Center.** This 18-floor hotel just a few metro stops from the Kremlin is one of the best mid-price options in the city for business travelers. It's a typical Novotel creation—functional and efficient, if a bit unimaginative. Rooms come with all the usual amenities, and some of them have rather interesting shapes because the building itself is cylindrical. The hotel stands next door to the Meyerhold complex, which includes a theatrical center, offices, and retail space. **Pros:** lots of cafés and bars in the area; reasonably priced. **Con:** staff cannot provide adequate tourist information. ✉*23 Novoslobodskaya ul., Northern Outskirts 127055* ☎*495/780–4000* ⊕*www.novotel.com* ↪*255 rooms, 1 suite* ♿*In-hotel: restaurant, bar, gym, public Wi-Fi* ☰*AE, DC, MC, V* Ⓜ*Mendeleyevskaya.* SEP 2007

$$$ 🏨**Novotel Moscow Sheremetyevo Airport.** If you need a room near Sheremetyevo II airport, try this hotel. The rooms and beds are comfortable, the halls quiet. In addition, the staff is eager to please, and the modern facilities are well maintained. A 24-hour shuttle bus runs to the airport, which is ¼ mi away, and there's a complimentary bus to the city center as well. Clients are, predictably, primarily businesspeople and airline personnel, though the Novotel also happens to be popular with professional European soccer teams because of its few distractions. Day rates of less than half the normal prices are available. **Pros:** ideal for passengers in transit; next to the airport. **Con:** far from the city center. ✉*Sheremetyevo II airport, Northern Outskirts 103339* ☎*495/926–5900, 7502/926–5900 outside Russia* ⊕*www. novotel.com* ↪*466 rooms, 22 suites* ♿*In-hotel: 2 restaurants, bar, pool, gym, public Wi-Fi* ☰*AE, DC, MC, V.*

$$
★ 🏨**Heliopark Empire Hotel.** This affordable hotel is located just a stone's throw from Tverskaya ulitsa and Belorussky station. Opened in March 2006 the hotel occupies a recently renovated seven-story building. Spacious guest rooms with high ceilings have soundproof windows that

1

ward off incessant street noise from the narrow 1st Brestskaya ulitsa which is always jammed with traffic. The surrounding shabby buildings still await their turn for renovation which makes the view less than desirable. Breakfast is hearty and tasty, but the breakfast room is somewhat small, so be prepared to share a table with strangers. **Pros:** central location; pleasant, attentive staff. **Cons:** poor views; tiny breakfast room; bathroom fixtures look rather cheap. ⊠60/1 Pervaya (1st) Brestskaya ul., Northern Outskirts 125047 ☎495/251–6413 🖷495/917–2314 ⬡33 rooms, 1 junior suite, 1 deluxe room ⌂In-room: Wi-Fi. In-hotel: restaurant, room service ▤AE, DC, MC, V Ⓜ Belorusskaya.

$$
★ **Kosmos.** This huge, 26-story hotel built by the French for the 1980 Olympics is popular with tour groups, for good reason: it's one of the city's best bargains. Years of heavy tourist traffic have dulled the shine on the French-furnished interiors, but the rooms are adequate, clean, and some have been recently renovated. The spacious, two-story lobby is decorated with a sculpture strongly reminiscent of the molecule models typically found in a sixth-grade science class. The hotel stands across the street from the All-Russian Exhibition Center, a part of town that has interesting sights, but is far from downtown; however, the metro is right across the street. **Pro:** bargain prices. **Con:** Soviet-style service. ⊠150 Prospekt Mira, Northern Outskirts 129366 ☎495/234–1212, 495/234–1000, 495/234–1206, or 495/234–1256 🖷495/215–8880 ⬡1,300 rooms ⌂In-hotel: 4 restaurants, bars ▤AE, DC, MC, V Ⓜ VDNKh.

$$
★ **Sovietsky Historical.** Plunge into Soviet-era grandeur at this historic hotel which recently considerably upgraded its facilities while still managing to preserve its nostalgic atmosphere. The hotel's public areas with massive marble columns, comfortable sofas, and grand chandeliers are extremely well looked after and guests receive a warm welcome with a glass of champagne when checking in. There is a gentlemen's club in the basement of the hotel where working girls can be met but the hotel security staff keeps them away from the guests. **Pros:** very spacious, clean, and well-lit rooms; great Russian restaurant (Yar) on premises. **Cons:** a 15-minute walk to the metro and 10- to 15-minute ride to the Kremlin; no air-conditioning; gentlemen's club downstairs. ⊠32/2, Leningradsky pr., Northern Outskirts 125040 ☎495/960–2000 ⊕www.sovietsky.ru ⬡130 rooms, 4 suites ⌂In-room: ethernet. In-hotel: restaurant, room service, bar, gym, sauna ▤AE, DC, MC, V Ⓜ Dinamo or Belorusskaya.

SOUTHERN OUTSKIRTS

$ **Danilovskaya.** Within the walls of the Orthodox Danilovsky (St. Daniel) Monastery—the official residence of Patriarch Alexei II of Moscow and All Russia—this hotel is serene and lovely, with fountains, religious-theme paintings, and domed monastery buildings. The church holds conferences here, and also sponsors concerts and exhibitions. Though basic, the rooms (breakfast included) are clean and spacious; some rooms have showers, but no tubs. Standard double rooms have

FodorśChoice
★

two twin beds, and suites have double beds. The restaurant's Russian menu is affordable, but the green decor feels institutional. The hotel is just a five-minute walk from the metro station. **Pro:** nice hotel grounds. **Cons:** remote location; very basic rooms. ⊠ *5 Bolshoi Starodanilovsky per., Southern Outskirts 113191* ☎ *495/954–0503* 🖷 *495/954–0750* 📞 *103 rooms, 13 suites* 👌 *In-room: refrigerator. In-hotel: restaurant, room service, bar, pool* ☰ *AE, DC, MC, V* Ⓜ *Tulskaya.*

EASTERN OUTSKIRTS

¢   ▦ **Gamma-Delta Izmailovo.** At one time this mammoth hotel complex included five buildings, making it Europe's largest lodging, with thousands of rooms. Now it's four hotels, Alfa, Beta, Gamma, and Delta, with the latter most commonly used by foreigners. A two-minute walk from the lively Izmailovsky flea market, this is a convenient place for the serious souvenir shopper. It's also adjacent to a metro station, close to Izmailovo Royal Estate (where Peter the Great learned to sail), and near Izmailovsky Park, one of the biggest in the city; otherwise this is a trek from most tourist sights. The rooms are basic. **Pro:** bargain prices. **Con:** Soviet-style service. ⊠ *71 Izmailovskoye shosse, Eastern Outskirts 105613* ☎ *495/166–4490 or 495/737–7000* 🖷 *495/166–7486* 📞 *2,000 rooms* 👌 *In-hotel: 3 restaurants, room service, bars* ☰ *AE, DC, V* Ⓜ *Partizanskaya.*

WESTERN OUTSKIRTS

$$$$ ▦ **Mezhdunarodnaya.** With a name that means "international," this big gray hotel, nicknamed "the Mezh" by foreign residents, is part of the huge World Trade Center complex, which also includes a shopping center and two buildings for offices and apartments. Although it has lost some of its original prestige, the Mezh is near the city exposition center and is a frequent site for conferences. The rooms are spacious, with elegant dark-wood furniture and cream-color walls. The hotel is within sight of the city center but far from the metro, and only one city bus stops near here. **Pro:** several great restaurants in the area. **Cons:** far from city center and metro stations; Soviet-style service; frequent conferences. ⊠ *12 Krasnopresnenskaya nab., Krasnaya Presnya 123610* ☎ *495/258–2122* ⊕ *www.wtcmoscow.ru/eng/hotel* 📞 *547 rooms, 33 suites* 👌 *In-hotel: 5 restaurants, room service, bars, pool, gym, public Wi-Fi* ☰ *AE, DC, MC, V* Ⓜ *Ulitsa 1905 Goda.*

$$$$ ▦ **Radisson SAS Slavyanskaya.** Designed for business travelers, the Radis-
★   son offers every modern American-style amenity and no-nonsense comfort. Its huge, two-story lobby—great for people-watching—is lined with restaurants, luxury shops, a popular English-language theater with first-run movies, a casino, and a health club. The hotel's location is not quite central and it is alongside Kiev station with its transients and homeless population. There are security guards at the hotel entrance, however. This is a good choice for those who favor comfort and service over character. **Pros:** a good selection of restaurants; the metro stop is five minutes away. **Cons:** some rooms are small and need renovation;

furniture is scratched. ✉ *2 Berezhkovskaya nab., Western Outskirts 121059* ☎ *495/941–8020, 800/333-3333 in U.S.* ⊕ *www.radisson. com* ⇗ *410 rooms, 20 suites* ⚿ *In-room: refrigerator. In-hotel: 4 restaurants, room service, bar, pool, gym, public Wi-Fi* ▭ *AE, DC, MC, V* Ⓜ *Kievskaya.*

$ 🏨 **Soyuz.** A distant location on the northwestern outskirts of town keeps the rates of this hotel inexpensive, and the service and atmosphere are good. With modern furnishings and a cheery atmosphere, flowery wallpaper decorates the rooms, and the bathrooms are tiled in a startling red. Some rooms overlook Moskva River, where in summer Muscovites come in droves to swim and sunbathe. **Pro:** one of the few truly inexpensive hotels in Moscow. **Con:** location is a serious drawback—the hotel is convenient only to Sheremetyevo II airport (15 minutes away), the closest metro stop is a 20-minute bus ride, and it can take more than an hour to drive to the city center. ✉ *12 Levoberezhnaya ul., Western Outskirts 125475* ☎ *495/457–2088* ⊕ *www. soyuz-hotel.ru* ⇗ *158 rooms* ⚿ *In-hotel: restaurant, bars* ▭ *AE, DC, MC, V* Ⓜ *Rechnoy Vokzal.*

$ 🏨 **Ukraina.** One of the seven Stalin Gothic skyscrapers, this hotel is a familiar landmark on the banks of the Moskva River. It has all the hallmarks of the Stalinist era inside, including red carpeting, grandiose socialist-realist decor (note the foyer's ceiling), redwood and oak furnishing, and fancy chandeliers. The rooms are worn but clean. Rooms on the higher floors have great views, particularly of the White House, where the government and prime minister work, across the river. The almost-central location places you where Kutuzovsky prospekt (a chic place to shop) meets up with the Novy Arbat. The nearest metro is a 10-minute trek away. **Pros:** great views and interiors. **Cons:** expect Soviet-style service; far from metro. ✉ *2/1 Kutuzovsky pr., Western Outskirts 121249* ☎ *495/933–5652, 495/243-3030 reservations* ⊕ *www.ukraina-hotel.ru* ⇗ *1,600 rooms* ⚿ *In-room: refrigerator. In-hotel: 4 restaurants, room service, bar* ▭ *AE, DC, MC, V* Ⓜ *Kievskaya.*

NIGHTLIFE & THE ARTS

A city of classical culture, Moscow also offers plenty of glamour and glitz. Ballet at the Bolshoi, concerts at the Tchaikovsky Conservatory, and theaters packed for Chekhov plays are among the highlights of the intense arts scene, while the nightlife takes in cozy cellar bars and glittering clubs for the elite.

Ticket booths on city streets testify to Muscovites' love of theater, and low prices ensure that high culture remains a mass pursuit. This enthusiasm means that the most popular shows can sell out weeks ahead, but smaller arts events, such as the regular free concerts at the Conservatory, are often equally rewarding. Although the Bolshoi's famous columned theater has been closed for repairs, the troupe still performs in a newly built venue whose elaborate interior rivals the original. On a much smaller scale, the Helikon Opera's innovative productions of classics such as *Carmen* gain critical raves, notwithstanding the theater's tiny stage.

The neon facades of downtown casinos and the ranks of Mercedes cars outside certain city clubs make it clear that Moscow is a city for big spenders. But you don't have to be one to have a good time. A more bohemian crowd gathers at bars and clubs that offer live concerts by local bands, cheap beers, and tasty eats.

THE ARTS

St. Petersburg may be most well known as Russia's cultural capital, but Moscow easily rivals its northern neighbor. Estimates differ, but the city has anywhere from 60 to 200 theaters, not to mention several prestigious acting schools and the increasingly popular International Chekhov Theater Festival, which usually takes place late August through early September. Every Thursday the free English-language newspaper, the *Moscow Times,* publishes a schedule of cultural events for the coming week. Pick up a copy at the airport when you arrive or at a hotel, restaurant, or bar in the city center.

Most theaters' tickets can be obtained at the theaters themselves or at the box offices (*teatralnaya kassa*) scattered throughout the city. Note that some theaters charge different prices for Russians and foreigners. If you're intimidated by the language barrier, ask your hotel's concierge for help. The prices are inflated, but a concierge can often get you tickets to otherwise sold-out performances. Scalpers usually can be found selling tickets outside theaters immediately prior to performances, but they have been known to rip off tourists, either charging exorbitant prices or selling fake tickets.

ART GALLERIES

Numerous private galleries sell Russian artwork, a nice alternative to the kitsch available at most of the tourist and riverside markets. The Friday edition of the *Moscow Times* carries a review of current exhibits. At group shows and festivals, watch out for the one-man Coat Gallery (aka Alexander Petrelli), who has paintings hidden inside his overcoat. Just go up to him and ask and he'll open up and show you his wares. For opening hours, check with the galleries themselves; some are open only by appointment, and most are closed on Sunday and Monday. Those looking for a truly grand spectacle can check out The Moscow World Fine Art Fair (⊕*www.moscow-faf.com*), considered by many to be the most exclusive fine art exhibition in Eastern Europe. Those with their sights set on buying should bring a wheelbarrow full of money.

Aidan Gallery. The artists displayed in this central gallery that was founded in 1992 are young, little known, and very stylish. ⊠*6 4th Syromantichesky per., Eastern Outskirts* ☎*495/228–1158* ⊕*www. aidan-gallery.ru* Ⓜ*Kurskaya.*

ArtStrelka. This bohemian arts center houses 11 galleries displaying contemporary art, photographs, and designer clothes. Cross the pedestrian bridge opposite the Cathedral of Christ Our Savior and turn right. ✉*14 Bersenevskaya nab., Bldg. 5, Zamoskvoreche* ☎*910/405–2428 cell phone* ⊕*www.artstrelka.ru* Ⓜ*Kropotkinskaya.*

Dom Nashchokina Gallery. A mixture of classic Russian art and crowd-pulling exhibitions by celebrity artists can be found at this established space. ✉*12 Vorotnikovsky per., Kitai Gorod* ☎*495/299–1178* ⊕*www.domnaschokina.ru* Ⓜ*Mayakovskaya.*

Fine Art. This was one of the first private galleries in post-Soviet Russia. Today it displays contemporary art from the best of the previous generation's nonconformists to the most current names. ✉*3/10 Bolshaya Sadovaya, Bldg. 10, Tverskaya* ☎*495/251–7649* Ⓜ*Mayakovskaya.*

★ **Guelman Gallery.** One of Moscow's first galleries, this is also one of its most controversial, due to the attention-loving nature of owner Marat Guelman. There's a definite shock value to many of the modern and avant-garde exhibits. It's a good bet for performance·art. ✉*1 4th Syromantichesky per., Eastern Outskirts* ☎*495/229–1339* ⊕*www.guelman.ru* Ⓜ*Chkalovskaya.*

Krokin Gallery. You'll find a focus on modern art, particularly photography and graphic art here. ✉*15 Bolshaya Polyanka, Zamoskvoreche* ☎*495/959–0141* ⊕*www.krokingallery.com* Ⓜ*Polyanka.*

NB Gallery. In the unlikely event that none of the contemporary landscape paintings displayed here catches your eye, proprietor Natalya Bykova, a friendly English-speaking art lover, is happy to offer advice on other top art venues in Moscow. The gallery is within an apartment, so it's best to call ahead. ✉*6/2 Sivtsev Vrazhek, Apartment 2, Kropotkinsky District* ☎*495/203–4006 or 495/737–5298* Ⓜ*Kropotkinskaya.*

★ **Stella Art.** Works by top names such as Andy Warhol are exhibited at this commercial gallery that opened in 2003. The art here can go for millions of dollars. ✉*7 Skaryatinksy per., Bolshaya Nikitskaya* ☎*495/291–3407* ⊕*www.stella-art.ru* Ⓜ*Krasnopresnenskaya.*

★ **Stella Art Russian.** Veteran Russian conceptual artists are featured at this sister of Stella Art. In 2004 it invited prominent, New York–based artist Ilya Kabakov for his first Moscow exhibition since emigrating. ✉*62 Mytnaya ul., Southern Outskirts* ☎*495/954–0253* ⊕*www.stella-art. ru* Ⓜ*Tulskaya.*

Tsentralny Dom Khudozhnika *(TsDKh).* Many different galleries are housed within this vast exhibition center, the Central House of Artists, and if you wander long enough you're sure to find something to fit your tastes, from traditional landscapes to the latest avant-garde outrage. In front of TsDKh a huge painting market snakes its way along the river. Among the piles of kitsch and tedious landscapes you can find some real gems. Be prepared to bargain. ✉*10 Krymsky Val, Zamoskvoreche* ☎*495/238–9843 or 495/238–9634* ⊕*www.cha.ru* Ⓜ*Park Kultury or Oktyabrskaya.*

Winzavod. In Soviet times, it was a massive wine factory. Today, Winzavod is the epicenter of Moscow's burgeoning contemporary arts scene, housing more than a half dozen galleries, as well as a tony clothing boutique called Cara & Co. ✉*1 4th Syromantichesky per., Bldg 6, Eastern Outskirts* ☎*495/917–3436* ⊕*www.winzavod.com* Ⓜ*Chkalovskaya.*

XL-Gallery. Russia's most renowned conceptual artists exhibit drawings, photographs, installations, and occasionally put on performances in this intimate space. ⊠*1 4th Syromantichesky per., Eastern Outskirts* ☎*495/775–8373* ⊕*xlgallery.artinfo.ru* Ⓜ*Chkalovskaya.*

MOVIES

Dome Cinema. A hotel movie house, Dome Cinema caters to the expatriate community with recent Hollywood releases. ⊠*Renaissance Moscow hotel, 18/1 Olympiisky pr., Eastern Outskirts* ☎*495/931–9873* ⊕*www.domecinema.ru* Ⓜ*Prospekt Mira.*

35mm. An artsy crowd frequents this simple theater with top-quality projection and sound. The films are always shown in their original language, usually with Russian subtitles. ⊠*47/24 Pokrovka, Kitai Gorod* ☎*495/917–5492 or 495/917–1883* Ⓜ*Krasniye Vorota.*

MUSIC

Moscow's musical life has always been particularly rich; the city has several symphony orchestras as well as song-and-dance ensembles. Moiseyev's Folk Dance Ensemble is well known in Europe and America, but the troupe is on tour so much of the year that when it performs in Moscow (generally at the Tchaikovsky Concert Hall), tickets are very difficult to obtain. Other renowned companies include the State Symphony Orchestra and the Armed Forces Song and Dance Ensemble. With the exception of special performances, tickets are usually easily available and inexpensive.

Glinka Music Museum Hall. This is one of many small concert halls scattered throughout the city. ⊠*4 ul. Fadeyeva, Tverskaya* ☎*495/251–1066* Ⓜ*Mayakovskaya.*

Moscow International Performing Arts Center (*Moscow International House of Music*). Opened in 2002, this architecturally striking center stages major classical concerts in its Svetlanov Hall, which contains Russia's largest organ. ⊠*52 Kosmodamianskaya nab., Bldg. 8, Zamoskvoreche* ☎*495/730–1011* ⊕*www.mmdm.ru* Ⓜ*Paveletskaya.*

Russian Army Theater. The Armed Forces Song and Dance Ensemble calls this venue home. ⊠*2 Suvorovskaya Pl., Northern Outskirts* ☎*495/681–2110 or 495/681–5120* Ⓜ*Novoslobodskaya.*

Scriabin Museum Hall. Performances are held usually on Wednesday in a small concert hall in the apartment building where the composer Alexander Scriabin lived. ⊠*11 Bolshoi Nikolopeskovsky per., Arbat* ☎*495/241–1901 or 495/299–1192* Ⓜ*Smolenskaya.*

Tchaikovsky Concert Hall. With seating for more than 1,600, this huge hall is home to the State Symphony Orchestra. ⊠*4/31 Triumfalnaya Pl., Tverskaya* ☎*495/299–3957 or 495/232–5353* Ⓜ*Mayakovskaya.*

FodorśChoice
★ **Tchaikovsky Conservatory.** Rachmaninoff, Scriabin, and Tchaikovsky are among the famous composers who have worked here. The acoustics of the magnificent Great Hall are superb, and portraits of the world's great composers hang above the high balcony. The adjacent Small Hall is usually reserved for chamber-music concerts. ⊠*13 Bolshaya Nikitskaya ul., Bolshaya Nikitskaya* ☎*495/629–2060* ⊕*www.mosconsv.ru* Ⓜ*Okhotny Ryad or Arbatskaya.*

Tsaritsyno Museum. A music hall nestled among the remains of Catherine the Great's partially completed Moscow estate regularly holds classical-music concerts. ✉*1 ul. Dolskaya, Southern Outskirts* ☎*495/321–0743* ⊕*www.tsaritsyno-museum.ru* Ⓜ*Orekhovo or Tsaritsyno.*

OPERA & BALLET

FodorsChoice
★ **Bolshoi Opera and Ballet Theatre.** The landmark building of this world-renowned theater is closed for restoration until 2009. Until then, performances are held on a second stage built in 2002. The quality of the Bolshoi's productions has been erratic at times, but recent guest foreign directors have made for more innovative shows. The Russian flair for set and costume design alone can be enough to keep an audience enthralled. Performances sell out quickly, so order tickets far in advance. ✉*1 Teatralnaya Pl., Kitai Gorod* ☎*495/692–9986, 495/250–7317 tickets* ⊕*www.bolshoi.ru* Ⓜ*Teatralnaya.*

★ **Helikon Opera.** In addition to delivering consistently appealing and critically acclaimed opera performances, the Helikon troupe is equally talented in space management: even the grandest of classics are fitted with ease onto the small stage. ✉*19 Bolshaya Nikitskaya ul., Bolshaya Nikitskaya* ☎*495/202–6584* ⊕*www.helikon.ru* Ⓜ*Pushkinskaya or Arbatskaya.*

Kolobov Novaya Opera. As fresh as the name *Novaya* ("new") indicates, this opera house has quickly established itself as one of the best and most innovative in the city. The surrounding Hermitage Garden is a perfect place for a pre- or post-theater stroll. The choir is ranked as the best in the city. ✉*3 Karetny Ryad, Tverskaya* ☎*495/694–0868* ⊕*www.novayaopera.ru* Ⓜ*Tverskaya.*

State Kremlin Palace. Formerly the hall where Soviet Communist Party congresses were held, this modern concert venue now hosts regular performances by opera and ballet troupes, including those from the Bolshoi. Of late it also has become the stage for international megastars such as Elton John, Bryan Adams, Cher, and Mariah Carey. Entrance is through the whitewashed Kutafya Gate. ✉*1 ul. Vozdvizhenka, in Kremlin, Kremlin/Red Square* ☎*495/620–7729 or 923-3877* Ⓜ*Aleksandrovsky Sad.*

THEATER

Even if you don't speak Russian, you might want to explore the intense world of Russian dramatic theater. Unfortunately, headphones providing English translations are virtually unheard of, so it's best to stick to something you already know in English (Shakespeare is, of course, widely performed, as are many plays based on classical works that would be familiar to readers of Russian literature, such as "The Master and Margarita" and "Brothers Karamazov"). The partial listings below cover Moscow's major drama theaters. Note that evening performances begin at 7 PM *sharp.*

Estrada Theater. The curtain goes up here for comedies starring some of Russia's best-known actors, along with a number of variety shows. ✉*20/2 Bersenyovskaya nab., Zamoskvoreche* ☎*495/959–0456* Ⓜ*Kropotkinskaya.*

LenKom Theater. Good, often flashy productions are on the playbill here. Tickets are frequently very hard to get. ⊠*6 Malaya Dmitrovka ul., Tverskaya* ☎*495/699–0708 or 495/699–9668* Ⓜ*Pushkinskaya.*

Maly Theater. Moscow's first dramatic theater, opened in 1824, the Maly is famous for its staging of Russian classics, especially those of the 19th-century satirist Alexander Ostrovsky—his statue stands outside the building. ⊠*1/6 Teatralnaya Pl., Kitai Gorod* ☎*495/623–2621* Ⓜ*Teatralnaya.*

Fodor's Choice ★ **Moscow Art Theater** *(MKhAT).* Founded in 1898, the MKhAT is the heart of the Moscow theater scene. The theater is famous for its productions of the Russian classics, but it also stages plenty of modern and foreign performances. The American Studio at the Chekhov Art Theater presents performances, typically Russian classics, in English a few times a year. ⊠*3 Kamergersky per., Tverskaya* ☎*495/248–9174* ⊕*www.chekhov.ru* Ⓜ*Okhotny Ryad.*

★ **Moscow Theater for Young Viewers.** Despite its name, this acclaimed theater mainly stages adult productions. It's famed for its dramatizations of Chekhov short stories, staged by director Kama Ginkas. ⊠*10 Mamonovsky per., Tverskaya* ☎*495/299–9917 or 495/299–5360* Ⓜ*Pushkinskaya.*

Mossoviet Theater. Contemporary drama shares the stage with comedies and musicals here. ⊠*16 Bolshaya Sadovaya, Tverskaya* ☎*495/299–2035* Ⓜ*Mayakovskaya.*

Operetta Theater. The Operetta stages lighthearted, and much humbler, versions of Western musicals, as well as the latest Russian musicals. ⊠*ul. 6 Bolshaya Dmitrovka, Kitai Gorod* ☎*495/292–1237* ⊕*www. mosoperetta.ru* Ⓜ*Teatralnaya.*

Sovremennik Theater. This well-respected theater stages a mix of Russian classics and foreign adaptations. ⊠*19a Chistoprudny bulvar, Kitai Gorod* ☎*495/621–6473* Ⓜ*Chistiye Prudy.*

★ **Taganka Theater.** Run by the legendary Yuri Lyubimov, the Taganka is one of the world's most famous theaters. The troupe's most redoubtable dramatization is of Mikhail Bulgakov's novel *The Master and Margarita.* Performances sell out far in advance. ⊠*76 Zemlyanoy Val, Eastern Outskirts* ☎*495/915–1015* ⊕*www.taganka.theatre.ru* Ⓜ*Taganskaya.*

Tereza Durova Clown Theater. Attracting children and adults, the shows here are based on the commedia dell'arte, filled with music, dance, and acrobatics. ⊠*6 Pavlovskaya ul., inside DK Zavoda Ilyicha, Southern Outskirts* ☎*495/637–1689* Ⓜ*Serpukhovskaya.*

NIGHTLIFE

The *Moscow Times, Element,* and *LifeStyle* (available for free at hotels, bars, and restaurants) publish up-to-date calendars of events in English.

⚠ **Foreigners make easy crime targets, so you should take special precautions at night. You're safest venturing out with other people. Do not drive under any circumstances if you drink; the laws in Russia are strict, and traffic police can and do stop cars at will.**

BARS

There are no cover charges for bars, unless live music is taking place there. At some clubs, there's a fee to be seated at a table.

Annushka. Housed on a tram that makes a constant and short loop around the picturesque Chistiye Prudy area, Annushka is a cozy bar and eatery. Wait outside the metro station, where it stops every 10 to 15 minutes. ✉*Stops outside Chistiye Prudy metro station, Kitai Gorod* ☎*495/507–5770* Ⓜ*Chistiye Prudy.*

Glavpivtorg. Live musicians perform songs from the Soviet era at this enormous retro-style eatery. It

has a comprehensive choice of beers, including its own brand. The traditional Russian dishes are expensive but served up with style. Book ahead, as it gets busy even on weeknights. ✉*5 Bolshaya Lubyanka ul., Kitai Gorod* ☎*495/628–2591 or 495/624–1996* Ⓜ*Lubyanka.*

GQ Bar. It's not cheap, and the face control gets strict from time to time, but if you're looking for an elite bar scene, it's hard to beat. This is where Moscow's upper crust—everyone from upwardly mobile execs to almost-oligarchs—comes to grab its after-work drink, or a bite in one of the three lavishly appointed dining halls. ✉*5 ul. Balchug, Zamoskvoreche* ☎*495/956–7775* Ⓜ*Novokuznetskaya.*

Hard Rock Cafe. It may be an international chain, but somehow the Moscow branch manages to maintain its own flavor. Locals come for the pop-music classics, and Westerners stop by for a taste of home. ✉*44 Arbat, Arbat* ☎*495/241–9853 or 495/205–8335* ⊕*www.hardrock cafe.ru* Ⓜ*Smolenskaya.*

Kitaiysky Lyotchik. Live music and tasty, affordable food draw a bohemian crowd to this cellar bar whose name translates to "Chinese Pilot." ✉*25 Lubyansky proyezd, Bldg. 1, Kitai Gorod* ☎*495/624–5611* Ⓜ*Kitai Gorod.*

Krasny Bar. The views of the city from this upscale 27th-floor bar, open until the last customer leaves, are excellent. ✉*nab. 23a Tarasa Shevchenko, Western Outskirts* ☎*495/730–0808* Ⓜ*Kievskaya.*

Proyekt O. G. I. This was one of the city's first bohemian clubs, complete with a bookstore and live music. It has since evolved into an increasingly commercial, expanding chain of cheap restaurants. The original, however, is still authentic. ✉*8/12 Potapovsky per., Kitai Gorod* ☎*495/627–5366* ⊕*www.proektogi.ru* Ⓜ*Chistiye Prudy.*

Real McCoy's. A speakeasy theme pervades this bar. Weekend nights, the place explodes into an alcohol-fueled party with customers dancing on the bar. ✉*1 Kudrinskaya Pl., Bolshaya Nikitskaya* ☎*495/255–4144* Ⓜ*Barrikadnaya.*

Silvers. This is the place to go for those desperate for authentic Irish pub atmosphere and a pint of Guinness. Wood-paneled walls, shamrocks, and tons of expatriates are enough to make even the weariest traveler feel at home. ✉5/6 *Tverskaya ul., Tverskaya* ☎495/290–4222 Ⓜ*Okhotny Ryad.*

Sally O'Brien's. Despite the country music often played here, this is a pub with a definite Irish feel. It's also a good place to meet other foreigners. ✉1/3 *Polyanka ul., Zamoskvoreche* ☎495/959–0175 Ⓜ*Polyanka.*

Sixteen Tons. A popular pub with a club upstairs, this spot serves its own home-brewed beer. ✉6 *Presnensky Val, Western Outskirts* ☎495/253–5300 ⊕*www.16tons.ru* Ⓜ*Ulitsa 1905 Goda.*

> ## COCKTAILS...NOT THE MOLOTOV KIND
>
> As much progress as the Moscow bar scene has made in recent years, many of the capital's bartenders have not yet mastered the art of mixology, resulting in the occasional mangled Martini (though nothing explosive yet). **Help** (✉27 [1st] Tverskaya-Yamskaya ul., Bldg. 1, Northern Ouskirts Ⓜ*Belorusskaya*) is on the way, however, at this bar which offers over 200 drink options, from classics like the Long Island Iced Tea (only 150R) to more exotic but well-made local creations.

Tinkoff. A futuristically styled beer restaurant run by Tinkoff brewery, this spot is popular with diplomats working in nearby embassies. ✉11 *Protochny per., Arbat* ☎495/777–3300 ⊕*www.tinkoff.ru* Ⓜ*Smolenskaya.*

CLUBS

Moscow's clubbing scene has finally grown up, with plenty of Western-quality places to go. However, *feis kontrol* (face control, or a velvet-rope mentality) is common at most high-end clubs. Most clubs don't get busy until between midnight and 2 AM. Live music is popular, and some larger clubs put on shows by famous foreign DJs and musicians.

B-2. One of the best places in Moscow for live rock performances, B-2 is an enormous five-story club that includes a sushi bar, a big-screen TV, a dance club, and several bars. ✉8 *Bolshaya Sadovaya, Tsverskaya* ☎495/650–9918 ⊕*www.b2club.ru* Ⓜ*Mayakovskaya.*

Club Che. This is a vibrant Latin American–theme club staffed by Cuban waiters. Drink service can be slow at night, when the staff often dances with the crowd. Show up early or you'll never get in. ✉10/2 *Nikolskaya ul., Kitai Gorod* ☎495/621–7477 ⊕*www.clubche.ru* Ⓜ*Lubyanka.*

Fabrique. Popular with expats and students, this two-story club features tasty food and sessions by top guest DJs. ✉2 *Kosmodamianskaya nab., Zamoskvoreche* ☎495/540–9955 or 495/953–6576 ⊕*www.fabrique.ru* Ⓜ*Novokuznetskaya or Paveletskaya.*

Garazh. Getting into this popular nightclub on the weekend isn't always easy, but if you make it you'll be among Moscow's most dedicated clubbers. Wednesday is hip-hop night. ✉16 *Tverskaya ul., Bldg. 2/2, Tsverskaya* ☎495/650–1848 Ⓜ*Tverskaya or Chekhovskaya.*

Hungry Duck. Once famed as Moscow's wildest and most depraved place to spend a weekend night, the Duck has lost its edge since its mid-'90s

SKIPPING VELVET ROPES

Although clubs the world over reserve the right to be choosy about who gets in and who gets left out in the cold, few doormen have a reputation for being as stringent—or as sadistic—as the ones working Moscow's nightspots. The truth is, many of the places listed below can easily be called *demokratichny,* meaning that they maintain a democratic door policy. If you do find yourself in a run-in with the face-control goons, however, there are a few strategies that can help you skip the velvet rope:

Dress to impress: Try to find out the type of crowd your club attracts, and don the appropriate attire. Keep in mind, however, that "appropriate" and "formal" are two different things.

A pair of Prada jeans may get you a lot further than a three-piece suit.

Speak English: Although foreigners seldom create the impression that they did, say, ten years ago, many clubs consider it desirable to have an international clientele. Speaking some English, flashing your passport, and saying you'll tell everybody back in Boise how cool the club is might be enough for you to waltz right in.

Let your money do the talking: If you really want to get in and are still getting the cold shoulder, call the club's PR manager over and ask to buy a club card. The card makes you face-control proof and may also get you a discount on drinks and food, but it won't come cheap. Club cards cost from a few hundred to a few thousand dollars.

heyday. Nevertheless, most visitors to Moscow still believe this sweaty, sticky dive is a must-see. Consider yourself warned. ⊠ *9/6 Pushechnaya ul., Bldg. 1, Kitai Gorod* ☎ *495/923–6158* ⊕ *www.hungryduck. com* Ⓜ *Kuznetsky Most.*

Karma Bar. Top 40 hits and a crew of die-hard regulars mean that hardly a weekend goes by without Karma's dance floor being packed wall to wall. Democratic face control also helps bring in the crowds. ⊠ *3 Pushechnaya ul., Kitai Gorod* ☎ *495/624–5633* ⊕ *www.karma-bar.ru* Ⓜ *Kuznetsky Most.*

Keks. Housed in a former factory, this retro-theme café turns into a club at night with guest DJs and a small dance floor. ⊠ *11/34 Timura Frunze ul., Kropotkinsky District* ☎ *495/246–0864* ⊕ *www.cafekeks. ru* Ⓜ *Park Kultury.*

Papa's. Nights at Papa's are all about strip egg-and-spoon races, wet T-shirt contests, or any other silly games the management can think of. Dirt-cheap happy-hour drinks are a big draw for students. ⊠ *22 Myasnitskaya ul., Kitai Gorod* ☎ *495/755–9554* Ⓜ *Chistiye Prudy.*

★ **Propaganda.** This is probably the city's most reliable club for trendy, yet laid-back crowds and good DJs. It's *the* place to be on Thursday night. On Sunday night it turns into one of the city's most popular gay clubs. ⊠ *7 Bolshoi Zlatoustinsky per., Kitai Gorod* ☎ *495/624–5732* ⊕ *www.propagandamoscow.com/home.html* Ⓜ *Kitai Gorod.*

Vermel. Cheap drinks and affordable concerts have made Vermel a big hit with students and other young clubbers. ⊠ *4/5 Raushskaya nab., Zamoskvoreche* ☎ *495/959–3303* Ⓜ *Tretyakovskaya.*

GAY & LESBIAN CLUBS

Three Monkeys. This gay club, a popular spot with students, is one of the most well established in town, with a regular rotation of good DJs. Mostly men come here, but women are welcome. ✉*11 Nastavnichesky per., Bldg. 1, Zamoskvoreche* ☎*495/916–3555* Ⓜ*Kurskaya or Chkalovskaya.*

12 Volt. This club for both men and women is tricky to find, but has a welcoming atmosphere. It has DJs, film screenings, karaoke, and cheap drink deals. ✉*12 Tverskaya ul., Bldg. 2, entrance in yard off Kozitsky per., Tsverskaya* ☎*495/933–2815* ⊕*12voltclub.ru* Ⓜ*Tverskaya.*

> **IN THE LIMELIGHT**
>
> Opened by the renowned Russian designer of the same name, the **Denis Simachev Bar** (✉*12 Stoleshnikov per., Tsverskaya* ☎*495/629–8085* Ⓜ*Teatralnaya*) combines kitsch, elegance, and a hot crowd for a unique bar experience that can be a treat for those keen on people-watching. Here's where Moscow's "Zoilotoy Molozyozh," or "Gilded Youth," go for their pre-party drinks.

JAZZ & BLUES

BB King Blues Club. The premiere opening featured the man himself, and visiting Western stars have continued to make appearances here, often for post-concert jams. ✉*4 Sadovaya-Samotyochnaya ul., Bldg. 2, Northern Outskirts* ☎*495/699–8206* Ⓜ*Tsvetnoy Bulvar.*

Blue Bird Jazz Café. Russian talent and the occasional odd foreign guest perform here, at one of Moscow's oldest jazz clubs. ✉*23/15 Malaya Dmitrovka ul., Kitai Gorod* ☎*495/299–2225* Ⓜ*Mayakovskaya.*

Jazz Town. Lit up like a Christmas tree year-round, this newcomer to Moscow's live music scene features bands performing nearly every night, as well as the occasional DJ. ✉*12 Taganskaya Pl., Eastern Outskirts* ☎*495/241–0644* Ⓜ*Taganskaya.*

SPORTS & THE OUTDOORS

Rollerblading and mountain biking are increasingly popular, as is skateboarding. Although rare in the city center (as streets are covered with snow, ice, or mud for more than half the year, and the air around roadways is unbearably smoggy in summer), joggers are common in parks; they are replaced in winter by cross-country skiers of all ages.

Tickets for sporting events can be purchased at the sports arena immediately prior to the game or at any of the numerous theater box offices (*teatralnaya kassa*) throughout the city. You can also ask your hotel's service bureau for assistance in obtaining tickets to sporting events, but the fee will probably far exceed the value of the ticket. Soccer is the most popular sport and Muscovites support local teams Dinamo and Lokomotiv.

On the banks of the Moskva River across from Sparrow Hills and Moscow State University, **Luzhniki Sports Palace** (✉*24 Luzhnetskaya nab., Southern Outskirts* ☎*495/785–9717 main number, 495/637–0802,*

495/637–0435 tennis, 495/637–0764 pool, 495/637–0210 ice-skating Ⓜ*Sportivnaya*) is probably the city's most easily recognizable stadium. It has high-quality facilities for professional soccer, but its other facilities are a bit outdated. There's a nice pool (although you have to bring a medical certificate to use it), and tennis courts are available for rent by the hour.

BANYAS

Of all Russia's traditions, perhaps none is more steeped in ritual than a trip to the steamy banya, a sauna-style bathhouse where the steam is produced by throwing a steady supply of water over heated rocks. In fact, for many banya lovers a trip to the bathhouse is almost a religious experience, complete with birch twigs for self-flagellation (to open pores and promote circulation). There's even a traditional garment—a peaked woolen hat (sold at numerous shops and sometimes at the banyas themselves) to keep the tips of your ears from burning and prevent heat from escaping through the top of your head. Manicures, pedicures, and massages are also often available, and some banyas are even attached to fitness centers.

A few stores around the city sell banya goods, including hats, chamomile-soaked towels, and herb-enriched lotions. **Perekryostok Supermarket** (✉*1 Tishinskaya Pl., Northern Outskirts* ☎*495/662–8888* ⊕*www.perekrestok.ru* Ⓜ*Be-lorusskaya*) stocks hats, aromatic oils, and ready-packed birch twigs at more than 50 branches around the city. **Novaya Zarya** (✉*4 Ulinka ul., in Gostiny Dvor, Kitai Gorod* ☎*495/298–0752* Ⓜ*Ploshchad Revolutsii*) is one of Russia's oldest perfume manufacturers, which makes its own line of fragrant essences that you can add to banya water (you can get your own tub even at a public banya).

> ### WORD OF MOUTH
>
> "I had prepared myself for the unexpected but nothing could have prepared me for the heat [of the banya].... Then Pavel came in, a man who looked like a body builder and would be the one to apply the birch branch treatment. You lay down on a board and he scrubs the living you-know-what out of your whole body with some birch leaves, with the coup de grâce being a mild whipping. Did I mention that Pavel was wearing a white loin cloth? He was. As awkward, strange and torturous as the whole process sounds, it felt pretty good."
>
> —ksose

Unless otherwise indicated, the banyas listed below are open daily. Note that over the summer, most banyas close for two or three weeks when hot water is turned off for a few weeks at a time in different parts of the city.

With a gym, salon, bar, pool, and massage, **Bani na Presne** (✉*7 Stolyarny per., Western Outskirts* ☎*495/255–0115* Ⓜ*Ulitsa 1905 Goda*) is a popular, casual banya. It's fairly expensive at about 500R to 600R for a two-hour visit. **Russkie Bani** (✉*25A Bolshoy Strochenovsky per., Zamoskvoreche* ☎*495/236–3171* Ⓜ*Dobrinskaya or Serpukhovs-*

CLOSE UP

Get Steamed: Banya Basics

The banya, or bathhouse, is a cultural tradition that became popular in the 17th century, when attending a communal bath was the only way for many Russians to stay clean. Today, it is still believed to have therapeutic benefits and is also valued as a place to relax, socialize, and even do business.

Though visiting a banya can be one of the highlights of a trip to Moscow, it can also be a confusing experience and there are a few ground rules you should know, like men and women are separated in general sections, although families and couples can hire a private bath for use together, and soap is strictly forbidden (the steam is supposed to clean you).

Here are a few easy steps that will help you get the best steam possible:

1. Check Yourself: If you have low or high blood pressure, a heart ailment, or some other health issue, you may want to stay away. Pregnant women and asthma sufferers are advised to do the same.

2. Check In: After paying the entrance fee, your valuables are handed to a special attendant who puts them in a locker and watches over them. Theft is rare, but you may be better off leaving valuables in a hotel safe. Tipping is customary, generally 50R–150R for the attendant, 300R–500R for a good masseur. You will then be given a towel and assigned a locker for your clothes. Bring a pair of flip-flops to walk around in.

3. Sweat It Out: Champions of the Russian banya believe that steaming helps combat respiratory problems, aids in circulation, and opens the pores to help rid you of all the nasty

toxins in your body—that's why the steam room is kept hotter than the fires of hell—a toasty 90°C (194°F) to be exact. Have a seat on one of the benches lining the walls (the higher up you sit, the hotter you'll be). You can wrap yourself in a towel but most bathers in gender-segregated rooms go nude. Towels are, however, very useful for sitting on. Are the tips of your ears burning? That means it's working. Don't overdo it: 10–15 minutes is more than enough for your first time.

4. Cool Down: Once you feel sufficiently steamed, dunk yourself in the pool, barrel, or bucket of icy water provided. This is an essential part of the process—if you don't get your body temperature down, your next trip to the steam room won't be much fun.

5. Relax: The banya will probably have a relaxation zone that provides everything from couches and cold drinks to meals. While the ultra-Russian ambience might seem ideal for doing a shot or two of vodka, keep in mind that you will be dehydrated. Stick to beer, juice, or best of all, water.

6. Repeat Steps 3–5: Once you're rested, reenter the steam room. You'll likely sweat more profusely this go round. This is an ideal time to engage in some self-flagellation with a bunch of soaked *veniki*, or birch twigs. Repeat the process as many times as you see fit, and when you're done, give your neighbors the traditional post-banya salutation: *s lyokhim parom*—may your steam be light!

kaya) is part of a fitness center across the street from the South African embassy. Two-hour sessions cost around 350R.

Dating to the late 1800s, the impeccably clean **Sandunovskiye Bani** (**Сандуновские Бани**) (✉ *14 Neglinniy per., Kitai Gorod* ☎ *495/625–4631 or 495/628–4633* ⊕ *www.sanduny.ru* ⊙ *Daily 8* AM*–10* PM Ⓜ *Kuznetsky Most*) is probably the city's most elegant bathhouse, with a lavish interior. Prices depend on your gender and which section you visit, but range from 600R to 1,000R. On-site facilities include a beauty parlor and, of course, massage. One of the better banya bargains in town, **Seleznyovskiye Bani** (✉ *15 Seleznyovsky ul., Northern Outskirts* ☎ *495/978–7521* Ⓜ *Novoslobodskaya*) combines quality service with low prices. Two hours cost around 400R, depending on what section you go into and the day of the week. Prices range from 300R to 700R. It's closed Monday.

ICE HOCKEY

The NHL snaps up most of Russia's best players, but you can still catch some budding stars before the United States and Canada lure them away.

Dinamo (✉ *36 Leningradskoe shosse, Northern Outskirts* ☎ *495/612–7092 or 495/612–3132* Ⓜ *Dinamo*), one of the city's largest hockey stadiums, with a seating capacity of 60,000, is home to the army's team, TsSKA. Spartak holds its home games at **Sokolniki Ice Palace** (✉ *1b Sokolnicheski Val, Eastern Outskirts* ☎ *495/645–2065* Ⓜ *Sokolniki*).

RUNNING

Runners should avoid city streets which are covered with snow, ice, or mud for more than half the year, and filled with noxious fumes and smoggy air in the summer. As in any city unaccustomed to joggers, it can be difficult to find a comfortable running route, and you probably will be in a conspicuous minority.

The Hash House Harriers, however, a social running and drinking club, meets weekly for a run through one of the city's parks followed by a bit of drinking and socializing. Meeting days and times are often listed in the *Moscow Times* community bulletin board section.

The best spot for jogging is along the path from Gorky Park to **Vorobyovy Gory** (✉ *Vorobyovskaya nab., Southern Outskirts* Ⓜ *Vorobyovy Gory*) near Moscow State University. The trails through **Nyeskuchny Sad** (✉ *Entrances between 8 and 10 Leninsky pr. and 28 and 30 Leninsky pr., Zamoskvoreche* Ⓜ *Leninsky Prospekt or Oktyabrskaya*) are also a good spot for jogging. You can avoid Moscow's heavy traffic and fumes at **Filyovsky** (✉ *24–26 Filyovskaya ul., Northern Outskirts* Ⓜ *Filyovsky Park*), Izmailovsky, Kolomenskoye, or Sokolniki Park.

SOCCER

Footage of Russian teenagers rioting outside the Kremlin after Russia lost to Japan in the 2002 World Cup was a reminder to the world of how seriously this country takes its soccer (*futbol*). As a general rule, Russian soccer teams fare poorly in international events, but that doesn't seem to bother Russia's die-hard fans. Riots were once common at some of Moscow's larger stadiums, but an overwhelming police presence and the prohibition of alcohol sales at nearby stores have managed to quell the problem. Still, before games, neighborhoods surrounding the stadiums are often full of hooligans looking for any excuse for a fight. The season usually runs from early spring to late fall. During the off-season, Duma deputies and other politicians hold games that tend to be more comedic and less crowded. Moscow mayor Yuri Luzhkov is a huge fan and has been known to hold matches with players from city hall. You can buy tickets for the matches outside the stadiums or at the teatralnaya kassa.

Old and dilapidated but still in working order, **Dinamo** (✉ *36 Leningradskoe shosse, Northern Outskirts* ☎ *495/612–7092 or 495/612–3132* Ⓜ *Dinamo*) is a favorite stadium for matches between Duma deputies and city hall officials. **Lokomotiv** (✉ *125a Bolshaya Cherkizovskaya, Eastern Outskirts* ☎ *495/161–4283* Ⓜ *Cherkizovskaya*), Moscow's newest and largest stadium, is probably the most comfortable place to watch a soccer match. **Luzhniki** (✉ *24 Luzhnetskaya nab., Southern Outskirts* ☎ *495/785–9717 main number, 495/637–0802, or 495/637–0435* Ⓜ *Sportivnaya*), the city's flagship stadium and home of the Spartak, is fully up to European standards. It sometimes hosts international matches.

SHOPPING

Gone are the Cold War images of long lines and empty shelves, the uneven and unpredictable distribution of goods. These days, Muscovites can shop in glossy malls, revamped department stores, and designer boutiques.

Keep in mind that you're forbidden to take some items out of the country. The law basically disallows the export of anything of "cultural value to the Russian nation." In practical terms, this means that anything older than 30 to 40 years is not allowed out without special permission from the Ministry of Culture or its local agent; the item will be confiscated at the border if you lack the necessary papers. Anything prerevolutionary is simply not let out at all. If you're buying paintings or art objects, it's important to consult with the seller regarding the proper documentation of sale for export. Keep receipts of your purchases.

Hours of operation can be capricious, but the general rule is Monday through Saturday 10 to 7 (occasionally closing for an hour sometime between 1 and 3). Food stores may open an hour earlier, and department stores may remain open later, with additional hours on Sunday (11 to 6). Most of the newer shopping malls stay open daily from 10 or 11 to 9 or 10.

SHOPPING DISTRICTS

Historically, the main shopping districts of Moscow have been concentrated in the city center, along Tverskaya ulitsa and Novy Arbat. Luxury designer stores like Cerutti, Versace, Hermès, Gucci, Armani, and Prada have settled along pedestrianized Stoleshnikov pereulok, Kuznetsky Most, and Tretyakovsky proyezd. On Kutuzovsky prospekt, off Novy Arbat, you'll find Dolce & Gabbana, Donna Karan, and Fendi boutiques. Cheaper Russian and Western fashion brands can be found in the giant new malls next to the Kursk and Kiev train stations, while Stary Arbat, which has been particularly spruced up for the tourist trade, is your best bet for speedy souvenir shopping.

DEPARTMENT STORES & MALLS

Atrium. A giant shopping mall in front of the Kursk station, Atrium is yet another symbol of Mayor Yuri Luzhkov's Moscow. With everything under one roof, including numerous clothing stores, a perfumes supermarket, huge grocery store, casino, and the Formula Kino movie theater, this is one of the best places to shop. There's a great coffee shop in the lobby, where classical and jazz musicians give live concerts every night, as well as a trendy Italian café and a sushi bar. ⊠ *33 Zemlyanoi Val, Eastern Outskirts* ☎ *495/927–3217* Ⓜ *Kurskaya.*

Detsky Mir. The famous "Children's World" department store now also hawks clothes, makeup, and a wide assortment of toys for grown-ups. The first and second floors are still a delight for kids. Don't miss the merry-go-round in the center. A New Year's market of trees, locally made glass ornaments, and lights starts in October, gradually taking over the first floor. Unfortunately, the building is set to be gutted and remodeled, which looks likely to spoil its nostalgic charm. It's near Lubyanskaya Ploshchad. ⊠ *5 Teatralny proyezd, Kitai Gorod* ☎ *495/781–0950* Ⓜ *Lubyanka.*

Gallery Aktyor. Next door to the high-end grocery Yeliseyevsky's, this space is smaller, more elegant, and often less crowded than GUM or Manezh. Popular brands like Naf Naf, Levi's, Chevignon, and Lacoste are for sale. The first floor houses a Swatch outlet and a Clinique cosmetics store. ⊠ *16/2 Tverskaya ul., Tverskaya* ☎ *495/290–9832* Ⓜ *Tverskaya or Pushkinskaya.*

★ **GUM.** A series of shops and boutiques inside a 19th-century arcade, this shopping emporium sits on Red Square, right across from the Kremlin. GUM, which stands for Gosudarstvenny Universalny Magazin, or State Department Store, now stocks only a handful of Russian brands in the upper-level stores. On the first floor you will find an arcade of boutiques, including MaxMara, Hugo Boss, and La Perla. Also here is the elegant Bosco restaurant, which overlooks Red Square and has a summer terrace. Cheaper eats are available at fast-food outlets on the top floor. ⊠ *3 Red Sq., Kremlin/Red Square* ☎ *495/788–4343* ⊕ *www.gum.ru* Ⓜ *Ploshchad Revolutsii.*

Kalinka-Stockmann. This major Finnish chain store combines several departments under one roof at Smolensky Passazh on the Garden Ring. A grocery shop with a broad assortment of fresh fruits, vegetables, and fish is below ground. A vast men's and women's clothing shop occupies the first floor, and housewares, linens, electronics, footwear, and children's clothing are on the second floor. ✉ *3 Smolenskaya Pl., Bldg. 5, Arbat* ☎ *495/974–0122* ⊕ *www.stockmann.ru* Ⓜ *Smolenskaya*.

Manezh. Although the proper name of this mall is Okhotny Ryad, everyone calls it Manezh for the square on which it sits. Brands like Benetton, Tommy Hilfiger, Motivi, and MEXX along with gift items are the strong point of this shopping showcase. Set under the main square adjacent to the Kremlin, the Manezh attracts crowds of Russian out-of-towners, who stroll, photograph the intricate cupola that extends aboveground, and window-shop. ✉ *Trade Center Okhotny Ryad, 1 Manezhnaya Pl., Kremlin/Red Square* Ⓜ *Okhotny Ryad*.

Petrovsky Passazh. MaxMara, Nina Ricci, Givenchy, Kenzo, and Bally boutiques and an antiques store bejewel this chic, glass-roof space, the most luxurious shopping *passazh* (arcade) in town. ✉ *10 ul. Petrovka, Kitai Gorod* ☎ *495/995–8899* Ⓜ *Kuznetsky Most*.

Ramstore. The huge outlets of this Turkish-owned superstore chain are the Russian version of Wal-Mart. The prices are slightly below normal Moscow levels. There are 22 Ramstore outlets in Moscow that differ only in size. ✉ *23B/1 ul. Krasnaya Presnya, Bolshaya Nikitskaya* ☎ *495/255–5412* Ⓜ *Krasnopresnenskaya* ✉ *60A Sheremetyevskaya ul., Northern Outskirts* ☎ *495/937–2600* Ⓜ *Rizhskaya or Belorusskaya* ✉ *13 Chasovaya ul., Northern Outskirts* ☎ *495/937–0510* Ⓜ *Aeroport or Sokol* ✉ *6 Komsololskaya Pl., Northern Outskirts* ☎ *495/207–0241* Ⓜ *Komsomolskaya*.

TsUM. TsUM, which stands for Central Department Store, has upgraded itself to an expensive store with collections of nearly all the top European designers. It's a two-minute walk down ulitsa Petrovka from Petrovsky Passazh. ✉ *2 ul. Petrovka, Kitai Gorod* ☎ *495/933–7300* ⊕ *www.tsum.ru* Ⓜ *Kuznetsky Most*.

SPECIALTY STORES

ARTS & CRAFTS

Arbatskaya Kollektsia. This nice souvenir shop sells the best of locally produced folk art, including *palekh* (colorful, lacquered wood with folklore designs) chess sets, cocktail glasses, and coffee sets made of amber. ✉ *12 Arbat, Arbat* ☎ *495/291–9300* Ⓜ *Arbatskaya*.

Arbatskaya Lavitsa. This large, old-fashioned store sells Gzhel china, linen tablecloths, nesting dolls, and wooden toys at reasonable prices and without the hard sell. ✉ *27 Arbat, Arbat* ☎ *495/290–5689* Ⓜ *Arbatskaya or Smolenskaya*.

Art boutiques of the Varvarka ulitsa churches. These boutiques are inside the Church of St. Maxim the Blessed, open daily 11–6, and the Church of St. George on Pskov Hill, open daily 11–7. Both carry a fine selection of handicrafts, jewelry, ceramics, and other types of native-Russian art. ✉ *6 Varvarka ul., Kitai Gorod* Ⓜ *Kitai Gorod* ✉ *12 Varvarka ul., Kitai Gorod* Ⓜ *Kitai Gorod*.

Culture Pavilion. Part of the Soviet showpiece now called the All-Russian Exhibition Center, the elegant white Pavilion No. 66 stocks a huge range of crafts, from Turkmen embroidery to earthenware pots from

Suzdal and carved stone animals from Perm. ✉*All-Russian Exhibition Center, Northern Outskirts* ☎*495/544–3400* Ⓜ*VDNKh.*

Ikonnaya Lavka. The Cathedral of Our Lady of Kazan, near Russian Museum World, houses this icon shop. In addition to icons, you can purchase religious books, silver crosses, and other Orthodox religious items. ✉*3 Nikolskaya ul., at Red Sq., Kremlin/Red Square* ☎*No phone* Ⓜ*Ploshchad Revolutsii.*

Novodel. This small store sells quirky contemporary crafts from local artists, including toys, clocks, and greetings cards. ✉*9 Bolshoi Palashevsky pereulok, Tverskaya* ☎*495/926–4538* Ⓜ*Mayakovskaya or Tverskaya.*

Russian Museum World. The Historical Museum's art shop deals in a

wide gamut of souvenirs, from jewelry, T-shirts, handmade crafts, and replicas of museum pieces to Russian- and Ukrainian-style embroidered shirts, Gzhel ceramics, and more. Wooden bowls and spoons decorated in *khokhloma* style—with bright oils painted on a black-and-golden background—fill the shelves. The store is on the right-hand side of the museum as you enter Red Square through the Resurrection Gates. ✉*1/2 Red Sq., Kremlin/Red Square* ☎*495/692–1320* Ⓜ*Ploshchad Revolutsii.*

Russkaya Vyshivka. Specializing in Russian linen, this store stocks beautiful embroidered christening gowns as well as table linens and rag rugs. ✉*31 Arbat, Arbat* ☎*495/241–2841* Ⓜ*Arbatskaya or Smolenskaya.*

CLOTHING

Most Western stores like Levi's and Nike can be found in shopping malls such as GUM and Yevropeisky. However, the prices will be much higher than in the United States. Instead, take a look at the stores of Russian designers, which sell clothes at prices ranging from reasonable to outrageous.

Denis Simachev. This up-and-coming Russian designer has opened a boutique selling his clothes in the heart of Moscow's designer district. He specializes in fur and enlarged folk art patterns. The outside of the store is decorated with designs based on red-and-gold *khokhloma* bowls. At night, the tiny bar within the store is one of the hottest spots in town. ✉*12 Stoleshnikov per., Bldg. 1, Tverskaya* ☎*495/629–8085* ⏱*24 hours* Ⓜ*Teatralnaya.*

Mir Shersti. Tucked away in a backstreet, this store specializes in Russian-made felt boots, or valenki, which it stocks in children's and adult sizes. You can also buy ribbon-trimmed felt slippers and fleece-lined clothing.

A small museum of valenki is next door. ✉*12 (2nd) Kozhevnichesky per., Northern Outskirts* ☎*495/775–2577* Ⓜ*Paveletskaya.*

Moskvichka. Although poorly laid out, this store purveys popular clothing brands like Guess, Sisley, Esprit, and MEXX and also stocks Russian brands Sultanna Frantsuzova, Yevgeniya Ostrovskaya, and Sunie Li, popular with the city's office girls. It's just a few doors down Novy Arbat from Novoarbatsky Gastronom. ✉*15 Novy Arbat, Arbat* ☎*495/202–5250* Ⓜ*Arbatskaya.*

Valentin Yudashkin Trading House. Make an appearance at Valentin Yudashkin for the latest Russian haute couture. The women's fashion designer is perhaps the only Russian designer known outside the country and many Russian celebrities prefer his work to that of Western designers. ✉*19 Kutuzovsky pr., Western Outskirts* ☎*495/240–1189* Ⓜ*Kievskaya or Kutuzovskaya.*

Yevropeisky. This huge, well laid-out new mall has a European theme and includes branches of Britain's Marks & Spencers and Top Shop as well as Spain's Bershka and Zara. The floaty and feminine Russian brands Sultanna Frantsuzova and Sunie Li both have stores here. ✉*2 Ploshchad Kievskogo Vokzala, Western Outskirts* ☎*495/101–4444* Ⓜ*Kievskaya.*

FOOD & SPIRITS

Caviar in Russia? Who can resist? Unfortunately, as of fall 2007 it was only possible to find the cheaper red caviar in city stores, due to restrictions on black caviar brought in to save sturgeon stocks. Black caviar is slowly making its way back into stores, albeit at exorbitant prices. Black-market caviar is produced by killing the endangered fish and is often packed in unsanitary conditions, so if you come across any at street markets, don't buy it there. A ban on selling caviar at street markets is still being debated.

Buying liquor—especially vodka—in Russia is a de rigueur activity fraught with danger. Alcohol counterfeiting is a big problem; according to various estimates, illegally produced vodka accounts for 40% to 70% of what is available on the market. If you don't follow safe buying practices, you could end up with a severe case of alcohol poisoning. Your best bet on price and safety is to buy well-known brands such as Kristall and Russky Standart at reputable supermarkets. Note that every bottle of vodka sold in Russia must bear a white excise stamp, glued over the cap, and those sold in Moscow must also bear a barcode stamp.

Western-style supermarkets are rapidly squeezing Soviet-style food stores such as bakeries out of business. Though there are still some bakers in operation, supermarket bakery counters are a good option for Russian bread for less than 20R a loaf. *Podmoskovny* and *nareznoi* sell for about 15R and are lighter than the black bread generally associated with Russia. Varieties of black rye bread (*borodinsky* and *khamovnichesky*) are the tastiest, and they still won't put you out more than 25R. Branches of Perekryostok, often open 24 hours, have proliferated like underbrush below the high-rise canopies of Moscow's suburbs. This supermarket offers good freshly baked bread including round *stolichny* loaves with a crisp crust. The delicious and hugely popular Armenian lavash—soft, thin flatbread—is made with flour and water. Perhaps the best bread in the city is baked at Volkonsky, a small French-owned chain that sells expensive, but great quality loaves baked on-site as well as cookies and pastries that you can enjoy in the store's café.

Bulochka Brioche. A much cheaper alternative for bread than Volkonsky, the Bulochka Brioche chain sells crusty olive bread and baguettes in kiosks outside metro stations. ⊠ *Gruzinsky Val outside the Circle Line exit of Belorusskaya metro station, Northern Outskirts.*

Globus Gourmet. Picky eaters will like this 24-hour grocery store that has been stocking its shelves with high-quality imported foodstuffs since its opening in 2005. Among the wide array of deli foods, Globus offers Italian raspberry-flavor balsamic vinegar, priced at 815R for a 250-milliliter jar. The store's cheese department has to be seen to be believed. According to the staff, an average sales receipt at Globus runs 750R–990R, making it reasonably priced compared to French competitor Fauchon. ⊠ *22 Bolshaya Yakimanka, Zamoskvoreche* ☎ *495/995–2170* Ⓜ *Oktyabrskaya and Polyanka* ⊠ *19 Novy Arbat, in the basement of Vesna shopping center, Arbat* ☎ *495/775–0918 or 495/775–0923* Ⓜ *Arbat.*

Konditersky. This cozy, old-fashioned candy store will weigh out chocolates for you and has a good choice of Russian brands, including Krasny Oktyabr. ⊠ *22 Pyatnitskaya ul., Zamoskvoreche* ☎ *495/951–3764* ⊙ *Weekdays 9–8, Sat. 10–6. Closed Sun.* Ⓜ *Tretyakovskaya.*

Korkunov. This is an upscale store selling individual chocolates and boxed candies produced in Russia by a newly established company that uses Italian manufacturing equipment. ⊠ *13/16 Bolshaya Lubyanka ul., Kitai Gorod* ☎ *495/625–6411* ⊙ *Mon.–Sat. 10–8* Ⓜ *Lubyanka.*

Krasny Oktyabr chocolate factory. Russian-made chocolates make a great, unexpected souvenir from Russia. Those from Moscow's Krasny Oktyabr (Red October) factory are the best. You can buy both individual candies, of various names—*Krasnaya Shapochka* (Little Red Riding Hood), *Mishka Kosolapaya* (Little Bear), and *Melodiya* (Melody)—and gift boxes. A nice box of *Nadezhda* (Hope) chocolates sells for just over 200R; a gift tin of Mishka Kosolapaya for about 350R. The chocolates are widely available in supermarkets and kiosks. The best assortment, including gift boxes and chocolate animal figures, is at the store next to the historic factory building. ⊠ *14 Bersenevskaya Naberezhnaya, Kropotkinsky District* ☎ *495/230–0049* Ⓜ *Kropotkinskaya.*

Volkonsky. This French-owned chain now has three branches in Moscow, where you can buy freshly baked cookies, pastries, and bread, and also drink coffee in a small café. This branch is perfect to combine with a walk around Patriarch's Pond. ⊠ *2/46 Bolshaya Sadovaya, Tverskaya* ☎ *495/699–3620* Ⓜ *Tverskaya.*

★ **Yeliseyevsky's.** Historic, sumptuous, gourmet—this turn-of-the-20th-century grocery store is the star of Tverskaya ulitsa. A late-18th-century classical mansion houses the store, and the interior sparkles with chandeliers, stained glass, and gilt wall decorations. Fine products abound, from cognac to Armenian berry juices and Russian chocolate and candy of all sorts. This is one of the best places to buy freshly baked goods. You'll find traditional favorite Russian rye breads such as borodinsky and stolichny, wheat nareznoi, as well as a wide variety of croissants (including dark and multigrain), brioches, and seven-grain loaves that were virtually unknown to Muscovites a decade ago. Another plus: the store is open 24 hours. ⊠ *14 Tverskaya ul., Tverskaya* ☎ *495/209–0760* Ⓜ *Tverskaya or Pushkinskaya.*

STREET MARKETS

FOOD

Moscow's wave of reconstruction and renovation has benefited fresh-food markets (*rynok*). At the same time many have been closed indefinitely, because of concerns over cleanliness and organized crime, and some are being redeveloped as malls. ■ TIP→ **Bargaining often takes place at food stalls since usually no price is shown for goods. Ask** *SkOlko stOit?* **or "how much is it?" If the price sounds too high, say the number of rubles you think is reasonable. If the offer is refused, and you don't like the price, say** *Nyet, dOrogo,* **or "no, it's expensive," and turn away. The trader may then tell you,** *Dlya vas skidka,* **or "you get a discount." You'll likely receive a realistic price then.**

Danilovsky Rynok. A bustling outdoor market surrounds a covered hall where you can buy meat in all its shapes and forms—including halal meat, a huge choice of pickled goods, spices, and even blue, white, and gold Uzbek tea sets. Outside, traders sell pyramids of fruits and vegetables. In fall, you can buy berries and mushrooms. Also on sale are flowers, woven baskets, and hand-knit wool socks. ⊠ *Pl. Serpukhovskaya Zastava, Southern Outskirts* Ⓜ *Tulskaya.*

Dorogomilovsky Rynok. This large covered hall is beyond the outdoor Veshchevoy Rynok (literally, "Market of Things," which is certainly an apt name). Inside are rows of vendors hawking homemade cheese and milk products, honey, flowers, and produce of all kinds. Against one wall are sellers of pickled goods, an understandably popular form of food preparation in this land of long winters; you may want to sample some of their cabbage and carrot slaws, salted cucumbers, or spiced eggplant or garlic. ⊠ *Off Mozhaisky ul., near Kiev station, Western Outskirts* ☎ *No phone* Ⓜ *Kievskaya.*

Preobrazhensky Rynok. This historic market is worth visiting more for its picturesque setting than its produce. It stands next to the Old Believers' church and cemetery and is surrounded by high walls topped with towers. Stalls sell household goods, from saucepans to blankets, as well as food. You can also buy felt boots, or valenki, here in winter. The covered section of the market is rather dingy and lacking in atmosphere. ⊠ *Cherkizovskaya ul., Northern Outskirts* Ⓜ *Preobrazhenskaya.*

SOUVENIRS

For good souvenir hunting, you can certainly head straight to the Arbat. Stores here cater to tourists and Moscow's expatriate community, so you can expect good selection and service, but prices are on the high end. The Arbat's individual outdoor vendors invariably charge much more than they should, so stick to the stores.

Izmailovsky flea market. You could easily spend a whole day at Moscow's Izmailovsky Park, with its reasonably priced souvenirs, handicrafts, used books, and such Soviet memorabilia as authentic army belts and gas masks. *Matryoshki* (nesting dolls) come in both classic and nouveau styles: some bear likenesses of Soviet and Russian leaders; others depict American basketball stars and George W. Bush. Nearby is the former royal residence of Izmailovo, situated in an old hunting preserve. The flea market is open weekends 9–6, but it's best to get here early. Many vendors close down by midday. ✉ *Take the metro to Partizanskaya station and follow crowds as you exit, Eastern Outskirts.*

> **TASTE OF RYNOK**
>
> *Rynoks* (outdoor markets) are places to find some strange and delicious foods. Look for lumpy red *churchkhely*, a kind of Georgian candy made from walnuts and grape juice. Stalls sell piles of bright-pink pickled garlic and strings of dried wild mushrooms. In fall, the berry selection might include rose hips; orange *oblepikha*, or sea buckthorn; and *brusnika*, or cowberry. You can also sample unfamiliar fruits including the small red plum, *kizil*, or Cornelian cherry, and aromatic green citruslike fruit *feikhua*.

DID YOU KNOW? Nesting dolls, or matryoshki, aren't one of Russia's oldest crafts. Dating only to the 19th century, they are said to be based on a Japanese tradition. The center for Matryoshka-making is Sergiyev Posad outside Moscow. In Soviet times, a Matryoshka was used as the symbol of the state-owned travel agency, Intourist, which had a monopoly on organizing trips for foreigners (its name is short for *inostranny*, or foreign) and ran its own hotels. It still exists as a travel agency, but the hotels have all closed down. Consequently, Russians came to think of the dolls chiefly as gifts for foreign visitors. In many Russian homes, you will find a simple matryosha doll wearing a headscarf, but the elaborately decorated dolls on sale at the Arbat are strictly for export.

MOSCOW EXCURSIONS

Within easy reach of half-day excursions from the city await majestic old palaces, estates, and former noble residences, all set in emblematic Russian countryside. To see them to the best advantage you should try to make your visits in spring or summer.

All of these sights can be accessed by metro, though you may have to take a connecting bus or trolley.

ARKHANGELSKOYE АРХАНГЕЛЬСКОЕ

26 km (16 mi) northwest of Moscow via Volokolamskoye shosse.

In addition to its fine location on the banks of the Moskva River, the town of Arkhangelskoye holds a beautiful example of a noble country palace of the late tsarist era, the imposing estate of Prince Yusupov.

Yusupov's neoclassical palace forms the centerpiece of a striking group of 18th- and 19th-century buildings that make up the **Arkhangelskoye Estate Museum.** The main palace has been closed for restoration work for several years and was scheduled to reopen in fall 2006, but the deadline was moved indefinitely. In 1997 the estate was named one of the world's most endangered sites by the World Monuments Fund. Excursions can still be made to the estate grounds, but with the exception of the closed palace's ongoing reconstruction, a definite sense of disrepair pervades.

The main palace complex was built at the end of the 18th century for Prince Golitsyn by the French architect Chevalier de Huerne. In 1810 the family fell upon hard times and sold the estate to the rich landlord, Yusupov, the onetime director of the imperial theaters and St. Petersburg's Hermitage Museum, and ambassador to several European lands.

The estate became home to Prince Yusupov's extraordinary art collection. The collection includes paintings by Boucher, Vigée-Lebrun, Hubert Robert, Roslin, Tiepolo, Van Dyck, and many others, as well as antique statues, furniture, mirrors, chandeliers, glassware, and china. Much of the priceless furniture once belonged to Marie Antoinette and Madame de Pompadour. There are also samples of fabrics, china, and glassware that were produced on the estate itself.

Allées and strolling lanes wind through the **French Park,** which is populated with statues and monuments commemorating royal visits. There's also a monument to Pushkin, whose favorite retreat was Arkhangelskoye. In the western part of the park is an interesting small pavilion, known as the Temple to the Memory of Catherine the Great, that depicts the empress as Themis, goddess of justice. It seems that Yusupov, reportedly a Casanova, had turned the head of Russia's empress, renowned herself for having legions of lovers. This "temple" was built as a compliment to a painting she had previously commissioned—one in which she was depicted as Venus, with Yusupov as Apollo.

Back outside the estate grounds on the right-hand side of the main road stands the **Estate (Serf) Theater,** built in 1817 by the serf architect Ivanov. Currently a museum, the theater originally seated 400 and was the home of the biggest and best-known company of serf actors in Russia. Serf theaters first appeared in Russia in the mid-18th century and disappeared a century later after 1861 when serf rule was abolished in Russia by Tsar Alexander II. Although serf theaters existed even in the most remote rural parts of Russia, the most prominent was housed by the Sheremetyev family at their Kuskovo estate that was later moved to Ostankino estate to the north of Moscow. The star of the troupe was serf actress Praskovya Kovalyova-Zhemchugova (1768–1803), who played more than 50 opera roles during her short stage career. In 1798 Count Nikolai Sheremetyev freed Kovalyova-Zhemchugova, who was by that time already suffering from tuberculosis, and married her in secret in 1801. The former actress died two years later, shortly after giving birth to their son. In his summer serf theater in Arkhangelskoye, Prince Nikolai Yusupov also favored weekly opera performances as well as dance shows with rich stage decorations. The well-preserved stage decorations are by the Venetian artist Pietrodi Gonzaga. Prince Yusupov was a kindly, paternalistic man and often opened his home and gardens to the public, a tradition that continues today. The Arkhangelskoye Estate Museum can be reached by Bus 541 from the Moscow metro station Sokolniki, or by car from the Rublevskoye shosse (turn right at the Militia Booth toward Ilinskoye and take a right turn after you pass the Russkaya Izba restaurant). Check first with your hotel's service bureau or your tour agency for updated information on the renovation project. ✉ *Arkhangelskoye* ☎ *495/363–1375* ⊕ *www.arkhangelskoe.ru* 🎫 *50R* ☉ *Park Wed.–Sun. 10–8, exhibits 10–5.*

WHERE TO EAT

$$ ✕ **Arkhangelskoye.** A palekh motif—a traditional lacquer design depicting characters from Russian fairy tales—decorates this restaurant. The convenient location (directly across the road from the entrance to the Arkhangelskoye Estate Museum) adds value to the decent food. Try the borscht, followed by veal with mushrooms. Grilled salmon is also delicious. ✉ *Ilyinskoye shosse, across from main entrance to Arkhangelskoye Estate Museum* ☎ *495/562–0328* 💳 *AE, MC, V.*

$$ ✕ **Russkaya Izba.** This wooden restaurant's rustic decor is patterned on the *izba,* a Russian country home. Caviar, blini, and other Russian dishes are served here. Reservations are recommended. ✉ *Ilyinskoye village, on road to Arkhangelskoye, near Moskva River* ☎ *495/561–4244* 💳 *No credit cards.*

VICTORY PARK ПАРК ПОБЕДЫ

10 km (6 mi) west of Moscow city center via Kutuzovsky pr.

This 335-acre park (Park Pobedy) near the landmark Triumphal Arch, on the western edge of the city, is historically linked to the defense of Moscow against invaders. Poklonnaya Gora, the hill that used to be here, is where Napoléon is said to have waited in vain for the keys to Moscow in 1812. Once the highest hill in Moscow, Poklonnaya Gora was razed in the 1970s to build Triumphal Arch, a World War II memorial, which was unveiled in 1995 in time for the 50th anniversary of the victory over Nazi Germany. Packed with all sorts of documentary evidence of the Soviet Army's victory, the memorial is the centerpiece of the park, but also here are a chapel and an outdoor display of vintage World War II arms. Victory Park is a popular spot for festivities on public holidays, including Victory Day, Orthodox Easter, and Christmas. On a warm day, expect to see strolling couples and hordes of rollerbladers, including whole families rollerblading together. The park is near the Park Pobedy metro station.

KOLOMENSKOYE КОЛОМЕНСКОЕ

★ 17 km (10½ mi) south of Moscow city center via Kashirskoye shosse, on west bank of Moskva River.

If you want to spend an afternoon in the great Russian outdoors without actually leaving the city, Kolomenskoye, on a high bluff overlooking the Moskva River, is just the right destination. The estate was once a favorite summer residence of Moscow's grand dukes and tsars. Today it's a popular public park with museums, a functioning church, old Russian cottages, and other attractions. It's also the site of the city's main celebration of the holiday Maslenitsa, or Butter Week, which usually falls at the end of February or beginning of March. Traditional Russian amusements such as mock fistfights, bag races, and tug-of-war are held on the park's grounds, with heaps of hot blini served as round reminders of the spring sun.

As you approach Kolomenskoye, the first sights you see are the striking blue domes of the **Church of Our Lady of Kazan,** a functioning church that is open for worship. It was completed in 1671. Opposite the church there once stood a wooden palace built by Tsar Alexei, Peter the Great's father. Peter spent much time here when he was growing up. Nothing remains of the huge wooden structure (Catherine the Great ordered it destroyed in 1767), but there's a scale model at the **museum,** which is devoted to Russian timber architecture and folk crafts. The museum lies inside the front gates of the park, at the end of the tree-lined path leading from the main entrance of the park.

The most remarkable sight within the park is the **Church of the Ascension,** which sits on the bluff overlooking the river. The church dates from the 1530s and was restored in the late 1800s. Its skyscraping tower is an example of the tent or pyramid-type structure that was popular in Russian architecture in the 16th century. The view from the bluff is impressive in its contrasts: from the 16th-century backdrop you can look north across the river to the 20th-century concrete apartment houses that dominate the contemporary Moscow skyline. In summer you'll see Muscovites bathing in the river below the church, and in winter the area abounds with cross-country skiers.

Examples of wooden architecture from other parts of Russia have been transferred to Kolomenskoye, turning the estate into an open-air museum. In the wooded area near the site of the former wooden palace you'll find a 17th-century prison tower from Siberia, a defense tower from the White Sea, and a 17th-century mead brewery from the village of Preobrazhenskaya. One of the most attractive original buildings on the site is the wooden cottage where Peter the Great lived while supervising the building of the Russian fleet in Arkhangelskoye. The cottage was relocated here in 1934.

To get to Kolomenskoye take the metro to Kolomenskaya station; a walk of about 10 minutes up a slight hill brings you to the park's entrance. ⊠ *39 Andropova pr.* ☏*499/612–5217 or 8499/612–1155* ✉ *Free* ⏱ *Exhibits Tues.–Sun. 10–5, Park 10–9.*

SARITSYNO ЦАРИЦЫНО

21 km (13 mi) south of Moscow city center via Kashirskoye shosse.

This popular boating and picnicking spot is the site of the 18th-century summer palace that was started but never completed for Catherine the Great. Tsaritsyno was always an ill-favored estate. The empress pulled down the work of her first architect; the second building phase was never completed, probably for financial reasons. Her heirs took no interest in Tsaritsyno, so the estate served all sorts of functions, from a wine factory to a testing ground for rock climbers. In 1984 the long-needed reconstruction began, and a museum was founded. By that time some buildings had been so neglected that tall trees grew inside the walls. The government allocated funds to restore the fabulous Opera House and the elegant Small Palace, but the funding dried up in 1996. In summer 2005, this most neglected of the Moscow estates was transferred to the control of the Moscow city government. Mayor Yury Luzhkov announced a plan to spend 410 million rubles ($14.38 million) on the ruins and surrounding park. Restoration of the bread house (kitchen) was completed in 2006, and is still under way on the bridge and other structures. The Gothic Revival architectural ensemble is worth checking out, along with a collection of porcelain, paintings, and sculptures on display at the Opera House. Tsaritsyno is close to the metro station of the same name, three metro stops south of Kolomenskoye. ⊠ *1 ul. Dolskaya* ☏*495/321–0743* ⊕*www.tsaritsyno-museum.ru* ✉ *Free* ⏱ *Wed.–Sun. 11–6.*

KUSKOVO ESTATE & PALACE MUSEUM
ДВОРЕЦ-УСАДЬБА КУСКОВО

18 km (11 mi) southeast of Moscow city center via Ryazansky pr.

In the 18th and 19th centuries the country estate of Kuskovo was the Moscow aristocracy's favorite summer playground. It belonged to the noble Sheremetyevs, one of Russia's wealthiest and most distinguished families, whose holdings numbered in the millions of acres. (Today, Moscow's international airport, built on land that once belonged to one of their many estates, takes their family name.)

The Sheremetyevs acquired the land of Kuskovo in the early 17th century, but the estate, often called a Russian Versailles, took on its current appearance in the late 18th century. Most of the work on it was commissioned by Prince Pyotr Sheremetyev, who sought a suitable place for entertaining guests in the summer. The park—one of the most beautiful spots in all of Russia—was created by Russian landscape artists who had spent much time in Europe studying the art. The French-style gardens are dotted with buildings representing the major architectural trends of Europe: the Dutch cottage, the Italian villa, the grotto, and the exquisite hermitage, where, in the fashion of the day, dinner tables were raised mechanically from the ground floor to the second-floor dining room.

The centerpiece of the estate is the **Kuskovo Palace,** built in the early Russian classical style by the serf architects Alexei Mironov and Fedor Argunov. Fronted by a grand horseshoe staircase and Greek-temple portico, this building is the absolute quintessence of Russian neoclassical elegance. The palace, which is made of timber on a white-stone foundation, overlooks a human-made lake. It has been a house museum since 1918, and its interior decorations, including fine parquet floors and silk wall coverings, have been well preserved. The bedroom, with its lovely canopy bed, was merely for show: the Sheremetyevs used the palace exclusively for entertainment and did not live here. The parquet floors, gilt wall decorations, and crystal chandeliers of the marvelous White Hall testify to the grandeur of the ballroom extravaganzas that once took place here. On display in the inner rooms are paintings by French, Italian, and Flemish artists; Chinese porcelain; furniture; and other articles of everyday life from the 18th and 19th centuries. The palace also houses a collection of 18th-century Russian art and a rather celebrated ceramics museum with a rich collection of Russian, Soviet, and foreign ceramics.

Pyotr Sheremetyev had more than 150,000 serfs, many of whom received architectural training and participated in the building of his estate. The serfs also constituted a theater troupe that gave weekly open-air performances, a common practice on nobles' estates—the crème de la crème of Moscow society made it a point to attend the Sheremetyev showings. Today, of course, only the setting for this spectacular lifestyle remains, but the dreamlike park and palace persist as mute and eloquent testimony to a royalty long vanished.

Kuskovo is just outside the ring road marking the city boundary, but you can reach it by public transportation. Take the metro to Ryazansky Prospekt station and then Bus 208 or Bus 133 six stops to Kuskovo Park. You may find it more convenient to book a tour that includes transportation. Whatever you do, be sure to phone ahead before making the trek, because the estate often closes when the weather is very humid or very cold. ✉2 *ul. Yunosti* ☎*495/370–0160* ⊕*www.kuskovo.ru* 🎫*200R* ⊗*Nov.–Apr., Wed.–Sun. 10–4; May–Oct., Wed.–Fri. 11–7, weekends 10–6. Closed last Wed. of month.*

MOSCOW ESSENTIALS

TRANSPORTATION

BY AIR

As the most important transportation hub in the Commonwealth of Independent States (CIS, a quasi-confederation of states including most of the former Soviet Union), Moscow has several airports. Most international flights arrive at Sheremetyevo II, north of the city center. The Russian carrier Aeroflot operates flights from Moscow to just about every capital of Europe, as well as to Canada and the United States. The airline also serves numerous domestic destinations. Transaero, another Russian carrier, has a large network of domestic flights as well as several international routes. Among the international airlines with offices in Moscow are Air France, Alitalia, Austrian Airlines, British Airways, Delta, Finnair, Japan Airlines, KLM, Lufthansa, Malev, SAS, and Swiss.

> ### STALIN'S EIGHTH SISTER?
>
> You may notice a new stepsister to the Seven Gothic Sisters on the drive in from Sheremetyevo II airport. Triumph Palace, near the Sokol metro station, is a modern copy of the original skyscrapers. This expensive block of apartments, the tallest residential building in Europe at 866 feet, has been criticized by architects, but its huge size and similarity to the original Seven Sisters will likely make it another city symbol.

One of the most modern airports in Russia when it was built in 1979, Sheremetyevo II is inadequate and old-fashioned these days, although it is now being renovated and extended. Be prepared for lines everywhere and a wait of up to an hour or two at passport control. The baggage area is directly beyond passport control. Luggage carts are free, but they often go quickly. You can also hire a porter for about 130R per suitcase (agree on a price before you give your bags to the porter). There's a bank and an ATM in the waiting area where you can exchange money or traveler's checks while you're waiting for your luggage. Beyond the baggage area is customs. If you have nothing to declare, you can walk right through the green aisle to the waiting area, where you'll be greeted by mobs of eager gypsy cab drivers shouting, "Taksi! Taksi!"

In addition to its international airport, the city has four domestic terminals. Sheremetyevo I, some 30 km (19 mi) northwest of the city center, services domestic flights to St. Petersburg and the former Baltic republics (Estonia, Latvia, and Lithuania). It also handles the international flights of some of the newer Russian airlines. Domodedovo, one of the largest airports in the world (and perhaps the nicest in Russia), is some 48 km (30 mi) southeast of Moscow. British Airways, Swiss, and Transaero fly out of Domodedovo. Flights also depart from Domodedovo to the republics of Central Asia. Vnukovo, 29 km (18 mi) southwest of the city center, services flights to Georgia, the southern republics, and Ukraine. Bykovo, the smallest of the domestic terminals, generally handles flights within Russia and some flights to Ukraine.

For general information on arriving international flights, call the airline directly. Calling the airports usually takes longer and fewer people speak English.

Airline Information **Aeroflot** (☎ *495/223–5555*). **Air France** (☎ *495/937–3839*). **Alitalia** (☎ *495/967–0110*). **Austrian Airlines** (☎ *495/995–0995*). **British Airways** (☎ *495/363–2525*). **Delta** (☎ *495/937–9090*). **Finnair** (☎ *495/933–0056*).

Japan Airlines (☎*495/730–3070*). **KLM** (☎*495/258–3600*). **Lufthansa** (☎*495/980–9999*). **Malev** (☎*495/202–8416*). **SAS** (☎*495/775–4747*). **Swiss** (☎*495/937–7760 or 495/937–7767*). **Transaero** (☎*495/788–8080*).

Airport Information **Bykovo** (☎*495/558–4933 or 495/558–4738*). **Domodedovo** (☎*495/933–6666*). **Sheremetyevo I Airport** (☎*495/232–6565*). **Sheremetyevo II Airport** (☎*495/956–4666, 495/578–9101, or 495/956–2372*). **Vnukovo** (☎*495/436–2813*).

TRANSFERS   It's wise to make advance arrangements for your transfer from the airport. Most hotels will provide airport transfers (for a fee, usually about 1,000R) upon request by prior fax (which you should confirm).

There are plenty of gypsy cabs available, but there's always a risk of being swindled. If you do take one, bargain, bargain, bargain. The standard rate from Shermetyevo II to Moscow's city center is 1,500R. Gypsy cab drivers will try to persuade you to pay 2,000R, but this is too much. Remember, too, that you will likely travel in an old, small, Soviet car with no guarantee of a smooth or safe ride. And don't get out of the taxi while the driver is still at the wheel and your luggage is in the trunk—he might just drive off with your belongings. It's better to use the services offered on the airport's ground floor. These private firms are less risky, can provide a receipt, and you may find their prices more reasonable than the gypsy cabs' prices. Traveling to the airport from the city is cheaper. You can hail a taxi on the street for about 800R–900R or book a taxi in advance for 900R–1,000R.

All of the airports are served by municipal buses operating out of Aerovokzal (City Airport Terminal) at 37 Leningradsky prospekt, near the Aeroport metro station. Even more convenient are the buses and the faster marshrutka minibuses that go from just outside the airport to the Rechnoy Vokzal metro station. From here it's about 25 minutes to the city center. Service is not very convenient, especially if you have a lot of luggage, but it's very inexpensive. Buses leave for Rechnoy Vokzal metro station every 5 to 10 minutes but are more erratic to the City Airport Terminal; service to Domodedovo and Vnukovo airports is more frequent. Domodedovo is the easiest airport, with a fast train running from the airport to Paveletsky train station (where you can check in immediately with some airlines), although newly renovated Vnukovo also now has an express train service running from Kiev train station. Buses and marshrutka minibuses also run frequently from Domodedovo to the Domodedovskaya metro station. A train runs from Bykovo airport to Kazansky train station.

BY BOAT & FERRY

Moscow has two river ports: Severny Rechnoy Vokzal (Northern River Terminal; used for long-distance passengers), on the Khimki reservoir, and Yuzhny Rechnoy Vokzal (Southern River Terminal). However, international cruise lines offering tours to Russia usually disembark in St. Petersburg and continue from here by land.

It is possible, however, to book river cruises which run between Moscow and St. Petersburg, making a detour down the Volga canal en route. More ambitious cruises that go from Moscow to the southern city of Astrakhan or even to Perm in the Urals are also offered. Both foreign and local companies run cruises aimed at Western travelers. Due to the incredibly cold temperatures in the winter (not to mention the freezing of the rivers), crusies only run from May to September.

All the companies listed below use Russian ships, but these vary greatly in standard from adequate Soviet-style accommodation to luxurious renovated cabins on high-end cruises. If you're sailing between Moscow and St. Petersburg, the cruises tend to have similar stop-offs, but the top lines offer more onboard activities and more varied excursions.

Smithsonian Journeys, the most expensive company listed here, has completely refurbished its ship, which has a wood-paneled lounge, a fitness center, and flat-screen televisions in each cabin. The company arranges behind-the-scenes museum visits and onboard lectures by top statesmen. It offers cruises from Moscow to St. Petersburg and vice versa as well as a Baltic cruise that calls at Moscow and St. Petersburg.

In a slightly lower price bracket, Amadeus Waterways offers a cruise on a ship with an indoor swimming pool that was built for top Kremlin officials. Each cruise only has 160 passengers and services include onboard Russian languagae classes. Uniworld provides a similar standard of comfort on a refurbished ship. It has a 16-day tour from St. Petersburg to Moscow and a 14-day tour from Moscow to St. Petersburg. The cruises on the Russian-owned ship call at Kizhi and go down the Volga to Yaroslavl and Uglich. If you just want to visit Moscow, the company has a tour that starts in Rostov-on-Don, takes in major Volga cities such as Volgograd, and goes as far east as Kazan. Passengers are flown to and from Moscow.

California company Cruise Marketing International is the most affordable option, although its ships have been renovated. It offers river cruises from Moscow to St. Petersburg and vice versa.

Contacts Amadeus Waterways (✉ *21625 Prairie St., Chatsworth, CA 91311* ☎ *800/626–0126* ⊕ *www.amadeuswaterways.com*). **Cruise Marketing International** (✉ *3401 Investment Blvd., Suite 3, Hayward, CA 94545* ☎ *800/578–7742* ⊕ *www.cruiserussia.com*). **Mosturflot** (✉ *59 Leningradskoye shosse 59, Suite 103, Northern Outskirts* ☎ *495/221–8070 or 495/221–8058* ⊕ *www.mosturflot. com* Ⓜ *Rechnoy Vokzal*). **Orthodox Cruise Company** (✉ *5 ul. Alabyana, Northern Outskirts* ☎ *495/943–8560 or 495/943–8561* ⊕ *www.cruise.ru* Ⓜ *Sokol*). **Severny Rechnoy Vokzal** (✉ *51 Leningradskoye shosse, Northern Outskirts* ☎ *495/459–7465 or 495/457–4050* Ⓜ *Rechnoy Vokzal*). **Smithsonian Journeys** (✉ *Box 23293, Washington, DC 20026* ☎ *202/633–6088 or 877/338–8687* ⊕ *www.smithsonianjourneys.org*). **Uniworld** (✉ *17323 Ventura Blvd., Encino, CA 91316* ☎ *818/382–7820 or 800/733–7820* 📠 *818/382–7829* ⊕ *www.uniworld. com*). **Viking River Cruises** (✉ *5700 Canooga Ave., Suite 200, Woodland Hills, CA 91367* ☎ *800/304–9616 or 818/227–1234* ⊕ *www.vikingrivers.com*). **Vodohod** (✉ *13 Oruzheiny per., Bldg. 1, Mayakovskaya* ☎ *495/730–5885* ⊕ *www.vodohod. com* Ⓜ *Mayakovskaya*). **Yuzhny Rechnoy Vokzal** (✉ *11 Andropov pr., Southern Outskirts* ☎ *495/118–7811* Ⓜ *Kolomenskaya*).

BY BUS, TRAM & TROLLEY

You're unlikely to want to travel by long-distance bus in Russia, since the trains are frequent, cheap, and reliable. Most bus services go to provincial towns that lack good rail links.

Buses, trams, and trolleys all use the same tickets (15R), which you can buy in special kiosks, usually near metro stations. You can also buy tickets from the driver, but then they cost 25R. You have to get on at the entrance next to the driver and put the ticket through an electronic turnstile. The ticket is valid for one ride only; if you change buses you must pay another fare. Buses, trams, and trolleys operate from 5:30 AM to 1 AM, although service in the late-evening hours and on Sunday tends to be unreliable. Trolleys are connected to overhead power lines, trams to metal rails.

Local bus and tram routes tend to be mysterious, since bus stops don't provide information and the vehicles only carry a terse lists of destinations, often referring to factories or landmarks, and the like that no longer exist. Newspaper kiosks sell a map that shows all of Moscow's transport routes called, *karta Moskvy so vsem transportom.*

A nice tram ride is the 39, which goes from Universitet metro station to Chistiye Prudy metro station past Donskoy Monastery and Danilovsky Market. The B trolley bus runs around the Garden Ring and can be a nice trip when the traffic's not heavy.

Contacts **Tsentralny Avtovokzal** (*Central Bus Station* ✉ *75 Shchelkovskoe shosse, Eastern Outskirts* ☎ *495/468–0400* Ⓜ *Shchelkovskaya*). **Mosgortrans** is the organization that runs all the city's surface transport. (☎ *495/953–0061* ⊕ *www.mosgortrans.com*).

BY CAR

You can reach Moscow from Finland and St. Petersburg by taking the Helsinki–St. Petersburg Highway through Vyborg and St. Petersburg and continuing from there on the Moscow–St. Petersburg Highway. Be warned that driving in Russia is invariably more of a hassle than a pleasure. Roads are very poorly maintained, and many streets in the city center are one-way. In addition you face the risk of car theft, a crime that is on the rise.

BY METRO

The Moscow metro, first opened in 1935, ranks among the world's finest public transportation systems. With more than 200 km (124 mi) of track, the Moscow metro carries an estimated 8 million passengers daily. Even though it scrapes by with inadequate state subsidies, the system continues to run efficiently, with trains every 50 seconds during rush hour. It leaves New Yorkers green with envy.

If you're not traveling with a tour group or if you haven't hired your own driver, taking the metro is the best way to get around the Russian capital. You'll be doing yourself a great favor and saving yourself a lot of frustration if you learn the Russian (Cyrillic) alphabet well enough to be able to transliterate the names of the stations. This will come in especially handy at transfer points, where signs with long lists of the names of metro stations lead you from one major metro line to another. You should also be able to recognize the entrance and exit signs *(⇨English-Russian Vocabulary, at the end of this book).*

Pocket maps of the system are available at newspaper kiosks and sometimes from individual vendors at metro stations. Be sure that you obtain a map with English transliterations in addition to Cyrillic. If you can't find one, try any of the major hotels (even if you're not a guest of the hotel they'll probably give you a map). Plan your route beforehand and have your destination written in Russian and its English transliteration to help you spot the station. As the train approaches each station, the station name will be announced over the train's public-address system; the name of the next station is given before the train starts off. Reminders of interchanges and transfers are also given. Some newer trains do have the transliterated names of stations on line maps in the trains, which are very helpful for non-Russian speakers.

Stations are built deep underground (they were built to double as bomb shelters); the escalators are steep and run fast, so watch your step. If you use the metro during rush hour (8:30–10 AM, 4–6 PM), be prepared for a lot of pushing and shoving. In a crowded train, just before a station, you're likely to be asked, *"Vy vykhódíte?"* or whether you're getting off at the next station. If not, you're expected to move out of the way. Riders are expected to give up seats for senior citizens and small children.

FARES & SCHEDULES The metro is easy to use and amazingly inexpensive. Stations are marked with a large illuminated "M" sign and are open daily 5:30 AM to 1 AM. The fare is the same regardless of distance traveled, and there are several stations where lines connect and you may transfer for free. You purchase a magnetic card (available at all stations) for 1, 5, 10, 20, or more journeys and insert it into the slot at the turnstile upon entering. The card will then pop out of a slot at the other end, after you've passed through the turnstile. Don't forget to take it when it pops up. A single ride costs 19R, and discounts are available for multiple-journey cards. A card for 10 trips costs 155R.

You can also purchase an unlimited monthly pass (*yediny bilyet*), which is valid for all modes of public transportation (buses, trams, trolleys). The passes, which are plastic cards that you place against a sensor at the turnstile, are on sale at the same windows as metro cards. At 1,300R, they are inexpensive and well worth the added expense for the convenience.

BY TAXI

Exercise caution when using taxis. There are standard taxis of various makes and colors, but professional ones all have taxi lights on top and can easily be hailed in the city center. Official taxis have a "T" and checkered emblem on the doors (but there are not many of them). When you enter a cab, check to see if the meter is working; if it is not, agree on a price beforehand. Generally, everyone with a car is a potential taxi driver in Moscow; it's common for Muscovites to hail an ordinary car and negotiate a price for a ride. This is generally a safe practice, but it's best to avoid it, particularly if you don't speak Russian. If you do choose to take a ride in an ordinary car, take some precautions: never get in a car with more than one person inside, and if the driver wants to stop for another fare, say no or get out of the car.

You can also call cabs by phone or through your hotel's service bureau. Moscow has numerous cab companies, most with 24-hour service. There is sometimes a delay, but the cab usually arrives within the hour. If you order a cab in this way, you usually pay a set rate for the first 30 minutes (around 300R) and then a set rate per minute (usually around 8R per minute) after that. Always ask for an approximate price when you telephone for a cab. Unfortunately, most operators don't speak English. Moscow Taxi provides city cabs as well as airport service (from hotels or private residences) in vans or buses. Novoye Zhyoltoye Taksi (New Yellow Taxi) is a cab firm with a good reputation.

Contact **Moscow Taxi** (☎ *495/747–2699*). **Novoye Zhyoltoye Taksi** (☎ *495/940– 8888*).

BY TRAIN

Moscow is the hub of the Russian railway system, and the city's several railway stations handle some 400 million passengers annually. There are several trains daily to St. Petersburg, and overnight service is available to Helsinki, Riga, and Tallinn. All the major train stations have a connecting metro stop, so they're easily reached by public transportation. Note that although there are phone numbers for each station, it's all but impossible to get through to them. If you have limited time, it's best to ask your hotel service bureau or a travel agent for railway information and schedules.

The most important stations are Belorussia station, for trains to Belorussia, Lithuania, Poland, Germany, and France; Kazan station, for points south, Central Asia, and Siberia; Kiev station, for Kiev and western Ukraine, Moldova, Slovakia, the Czech Republic, and Hungary; Kursk station, for eastern Ukraine, the Crimea, and southern Russia; Leningrad station, for St. Petersburg, northern Russia, Estonia, and Finland; Pavelets station, for eastern Ukraine and points south; Riga station, for Latvia; and Yaroslav station, for points east, including Mongolia and China. The Trans-Siberian Express departs from Yaroslav station every day at 9:56 AM.

Both overnight trains and high-speed day trains depart from Leningrad station for St. Petersburg. The daytime express trains *Nevsky Express* and *ER-200* take 4½ hours and arrive in St. Petersburg in the evening. The *Avrora* day train makes the trip in just under six hours. Of the numerous overnight trains, the most popular is the *Krasnaya Strela* (Red Arrow), which leaves Moscow at 11:55 PM and arrives the next day in St. Petersburg at 7:55 AM. The Nikolayevsky Express leaves Moscow at 11:30 PM and reaches St. Petersburg at 7:40 AM. A new overnight service, the *Grand Express,* has showers in the compartments of the higher classes, and sinks in economy classes, as well as satellite television and other luxuries.

FARES & SCHEDULES For information on train schedules, reservations, and ticket delivery, call the Moscow Railways Agency. You can also purchase tickets at the railway stations. Bring your passport or a photocopy with you. You need it to buy tickets (they print your name and your passport number on the ticket), and you'll need to show your passport to the attendant on the train.

Train Information **Moscow Railways Agency** (✉ *6/11 Maly Kharitonevsky per., Chistiye Prudy* Ⓜ *Chistiye Prudy or Krasniye Vorota* ☎ *495/266–9333* ⊕ *www. mza.ru*).

Train Station Information **Belorussia station** *(Belorussky Vokzal)* (✉ *Northern Outskirts* ☎ *495/251–6093* Ⓜ *Belorusskaya*). **Kazan station** *(Kazansky Vokzal)* (✉ *Northern Outskirts* ☎ *495/264–6656* Ⓜ *Komsomolskaya*). **Kiev station** *(Kievsky Vokzal)* (✉ *Krasnaya Presnya* ☎ *495/240–1115* Ⓜ *Kievskaya*). **Kursk station** *(Kursky Vokzal)* (✉ *Eastern Oustkirts* ☎ *495/916–2003* Ⓜ *Kurskaya*). **Leningrad station** *(Leningradsky Vokzal)* (✉ *Northern Outskirts* ☎ *495/262–9143*). **Pavelets station** *(Paveletsky Vokzal)* (✉ *Southern Outskirts* ☎ *495/235–0522* Ⓜ *Paveletskaya*). **Riga station** *(Rizhsky Vokzal)* (✉ *Northern Outskirts* ☎ *495/631–1588* Ⓜ *Rizhskaya*). **Yaroslav station** *(Yaroslavsky Vokzal)* (✉ *Northern Outskirts* ☎ *495/621–5914* Ⓜ *Komsomolskaya*).

CONTACTS AND RESOURCES

EMERGENCIES

The state medical system is plagued by poor service, low hygiene standards, and a lack of medicines and basic medical equipment. If you're ill, contact one of several Western clinics, which are used by the foreign community as well as Russians who can afford the higher fees. Some of these clinics are membership organizations, but all will provide service to tourists, though perhaps not with 24-hour access; costs will be higher than for members, too. Usually you must pay with rubles or a credit card, and you'll need to settle accounts up front.

In an emergency, you can also contact your country's consular section for help with the logistics of serious medical treatment. For U.S. citizens, contact American Citizens Services. British citizens can call their embassy, or during workdays get a referral from the embassy clinic. Canadian citizens should call the embassy number, where they will be connected to a duty officer.

Emergency Services **Ambulance** (☎ *03*). **American Citizens Services** (☎ *495/728–5577 after-hours emergency*). **British Embassy clinic** (☎ *495/956–7270*). **Fire** (☎ *01*). **Police** (☎ *02*).

Contacts **German Dental Clinic** (✉ *2 Volochayevskaya ul., Bldg. 1, Western Outskirts* ☎ *495/362–4902* Ⓜ *Ploshchad Ilycha*). **U.S. Dental Care** (✉ *7/5 Bolshaya DmitrovkaPushkinskaya* ☎ *495/933–8686* Ⓜ *Pushkinskaya*).

HOSPITALS & CLINICS The American Medical Center offers full-range family practice and emergency services, including evacuation assistance. If treatment is needed outside the clinic, they use various hospitals. The office is open

24 hours, and doctors make house calls 24 hours a day. Medicine can be provided at the clinic. A tourist plan is available.

The European Medical Centre, which is not a membership group, offers a full range of services, including day and night house calls. Hospital referral is usually to the ZKB Presidential Hospital. English and French are spoken. Medicine can be provided at the clinic.

International SOS Clinic is a nonmember service that provides comprehensive care, hospitalization referral to the Kuntsevo (Kremlin VIP) Hospital, and evacuation via an in-house company (they are part of International SOS). English, French, and German are spoken, and there's a pharmacy on-site.

Mediclub Moscow is a Russian clinic that provides full medical service and hospital referral to Glavmosstroy Hospital. It's open weekdays 9–4, with last appointments at 3; you may call after hours for an emergency.

Contacts **American Medical Center** (⊠ *1 Grokholsky per., Northern Outskirts* ☎ *495/933–7700* Ⓜ *Prospekt Mira*). **European Medical Centre** (⊠ *5 Spiridonevsky per., Bldg. 1, Patriarshiye Prudy* ☎ *495/933–6655* Ⓜ *Mayakovskaya or Pushkinskaya*). **International SOS Clinic** (⊠ *31 Grokholsky per., 10th fl., Northern Outskirts* ☎ *495/937–5760* Ⓜ *Prospekt Mira*). **Mediclub Moscow** (⊠ *56 Michurinsky pr., Southern Outskirts* ☎ *495/931–5018 or 495/931–5318* Ⓜ *Prospekt Vernadskovo*).

PHARMACIES Pharmacies are plentiful, and many stay open around the clock in the city center. One highly rated pharmacy is 36.6, which has many branches, including one in Central Telegraph (at 7 Tverskaya ulitsa) and a 24-hour branch near the Pushkin metro. Western-brand medicines may not be recognizable to you in their Russian packaging; however, you often can buy medicine over the counter in Russia that requires a prescription in the United States. For prescriptions, you can contact one of the foreign clinics' pharmacies, though prices will be high. Some hotels also have small pharmacies.

Contacts **36.6** (⊠ *7 Tverskaya ul., Okhotny Ryad* ☎ *495/504–1119* Ⓜ *Okhotny Ryad* ⊠ *15 Novy Arbat ul., Bldg. 1, Arbat* ☎ *495/203–0321* Ⓜ *Arbatskaya*). **Rigla** (⊠ *27 Tverskaya ul., Bldg. 1, Tverskaya* ☎ *495/915–8926* Ⓜ *Mayakovskaya* ⊠ *2/15 Maroseika ul., Bldg. 1, Kitai Gorod* ☎ *495/628–9189* Ⓜ *Kitai Gorod*).

INTERNET, MAIL & SHIPPING
Internet access shouldn't be a problem in Moscow since there are many Internet cafés and Wi-Fi is quite commonly found in cafés and restaurants. Some of the city post offices also have Internet access.

Internet **Timeonline** (⊠ *Okhotny Ryad mall, on the lowest level, 1 Manezhnaya Ploshchad, Kremlin/Red Square* ☎ *495/988–6426* ⊗ *24 hours* Ⓜ *Okhotny Ryad*). **Café Max Internet Center** (⊠ *25 Pyatnitskaya ul., Bldg. 1, Novokuznetskaya* ☎ *495/787–6858* ⊗ *24 hours*). **Soyuz** (⊠ *8a Strastnoi bulvar, in the basement of mall, na Strastnom, Tverskaya* ☎ *303/937–4404* ⊗ *10 AM–10 PM*).

Mail & Shipping **Central Telegraph Office.** This has a post office, telegram services, and telephone booths. ⊠ *7 Tverskaya ul., Kremlin/Red Square* Ⓜ *Okhotny Ryad*.

DHL. ✉ *11 (1st) Pervaya-Yamskaya ul., Belorusskaya* ☎ *495/956–1010* ⊕ *www. dhl.ru* Ⓜ *Mayakovskaya.*

Federal Express. ✉ *17 Gogolevsky bulvar, Kropotkinsky District* ☎ *495/788–8881* ⊕ *www.fedex.com/ru* Ⓜ *Kropotkinskaya.*

Pochtamt, or Central Post Office. This has a post office, telegram services, and telephone booths. ✉ *26 Myasnitskaya ul., Chistiye Prudy* Ⓜ *Chistiye Prudy.*

MEDIA

ENGLISH-LANGUAGE BOOKSTORES

You'll pay a premium for most imported books, though books in Russian are remarkably inexpensive. Bright and comfortable Anglia British Bookshop carries a good selection of literature and books about Russia—mostly books from Britain. It also holds readings and other events. The bookshop is open weekdays 10–7, Saturday 10–6, and Sunday 11–5.

The Dom Inostrannoi Knigi (House of International Books), a British oasis, is just around the corner from the Kuznetsky Most metro station. The staff can be very grumpy. It's open weekdays 10–9, Saturday 10–9, and Sunday 10–8.

Dom Knigi, open weekdays 9–9 and weekends 10–9, is Russia's largest bookstore. It has a small foreign-literature section and a large section for students of Russian language. Be sure to examine the selection outside the front door, where individual sellers spread out their wares.

Contacts Anglia British Bookshop (✉ *6 Vorotnikovsky per., Mayakovskaya* ☎ *495/699–7766* Ⓜ *Mayakovskaya).* **Dom Inostrannoi Knigi** (✉ *18 Kuznetsky Most, Kuznetsky Most* ☎ *495/628–2021* Ⓜ *Kuznetsky Most).* **Dom Knigi** (✉ *26 Novy Arbat, Arbat* ☎ *495/789–3591* Ⓜ *Arbatskaya).*

NEWSPAPERS & MAGAZINES

You can read up on world and local news in the city's English-language newspaper, the *Moscow Times* (⊕ *www.themoscowtimes. com*), published weekdays. It's available in just about any Western store, restaurant, or major hotel. Other free publications include weekly entertainment guide *Element* and the outrageous biweekly newspaper *The Exile,* which writes satirically about life in Moscow and Russian politics.

BANKS & EXCHANGE SERVICES

ATMS

You'll find ATMs all around the city center, though they're nowhere near as common as in U.S. cities.

CURRENCY EXCHANGE

Most hotels have currency-exchange bureaus, some operating 24 hours a day. Additionally, throughout the city you can find exchange bureaus bearing the OBMEN VALUTY/EXCHANGE sign—these are often in Cyrillic, but just look for the signs with daily rates posted in easy view, often on freestanding sidewalk signboards. Exercise reasonable caution when using them, and don't be surprised to find a security guard, who may let only one or two people inside at a time. By law it's required that you be issued a receipt, but you may find this erratic in practice; be sure to ask for one. You can also exchange currency or traveler's checks at the Russian banks; one of the most reliable is Sberbank, the Russian state bank. You can also try the Moscow Bank office in the Radisson Slavyanskaya hotel. The American Express office, listed under Travel Agencies in the Essentials chapter of this book, will cash American Express traveler's checks for rubles and, if it has cash available, for dollars.

Contacts **Moscow Bank** (⊠ *Radisson Slavyanskaya hotel, 2 Berezhkovskaya nab., Krasnaya Presnya* ☎ *495/941–8128* Ⓜ *Kievskaya*). **Sberbank** (⊠ *19 ul. Tverskaya* ☎ *495/299–7995* Ⓜ *Pushkinskaya*).

TOUR OPTIONS
Every major hotel maintains a tourist bureau that books individual and group tours to Moscow's main sights. In addition, there are numerous private agencies that can help with your sightseeing plans.

Patriarshy Dom Tours conducts unusual day and overnight tours in and around Moscow and St. Petersburg for groups or individuals. Among the tours are the Red October chocolate factory, the KGB museum, literature or architectural walks, and the space-flight command center. You can call for schedules or pick up copies in some hotels and Western stores. Sputnik handles group and individual tours in Moscow and some day trips out of town. The company can tailor plans to suit your needs.

Contacts **Patriarshy Dom Tours** (⊠ *6 Vspolny per., Southern Outskirts* ☎ *495/795–0927, 650/678–7076 in U.S.*). **Sputnik** (⊠ *15 Kosygina ul., Southern Outskirts* ☎ *495/939–8374*).

VISITOR INFORMATION
The service bureaus of all the major hotels offer their guests (and anyone else willing to pay their fees) various tourist services, including help in booking group or individual excursions, making a restaurant reservation, or purchasing theater or ballet tickets. You can also find help (as the hotels themselves often do) from Intourist, today's reincarnation of the old Soviet tourist service or from some of the tour agencies.

Contact **The Moscow Committee for Tourism office** (⊠ *4 Ilyinka, Kremlin/Red Square* ☎ *495/232–5657* Ⓜ *Kitai Gorod*).

Moscow Environs & the Golden Ring

2

WORD OF MOUTH

"Golden Ring is well worth visiting. I would suggest Sergiev-Posad, Suzdal and Yaroslavl are the best, but a lot depends on how you travel."

—wasleys

"If you have 2 weeks, I would definitely squeeze in something else: Golden Ring is great and you may do it by car in 2–3 days. My husband and I did it 3 years ago with a private guide, and loved every minute of it."

—yn10

www.fodors.com/forums

Updated
by Oksana
Yablokova

THE RIVER VALLEYS EAST AND north of Moscow hold a unique realm you might call Russia's Capital-That-Might-Have-Been—Suzdalia, the region that encompassed the historic centers of Rostov, Vladimir, Suzdal, and Yaroslavl. These small towns, all within easy striking distance of Moscow, witnessed nothing less than the birth of the Russian nation nearly a millennium ago and, consequently, are home to some of the country's most beautiful churches and monasteries, romantic kremlins (fortresses), and famous works of art, such as Andrei Rublyov's frescoes in the cathedral at Vladimir.

Many of these towns and districts have more than 10 centuries of history to share, but their story really begins early in the 12th century, when Prince Yuri Dolgoruky, son of Vladimir Monomakh, the Grand Prince of Kiev, was given control over the northeastern outpost of what was then Kievan Rus' (the early predecessor of modern-day Russia and Ukraine). Dolgoruky established his power and authority, and founded the towns that would become Pereslavl-Zalessky and Kostroma. He also built frontier outposts to guard against his neighbors, including one on the southwest border, called Moscow.

Yuri Dolgoruky's son, Andrei Bogolyubsky, amassed considerable power within Kievan Rus', centered on his inherited lands of Suzdalia. He made Vladimir his capital and built up its churches and monasteries to rival those of Kiev, the capital of Kievan Rus'. In 1169, unhappy with the pattern of dynastic succession in Kiev, Bogolyubsky sent his and allied troops to sack Kiev and placed his son on the throne as grand prince. From that point forward, political and ecclesiastical power began to flow toward the northeastern region of Rus'.

Had not the Mongol invasion intervened a century later in 1237, Vladimir might have continued to grow in power and be the capital of Russia today. But invade the Mongols did, and within three years every town in the region was nearly decimated; the region remained subjugated for more than 200 years. Moscow, meanwhile, with the cunning it's still known for today, slowly rose to prominence by becoming tax (or tribute) collector for the Mongols. Ivan Kalita ("Ivan Moneybags") was a particularly proficient go-between, and, as Mongol power receded in the 14th century, he began gathering together the lands surrounding Moscow, beginning with Vladimir.

The ancient Russian towns north and east of Moscow that make up what is most commonly called the "Golden Ring" seem quite unassuming now in comparison to the sprawling, bustling capital. Before the Mongol invasion, Rostov, Vladimir, Suzdal, and Yaroslavl were the centers of Russian political, cultural, and economic life. Although they may lack some of the amenities you can easily find in Moscow, they have a provincial charm and aura of history that make them an important stop for anyone seeking to become acquainted with Mother Russia.

2

TOP REASONS TO GO

Architecture: These towns are home to some of the finest examples of Russian architecture; the oldest, most beautiful kremlins; and religious buildings decorated with ancient frescoes.

Onion Domes: The Troitse-Sergieva Lavra's Cathedral of the Assumption has some of the most beautiful and most photographed blue and gold onion domes, and is also the main pilgrimage site for all of Russia.

Experience the "Real" Russia: Moscow's bustling city center is markedly different from the rest of Russia—a visit to a quiet provincial town like Vladimir or Rostov provides a look at how Russians outside the outer ring road live. Their proximity to Moscow makes these towns easy for day or overnight trips.

Tchaikovsky and Tolstoy's Homes: Visit the home in Klin where Russia's best-known classical music composer, Tchaikovsky, wrote *The Nutcracker* and *Sleeping Beauty*. See the desk where Tolstoy penned *Anna Karenina* and *War and Peace* in his home in Yasnaya Polyana.

EXPLORING MOSCOW ENVIRONS & THE GOLDEN RING

With some exceptions, what you'll be traveling to see are churches and monasteries—the statement-making structures that princes, metropolitans, and merchants in old Russia built to display their largesse and power. And because most civil and residential buildings until the 18th century were constructed from wood, it turns out that these religious buildings, constructed of stone, have best survived the ravages of time, invading armies, and fire. Today, many are being returned to their original, ecclesiastical purposes, but most are still museums. In either instance, neglect and funding shortages have taken their toll on preservation and restoration efforts, and at times it can be difficult to imagine these historic monuments in their original glory.

A few of the attractions of the Moscow Environs section, such as the Abramtsevo Estate Museum and Sergiev-Posad, can be combined in one visit, but most of the sights of this region will require individual day trips. The towns of the Golden Ring lie on two main routes that most visitors travel as two separate excursions—north of Moscow to Sergiev-Posad, Pereslavl-Zalessky, Rostov, and Yaroslavl; and east of Moscow to Vladimir and Suzdal.

The easiest way to get to the towns of the Golden Ring is by train. Trains going from Moscow's Yaroslavsky train station will take you to Yaroslavl and Rostov. Trains from Moscow's Kursk train station run to Vladimir several times a day, while trains for Nizhny Novgorod always stop in Vladimir. Unless you speak some Russian you might find it easier to ask a hotel concierge to check the train schedule for you; buying the tickets at a train station is hardly ever a problem even for foreigners.

ABOUT THE RESTAURANTS

Although the tourist traffic to some towns near Moscow helps sustain a sufficient infrastructure, there are still few private restaurants, largely because Russians themselves do not dine out that frequently. The most reliable restaurants are in hotels catering to tourists or, occasionally, in downtown locations near main tourist sights. This is slowly changing, and some of the restaurants outside hotels can be quite cozy. Happily, restaurant prices here are considerably lower than in Moscow as reflected in the What It Costs chart, below.

ABOUT THE HOTELS

None of the towns covered in this section has a long list of lodging options, let alone good, tourist-class hotels. Although basic amenities are not usually a problem, it will be some time before the hotels in these towns catch up with Moscow's two- and three-star hotels. The one exception is Suzdal, which has opened up almost a dozen small private guesthouses in the past few years. As with restaurants, these hotels' prices are far below Moscow levels.

WHAT IT COSTS IN RUBLES					
	¢	$	$$	$$$	$$$$
RESTAURANTS	under 125R	125R–250R	251R–375R	376R–500R	over 500R
HOTELS	under 1,500R	1,500R–2,000R	2,001R–2,500R	2,501R–3,000R	over 3,000R

Restaurant prices are for a main course at dinner. Hotel prices are for two people in a standard double room in high season, excluding tax

TIMING

To see the monasteries, churches, and kremlins of the region to the best advantage you should try to make your visits in spring or summer.

MOSCOW ENVIRONS

Within easy distance of Moscow are several sights of interest, including two monasteries: the New Jerusalem Monastery near Istra and the Troitse-Sergieva Lavra in Sergiev-Posad. Russian-culture buffs may want to explore Tchaikovsky's former home in Klin, Tolstoy's estate in Yasnaya Polyana, and the Abramtsevo Estate Museum, a beacon for Russian artists in the 19th century.

TCHAIKOVSKY'S HOUSE MUSEUM IN KLIN
ДОМ-МУЗЕЙ ЧАЙКОВСКОГО В КЛИНУ

84 km (52 mi) northwest of Moscow via Leningradskoye shosse and M10.

Visiting Tchaikovsky's home in Klin is simply a must for classical-music lovers, despite the town's relatively remote location. Pyotr Tchaikovsky (1840–93) spent a total of eight years in Klin, where he wrote Symphony *Pathétique* and two of his three ballets, *Sleeping Beauty* and *The*

GREAT ITINERARIES

IF YOU HAVE 1 OR 2 DAYS
The **Tchaikovsky's House Museum in Klin, Leo Tolstoy's Museum in Yasnaya Polyana, Sergiev-Posad,** and **Abramtsevo Estate Museum** can all be easily visited as separate day trips from Moscow.

If you have two days to explore the towns of the Golden Ring, drive or take a morning train to **Vladimir.** Explore the town, being sure to take in the Church of the Intercession on the Nerl, then travel on to **Suzdal** and overnight in the beautiful Convent of the Intercession. This will put you right in the thick of things to start exploring Suzdal early the next morning. Return to Moscow via Vladimir late in the day.

Alternatively, take a morning train to **Yaroslavl** and spend the day and night there. The next morning catch a return train on the same route, stopping off in **Rostov** (1½ hours from Yaroslavl) to spend the day before catching a late-afternoon train back to Moscow.

IF YOU HAVE 3 OR 4 DAYS
Follow any of the itineraries above. But for the Vladimir and Suzdal trip, devote another full day to Suzdal. For the Yaroslavl and Rostov trip, overnight in **Rostov** and then stop for several hours in **Pereslavl-Zalessky** before returning to Moscow.

Nutcracker. He resided at a series of addresses, but this house was his last home. It's a typical, wooden residential building of the late 19th century, eclectic in style. It's standout features are the lantern-shape balcony with stained-glass windows and a tower-shape roof.

Russia's best-known composer departed from this abode on October 7, 1893, for St. Petersburg, where he performed his last concert before his death on November 6 of that year. Less than a year after his death, the composer's brother, Modest Tchaikovsky, transformed the house into a museum. A gifted playwright and translator, Modest also played an outstanding role in preserving his brother's heritage. He preserved the original appearance of the second-floor rooms, and secured personal belongings, photographs, and a unique library of some 2,000 volumes. Some of the original scores, drafts, and letters that Modest collected are now permanently displayed in Klin. The centerpiece of the museum is Tchaikovsky's Becker piano, on which only renowned musicians are permitted to play on special occasions. During World War II the house suffered major damage when the Nazis turned the first floor into a bike garage, and the second-floor rooms into soldiers' barracks. In the late 1940s the museum underwent major renovations, and a brick building with a concert hall was constructed next to the composer's house. The finalists of the annual Tchaikovsky International Competition of Young Musicians (held in May or June) perform in this Soviet-era hall. Additionally, on the anniversary of the composer's birth (May 7) and death (November 6) memorial concerts are held in the hall. Tchaikovsky's music plays continuously in the museum. ■ TIP→**The museum cafeteria serves a traditional Russian tea service from a samovar.** ⊠*48 ul.*

Tchaikovskovo, Klin ☎224/581–96 🎫80R ⏰*Mon. and Tues., and Fri.–Sun. 10–6, ticket office closes at 5. Closed last Mon. of month.*

NEW JERUSALEM MONASTERY
НОВО-ИЕРУСАЛИМСКИЙ МОНАСТЫРЬ

65 km (40 mi) northwest of Moscow via Volokolamskoye shosse and the M9.

Far from the crowds, the captivating Russian countryside surrounding the New Jerusalem Monastery (Novoierusalimsky Monastyr) is a marvelous setting for walks and excursions. This is not the most visited locale in Russia, and it's included in the standard offerings of tourist agencies only in summer. If you can't book a tour and are feeling adventurous, you could try an excursion on the commuter train. The monastery is near the town of Istra, at a bend in the river of the same name. Trains leave from Riga station and take about an hour and a half. Or, you could ask your concierge to arrange for a car and driver to take you there. Be sure to pack your lunch—the best you'll find in Istra is an occasional cafeteria or outdoor café.

The monastery was founded in 1652 by Nikon (1605–81), patriarch of the Russian Orthodox Church. It lies on exactly the same longitude as Jerusalem, and its main cathedral, **Voskresensky Sobor** (Resurrection Cathedral), is modeled after the Church of the Holy Sepulchre in Jerusalem. Nikon's objective in re-creating the original Jerusalem in Russia was to glorify the power of the Russian Orthodox Church and at the same time elevate his own position as its head. It was Nikon who initiated the great church reforms in the 17th century that eventually led to the *raskol* (schism) that launched the Old Believer sects of the Russian Orthodox faith. As a reformer he was progressive and enlightened, but his lust for power was his eventual undoing. In 1658, before the monastery was even finished, the patriarch quarreled with Tsar Alexei Mikhailovich over Nikon's claim that the Church was ultimately superior to the State. Nikon was ultimately defrocked and banished to faraway Ferapontov Monastery, in the Vologda region, some 400 km (246 mi) north of Moscow. He died in virtual exile in 1681, and was then buried in the monastery that was supposed to have glorified his power. You can find his crypt in the Church of St. John the Baptist, which is actually inside the Resurrection Cathedral. Ironically, the same church commission that defrocked Patriarch Nikon later voted to institute his reforms. ✉*On the banks of the river Istra, Istra* ☎8231/46549 🎫*Monastery grounds free; small fees for exhibits* ⏰*Tues.–Sun. 10–4. Closed last Fri. of month.*

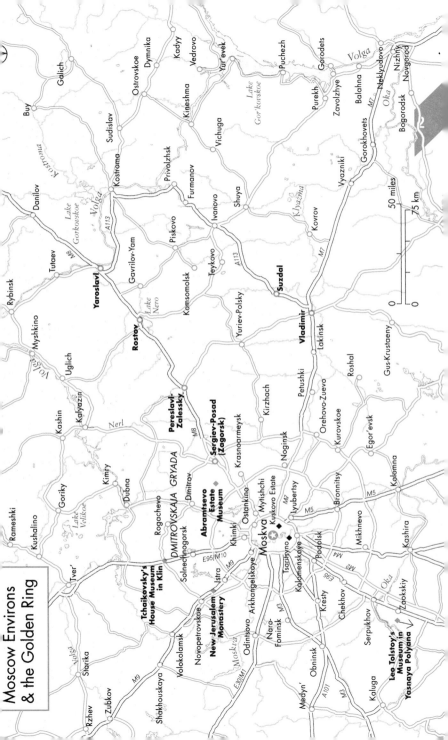

Moscow Environs
& the Golden Ring

Yaroslavl

Rostov

Pereslavl-Zalessky

Sergiev-Posad (Zagorsk)

Suzdal

Vladimir

DMITROVSKAJA GRYADA

Abramtsevo Estate Museum

Tchaikovsky's House Museum in Klin

New Jerusalem Monastery

Kuskovo Estate

Ostankino

Moskva

Leo Tolstoy's Museum in Yasnaya Polyana

Volga

Oka

Lake Gorkovskoe

Lake Nero

Lake Velikoe

Nizhniy Novgorod

Kostroma

Ivanovo

Kaluga

Serpukhov

50 miles

75 km

LEO TOLSTOY'S MUSEUM IN YASNAYA POLYANA
МУЗЕЙ ЛЬВА ТОЛСТОГО В ЯСНОЙ ПОЛЯНЕ

190 km (118 mi) south of Moscow via Simferopolskoye shosse and M2.

More than 50 years of Leo Tolstoy's life (1828–1910) passed at Yasnaya Polyana where he was born, wrote his most significant works, undertook social experiments, and was buried. Here he freed his serfs and taught peasant children at a school that he opened, attempting to transfer his ideal of a perfect world of universal equality to reality. Disappointed with his way of life and nobleman status, he decided at the age of 82 to depart from home forever, venturing out shortly before his death in October 1910.

In his home's upstairs dining room, you're greeted by numerous portraits of the Tolstoy aristocratic dynasty. Under their eyes, Tolstoy held significant social discussions with his family and his many visitors. Next door is the study where Tolstoy wrote *Anna Karenina* and *War and Peace* at his father's Persian desk. Tolstoy seemed to prefer moving around his house to work on different books, however: another room downstairs was also used as a study. This is usually the last room on a visit to the main house. In November 1910, the writer's body lay here in state as some 5,000 mourners passed to pay their last respects.

The far wing of the building houses a literary museum dedicated to Tolstoy's writing career. Drawings and prints produced by Tolstoy's contemporaries, derived from the plots and characters of his novels, as well as Tolstoy's original manuscripts are displayed in the six halls. A path from the main house into the forest leads to Tolstoy's simple, unadorned grave. On the edge of a ravine in the Stary Zakaz forest, the site was a favorite place of Tolstoy's and is now a popular pilgrimage destination for wedding parties. The walk to the grave takes about 20 minutes.

The estate-turned-museum is run by Tolstoy's great-great-grandson Vladimir Tolstoy, who is striving to turn it into a major cultural center. His concept is to purge the great author's home of modern technology (not that there's much modern technology there now) and turn the area back into a working 19th-century estate. Around this "living museum," however, Tolstoy plans to construct a tourist complex with a hotel, restaurants, and parking lots—none of which now exist.

A visit to the estate requires the whole day, because the trip from Moscow takes 2½ to 3 hours. If you plan to explore the grounds of Yasnaya Polyana independently you should strive to arrive there as early in the morning as possible, especially on Friday and weekends, to avoid busloads of tourists and crowds of newlyweds who flock to places such as this on their wedding day. A guided tour of the museums and the grounds, however, does give a better idea of all the important sights and Tolstoy's favorite spots. The cafeteria and the bookstore are directly opposite the main entrance.

Yasnaya Polyana is reached through the industrial town of Tula, some 170 km (105 mi) south of Moscow along Simferopolskoye shosse. After you pass through Tula's southern outskirts, Tolstoy's estate, only 14 km (9 mi) away, is easy to find thanks to clear signs in Russian and English; the roads, however, are notoriously bad. If you are traveling in the summer avoid driving on Saturday morning as there is often heavy traffic due to hordes of Muscovites traveling to their *dachas* (summer cottages). You can also get to Tula by commuter train from Moscow's Kursk station; once in Tula, take a bus traveling to Shchyokino from the station at prospekt Lenina. ⊠*Near Tula Yasnaya Polyana* ☎*0872/33–9118 or 0872/33–9832* ⊕*www.yasnayapolyana. ru* ⌁*25R, foreign-language guided tours 200R* ⊙*Tues.–Sun. 10–4. Closed last Wed. of month.*

WHERE TO STAY & EAT

$ ✕**Voronka Cafe.** Only 1½ km (1 mi) from Yasnaya Polyana on the way to Tula, Voronka is a good way to end a trip to Tolstoy's estate. The menu has an extensive selection of Russian dishes, including *solyanka* (a sharp-tasting soup of vegetables and meat or fish), borscht, *shashlyk* (kebabs), blini, and *ikra* (caviar). ⊠*152 Orlovskoye shosse* ☎*0872/38–3327* ▭*No credit cards.*

$$ ☖**Premiera.** The first Western-style hotel in Tula opened in May 2004. The petite hotel, close to the center, has seven rooms and two suites. Air-conditioned rooms are clean and spacious, with rainbowlike striped curtains that match the bedspreads. Bathrooms have hair dryers and the huge wall mirrors gleam. **Pro:** the only Western-style lodging option in town. **Cons:** few dining options in the area; no restaurant in the hotel, just a bar that also serves breakfast in the mornings. ⊠*3 ul. Maksimovskovo, Tula 630114* ☎*0872/49–0262 or 0872/49–9934* ⊕*www. premieratula.ru* ⇆*7 rooms, 2 suites* ⌂*In-hotel: bar* ▭*AE, MC, V.*

SERGIEV-POSAD (ZAGORSK) СЕРГИЕВ ПОСАД (ЗАГОРСК)

Fodor'sChoice ★ *75 km (47 mi) northeast of Moscow via Yaroslavskoye shosse and the M8.*

Sergiev-Posad is a comfortable and popular day trip from Moscow. The town's chief attraction is the Troitse-Sergieva Lavra, which for 500 years has been the most important center of pilgrimage in Russia and remains one of the most beautiful of all monasteries—the fairy-tale gold and azure onion domes of its Cathedral of the Assumption are among the most photographed in the country. Until 1930 the town was known as Sergiev, after the monastery's founder, and in 1991 it was officially renamed Sergiev-Posad. But the Soviet name of Zagorsk—in honor of a Bolshevik who was assassinated in 1919—has stuck, and you're as likely to hear the town and the monastery itself called one as the other.

The ride to Sergiev-Posad takes you through a lovely stretch of Russian countryside, dotted with colorful wooden cottages. As you approach the town, you see the sad and monolithic apartment buildings of the

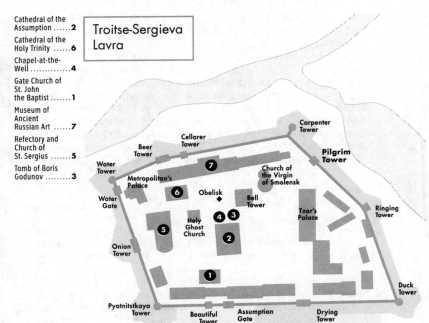

modern era. Then, peeking out above the hills, the monastery's golden cupolas and soft-blue bell tower come into view.

The best way to visit the town is to join an organized tour, because it's a full-day affair out of Moscow. The cost usually includes lunch in addition to a guided tour and transportation. You can also visit on your own by taking the commuter train from Moscow's Yaroslavsky station. The ride takes about two hours. This is much less expensive than an organized tour, but far from hassle-free. If you choose this alternative, be sure to pack your own lunch, because Sergiev-Posad's few restaurants fill up fast with prebooked tourist groups, especially in summer. ■TIP→ Be sure to dress appropriately for your visit to the functioning monastery: men are expected to remove their hats, and women are required to wear below-knee-length skirts or slacks (never shorts) and bring something to cover their heads.

The heart of Holy Russia until 1920 (when the Bolsheviks closed down most monasteries and shipped many monks to Siberia), the **Troitse-Sergieva Lavra** *(Trinity Monastery of St. Sergius)* was founded in 1340 by Sergius of Radonezh (1314–92), who would later become Russia's patron saint. The site rapidly became the nucleus of a small medieval settlement, and in 1550 the imposing white walls were built to enclose the complex of buildings, whose towers and gilded domes make it a smaller, but still spectacular, version of Moscow's Kremlin. The monastery was a Russian stronghold during the Time of Troubles (the Polish assault on Moscow in the early 17th century), and, less than a century later, Peter the Great (1672–1725) took refuge here during a bloody revolt of the *streltsy* (Russian militia), which took the lives of some of his closest rela-

tives and advisers. After the Bolshevik Revolution, the monastery was closed and turned into a museum. During World War II, however, in an attempt to mobilize the country and stir up patriotism, the Soviet government gained the support of the Orthodox Church by returning to religious purposes some of the Church property that had been confiscated earlier, including the Troitse-Sergieva Lavra. Today the churches are again open for worship, and there's a flourishing theological college here. Until the reopening in 1988 of the Danilovsky (St. Daniel) Monastery in Moscow, this monastery was the residence of the patriarch and administrative center of the Russian Orthodox Church.

You enter the monastery through the archway of the **Gate Church of St. John the Baptist**, which was erected in the late 17th century and is decorated with frescoes telling the life story of St. Sergius. One of the most important historic events in his life occurred prior to 1380, when the decisive Russian victory in the Battle of Kulikovo led to the end of Mongol rule in Russia. Before leading his troops off to battle, Prince Dmitri Donskoy sought the blessing of the peace-loving monk Sergius, a move that is generally thought to have greatly aided the Russian victory.

Although all of the monastery's cathedrals vie for your attention, the dominating structure is the massive, blue-domed, and gold-starred, **Cathedral of the Assumption** *(Uspensky Sobor)* in the center. Built between 1554 and 1585 with money donated by Tsar Ivan the Terrible (1530–84)—purportedly in an attempt to atone for killing his own son in a fit of rage—it was modeled after the Kremlin's Uspensky Sobor. Its interior contains frescoes and an 18th-century iconostasis. Among the artists to work on it was Simon Ushakov, a well-known icon painter from Moscow. The cathedral is open for morning services.

The small building just outside the Cathedral of the Assumption (near the northwest corner) is the **tomb of Boris Godunov and his family.** Boris Godunov, who ruled as regent after Ivan the Terrible's death, died suddenly in 1605 of natural causes. This was during the Polish attack on Moscow led by the False Dmitri, the first of many impostors to claim he was the son of Ivan. The death of Godunov facilitated the invaders' victory, after which his family was promptly murdered. This explains why Godunov was not bestowed the honor of burial in the Kremlin normally granted to tsars.

Opposite Boris Godunov's tomb is a tiny and colorful chapel, the **Chapel-at-the-Well**, built in 1644 above a fountain that is said to work miracles. According to legend, the spring here appeared during the Polish Siege (1608–10), when the monastery bravely held out for 16 months against the foreign invaders (this time led by the second False Dmitri). You can make a wish by washing your face and hands in its charmed waters. Towering 86 meters (285 feet) next to the chapel is the five-tier baroque belfry. It was built in the 18th century to a design by the master of St. Petersburg baroque, Bartolomeo Rastrelli.

Along the southern wall of the monastery, to your far left as you enter, is the 17th-century **Refectory and Church of St. Sergius**. The church is at the eastern end, topped by a single gilt dome. The long building of the refectory, whose colorful facade adds to the vivid richness of the monastery's architecture, is where, in times past, pilgrims from near and far gathered to eat on feast days. The pink building just beyond the refectory is the metropolitan's residence.

Across the path from the residence is the white-stone **Cathedral of the Holy Trinity** *(Troitsky Sobor)*, built in the 15th century over the tomb of St. Sergius. Over the centuries it has received many precious gifts from the powerful and wealthy rulers who have made the pilgrimage to the church of Russia's patron saint. The icons inside were created by famous master Andrei Rublyov and one of his disciples, Danil Chorny. Rublyov's celebrated *Holy Trinity*, now on display at the Tretyakov Gallery in Moscow, originally hung here; the church's version is a copy. The interior's beauty is mainly due to its 17th-century gilded iconostasis (which separates the sanctuary from the altar and body of the church). The upper tier of the church was once used by monks as a manuscript library. A continual service in memoriam to St. Sergius is held all day, every day.

The vestry, the building behind the Cathedral of the Holy Trinity, houses the monastery's **Museum of Ancient Russian Art**. It's often closed for no apparent reason or open only to groups, which is yet another reason to visit Sergiev-Posad on a guided tour. The museum contains a spectacular collection of gifts presented to the monastery over the centuries. On display are precious jewels, jewel-encrusted embroideries, chalices, and censers. Next door to the vestry are two more museums, which are open to individual tourists. The first museum contains icons and icon covers, portrait art, and furniture. The other museum (on the second floor) is devoted to Russian folk art, with wooden items, toys, porcelain, and jewelry. There's also a gift shop here. ✉*Sergiev-Posad* ☎*254/45–334* ⊕*www.lavra.ru* 🎫*60R* ⊙*Daily 10–5.*

DID YOU KNOW?   The world's first *matryoshka* (the familiar colorful, wooden nesting doll) was designed in Sergiev-Posad at the beginning of the 20th century, and most of the matryoshkas you see for sale in Moscow and St. Petersburg are made here. The Toy Museum *(Muzey Igrushki)* is evidence of Sergiev-Posad's claim to fame as a center for toy making. Although it is rarely included on organized tours, it is well worth an hour of your time and is within walking distance of the Troitse-Sergieva Lavra monastery. It boasts a collection of toys that amused, educated, and illuminated the lives of Russian children for generations. ✉*136 pr. Krasnoy Armii* ☎*254/44–101* 💳*90R* 🕐*Wed.– Sun. 10–5.*

WHERE TO STAY & EAT

$ ✕**Russky Dvorik.** A pleasant downtown café popular with tourist groups, this spot is right across from the Lavra. Be prepared for slow service. ✉*134 ul. Krasnoy Armii, Sergiev-Posad* ☎*254/45–114* 💳*AE, MC, V.*

$ ✕**Zolotoye Koltso.** The "Golden Ring" is considered the best restaurant in town. It caters to tour groups and has a good service record for preparing basic Russian fare: a selection of salads, soups, and (mostly) meat dishes. ✉*121 ul. Krasnoy Armii, Sergiev-Posad* ☎*254/41–517* 💳*No credit cards.*

$$ 🏨**Hotel Aristokrat.** This recently built, redbrick hotel is in the town center on Blinnaya Gora (Pancake Hill), a five-minute walk from the Lavra. Cozy guest rooms that overlook the Lavra have all the amenities, such as televisions and refrigerators. The Aristokrat restaurant serves traditional Russian food. **Pro:** great views of the Lavra. **Con:** in summer, rooms must be booked in advance. ✉*1A ul. Sergiyevskaya, Sergiev-Posad 141300* ☎*254/725–94 or 254/480–21* 🛏*18 rooms* 🛎 *In-room: refrigerator, TV. In-hotel: restaurant, pool* 💳*No credit cards.*

BRAMTSEVO ESTATE MUSEUM МУЗЕЙ-УСАДЬБА АБРАМЦЕВО

61 km (38 mi) northeast of Moscow via Yaroslavskoye shosse and the M8.

The 18th-century, wooden Abramtsevo estate served as the center of Russia's cultural life in two different periods of the 19th century. In 1918 it was nationalized and turned into a museum. Its guest list from different years includes writers Nikolai Gogol and Ivan Turgenev, opera singer Fyodor Chaliapin, and theater director Konstantin Stanislavsky. The artists Valentin Serov, Mikhail Vrubel, Ilya Repin, Viktor Vasnetsov, and Vasily Polenov were just a few of the luminaries who frequented the estate. It's easier to name those cultural figures of the 19th and early 20th centuries who have not visited Abramtsevo than all of those who have.

Until 1870 Abramtsevo belonged to Sergei Aksakov, a Slavophile who advocated the exportation of Orthodox Christianity to the West. A very religious man, Aksakov chose Abramtsevo as his residence because it was close to the Troitse-Sergieva Lavra. He opened his home to sympathetic writers and intellectuals of the 1840s. Nowadays only two rooms in the main house—Aksakov's dining room and study with his memorabilia—recall his presence. The rest of the house is dedicated to luminous Abramtsevo guests and the next (and final) private owner.

After Aksakov's death, railway tycoon Savva Mamontov purchased the estate in 1870 and turned it into an artists' colony. Here Mamontov and a community of resident artists tried to revive traditional Russian arts, crafts, and architecture to stimulate interest in Russian culture and make arts more accessible to the people.

In the 1880s half a dozen resident artists participated in the construction of the prettiest structure on Abramtsevo's grounds, the diminutive **Tserkov Ikony Spasa Nerukotvornovo** (Church of the Icon of the Savior Not Made by Hands). The idea to build a church was born when a flood prevented the local community from attending the festive Easter church service. The artist Polenov chose a 12th-century church outside Novgorod as a model. He and fellow artists Repin and Nesterov painted the gilt iconostasis; Vasnetsov laid the mosaic floor he had designed in the shape of a giant blooming flower. Some of the resident artists created their finest works in Abramtsevo. Serov painted his *Girl with Peaches,* an 1870 portrait of Mamontov's daughter, Vera, which now decorates Mamontov's dining room. Vasnetsov worked on his 1898 *Bogatyri* (Russian epic heroes) in Abramtsevo as well. Other structures on Abramtsevo's grounds include the wooden Izbushka Na Kuryikh Nozhkakh (House on Chicken Legs), the residence of the witch Baba-Yaga from Russian fairy tales; Polenov's dacha; and an artists' workshop. In 1889 the troubled artist Mikhail Vrubel joined the Abramtsevo colony to participate in the ceramics workshop, where his provocative grotesque designs are still evident in the tile stoves, ceramic inlay, and furniture.

The estate can easily be visited on the way back from Sergiev-Posad. For Russian art aficionados, however, it may be worth a single one-day trip. You can visit the estate on a tour or head there yourself by commuter train; take the train from Yaroslavsky station to Sergiev-Posad or Alexandrov and get off at the Abramtsevo station. ⊠*Sergiev-Posad district, Abramtsevo station* ☎*8254/306–68 or 8254/302–78* ⊠*90R* ⊙ *Wed.–Sun. 10–6. Closed last Thurs. of month.*

WHERE TO EAT

$$ ✕ **Galereya.** The extensive menu of traditional Russian food served at this restaurant, which is right across the street from the central gate of the estate, makes it a solid lunch option. If you don't feel like dining in, order a few *pirozhki* (small pies of cabbage, apple, or potatoes) to go. They're particularly delicious with *mors,* a traditional Russian cranberry drink. ⊠*3 Muzeynaya ul.* ☎*8254/350–53* ▭*No credit cards.*

THE NORTHERN GOLDEN RING

Within this historic region northeast of Moscow are ancient towns, venerable churches, and the magnificent Rostov kremlin and Monastery of St. Ipaty. There are plenty of guided-tour options, ranging from one-day outings to 1,000-km (620-mi) bus tours. And if you want to visit this region on your own, you're in luck: these towns are tourist-friendly.

ERESLAVL-ZALESSKY ПЕРЕСЛАВЛЬ-ЗАЛЕССКИЙ

127 km (79 mi) northeast of Moscow via the M8.

Pereslavl-Zalessky was founded in 1157 by Yuri Dolgoruky for two very important reasons. The first was political: he sought to draw parallels between the power base he was building in northeast Rus' and the center of power in Kiev, to the southeast. So he named this town Pereyaslavl (meaning "to achieve glory"; the "ya" was later dropped) after a town outside of Kiev, and he named the river alongside the town Trubezh, just as in the Kievan Pereyaslavl. The "Zalessky" appellation, added in the 15th century, means "beyond the forests" and was used to distinguish the town from many other Pereyaslavls (not least the one near Kiev).

The second reason was economic. The location of the town on the southern shore of Lake Pleshcheyevo was ideal for defending the western approaches to vital trade routes along the Nerl River to the Klyazma, Oka, and Volga rivers. The topography only accentuates this role. From the hills, the impressive Danilovsky and Goritsky monasteries peer down on the low wooden and stone buildings of town.

As the birthplace of Alexander Nevsky (1220–63), Pereslavl-Zalessky has yet another claim to fame. Nevsky entered the pantheon of Russia's great heroes when, as Prince of Novgorod, he beat back invading Swedes in 1240 at the Battle of the Neva (thus his last name). For his victory, the Mongol Khan awarded Nevsky the title of Grand Prince of Vladimir. There's a small church in town honoring Nevsky.

■TIP➔**Note that the town can be reached by bus or car, but not by train.**

The fortresslike **Goritsky Monastyr,** high on a hill south of the town center, was founded in the first half of the 14th century and is now an art and history museum. It displays ancient manuscripts and books found in this area, jewelry, and sculptures. An impressive collection of icons includes the 15th-century treasure, *Peter and Paul Apostles,* the oldest icon in the region, and a small collection of paintings with works of Konstantin Korovin. Outside the entrance to the museum is a proud monument to the T-34 tank, which was the tank that saved Russia from the Germans in World War II. Inside is the large Uspensky Sobor (Cathedral of the Assumption), built in 1544. ☎*48535/381–00* 🖂*100R* ☾ *Wed.–Mon. 10–4:30. Closed last Mon. of month.*

In the center of town, along Sovetskaya ulitsa, is the 12th-century limestone **Cathedral of the Transfiguration** *(Spaso-Preobrazhensky Sobor).* Construction began on this church in the same year as the Church of Saints Boris and Gleb in Kideksha, near Suzdal, making it one of the oldest stone buildings standing in Russia. ✉*Sovetskaya ul.* ☎*No phone* 🖂*Free* ☾*May–Oct., Wed.–Mon. 10–6.*

Pereslavl-Zalessky was the birthplace of the Russian navy. The **Botik museum,** a few miles outside of town, houses the only remaining boat of the more than 100 Peter the Great built for the fleet he sailed on Lake Pleshcheyevo. The *botik,* a small sailboat, usually single-mast, is often called the grandfather of the Russian fleet. The museum also displays several naval guns, a triumphal arch, and a monument to Peter the Great. To get to the museum (3 km [2 mi] away), you take a narrow-gauge train running south and west along the lake from the bus station, which is on ulitsa Kardovskovo, just below the Goritsky Monastery. It departs the bus station at 9 AM, 1 PM, and 4:30 PM and returns from the museum at 12:30 PM, 4 PM, and 8:30 PM. ⊠*Near Veslevo village* ☎*48535/22–788* ✉*25R, English-guided tours 200R* ☉*Tues.–Sun. 10–5. Closed last Thurs. of month.*

WHERE TO STAY & EAT

¢   ✕▥ **Botik Tourist Complex.** A café and six pretty wooden houses that accommodate two people each are down the path from the Botik museum on the bank of Pleshcheyevo Lake. Houses need to be booked in advance. Besides accommodation, the complex also has a sauna, beach, and bar. The Botik Café ($), designed in the shape of a ship, serves moderately priced traditional Russian cuisine. **Pros:** great views of the lake; beachfront location. **Cons:** rooms look a bit shabby and need to be booked in advance. ⊠*Near Veslevo village, 152020* ☎*08535/98–085* ☎*08535/98–865* ⚓*6 houses* ⚐*In-hotel: bar, beachfront* ▤*No credit cards.*

$ ✕▥ **Hotel Pereslavl.** The Pereslavl is a Soviet-era hotel with a convenient downtown location. It recently underwent a major renovation which raised the prices considerably (though they are still moderate), but the rooms are the better for it—clean and light with nice furniture and decent bathroom fixtures. Bar Rita ($), which serves Russian food, has a staff that prides itself on service—the owner learned quite a few things on his trips to the United States. The Russian flavored vodkas are worth sampling; try *pertsovka* (hot pepper) or *zubrovka* (bison grass). **Pro:** convenient location. **Con:** bar can get loud on weekends. ⊠*27 Rostovskaya ul., Pereslavl-Zalessky 152020* ☎*08535/21–788 hotel, 08535/21–633 restaurant* ⊕*www.hotelpereslavl.ru* ⚓*59 rooms* ⚐*In-hotel: restaurant, bar* ▤*No credit cards.*

$$$$ ▥ **Hotel Zapadnaya.** On the bank of the Trubezh River, this hotel has a superb, picturesque location in the historical center of town. Rooms are clean and spacious, and the staff is friendly. **Pros:** great location; helpful staff. **Con:** a bit overpriced. ⊠*1-A Pleshcheyevskaya ul., Pereslavl-Zalessky 152020* ☎*08535/34–378 or 08535/34–380* ⊕*www. westhotel.ru* ⚓*11 rooms* ⚐*In-room: dial-up. In-hotel: restaurant* ▤*No credit cards.*

ROSTOV РОСТОВ

225 km (140 mi) northeast of Moscow via the M8, 58 km (36 mi) southwest of Yaroslavl.

Rostov, also known as Rostov-Veliky ("the Great") so as not to confuse it with Rostov-on-the-Don, is one of the oldest towns in Russia. Founded even before Riurik, a semi-legendary Viking prince, came to rule Russia in the 9th century, Rostov is first mentioned in historical chronicles in 862. It became an independent principality at

2

the beginning of the 13th century and soon became one of the most prosperous and influential political centers of ancient Rus. However, the city was destroyed when the Mongols invaded in 1238. In the 15th century Rostov ultimately lost its political independence but retained its influence as a major religious center. It became the seat of the metropolitan, the leader of the Orthodox Church, in the late 16th century.

The small town, with a population of 36,000, is beautifully situated on the edge of Lake Nero, with earthen ramparts and radial streets.

odor$Choice ★ At the center of Rostov is the incomparable **Rostov kremlin,** a fortress with 6-foot-thick white-stone walls and 11 circular towers topped with wood-shingle cupolas. The kremlin dates from 1631, but it was built to its current glory between 1670 and 1690 by Rostov Metropolitan Jonah. Its main purpose was to serve as court and residence for the metropolitan, though Jonah saw himself as creating an ideal type of self-enclosed city focused on spiritual matters. As such, it was Russia's first planned city.

The huge, blue-dome **Cathedral of the Assumption** (Uspensky Sobor) stands just outside the walls of the kremlin. Inside are frescoes dating to 1675. But the truly memorable site is the adjacent four-tower **belfry.** The famous 13 bells of Rostov chime on the half hour and full hour and can play four tunes. It's said that the largest of the bells, which weighs 32 tons and is named Sysoi, for Jonah's father, can be heard from 19 km (12 mi) away.

You enter the kremlin through the richly decorated northern entrance, past the **Gate Church of the Resurrection** (Nadvratnaya Voskresenskaya Tserkov). Well-groomed pathways and a pleasant, tree-lined pond lend themselves to a contemplative walk. Just to the right of the entrance into the kremlin is the **Church of the Mother of God Hodegetria** (Tserkov Bogomateri Odigitrii), whose faceted baroque exterior rises to a single onion dome.

The **Church of John the Theologian** (Tserkov Ioanna Bogoslova), another gate church, is on the west side of the kremlin. Adjacent to this church is the two-story **Red Palace** (Krasnaya Palata), once known as the Chamber for Great Sovereigns. Built first for Ivan the Terrible for his visits to the town, it was later used by Peter the Great and Catherine the Great. It's now a hotel known as the International Youth Tourism Center.

Adjacent is the **White Palace** (*Belaya Palata* ☎*No phone* ☉*May–Oct. daily 10–5*)—the metropolitan's residence—most notable for its large hall (3,000 square feet) supported by a single column. Connected to the residence is the private church of the metropolitan, the Church of the

Savior on the Stores, which was built over a food-storage shelter. This church has the most beautiful wall paintings in the entire complex, as well as gilded columns and handsome brass doors. The metropolitan's residence now houses a museum of icons and Rostov enamel (*finift*), a craft the town is famous for throughout Russia. The southern portion of the kremlin features the tall **Church of Grigory the Theologian** (Tserkov Grigoria Bogoslova). ☎48536/61–717 ⊕*www.rostmuseum. ru* ✉*140R for all churches and palaces inside the kremlin* ☉*Daily 10–5, except Jan. 1. Churches: May–Oct., daily 10–5.*

On your way out of the kremlin complex, be sure to explore the shop arcade called **Torgoviye Ryady** *(trade rows)*, across the square from Uspensky Sobor. In the early 19th century, after Rostov had lost its metropolitanate to nearby Yaroslavl, it became an extremely important trading center. Rostov's annual market was the third largest in Russia.

Along the lakefront and southwest of the kremlin is the rather eclectic **Yakovlevsky (Jacob) Monastery.** Dominating the ensemble is the huge, Romanesque Dmitriyev Church, crowned by a large spherical central dome and four smaller corner domes. The monastery was founded in 1389. Take the guided tour for access to the premises of the working monastery. ☎48536/743–69 ✉*Monastery grounds free, guided tours 150R* ☉*Daily 9–5.*

The oldest monastery in Russia, **Avraamiyev (Abraham) Monastery** was founded at the end of the 11th century. Interestingly, it was erected on the site of a former pagan temple to Veles, god of cattle. The five-dome Epiphany Cathedral in the monastery complex dates from 1553 and is the oldest standing building in Rostov. The nuns' cloister, which is still working, is on the lakefront, northeast of the kremlin. ☎48536/637–12 or 48536/740–05 ✉*Free* ☉*Daily 9–5.*

WHERE TO STAY & EAT

$$ ✕**Krasnaya Palata.** The large, single hall of this eatery within the kremlin brings those visiting the sights of historic Rostov together. ⊠*Rostov kremlin* ☎48536/31–717 ▭*No credit cards.*

$ ✕**Teremok.** Borscht, solyanka, and blini with caviar are among the good Russian dishes served at this cozy restaurant in front of the kremlin. ⊠*9 ul. Moravskovo* ☎48536/31–648 ▭*No credit cards.*

$ ✕▦**Boyarsky Dvor.** Just 50 meters away from the kremlin, this recently-renovated 18th-century, two-story historic mansion-turned-hotel has all the amenities you could ask for from a provincial hotel. Cheerfully decorated in pastel colors, the rooms are clean and spacious. Restaurant Rasstegai ($), on the ground floor, serves hearty Russian meals. **Pros:** great location; comfortable beds. **Con:** advance booking required in summer. ⊠*4, Kammeny Most ul.* ☎7495/231–3670 ⊕*www.reinkap-hotel.ru* ⏎*53 rooms* ⚴*In-hotel: restaurant* ▭*No credit cards.*

$ ▦**Dom na Pogrebakh.** If you've ever wanted to stay overnight in a kremlin, here's your chance. Built over the food stores or *pogreba* of the kremlin, this modern hotel is in a two-story building of stone and wood. Although a bit Soviet in style and presentation, the wooden-wall rooms of varying sizes do have all the basic amenities. The hotel's great advantage is location as it allows you the privilege of wandering the grounds of the kremlin at night, though you should not be too loud. **Pro:** the opportunity to stay inside a 17th-century kremlin. **Con:** rooms are a bit shabby. ⊠ *Rostov kremlin, in Red Palace* ☎*48536/61–244* 🖷*48536/61–502* ⊕*www.rostmuseum.ru/hotel/hotel.html* 🗱*13 rooms with shared bath* 🝤*In-hotel: restaurant* 🗖*No credit cards.*

AROSLAVL ЯРОСЛАВЛЬ

282 km (175 mi) northeast of Moscow on the M8.

Yaroslavl has a very storied history, beginning with an apocryphal founding. It's said that local inhabitants set loose a bear to chase away Prince Yaroslav the Wise (978–1054). Yaroslav wrestled and killed the bear and founded the town on the spot. If true, these events happened early in the 11th century; Yaroslav decreed the town's founding as a fortress on the Volga in 1010. About 600 years later, in 1612, during the Time of Troubles, the town was the center of national resistance against the invading Poles, under the leadership of Kuzma Minin and Dmitri Pozharsky.

The town rests at the confluence of the Volga and Kotorosl rivers, which made it a major commercial center from the 13th century until 1937, when the Moscow-Volga canal was completed, allowing river traffic to proceed directly to the capital. This commercial heritage bequeathed the city a rich legacy that offers a glimpse of some of the finest church architecture in Russia.

In the town center, proceed northwest along Pervomaiskaya ulitsa, a favorite pedestrian area for locals that follows the semicircular path of the town's former earthen ramparts. Peruse the impressive, colonnaded **trade rows** and walk on to the Znamenskaya watchtower, which in the middle of the 17th century marked the western edge of the town—another watchtower stands on the Volga embankment. The yellow building directly across the square is the **Volkov Theater.** The theater and square are named for Fyodor Volkov, who founded Russia's first professional drama theater here in 1750—the theater was the first to stage *Hamlet* in Russia. Continue along Pervomaiskaya and it will take you to the banks of the Volga, which is 1 km (½ mi) wide at this point. Look for the monument to the great Russian poet Nikolai Nekrasov, who came from nearby Karabikha.

The mid-17th-century **Church of Elijah the Prophet** *(Tserkov Ilyi Proroka)* stands at the center of town on Sovetskaya Ploshchad (Soviet Square), some say on the site of Yaroslav's alleged wrestling match with the bear (though a monument down by the Volga commemorates the spot of the town's founding). Its tall, octagonal belfry and faceted green onion domes make the church the focal point of the town. Inside the ornamental church are some of the best-preserved frescoes (1680) by Gury Nikitin and Sila Savin, whose works also adorn Moscow Kremlin cathedrals, as well as churches throughout the region. The frescoes depict scenes from the Gospels and the life of Elijah and his disciple Elisha. ✉ *22 Sovetskaya Pl.* ☎ *4852/3040–72* 💰 *60R* ☉ *Apr.–Oct., daily 10–1 and 2–6.*

The **Monastery of the Transfiguration of the Savior** *(Spaso-Preobrazhensky Monastyr)*, surrounded by white, 10-foot-thick walls, was the site of northern Russia's first school of higher education, dating to the 13th century. It houses several magnificent churches and is where Ivan the Terrible took refuge in 1571, when the Mongols were threatening Moscow. Dating to 1516, the **Holy Gates** entrance to the monastery, on the side facing the Kotorosl River, is the oldest extant structure in the compound. A six-story **belfry** rises high above the round-dome Cathedral of the Transfiguration of the Savior, which was under restoration at this writing. Climb to the top of the belfry for a panoramic view of the city. The clock in the belfry hung in the famous Spasskaya Tower of the Moscow Kremlin until 1624, when it was purchased by the merchants of Yaroslavl. ✉ *25 Bogoyavlenskaya Pl.* ☎ *4852/3292–40* 💰 *Free, small fee for individual churches and belfry within monastery* ☉ *Tues.–Sun. 10–5. Closed 1st Wed. of month.*

A **statue of Yaroslav the Wise,** unveiled in 1993 by Russian president Boris Yeltsin and Ukrainian president Leonid Kravchuk, stands not far from the monastery. Yaroslav is depicted holding a piece of the kremlin and staring off in the direction of Moscow. To see the statue, walk away from the river down ulitsa Nakhimsona toward the monastery.

The large, redbrick, blue-cupola **Church of the Epiphany** *(Tserkov Bogoyavleniya)* is renowned for its fine proportions, enhanced by splendid decorative ceramic tiles and unusually tall windows. Inside are eight levels of wall paintings in the realistic style that began to hold sway in the late 1600s. The church is directly west of the Monastery of the Transfiguration of the Savior. ✉ *Bogoyavlenskaya Pl.* ☎ *4852/3034–29 or 4852/7256–23* 💰 *Free* ☉ *Wed.–Mon. 10–1 and 2–5.*

The 100-foot-tall **"candle of Yaroslavl"** is actually a belfry for two churches, Ioann Zlatoust (St. John Chrysostom, 1649) and the miniature Tserkov Vladimirskoi Bogomateri (Church of the Vladimir Virgin, 1678). The former is a larger summer church, ornately decorated with colorful tiles; the latter is the more modest and easy-to-heat winter church. From the Monastery of the Transfiguration of the Savior, it's a 1-km (½-mi) walk (or two stops on Bus 4) across the bridge and along the mouth of the Kotorosl to the churches and belfry.

Although it looks as though it's made from wood, the 17th-century five-dome **Church of St. John the Baptist** *(Tserkov Ioanna Predtechi)* is actually fashioned from carved red brick. The church is on the same side of the Kotorosl River as the candle of Yaroslavl, but it's west of the bridge by about 1 km (½ mi). ✉ *69 Kotoroslnaya nab.* ☎ *No phone.*

2

$–$$ ✕**Premiera.** St. Petersburg–brewed Baltika beer accompanies the moderately priced traditional Russian dishes served at this café right behind the Volkov Theater. ⊠*5 Pervomaiskaya ul.* ☎*4852/728–601* ▭*No credit cards.*

$ ✕**Golden Bear Café.** In this pleasant café you'll find tasty Russian-style cooking, good service, and a modern interior. If the *salat* (salad) selection doesn't appeal, try the *buterbrod* (open-face sandwich), a dependable choice. ⊠*3 Pervomaiskaya ul.* ☎*4852/328–532* ▭*No credit cards.*

$$$$ ✕▣ **Ring Premier Hotel.** Five minutes by foot from the Transfiguration monastery and just steps from Shinnik soccer stadium, this four-star hotel has the most luxurious accommodations in town. All guest rooms are reasonably large, nicely furnished, air-conditioned, and have satellite television and Internet access. The hotel's Sobinov ($$) restaurant serves European-style cuisine. **Pros:** staff speaks excellent English; great sauna and pool. **Con:** hotel bar and restaurant are a bit overpriced. ⊠*55 ul. Svobody, 150040* ☎*4852/5811–58 or 4852/5808–58* ⊕*www.ringpremier-hotel.ru* ⇱*122 rooms* ⌂*In-hotel: restaurant, bar, pool, public Wi-Fi* ▭*MC, V.*

$$$$ ✕▣ **Yubileynaya.** Located near the monastery, the recently renovated Yubileynaya overlooks the Kotorosl River and the historic town. The renovation included new wooden furniture, upgraded bedsheets and carpets, and the addition of 20 new rooms. The hotel restaurant, Znamensky ($), with its European-style cuisine is a nice plus. **Pros:** central location on the riverbank; Wi-Fi; nice buffet breakfast. **Con:** a bit overpriced. ⊠*11a Kotoroslnaya nab., Yaroslavl 150000* ☎*4852/309–259* ⊕*www.yubil.yar.ru* ⇱*220 rooms* ⌂*In-hotel: restaurant, bar, public Wi-Fi* ▭*No credit cards.*

$$ ✕▣ **Kotorosl.** This decent, renovated, tourist-class hotel is not far from the city center, near the railway station. The restaurant ($) serves basic Russian fare with little luster. **Pro:** close to train station. **Con:** standard rooms are overpriced, given that bathrooms are shared between two rooms. ⊠*87 Bolshaya Oktyabrskaya ul., 150000* ☎*4852/211–581* ⊕*www.kotorosl.yaroslavl.ru* ⇱*184 rooms* ⌂*In-hotel: restaurant, bar, gym* ▭*No credit cards.*

HE EASTERN GOLDEN RING

Vladimir and Suzdal, which together make up a World Heritage Site, hold some of Russia's most beautiful medieval kremlins, churches, and monasteries. The towns lie to the east of Moscow.

LADIMIR ВЛАДИМИР

190 km (118 mi) east of Moscow via the M7.

Although this fairly peaceful city of 350,000 seems unassuming today, half a millennium ago it was the cultural and religious capital of northeastern Rus'. Several of the monuments to this time of prosperity and prestige remain, and a visit to this city, and nearby Suzdal, is vital to understanding the roots from which contemporary Russia grew.

Vladimir was founded in 1108 on the banks of the Klyazma by Vladimir Monomakh, grandson of Yaroslav the Wise and father of Yuri Dolgoruky. Yuri, as he increased his power en route to taking the throne in Kiev, preferred Suzdal, however, and made that town his de facto capital in 1152. Upon Yuri's death five years later, his son, Andrei Bogolyubsky, moved the capital of Suzdalia to Vladimir and began a massive building campaign.

Cathedral of the Assumption *(Uspensky Sobor)*, a working church in the center of town, is an important city landmark from Andrei Bogolyubsky's time, completed in 1160. Its huge, boxy outline and golden domes rise high above the Klyazma River. After a fire in 1185, the cathedral was rebuilt, only to burn down again in 1237 when the Mongols attacked the city. The town's residents took refuge in the church, hoping for mercy. Instead, the invaders burned them alive. The cathedral was again restored, and in 1408 the famous artist Andrei Rublyov repainted the **frescoes of the** *Last Judgment,* which in themselves make this impressive monument worth a visit. Ivan the Great (1440–1505) had his architects use this cathedral as a model to build the Assumption Cathedral in the Moscow Kremlin. The cathedral also houses a replica of Russia's most revered icon, the Virgin of Vladimir; the original was moved from here to Moscow in 1390. Andrei Bogolyubsky is entombed here. ⌂*Sobornaya Pl.* ☎*4922/3242–63 or 4922/3252–01* 🖼*100R* ☉*Tues.–Sun. 1:30–4:45.*

Andrei Bogolyubsky was succeeded by Vsevolod III, also known as "the Great Nest" because of the great number of his progeny. Although he focused much of his energy in the neighboring regions of Ryazan and Murom, he was instrumental in rebuilding Vladimir's town center in 1185 after a fire caused much damage. He also built the remarkable **Cathedral of St. Dmitri** *(Dmitriyevsky Sobor)*, finished in 1197. The cathedral stands adjacent to Vladimir's much larger Cathedral of the Assumption, where he is buried, and is covered in ornate carvings with both secular and religious images. The lower images are quite precise and detailed; the upper ones have fewer details but deeper grooves for better visibility. The Cathedral had been closed for a complex, five-year restoration and reopened its doors for visitors in summer 2005. ⌂*Sobornaya Pl.* ☎*4922/3242–63* 🖼*80R* ☉*Wed.–Sun. 11–5.*

Originally, Vladimir had four gates guarding the main approaches to the town. The 12th-century **Golden Gates** *(Zolotye Vorota)*, which stand in the middle of Moskovskaya ulitsa, a few hundred yards west of the Cathedral of the Assumption, guarded the western approach. The main road from Moscow to Siberia passed through these gates, which, starting in the 1800s, became a significant monument on the infamous Vladimirka—the road prisoners took east to Siberia.

Most of Andrei Bogolyubsky's construction projects were built in **Bogolyubovo,** 10 km (6 mi) east of Vladimir. Near the convergence of the Nerl and Klyazma rivers, he built an impressive fort and living compound. The dominant building in the compound today is the richly decorated **Cathedral of the Assumption** (Uspensky Sobor), rebuilt in the 19th century. Remnants of his quarters—a tower and an archway—still stand. It was on the stairs of this tower that Andrei, despised by many for his authoritarian rule, was stabbed to death by several members of his inner circle. In the 13th century, Bogolyubovo became a convent, which it remains today. In 1702 Andrei was canonized. ⊠ *Bogolyubovo village* ☎ *4922/3242–63 tour reservations* 🎫 *Free, fee for tour* ☉ *Daily 10–5.*

★ Andrei's greatest creation and, some feel, the most perfect medieval Russian church ever built, is the 1165 **Church of the Intercession on the Nerl** *(Khram Pokrova Na Nerli)*, less than 2 km (1 mi) from Bogolyubovo. On a massive limestone foundation covered with earth, the church sits near the confluence of the Nerl and Klyazma rivers and appears to be rising out of the water that surrounds it. Andrei built the church in memory of his son Izyslav, who was killed in a victorious battle with the Bulgars. Look for the unique carvings of King David on the exterior, the earliest such iconographic carvings in this region. Inside, the high, narrow arches give an impressive feeling of space and light. To get to the church from Bogolyubovo, walk a few hundred yards west of the monastery, down ulitsa Frunze and under a railway bridge; then follow the path through a field to the church.

WHERE TO STAY & EAT

$ ✕ **Stary Gorod.** This "Old Town" restaurant serving Russian and European cuisine is a good option for a meal, only steps away from Sobornaya Ploshchad. The place is quiet, and the staff is friendly. The summer terrace is open May through September. ⊠ *41 Bolshaya Moskovskaya ul., Vladimir* ☎ *4922/3229–54* ⊕ *www.oldcity33.ru* ▤ *No credit cards.*

¢ ✕ **Tri Peskarya.** The "Three Minnows" is a cozy wood-lined place that resembles a beer cellar. The service is good and the Russian cuisine, such as *ukha* (fish soup), grilled sturgeon, and fish *kulebyaka* (pie) is agreeable. ⊠ *88 Bolshaya Moskovskaya ul., Vladimir* ☎ *4922/3254–01* ▤ *No credit cards.*

$$$ 🏨 **Monomah Hotel.** The latest addition to the Vladimir hotel scene, Monomah offers one of the best accommodations in the city, though a bit on the pricey side. Rooms are very clean, new, and cozy, and the staff is very friendly. **Pros:** central location; slippers in each room. **Con:** a bit overpriced. ⊠ *20 ul. Gogolya, Vladimir 600000* ☎ *4922/4404–44* ⊕ *www.monomahhotel.ru* ⇗ *16 rooms* ⌂ *In-room: refrigerator. In-hotel: restaurant, bar* ▤ *MC, V.*

$ 🏨 **U Zolotykh Vorot.** This elegant hotel is in a recently renovated 19th-century building, next to the Golden Gates. Doubles and singles, tastefully decorated in beige and pink, are available along with one two-room suite. **Pros:** central location; great breakfast. **Con:** rooms with a street view can be noisy. ⊠ *17 Bolshaya Moskovskaya ul., Vladimir* ☎ *4922/4208–23* ⊕ *www.golden-gate.ru* ⇗ *13 rooms, 1 suite* ⌂ *In-hotel: restaurant, bar* ▤ *MC, V.*

SUZDAL СУЗДАЛЬ

★ *190 km (118 mi) east of Moscow on the M7 via Vladimir, then 26 km (16 mi) north on the A113.*

Suzdal is the crown jewel of the Golden Ring, with more than 200 historic monuments and some of the most striking churches in Russia. This quiet tourist town of 12,000 on the Kamenka River is compact enough to be explored entirely on foot, but to do it justice, give it two days.

One of the earliest settlements in central Russia, Suzdal has been inhabited since the 9th century and was first mentioned in the *Russian Chronicle* (Russia's ancient historical record) in 1024. In 1152 Yuri Dolgoruky made Suzdal the capital of his growing fiefdom in northeastern Russia. He built a fortress in nearby Kideksha (the town, 4 km [2½ mi] to the east, is the site of the oldest stone church in northeastern Russia—the Church of Saints Boris and Gleb, built in 1152). His son, Andrei Bogolyubsky, preferred nearby Vladimir and focused much of his building efforts there. Still, Suzdal remained a rich town, largely because of donations to the many local monasteries and church building commissions. Indeed, medieval Suzdal had only about 400 families, but some 40 churches.

The **Suzdal kremlin,** which may have first been built in the 10th century, sits on an earthen rampart, with the Kamenka River flowing around all but the east side (demarcated by ulitsa Lenina). The dominant monument in the kremlin (and indeed the town) is the mid-13th-century **Sobor Rozhdestva Bogorodnitsy** (Cathedral of the Nativity of the Virgin), topped by deep-blue cupolas festooned with golden stars. It has been subjected to many calamities and reconstructions, and is closed to the public. Original limestone carvings can still be found on its corners and on its facade. Its exquisite bronze entry doors are the oldest such doors in Russia, having survived since the 13th century. Inside, the brilliant and colorful frescoes dating from the 1230s and 1630s are without compare.

The long, white, L-shaped three-story building that the cathedral towers over is the **Archbishop's Chambers.** Behind its broad windows you'll find the superb "cross chamber" (named for its shape), which is a large hall without any supporting pillars—the first hall of its type in all Russia. The kremlin also holds museums of antique books and art. ⊠*Southern part of town Suzdal* ☎*49231/20–937* 🎫*150R for entire kremlin* ⊙ *Wed.–Mon. 10–5. Closed last Fri. of month.*

The **Museum of Wooden Architecture** *(Muzey Derevyannovo Zodchestva)* contains interesting wooden buildings moved here from around the region. Of particular interest is the ornate **Church of the Transfiguration,** dating from 1756; it was moved here from the village of Kozlyatievo. The buildings can be viewed from the outside any time of year, but from the inside only from May to October. The museum is just below the kremlin and across the river to the south; to get here you'll need to go south on ulitsa Lenina, cross the river, and turn right on Pushkarskaya ulitsa. 💳*150R* 🕐*May–Oct., Wed.–Mon. 9:30–4. Closed last Fri. of month.*

Walking north from the kremlin on ulitsa Lenina, you'll pass several churches on your left and the pillared trading arcades. Just beyond the arcades are the beautiful **Churches of St. Lazarus and St. Antipy** *(Tserkov Svyatovo Lazarya and Tserkov Svyatovo Antipiya)*, their colorful bell tower topping the unique, concave tent-roof design. This ensemble is a good example of Russian church architecture, where a summer church (St. Lazarus, with the shapely onion domes, built in 1667) adjoins a smaller, easier-to-heat, and more modest winter church (St. Antipy, built in 1745). ✉*Ul. Lenina* ☎*No phone* 💳*Free.*

Rising 236 feet high, the bell tower in the **Monastery of the Feast of the Deposition of the Robe** *(Rizopolozhensky Monastyr)* complex is the tallest building in Suzdal. It was built by local residents in 1819 to commemorate Russia's victory over Napoléon. The monastery is on ulitsa Lenina, opposite the post office.

Fodor'sChoice The impressive **Monastery of St. Yefim** *(Spaso-Yefimsky Monastyr)* dates
★ from 1350. The tall brick walls and 12 towers of the monastery have often been the cinematic stand-in for the Moscow Kremlin. The main church in the monastery, the 16th-century **Church of the Transfiguration of the Savior,** is distinctive for its extremely pointed onion domes and its New Testament frescoes by Gury Nikitin and Sila Slavin, the famous 17th-century Kostroma painters. A museum in the monastery is devoted to their lives and work. The church also houses the tomb containing the remains of Dmitri Pozharsky, one of the resistance leaders against the Polish invaders in the Time of Troubles. Adjoining the church is a single-dome nave church, which is actually the original Church of the Transfiguration; it was built in 1509, constructed over the grave of St. Yefim, the monastery's founder. Every hour on the hour there's a wonderful chiming of the church's bells. The 16th-century **Church of the Assumption** (Uspenskaya Tserkov), next door to the larger Church of the Transfiguration of the Savior, is one of the earliest examples of tent-roof architecture in Russia.

In the middle of the 18th century, part of the monastery became a place for "deranged criminals," many of whom were in actuality political prisoners. The prison and hospital are along the north wall and closed to visitors. ✉*Ul. Lenina* ☎*No phone* 💳*Monastery grounds 50R, for grounds and all museums 300R* 🕐*Tues.–Sun. 10–4. Closed last Thurs. of month.*

In addition to being a religious institution, the **Convent of the Intercession** *(Pokrovsky Monastyr)* was also a place for political incarcerations. Basil III divorced his wife Solomonia in 1525 and banished her here when she failed to produce a male heir. Basil may have chosen this monastery because, in 1514, he had commissioned the splendid octagonal, three-dome Cathedral of the Intercession here, as supplication for a male heir. Interestingly, local legend has it that Solomonia subsequently gave birth to a boy and then staged the child's death to hide him from Basil. You can overnight in cozy *izbas* (wooden cabins) inside the convent, and dine in one of the town's best restaurants, here on the convent grounds. The convent sits across the Kamenka River from Spaso Yefimsky, in an oxbow bend of the river. To get here, turn east off ulitsa Lenina onto ulitsa Stromynka, and then go north on Pokrovskaya ulitsa. ☎*09231/20–889* 🎫*50R* ⊙ *Wed.–Mon. 9:30–4. Closed last Fri. of month.*

WHERE TO STAY & EAT

Unlike other towns of the Golden Ring, Suzdal offers various accommodations to choose from. The town's older hotels have improved their facilities in recent years; several new hotels and a dozen small guesthouses have also opened. For a more comprehensive list of Suzdal accommodations, see ⊕*www.suzdal.org.ru.*

$$ ✕**Trapeznaya.** Excellent Russian fare such as grilled sturgeon and pancakes with red caviar is served in the Convent of the Intercession itself, making this place one of the best dining options around, if you can get past the slow service. ⊠*Convent of the Intercession* ☎*49231/20–889* ▤*No credit cards.*

$$ ✕**Trapeznaya Kremlya.** Arguably the best restaurant in town, and not to be confused with the restaurant of the same name in the Convent of the Intercession, this is a pleasant Russian-style eatery within the Suzdal kremlin. The quality of your meals may depend on the day of the week you visit; it's likely to be better on weekdays than on weekends when the restaurant is crowded. If you don't want to order a full meal, consider trying some tea and *keks* (cakes) or *pirozhnoye* (pastry), all-day selections in Russia. ⊠*Archbishop's Chambers, Suzdal kremlin* ☎*49231/20–937* ▤*No credit cards.*

$$$ 🏨**Tourcenter.** Formerly known as the GTK Tourist Complex, a large complex divided into separate functioning units, this hotel used to be a rather basic, Soviet-style property, with middling service. However, it is now under new management and has considerably improved its amenities and service. The motel section has two-story rooms with separate street entrances; some even have garages. The Suzdal section offers 30 big rooms, plus winning personal service. A good way to explore the appealing grounds around Suzdal is to rent a snowmobile at Tourcenter in winter. **Pros:** nice pool; bowling alley in hotel. **Con:** the complex is huge but can get crowded with tour groups on some weekends and public holidays. ⊠*7 ul. Korovniki, 601260* ☎*49231/21–530 or 49231/20–908* 🖷*49231/207–66* ⬦*430 rooms* ⌂*In-hotel: restaurant, pool* ▤*No credit cards.*

$$–$$$ 🏨**Pokrovskaya.** These rustic accommodations are in 19th-century log cabins, also known as *izbas* (peasant wood cottages), on the grounds of the Convent of the Intercession. **Pros:** nice views of the monastery and its grounds; delicious pancakes for breakfast. **Cons:** staying inside the functioning monastery requires that you dress appropriately and be relatively quiet. ⊠*Pokrovsky Monastyr, 601260* ☎*49231/20–889* ⬦*30 rooms* ⌂*In-hotel: restaurant* ▤*No credit cards.*

$–$$ 🏨**Sokol Hotel.** This recently opened hotel is in the historic part of the town, a pleasant 10-minute walk to the kremlin. Guest rooms are clean, have all amenities, and have great views of the churches. The hotel offers tours of Suzdal, horseback riding, and snowmobile trips around the town. **Pro:** hearty breakfast included. **Con:** some staff may not speak English. ✉*2A Torgovaya Pl., 601260* ☎*495/925–1566 or 495/916–3364* ⊕*www.hotel-sokol.ru* ➾*39 rooms* ⚑*In-hotel: restaurant* ⊟*No credit cards.*

$ 🖼**Dom Kuptsa Likhonina.** A cozy bed-and-breakfast option in a 17th-century house, this was formerly the abode of a rich merchant. **Pro:** cozy. **Con:** must book in advance. ✉*34 Slobodskaya ul., 601260* ☎*49231/21–901* ➾*8 rooms* ⚑*In-room: refrigerator* ⊟*No credit cards* ⊟*No credit cards.*

$ 🖼**Tatyana's House.** A good alternative to a hotel, this guesthouse in a white-brick two-story building is just a five-minute walk to the Museum of Wooden Architecture and the kremlin. Guests are welcomed by the owner, Tatyana, with a hearty traditional Russian meal and vodka and awake to a breakfast of pancakes, eggs, and sandwiches. The host can also arrange for a traditional Russian banya experience, tours of the town, and horseback riding. This is an ideal option for groups as you can rent out either floor (3,000R–4,000R) for six to eight people or the whole house (8,000R) for 10 to 15 people. **Pro:** cozy; central location; warm welcome. **Con:** guests share bathrooms. ✉*46B Lenina ul., 601260* ☎*49231/2–3006* ➾*5 rooms with shared bath* ⊟*No credit cards.*

MOSCOW ENVIRONS & THE GOLDEN RING ESSENTIALS

TRANSPORTATION

BY BOAT

Cruises from Moscow to St. Petersburg along the Moscow-Volga canal, visit just one city of the Golden Ring, Yaroslavl. *For more information, see Moscow Essentials in Chapter 1.*

BY BUS

Though it's not as comfortable as traveling by train, the bus can be a decent way to travel as long as it's not the height of summer, when the vehicles can be exceedingly stuffy. Buses run on direct routes to all the towns of the Golden Ring. And, to get to two towns—Pereslavl-Zalessky and Suzdal—by public transport, you'll need to travel by bus at least part of the way.

For short-distance travel between towns, buses can't be beat. But buses are the most unreliable form of long-distance transport. Be sure to check schedules before you leave Moscow to make sure that there are plenty of return buses if you need one.

FARES & SCHEDULES Pereslavl-Zalessky is a three-hour journey from Moscow's Central Bus Station (Tsentralny Avtovokzal). There are four buses daily that run between the capital and Pereslavl-Zalessky; many other buses travel farther on and simply stop here. There are also four buses each day between Pereslavl-Zalessky and Sergiev-Posad (about a one-hour ride).

From Moscow it's a five-hour trip to Rostov and a 1- or 1½-hour trip to Sergiev-Posad. Vladimir is four hours and Yaroslavl is six hours from Moscow. Just one daily bus goes directly to Suzdal from Moscow, departing at 5 PM and taking five hours. It's best to take the train or bus to Vladimir and then change to a bus (running nearly every hour) between Vladimir and Suzdal.

Contact **Central Bus Station** (⊠ *75 Schelkovskoe shosse, Moscow* ☎ *495/468–0400* ⊕ *www.mostransavto.ru/index.php?page=avshelk* Ⓜ *Schelkovskaya*).

BY CAR

For the towns of the Golden Ring, which lie relatively close to one another and are connected by some of Russia's best paved roads, travel by car is by far the most flexible option. There's no problem getting gas in these towns.

BY TAXI

You'll usually have no trouble getting a taxi at a train or bus station in these towns, which is important, because the stations are often far from the town center. Most of the towns are small enough to be navigated easily on foot, but a taxi may be a desirable alternative to short bus trips (e.g., from Vladimir out to Bogolyubovo, from Vladimir to Suzdal, or from Tula to Yasnaya Polyana).

BY TRAIN

There are plenty of trains running on the main routes (Moscow–Yaroslavl and Moscow–Nizhny Novgorod) on which most all the towns in this region lie, so it's quite easy to travel between towns here, as well as to and from Moscow. Two types of trains will get you to most of these towns: *elektrichkas* (suburban commuter trains) and normal long-distance trains. In addition to being cheaper, elektrichkas run more frequently. But they are also a bit less comfortable, and there's no reserved seating. Check with a local travel agent in Moscow or at the station itself for train schedules. With the exception of traveling by elektrichka at busy times (Friday evenings and weekends), you should not have trouble getting a ticket the same day you wish to travel.

FARES & SCHEDULES

Most elektrichkas will stop in all the towns listed here; it's best to double-check, however, which stops your long-distance train makes.

Commuter trains to Klin, site of Tchaikovsky's House Museum, depart from Moscow's Leningrad station. For the New Jerusalem Monastery, take an elektrichka from Moscow's Rizhsky station and get off at Istra. From there take any local bus to the Muzey (museum) stop. Rostov is four hours by long-distance train from Yaroslavsky station in Moscow, and five hours by elektrichka (changing in Aleksandrov). Elektrichkas also run regularly between Rostov and Yaroslavl (originating in Moscow's Yaroslav station); the trip lasts 1–1½ hours. Sergiev-Posad is 1½ hours by elektrichka from Yaroslavsky station. Vladimir is a three- to four-hour train ride by long-distance train from Moscow's Kursk station. There is no train directly to Suzdal. To get there, take the train to Vladimir, then catch one of the frequent buses to Suzdal that run every hour from Vladimir bus station. Although there's a train station near Yasnaya Polyana, the commuter trains departing from Moscow's Kursk station run only to Tula. The trip takes about three hours. Yaroslavl is five hours by long-distance train from Moscow's Yaroslav station. *For train station information, see Moscow Essentials in Chapter 1.*

CONTACTS & RESOURCES

BANKS & EXCHANGE SERVICES

You'll find far fewer exchange points or ATMs in these smaller towns than in Moscow and St. Petersburg. Look for bureaus in the larger hotels or banks downtown.

TOUR OPTIONS

There are several local and international travel agents who specialize in tours to the Golden Ring and Moscow environs. Seattle-based Mir Corporation is particularly good for individual travelers and also conducts regular tours to Russia that include the Golden Ring. Moscow-based Patriarshy Dom Tours offers a variety of one-day and multiday tours throughout the Golden Ring at very reasonable rates.

Contacts **Mir Corporation** (☎ 800/424–7289 ⊕ www.mircorp.com).

Patriarshy Dom Tours (☎ 495/795–0927 in Moscow or 650/678–7076 in the U.S. ⊕ www.russiatravel-pdtours.netfirms.com).

VISITOR INFORMATION

There's no regional tourist office dealing with the Golden Ring region. Any questions should be directed to travel agencies and guided tour companies in Moscow. The State Historical Architecture and Art Vladimir-Suzdal Museum-Reserve Web site (⊕ *www.museum.vladimir.ru*) has some interesting information on Vladimir and Suzdal.

St. Petersburg

WORD OF MOUTH

"OMG—Of course it is 'worth it'! St Petersburg is an amazing place with one museum alone (the Hermitage) worth a day by itself. Plus palaces, gardens and so on."

—janisj

"I thought all the little canals and bridges were magical. For me, [St. Petersburg] was a lovely city to wander around. A boat cruise was fun too, as was this great evening event on summer weekends, where they timed a fountain in the middle of the Neva to lights and music—nice crowds of locals enjoying the evening, with drinks and snacks from little carts. Peterhof and the museums are great too, but there are plenty of 'small' moments here."

—alyssabc

Updated by
Matt Brown &
Irina Titova

COMMISSIONED BY TSAR PETER THE Great (1672–1725) as "a window looking into Europe," St. Petersburg is a planned city whose elegance is reminiscent of Europe's most alluring capitals. Little wonder it's the darling of today's fashion photographers and travel essayists: built on more than a hundred islands in the Neva Delta linked by canals and arched bridges, it was first called the "Venice of the North" by Goethe, and its stately embankments are reminiscent of those in Paris. An Imperial city of golden spires and gilded domes, of pastel palaces and candlelit cathedrals, it's filled with pleasures and tantalizing treasures.

3

"The most abstract and intentional city on earth"—to quote Fyodor Dostoyevsky—became the birthplace of Russian literature, the setting for Dostoyevsky's Crime and Punishment and Pushkin's *Eugene Onegin*. From here, Tchaikovsky, Rachmaninov, Prokofiev, and Rimsky-Korsakov went forth to conquer the world of the senses with unmistakably Russian music. It was in St. Petersburg that Petipa invented—and Pavlova, Nijinsky, and Ulanova perfected—the ballet, the most aristocratic of dance forms. Later, at the start of the 20th century, Diaghilev enthralled the Western world with the performances of his Ballets Russes. Great architects were summoned to the city by 18th-century empresses to build palaces of marble, malachite, and gold. A century later it was here that Fabergé craftsmen created those priceless objects of beauty that have crowned the collections of royalty and billionaires ever since.

The grand, new capital of the budding Russian empire was built in 1703, its face to Europe, its back to reactionary Moscow, which had until this time been the country's capital. It was forcibly constructed, stone by stone, under the might and direction of Peter the Great, for whose patron saint the city is named. But if Peter's exacting plans called for his capital to be the equal of Europe's great cities, they always took into account the city's unique attributes. Peter knew that his city's source of life was water, and whether building palace, fortress, or trading post, he never failed to make his creations serve it.

St. Petersburg is not just about its fairy-tale setting, however, for its history is integrally bound up in Russia's dark side, too—a centuries-long procession of wars and revolutions. In the 19th century, the city witnessed the struggle against tsarist oppression. Here the early fires of revolution were kindled, first in 1825 by a small band of starry-eyed aristocratic officers—the so-called Decembrists—and then by organized workers' movements in 1905. The full-scale revolutions of 1917 led to the demise of the Romanov dynasty, the foundation of the Soviet Union, and the end of St. Petersburg's role as the nation's capital as Moscow reclaimed that title. But the worst ordeal by far came during World War II, when the city—then known as Leningrad—withstood a 900-day siege and blockade by Nazi forces. Nearly 1.1 million civilians were killed in air raids, as a result of indiscriminate shelling, or died of starvation and disease.

TOP REASONS TO GO

The State Hermitage Museum: The pearl of the world's historical and art collections, you can see everything from works by Monet, Picasso, and Matisse to the opulence of tsarist Russia, from Egyptian mummies to Scythian gold.

St. Isaac's Cathedral: The third largest cathedral in the world dominates St. Petersburg's skyline, with a gilded dome covered in 100 kg (220 lbs) of pure gold. Climb the colonnade for a great panoramic view of the city.

White Nights: If you are planning to visit in May through July you'll be witness to this unusual phenomenon where the city is aglow in daylight throughout the night. Enjoy the romance and the beauty of the illu-

minated nights on the banks of the Neva River.

Mariinsky Opera and Ballet Theatre: Known for ballet stars such as Anna Pavlova, Vaslav Nijinsky, Rudolf Nureyev, and Mikhail Baryshnikov who once graced its stage, this theater also turns out great modern ballet as well as opera performances by the likes of Anna Netrebko.

Peter and Paul Fortress: St. Petersburg was founded at this site which Peter the Great built. It never saw battle, though, and instead became a political prison for Peter's rebellious son, Alexei and later held Dostoyevsky, Gorky, and Trotsky to name a few. The dynasty of Russian tsars is buried within the fortress.

St. Petersburg has had its name changed three times during its brief history. With the outbreak of World War I, it became the more Russian-sounding Petrograd. After Lenin's death in 1924, it was renamed Leningrad in the Soviet leader's honor. After the demise of the Soviet Union, the city's original name was restored by popular vote. But for all the controversy surrounding the name, residents have generally referred to the city simply—and affectionately—as Piter.

EXPLORING ST. PETERSBURG

The city's focal point is the Admiralteistvo, or Admiralty, a spire-top golden-yellow building; a stone's throw away is the Winter Palace, the city's most visited attraction. Three major avenues radiate outward from the Admiralty: Nevsky prospekt (St. Petersburg's main shopping street), Gorokhovaya ulitsa, and Voznesensky prospekt. Most visitors begin, however, at Palace Square, site of the fabled Hermitage.

Wherever you go exploring in the city, remember that an umbrella can come in handy. In winter be prepared for rather cold days that alternate with warmer temperatures, often resulting in the famous Russian snowfalls. One note: as with most Russian museums, you will find that St. Petersburg's museums charge a small extra fee to entitle you to use your camera or video camera within their walls.

Prices in this chapter are provided in rubles for sightseeing attractions, restaurants, and hotels. In Russia prices are officially listed in rubles.

However, you may still see some prices listed in "conditional units." The "unit" is basically that day's dollar rate, or increasingly in St. Petersburg, that day's euro rate.

GETTING ORIENTED

The city can be divided into approximately nine neighborhoods. The City Center embraces Palace Square, the Hermitage, and the northern end of Nevsky prospekt, with the Fontanka River as its southeastern border. Most of St. Petersburg's major attractions are within this area. To the west of the City Center is the smaller neighborhood of the Admiralteisky, surrounding the Admiralty building.

Second in number of sights, including the Chamber of Art and the Rostral Columns, is Vasilievsky Island, opposite the Admiralty and set off from the City Center by the Little and Great Neva rivers.

North of the City Center and the Neva River is the Petrograd Side, which holds Peter and Paul Fortress and the sights of Petrograd Island. Back on the mainland, Vladimirskaya is an area south of the Fontanka, taking in the lower part of Nevsky prospekt and bordered by the Obvodny Canal. The Liteiny/Smolny region lies to the northeast of Vladimirskaya and includes the Smolny cathedral. The Kirov Islands (north of the city), the Southern Suburbs, and the Vyborg Side (in the northeast corner of the city) have just a few sights.

St. Petersburg is a large city of almost 5 million inhabitants, which makes it as likely a place for petty crime as any other metropolis. As a foreigner, you're an even more likely target. Whatever you've heard about crime and poverty in Russia has probably been exaggerated, but you should still exercise caution if you wander too far off the beaten path.

Numbers in the text correspond to numbers in the margin and on the St. Petersburg map.

CITY CENTER: PALACE SQUARE & THE HERMITAGE
ДВОРЦОВАЯ ПЛОЩАДЬ & ЭРМИТАЖ

The best place to get acquainted with St. Petersburg is the elegant Dvortsovaya Ploshchad, or Palace Square. Its scale alone can hardly fail to impress—the square's great Winter Palace was constructed to clearly out-Versailles Versailles—and within the palace is the best reason to come to St. Petersburg, the Hermitage. Renowned as one of the world's leading picture galleries, it also served as a residence of the Russian Imperial family, and provides a setting of unparalleled opulence for its dazzling collections, which include some of the greatest old master paintings in the world. As a relief from all this impressive glitz and grandeur, tucked away in the shadows of the great Imperial complex is the moving apartment museum of Alexander Pushkin, that most Russian of writers, set in a neighborhood that still enchantingly conjures up early-19th-century Russia.

GREAT ITINERARIES

IF YOU HAVE 3 DAYS
If you have only three days, begin your visit of the city on Vasilievsky Island and the Left Bank. Most of the city's historic sites are here, including the Rostral Columns, the Admiralty (Admiralteistvo), and St. Isaac's Cathedral. If you have the energy after lunch, dedicate some time to the State Museum of Russian Art, one of the country's most important art galleries. On your second day, rise early to tackle the gargantuan Hermitage, one of the world's richest repositories of art. Don't try to see it all in one visit, instead, cross the river to the Petrograd Side and have lunch by the Peter and Paul fortress. After lunch spend the afternoon touring the Peter and Paul Fortress. On your third day, consider an excursion to Pushkin (formerly Tsarskoye Selo), south of St. Petersburg, once the summer residence of the Imperial family and a popular summer resort for the Russian aristocracy.

The main attraction here is the Catherine Palace, with its magnificent treasures including the famed Amber Room. If you have the energy, take in a performance at the famed Mariinsky Theatre.

IF YOU HAVE 5 DAYS
Follow the three-day itinerary described above. Devote your fourth day to St. Petersburg's inner streets, squares, and gardens. Begin with the grandeur of Ploshchad Iskusstv, or Square of the Arts. Here you can visit the Ethnography Museum before moving on to the colorful Church of the Savior on Spilled Blood and the Field of Mars (*Marsovo Pole*). Finish your walk at the Summer Garden with its famous railing designed by Yuri Felten in 1779. After lunch, visit the Kazan Cathedral. On the fifth day, head west of St. Petersburg to Peterhof (*Petrodvorets*), accessible by hydrofoil. The fountains, lush parks, and the magnificent Great Palace are at their best in the summer.

TIMING   Strolling through the Palace Square and taking in the sights from the outside may only take an hour or so, but it is a great introduction to St. Petersburg. The entire Hermitage cannot be seen in one day; you'll want to devote anywhere from a morning to two days to wander through it.

MAIN ATTRACTIONS

④ Alexander Column (*Aleksandrovskaya Kolonna*, Александровская Колонна). The centerpiece of Palace Square is a memorial to Russia's victory over Napoléon. Approximately 156 feet tall, it was commissioned in 1830 by Nicholas I in memory of his brother, Tsar Alexander I, and was designed by Auguste Ricard de Montferrand. The column was cut from a single piece of granite and, together with its pedestal, weighs more than 650 tons. It stands in place by the sheer force of its own weight; there are no attachments fixing the column to the pedestal. When the memorial was erected in 1832, the entire operation took only an hour and 45 minutes, but 2,000 soldiers and 400 workmen were required along with an elaborate system of pulleys and ropes. Crowning the column is an angel (symbolizing peace in Europe) crushing a snake, an allegorical depiction of Russia's defeat of Napoléon. ⌂*Dvortsovaya Pl., City Center* Ⓜ*Nevsky Prospekt.*

1 **Dvortsovaya Ploshchad** (*Palace Square*, Дворцовая Площадь). One of
the world's most magnificent plazas, the square is a stunning ensemble of buildings and open space, a combination of several seemingly
incongruous architectural styles in perfect harmony. It's where the city's
Imperial past has been preserved in all its glorious splendor, but it also
resonates with the history of the revolution that followed. Here, the
fate of the last Russian tsar was effectively sealed, on Bloody Sunday in
1905, when palace troops opened fire on peaceful demonstrators, killing scores of women and children. It was across Palace Square in October 1917 that Bolshevik revolutionaries stormed the Winter Palace in a
successful attempt to overthrow Kerensky's Provisional Government,
an event that led to the birth of the Soviet Union. Almost 75 years later,
during tense days, huge crowds rallied on Palace Square in support of
perestroika and democracy. Today, the beautiful square is a bustling
hubbub of tourist and marketing activity, lively yet seemingly imper-
turbable as ever. Horseback and carriage rides are available for hire
here. A carriage ride around the square costs about 200R per person. A
20-minute tour of the city in the direction of your choosing costs about
2,000R, for up to six people. ⊠ *City Center* Ⓜ *Nevsky Prospekt.*

3 **State Hermitage Museum** (*Gosudarstvenny Ermitazh Muzey,*
Государственный Эрмитаж). Leonardo's *Benois Madonna* . . . Rembrandt's *Danaë* . . . Matisse's *The Dance* . . . you get the picture. As the
former private art collection of the tsars, this is one of the world's most
famous museums, virtually wallpapered with celebrated paintings. In
addition, the walls are works of art themselves, for this collection is
housed in the lavish Winter Palace, one of the most outstanding examples of Russian baroque magnificence. The museum takes its name
from Catherine the Great (1729–96), who used it for her private apartments, intending them to be a place of retreat and seclusion. "Only the
mice and I can admire all this," the empress once declared.

Between 1764 and 1775, the empress undertook, in competition with
rulers whose storehouses of art greatly surpassed Russia's, to acquire
some of the world's finest works of art. In doing so, sometimes acquir-
ing entire private collections outright, she quickly filled her gallery
with masterpieces from all over the world. This original gallery section
of the Hermitage, completed in 1770 by Vallin de la Mothe, is now
known as the Maly (Little) Hermitage. It's attached to the Stary (Old)
Hermitage, which was built in 1783 by Yuri Felten to house the overflow of art, and also contained conference chambers for the tsarina's
ministers. Attached to the Hermitage by an arch straddling the Winter
Canal is the **Hermitage Theater** built between 1783 and 1787, created
for Catherine the Great by the Italian architect Giacomo Quarenghi.
Yet another addition, the New Hermitage, was built between 1839
and 1852 under Catherine's grandson, Nicholas I; it became Russia's
first public museum, although admission was by royal invitation only
until 1866. Its facade is particularly striking, with 10 male figures cut
from monolithic gray granite supporting the portico. Today's Hermitage is one of the world's richest repositories of art; it was continually
enlarged with tsarist treasures and acquisitions, all later confiscated and

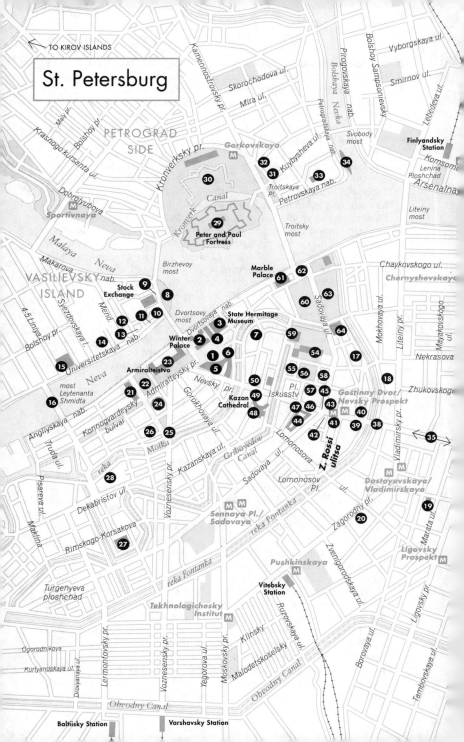

Minerainaya ul.

Zhukova ul.

VYBORG
SIDE

Arsenalnaya ul.

Kondratyevsky pr.

Sverdlovskaya nab.

hchad
na

Neva

nab.

palernaya ul.

53

Tavrichesky
Park

ova-Shchedrina ul.

LITEINY
SMOLNY

Suvorovsky pr.

Grechesky pr.

8 Sovetskaya ul.

Moiseyenko ul.

Mytninskaya ul.

Novgorodskaya

shchad
sstaniya/
yakovskaya

skovsky
ion

VLADIMIRSKAYA

Staro Nevsky pr.

A. Nevsky
Pl.

most
A. Nevsky

Ploshchad
Aleksandra Nevskovo

Alexander
Nevsky Lavra

36

Bolsheokhtinsky
most

Tulskaya ul.

Neva

Bakunina

Obuchovsky pr.

Glinyanaya ul.

51 52

53

3

KEY

Ⓜ *Metro stops*

nationalized, along with numerous private collections, by the Soviet government after the 1917 Bolshevik Revolution.

The entrance to the museum is through the main gates on Palace Square. When you first enter the Hermitage you'll see a *kassa* (ticket window) on both the right and left. Once you purchase your tickets, you can check your belongings and then return to enter the hall that was to your left as you entered the museum. Be forewarned that the ticket-takers are strict about oversize bags and about foreigners trying to enter on Russian-rate tickets.

> **BEST BETS**
>
> ■ **For Architecture**: Dvortsovaya Ploshchad, St. Isaac's Cathedral
>
> ■ **For Art**: State Hermitage Museum
>
> ■ **For Romance**: Strelka
>
> ■ **For Kids**: Zoological Museum
>
> ■ **For Military Sight**: *Avrora* cruiser ship
>
> ■ **For History**: Peter and Paul Fortress

With more than 400 exhibit halls and gilded salons, it's impossible to see everything here in a single day. It has been estimated that in order to spend one minute on each object on display, you would have to devote several years to the museum. Since you probably only have a few hours, be sure to take in the major attractions such as: Egyptian mummies and Scythian gold; the splendid halls of Russian tsars; the Peacock Clock; the great paintings of Leonardo, Rembrandt, Van Dyck, and Velaskes; and the outstanding collection of impressionists and postimpressionists.

Official guided tours (in English) tend to be rushed and you may want to return on your own. Consider hiring a private guide from outside the museum instead—their licensing requires a year of study and training and they'll take their time explaining the artwork to you. For information on private guides, *see* the Tour Options *in* the Essentials section of this chapter. During peak tourist season, or when there's a special exhibition, you may encounter long lines at the museum entrance. Note that the Hermitage is closed on Monday.

Although the museum is divided into eight sections, they are not clearly marked, and the floor plans available are not very useful, though they are in English as well as Russian. To orient yourself before your trip, you can go on a virtual tour of the museum on the Web site (⊕*www.hermitagemuseum.org*). Just after you have your ticket checked at the front entrance, head straight to the computer consoles in front of you—the plans shown here are similarly short on information, but you can print them out, complete with instructions on how to get to various rooms. Enjoy your wander, and don't be shy about asking the guards to point you in the right direction. There's also a helpful information desk in the main hall, before you go into the museum, where you can ask specific questions.

There are three floors to wander through. The **ground floor** covers prehistoric times, displaying discoveries made on former Soviet territory,

The Peacock Clock

The Peacock Clock (*Tchasy Pavlin*), one of the most delightful pieces on display at the State Hermitage Museum, is found in the Pavilion Hall on the first floor. The clock consists of a gilded peacock on a branch, a rooster, and an owl in a cage. Designed by the famous London jeweler and goldsmith James Cox and brought in pieces to St. Petersburg for Russian empress Catherine the Great in 1781, the clock is still in working order. Over the past decades it has been wound once a week to activate the moving pieces—the peacock spreads its wings and turns in a circle, the rooster crows, and the owl opens and closes its eyes—but recently the museum has cancelled this weekly ritual to save the aging mechanisms. Even without motion the clock is still a must-see. If you have kids with you, ask them to count all the creatures on the clock. There are more than just the three birds, like the dragonfly that acts as the tiny second hand on the mushroom dial.

including Scythian relics and artifacts; art from the Asian republics, the Caucasus, and their peoples; and Greek, Roman, and Egyptian art and antiquities. On the ground floor, head for the Hall of Ancient Egypt, the Pazyryk exhibition, and the Hall of the Big Vase. The first contains the remains of a mummified priest; the second, a mummified Scythian tsar and his horses as well as the most ancient carpet in the world; the third, a magnificent example of Russian stone-carving—the huge Kolyvan vase in the center of the hall. It's 2.57 meters (2.81 yards) high and weighs 19 tons.

Possibly the most prized section of the Hermitage—and definitely the most difficult to get into—is the ground floor's **Treasure Gallery**, also referred to as the Zolotaya Kladovaya (Golden Room). This spectacular collection of gold, silver, and royal jewels is well worth the hassle and expense of admission. The collection is divided into two sections. The first section, covering prehistoric times, includes Scythian gold and silver treasures of striking simplicity and refinement recovered from the Crimea, Ukraine, and Caucasus. The second section contains a dizzying display of precious stones, jewelry, and such extravagances as jewel-encrusted pillboxes and miniature clocks, all from the 16th through the 20th centuries.

You'll find the Pavilion Hall on the **first floor** which is known for the wonderous Peacock Clock. The hall itself, with 28 crystal chandeliers, is impressive in its own right. The Knights' Room is also on this floor, with knights' armor on display, including a child-size and a horse suit of armor.

You'll also find many rooms that have been left as they were when the Imperial family lived in the Winter Palace on the first floor. Through the entrance hall you can reach the first-floor galleries by way of the Jordan Staircase, a dazzling 18th-century creation of marble, granite, and gold. One of the first rooms you pass through on the first floor is the Malachite Room, with its displays of personal items from the

Imperial family. In the White Dining Room the Bolsheviks seized power from the Provisional Government in 1917. Balls were staged in the small Concert Hall (which now also holds the silver coffin, and just the coffin, of the hero Alexander Nevsky) and, on grand occasions, in the Great Hall.

A wealth of Russian and European art is also on this floor: Florentine,

Venetian, and other Italian art through the 18th century, including Leonardo's *Benois Madonna* and *Madonna Litta* (Room 214), Michelangelo's *Crouching Boy* (Room 229), two Raphaels, eight Titians, and works by Tintoretto, Lippi, Caravaggio, and Canaletto. The Hermitage also houses a superb collection of Spanish art, of which works by El Greco, Velázquez, Murillo, and Goya. Its spectacular presentation of Flemish and Dutch art contains roomfuls of Van Dycks, including portraits done in England when he was court painter to Charles I. Also here are more than 40 canvasses by Rubens (Room 247) and an equally impressive number of Rembrandts, including *Flora, Abraham's Sacrifice,* and *The Prodigal Son* (Room 254). The famous *Danaë,* which was mutilated by a knife- and acid-wielding lunatic in 1985, is back on exhibition once again. A smattering of excellent British paintings, extending also to the next floor, includes works by Joshua Reynolds, Thomas Gainsborough, and George Morland.

Reflecting the Francophilia of the Empresses Elizabeth and Catherine, the museum is second only to the Louvre in its collection of French art. The scope is so extraordinary that the collection must be housed on both the first and second floors. Along with masterpieces by Lorrain, Watteau, and Poussin—including Poussin's *Tancrède et Herminie* (Room 279)—there are also early French art and handicrafts, including some celebrated tapestries.

On the **second floor,** you can start with the French art of the 19th century, where you'll find Delacroix, Ingres, Corot, and Courbet. You then come to a stunning collection of impressionists and postimpressionists, originally gathered mainly by two prerevolutionary industrialists and art collectors, Sergei Shchukin and Ivan Morozov. They include Monet's deeply affecting *A Lady in the Garden,* Degas's *Woman at Her Toilette* and *After the Bath,* and works by Sisley, Pissarro, and Renoir. Sculptures by Auguste Rodin and a host of pictures by Cézanne, Gauguin, and van Gogh are followed by Picasso and a lovely room of Matisse, including one of the amazing *Joys.* Somewhat later paintings—by the Fauvist André Derain and by Cubist Fernand Léger, for example—are also here. Rounding out this floor is the museum's collection of Asian and Middle and Near Eastern art, a small American collection, and two halls of medals and coins.

The Fate of Rembrandt's Danaë

One of the most celebrated of Rembrandt's works, and among the most beautiful examples of European painting, the *Danaë* was almost irreparably damaged in 1985 when a mentally deranged man twice knifed and then splashed sulfuric acid on the painting in front of a stunned tour group. Acquired by Catherine the Great in 1772, it was one of the jewels of her collection. After the shocking act of vandalism the canvas, completed by the Dutch master in 1636, was a mess of brown spots and splashes. The process of restoration began the same day, when after consulting chemists, the Hermitage restorers washed the canvas with water to stop the chemical reaction. It then took 12 years to reconstruct the picture, which was finally placed on view again in 1997. It's now covered with armored glass to prevent any further damage. The painting is not 100% Rembrandt anymore, but the original spirit of the work remains intact.

The best deal is to buy a two-day combined-entrance ticket, which allows you to visit the State Hermitage Museum and three other splendid museums: the original, wooden Winter Palace of Peter the Great, accessible through a tunnel (historians believe this is the site where Peter the Great died) from the museum; the General Staff Building; and Menshikov Palace. Tours in English (of several sections of the museum or just the Treasure Gallery) are available and highly recommended. Tours are normally given once or twice a day at 11:40 AM and 2:40 PM, but it's best to call ahead to be sure. An exchange bureau, Internet café, and theater ticket office are on the premises. ⊠*2 Dvortsovaya Pl., City Center* ☎*812/710–9625, or 812/710–9079, 812/571–8446 tours* ⊕*www.hermitagemuseum.org* ✉*State Hermitage Museum 350R (free 1st Thurs. of month), two-day combined-entrance ticket 700R (this can only be purchased through the Web site), Treasure Gallery 300R* ☉*Tues.–Sat. 10:30–6, Sun. 10:30–5; kassa open Tues.–Sat. until 5, Sun. until 4* Ⓜ*Nevsky Prospekt.*

2 **Winter Palace** *(Zimny Dvorets,* Зимний Дворец*).* With its 1,001 rooms swathed in malachite, jasper, agate, and gilded mirrors, this famous palace—the residence of Russia's rulers from Catherine the Great (1762) to Nicholas II (1917)—is the focal point of Palace Square. The palace, now the site of the State Hermitage Museum, is the grandest monument of that strange hybrid, the Russian rococo, in itself an eye-popping mix of the old-fashioned 17th-century baroque and the newfangled 18th-century neoclassical style (at the time of the palace's construction a chic import from France).

Fodor's Choice
★

The palace, which was created by the Italian architect Bartolomeo Francesco Rastrelli, stretches from Palace Square to the Neva River embankment. The current palace was commissioned in 1754 by Peter the Great's daughter Elizabeth. By the time it was completed, in 1762, Elizabeth had died and the craze for the Russian rococo style had waned. Catherine the Great left the exterior unaltered but had the interiors redesigned in the neoclassical style of her day. In 1837, after the palace was gutted by fire, the interiors were revamped once again. Three of the most celebrated rooms are the **Gallery of the 1812 War,** where portraits of Russian commanders who served against Napoléon are on display; the **Great Throne Room,** richly decorated in marble and bronze; and the **Malachite Room,** designed by the architect Alexander Bryullov and decorated with columns and pilasters of malachite. These rooms and parts of the Winter Palace that encompass the State Hermitage Museum are the only bits of the palace on view to the public. When touring the museum, you must therefore think of portions of it as the Imperial residence it once was. ✉ *Dvortsovaya Pl., City Center* ☎ *812/710—9625 or 812/710–9079* ⊕ *www.hermitagemuseum.org* 🎫 *200R* ⊙ *Tues.—Sat. 10:30—5, Sun.10:30—4 kassa open Tues.–Sat. until 4, on Sun. until 3* Ⓜ *Nevsky Prospekt.*

ALSO WORTH SEEING

❼ **Alexander Pushkin Apartment Museum** *(Muzey Kvartira Alexandra Push-*
★ *kina,* **Музей-квартира Александра Пушкина***)*. After fighting a duel to defend his wife's honor, the beloved Russian poet Alexander Pushkin died in a rented apartment in this building (which, at the end of the 18th century, had been the palace of Prince Volkhonsky) on January 27, 1837. The poet lived out the last act of his illustrious career here, and what a life it was. Pushkin (b. 1799) occupies in Russian belles lettres the position enjoyed by Shakespeare and Goethe in the respective literatures of England and Germany. He is most famous as the author of *Eugene Onegin*, the ultimate tale of unrequited love, whose Byronic hero is seen more as the victim than as the arbiter of his own fate (a new sort of "hero" who cleared the path for the later achievements of Tolstoy and Chekhov). At the heart of this story—which involves a young genteel girl who falls in love with Onegin only to be rejected, then years later winds up rejecting Onegin when he falls in love with her—is a sense of despair, which colored much of Pushkin's own life and death. The poet, alas, was killed by a dashing count who had openly made a play for Pushkin's wife, Natalya Goncharova, reputedly "the most beautiful woman in Russia."

Pushkin actually lived at this address less than a year (and could afford it only because of the palace owners, the noble Volkhonsky family, co-sympathizers with the poet for the Decembrist cause). The apartment museum has been restored to give it the appearance of an upper-middle-class dwelling typical of the beginning of the 19th century. Pushkin had to support a family of six with his writing, so it's not surprising that his apartment was actually less luxurious than it looks now. Although few of the furnishings are authentic, his personal effects (including the waistcoat he wore during the duel) and those of his wife are on display. The library, where Pushkin actually expired, has been rebuilt according to sketches made by his friend and fellow poet Vasily Zhukovsky, who was holding vigil in his last hours. A moving tape-recorded account leads you through the apartment and retells the events leading up to the poet's death.

After you've seen Pushkin's deathbed, it's worth visiting the small **Konyushennaya Church** (✉ *1 Konyushennaya Pl., City Center*) around the corner, where his funeral was held on February 1, 1837. Coming out of Moika 12, turn right, and right again at the bridge; the Imperial stables and Konyushennaya Square are on your left. The door to the left of the passageway in the central portion of the stables is the entrance to the church. Pushkin's funeral was held here, some say, to keep a low profile (the church was too small for a big crowd to attend), and perhaps as a special favor from Emperor Nicholas I, since the church was attached to the palace and not open to the public. Its coziness, light, and warmth make the church, which was built between 1816 and 1823 by Stassov, a very tranquil stop. It's open daily 9 to 7. ✉ *12 nab. Moika, City Center* ☎ *812/314–0006* ⊕ *www. museumpushkin.ru* ✉ *100R; audioguide in English, German, French, or Italian 100R* ☾ *Wed.–Mon. 10:30–5. Closed last Fri. of month* Ⓜ *Nevsky Prospekt.*

> ## PUSHKIN: RUSSIA'S POETIC LOVE
>
> Alexander Pushkin is undoubtedly the most beloved poet in Russia and most any citizen can quote from his poetry the way Westerners may quote Shakespeare. "Moroz I solntse! Den chudesnyi!" ("Snow, frost and sunshine. Lovely morning!") Russians exclaim on a clear winter day, reciting lines from "Winter Morning" ("Zimneye Utro"). Though he only lived to be 37, he had many loves, was exiled by Tsar Alexander I for his criticism of the monarchy, and married one of the most beautiful women of his time, Natalya Goncharova.

NEED A BREAK?

The **Pushka Inn** (✉ *14 nab. Moika, City Center* ☎ *812/312–0957* Ⓜ *Nevsky Prospekt*), a business-class hotel and bar-restaurant right next to the Alexander Pushkin Apartment Museum, is a great place to grab a refreshing drink and something to eat at any time of the day. The extensive menu includes *blini* (pancakes) with caviar, homemade *pelmeni* (meat dumplings), borscht, and *vareniki* (a Ukrainian dish—dumplings filled with all kinds of stuffing such as cabbage, cherries, and mushrooms). The name is both a play on Pushkin's name and the Russian word for cannon—which explains the military-theme paintings and the miniature cannon near the entrance. The spot is popular with members of the expatriate community.

❺ **General Staff Building** (*Glavny Shtab*, Главный Штаб). The eastern side of Palace Square is formed by the huge arc of this building whose form and size give the square its unusual shape. During tsarist rule this was the site of the army headquarters and the ministries of foreign affairs and finance. Created by the architect Carlo Giovanni Rossi in the neoclassical style and built between 1819 and 1829, the General Staff Building is actually two structures connected by a monumental archway. Together they form the longest building in Europe. The arch itself is another commemoration of Russia's victory over Napoléon. Topping it is an impressive 33-foot-tall bronze of Victory driving a six-horse chariot, created by the artists Vasily Demut-Malinovsky and Stepan Pimenov. An errant flare partly melted the statue on New Year's

Eve 2000, necessitating lengthy repairs. The passageway created by the arch leads from Palace Square to St. Petersburg's most important boulevard, Nevsky prospekt. Part of the Hermitage, the building has a permanent display on its history and architecture, plus temporary exhibits of local and international artwork. ⊠ *Dvortsovaya Pl., City Center* 🕾 *812/311–3420* 🌐 *www.hermitagemuseum.org* 🎫 *200R, 700R for multi-access ticket to several branches of State Hermitage Museum* ⊙ *Tues.–Sun. 10:30–6, kassa open until 5* Ⓜ *Nevsky Prospekt.*

❻ **Headquarters of the Guard Corps** *(Shtab Gvardeiskovo Korpusa,* **Штаб Гвардейского Корпуса***).* This modest structure serves as an architectural buffer between the neoclassical General Staff Building to the left of it and the baroque Winter Palace. Designed by the architect Alexander Bryullov and built between 1837 and 1843, the building is noteworthy for the very fact that it easily goes unnoticed. Instead of drawing attention to itself, it leads the eye to the other architectural masterpieces bordering Palace Square. The restraint shown in Bryullov's creation was considered the ultimate architectural tribute to the masters who came before him. ⊠ *Dvortsovaya Pl., City Center* Ⓜ *Nevsky Prospekt.*

THE ADMIRALTEISKY & VASILIEVSKY ISLAND
АДМИРАЛТЕЙСТВО & ВАСИЛЬЕВСКИЙ

The Admiralteisky is the area just west of the City Center. It is centered around the famous golden-yellow Admiralteistvo, or Admiralty building. This neighborhood is also home to Decembrists' Square, the site of the December 14, 1825 Decembrist revolt. One of the city's most famous monuments, the Bronze Horseman dedicated to Peter the Great, is located in the middle of the square. Across the Neva river is Vasilievsky Island. Peter the Great wanted his city center to be on Vasilievsky Ostrov (Vasilievsky Island), the largest island in the Neva Delta and one of the city's oldest developed sections. His original plans for the island called for a network of canals for the transport of goods from the main sea terminal to the city's commercial center at the opposite end of the island. These plans to re-create Venice never materialized, although some of the smaller canals were actually dug (and later filled in). These would-be canals are now streets, and are called "lines" *(liniya)*. Instead of names they bear numbers, and they run parallel to the island's three main thoroughfares: the Great (Bolshoi), Middle (Sredny), and Small (Maly) prospekts. Now the island is a popular residential area, with most of its historic sites concentrated on its eastern edge. The island's western tip, facing the Gulf of Finland, houses the city's main sea terminals.

TIMING The two neighborhoods, Admiralteisky and Vasilievsky Island, are separated by the Neva River and linked by the bridge Most Leytenanta Shmidta. If you don't want to linger very long at each sight, touring the neighborhoods should take four or five hours and you should plan to take a lunch break midday.

St. Petersburg in Literature

"On an exceptionally hot evening early in July, a young man came out of the garret in which he lodged in S. Place and walked slowly, as though in hesitation, towards K. Bridge." Thus opens Fyodor Dostoyevsky's *Crime and Punishment,* one of the greatest crime stories ever written, with the protagonist Rodion Raskolnikov making his way through 19th-century St. Petersburg. Both the grand landmarks and miserable details of St. Petersburg were so powerfully inspiring to the giants of Russian literature that the city became as much an inseparable part of their writing as it was of their lives.

The beloved Russian poet Alexander Pushkin (1799–1837) lived and died in St. Petersburg, and he honored the mighty capital in his works. In his epic *Bronze Horseman,* he immortalized the equestrian statue of Peter the Great on Decembrists' Square. In the poem, a poor clerk imagines that the rearing statue—which evokes the creative energy and ruthlessness of Peter—comes to life and chases him though the streets. In his poetic novel *Eugene Onegin,* Pushkin writes of St. Petersburg's early-19th-century high society—of balls, receptions, theaters, and ballets.

In contrast, Dostoyevsky's St. Petersburg is a place of catastrophes, strange events, crimes, and dramas. His heroes live desperate lives in a dank city of slums, poverty, and hopelessness. Fyodor Dostoyevsky (1821–81) was born in Moscow but spent much of his life in St. Petersburg, and was so scrupulous about describing the city that you can find many of the places where his "brainchildren"—as he called his characters—lived. Dostoyevsky lived at 19 ulitsa Grazhdans-

kaya for a time, and many believe this is the apartment he used as a model for Raskolnikov's home. Dostoyevsky wrote that on his way to murder the elderly pawnbroker, Raskolnikov took 730 steps from his lodgings to the victim's lodging at 104 Kanal Griboyedova/25 ulitsa Rimskovo-Korsakova. You can re-create this walk, though it requires more than 730 steps.

Nikolai Gogol (1809–52) also portrayed a shadowy St. Petersburg—a city of nonsensical businesslike character and ridiculous bureaucratic fuss. In Gogol's short story "The Nose," the protagonist, low-rank civil servant Kovalyov, loses his nose and must search through St. Petersburg to find it. The nose starts boosting its own bureaucratic career, obtains a higher rank than its owner, and ignores the desperate Kovalyov. To mark Gogol's satirical story, a bas-relief nose is displayed at the corner of Voznesenskii prospekt and ulitsa Rimskogo-Korsakova. The "memorial" regularly gets stolen.

The poetry of Anna Akhmatova (1889–1966) reflects the changing face of St. Petersburg (renamed Petrograd and then Leningrad) during her lifetime. Born in the St. Petersburg suburb of Tsarskoye Selo, Akhmatova wrote romantic and nostalgic verse about her beloved city at the beginning of her career. As the city changed, so did her poetry, based in part on her firsthand experience of Stalin's repression. Her son was imprisoned and her works were harshly denounced by government officials. Her poem "Requiem" describes the horrors of those times. During the siege of Leningrad, Akhmatova read on the city radio her poems of support for the hungry and dying city residents.

MAIN ATTRACTIONS

㉓ Admiralty *(Admiralteistvo,* **Адмиралтейство***)*. The Admiralty is considered the city's architectural center, and its flashing spire—visible at various points throughout the city—is one of St. Petersburg's most renowned emblems. To get the picture-perfect first impression, walk around to the front of this lovely golden-yellow building.

A series of important constructions, all related to the naval industry, predate the current building. The first was a shipyard of Peter the Great's, followed by an earthen fortress that guarded the port; after these came the first Admiralty, made of stone and topped by the famous spire that has endured to grace each successive structure.

Used as a shipbuilding center through the 1840s, it has belonged to the Higher Naval Academy since 1925 and is closed to the public. ✉*Admiralteisky pr., Admiralteisky* Ⓜ*Nevsky Prospekt.*

⑪ Chamber of Art *(Kunstkammer,* **Кунсткамера***)*. The Chamber of Art, also called the Chamber of Curiosities, is a fine example of the Russian baroque. Painted bright azure with white trim, the building stands out from the surrounding classically designed architecture. Its playful character seems to reflect its beginnings; it was originally commissioned in 1718 to house Peter the Great's collection of oddities, gathered during his travels. Completed by 1734, the Kunstkammer (from the German *Kunst,* "art," and *Kammer,* "chamber") was destroyed by fire in 1747 and almost entirely rebuilt. Today it houses the **Museum of Anthropology and Ethnography** but still includes a room with Peter's original collection, a truly bizarre assortment ranging from rare precious stones to preserved human organs and fetuses. The museum is enormously popular, so purchase entrance tickets early in the day. ✉*3 Universitetskaya nab., Vasilievsky Island* ☎*812/328–1412* 💳*200R* ☾*Tues.–Sun. 11–6, kassa open until 4:45. Closed last Tues. of month.* Ⓜ*Vasileostrovskay.*

㉒ Decembrists' Square *(Ploshchad Dekabristov,* **Площадь Декабристов***)*. This square, which was originally called Senatskaya Ploshchad (Senate Square), holds one of St. Petersburg's best-known landmarks: the gigantic equestrian statue of Peter the Great. The name "Decembrists' Square" refers to the dramatic events that unfolded here on December 14, 1825, when, following the death of Tsar Alexander I (1777–1825), a group of aristocrats staged a rebellion on the square in an attempt to prevent the crowning of Nicholas I (1796–1855) as the new tsar and perhaps do away with the monarchy altogether. Their coup failed miserably, as it was suppressed with much bloodshed by troops already loyal to Nicholas, and those rebels who were not executed were banished to Siberia. Although the Decembrists, as they came to be known, did not bring significant change to Russia in their time, their attempts at liberal reform were often cited by the Soviet regime as proof of deep-rooted revolutionary fervor in Russian society. In 1925 the square was renamed in their honor; it has since reverted to its original name of Senate Square, but nobody uses this title.

In the center of the square is the grand statue called the **Medny Vsadnik** (Bronze Horseman), erected as a memorial from Catherine the Great to her predecessor, Peter the Great. The simple inscription on the base reads, TO PETER THE FIRST FROM CATHERINE THE SECOND, 1782. Created by the French sculptor Étienne Falconet and his student Marie Collot, the statue depicts the powerful Peter, crowned with a laurel wreath, astride a rearing horse that symbolizes Russia, trampling a serpent representing the forces of evil. The enormous granite rock on which the statue is balanced comes from the Gulf of Finland. Reportedly, Peter liked to stand on it to survey his city from afar. Moving it was a Herculean effort, requiring a special barge and machines and nearly a year's work. The statue was immortalized in a poem of the same name by Alexander Pushkin, who wrote that the tsar "by whose fateful will the city was founded beside the sea, stands here aloft at the very brink of a precipice, having reared up Russia with his iron curb." ⊠ *Ploshchad Dekabristov, Admiralteisky* Ⓜ *Sennaya Ploshchad.*

❾ Rostral Columns (*Rostralnyie Kolonny,* **Ростральные Колонны**)*.* Swiss architect Thomas de Thomon designed these columns, which were erected between 1805 and 1810 in honor of the Russian fleet. The monument takes its name from the Latin *rostrum,* meaning "prow." Modeled on similar memorials in ancient Rome, the columns are decorated with ships' prows; sculptures at the base depict Russia's main waterways, the Dnieper, Volga, Volkhov, and Neva rivers. Although the columns originally served as lighthouses—until 1855 this was St. Petersburg's commercial harbor—they are now lit only on special occasions, such as City Day on May 27. They were designed to frame the architectural centerpiece of this side of the embankment—the old Stock Exchange, which now holds the Naval Museum. ⊠ *Birzhevaya Pl., Vasilievsky Island* Ⓜ *Vasileostrovskaya.*

㉔ St. Isaac's Cathedral (*Isaakievsky Sobor,* **Исаакиевский Собор**)*.* Of the grandest proportions, St. Isaac's is the world's third-largest domed cathedral and the first monument you see of the city if you arrive by ship. Its architectural distinction is a matter of taste; some consider the massive design and highly ornate interior to be excessive, whereas others revel in its opulence. Tsar Alexander I commissioned the construction of the cathedral in 1818 to celebrate his victory over Napoléon, but it took more than 40 years to actually build it. The French architect Auguste Ricard de Montferrand devoted his life to the project, and died the year the cathedral was finally consecrated, in 1858.

Tickets, which can be bought at the kassa outside, are sold both to the church ("the museum") and to the outer colonnade; the latter affords an excellent view of the city. Follow the signs in English. The interior of the cathedral is lavishly decorated with malachite, lazulite, marble, and other precious stones and minerals. Gilding the dome required 220 pounds of gold. At one time a Foucault pendulum hung here to demonstrate the axial rotation of the earth, but it was removed in the late 20th century. After the Revolution of 1917 it was closed to worshippers and in 1931 was opened as a museum; services have since resumed. St. Isaac's was not altogether returned to the Orthodox Church, but

Christmas and Easter are celebrated here (note that Orthodox holidays follow the Julian calendar and fall about 13 days after their Western equivalents).

When the city was blockaded during World War II, the gilded dome was painted black to avoid its being targeted by enemy fire. Despite efforts to protect it, the cathedral nevertheless suffered heavy damage, as bullet holes on the columns on the south side attest.

Opening up in front of the cathedral is **Isaakievskaya Ploshchad** (St. Isaac's Square), which was completed only after the cathedral was built. In its center stands the **Nicholas Statue.** Unveiled in 1859, this statue of Tsar Nicholas I was commissioned by the tsar's wife and three children, whose faces are engraved (in the allegorical forms of Wisdom, Faith, Power, and Justice) on its base. It was designed, like St. Isaac's Cathedral, by Montferrand. The statue depicts Nicholas on a rearing horse. Other engravings on the base describe such events of the tsar's reign as the suppression of the Decembrists' uprising and the opening ceremonies of the St. Petersburg–Moscow railway line.

To one side of the cathedral, where the prospekt meets Konnogvardeisky bulvar, is the early-19th-century **Konnogvardeisky Manège**, gracefully designed by Giacomo Quarenghi and decorated with marble statues of the mythological twins Castor and Pullox. This former barracks of the Imperial horse guards is used as an art exhibition hall. Every January it hosts an exhibition of new works by St. Petersburg artists. ⊠*1 Isaakievskaya Pl., Admiralteisky* ☎*812/315–9732* 🖅*Cathedral 300R, colonnade 150R* ⊙*Cathedral May–Sept., Thurs.–Tues. 10 AM–7 PM and 8 PM–10:30 PM; Oct.–Apr., Thurs.–Tues. 11–6, and ? PM–9:30 PM* Ⓜ*Sennaya Ploshchad.*

ALSO WORTH SEEING

Anglijskaya naberezhnaya *(English Embankment,* **Английская набережная***)*. Before the Revolution of 1917 this was the center of the city's English community. Here you can find some of St. Petersburg's finest aristocratic estates–cum–overcrowded communal apartments. No. 28 (east of most Leytenanta Shmidta), for example, was formerly the mansion of Grand Duke Andrei Vladimirovich Romanov. Today it's called the **Palace of Marriages** and was once the only place under Communism where marriages could be performed; the state-run, secular ceremonies, still the usual type held here, are perfunctorily recited with assembly-line efficiency. Its baroque-style interiors are decorated with marble stairwells, statuary, golden candelabra, and huge mirrors. Many of the mansions on the embankment have been renovated and have become once again luxury real estate, whether office space or housing. ⊠*Admiralteisky* Ⓜ*Nevsky Prospekt.*

⓯ Egyptian Sphinxes *(Yegipetskiye Sfinksy,* **Египетские Сфинксы***).* On the landing in front of the Repin Institute, leading down to the Neva, stand two of St. Petersburg's more magnificent landmarks, the famous Egyptian Sphinxes. These twin statues date from the 15th century BC and were discovered during an excavation at Thebes in the 1820s. They were apparently created during the era of Pharaoh Amenhotep III, whose features they supposedly bear. It took the Russians more than a year to transport the sphinxes from Thebes. ⊠*Universitetskaya nab., Vasilievsky Island* Ⓜ*Vasileostrovska.*

NEED A BREAK? The restaurant **Idiot** (⊠ *82 nab. Moika, City Center* ☏*812/315–1675* Ⓜ*Sennaya Ploshchad*), about 100 meters from St. Isaac's Square along the Moika River in the direction of Yusupov Palace, is a favorite among St. Petersburg expatriates. Its entrance is marked by a discreet white globe with IDIOT inscribed on it. The cozy café would be at home in New York's East Village and serves hearty vegetarian Russian food, good seafood, and a nice cappuccino.

⓮ Menshikov Palace *(Menshikovsky Dvorets,* **Меншиковский Дворец***).* Alexander Menshikov (1673–1729), St. Petersburg's first governor, was one of Russia's more flamboyant characters. A close friend of Peter the Great (often called his favorite), Menshikov rose from humble beginnings as a street vendor, reportedly getting his start when he sold a cabbage pie to the tsar—or so the legend goes. He eventually became one of Russia's most powerful statesmen, but Menshikov was famous for his corruption and political maneuvering. He is said to have incited Peter the Great against his son Alexei, and later attempted to take power from Peter II by arranging the young tsar's engagement to his daughter. The marriage did not take place and the young tsar exiled Menshikov and his family to Siberia.

His palace, the first stone building in St. Petersburg, was, at the time of its completion in 1720, the city's most luxurious building. Although only a portion of the original palace has survived, it easily conveys a sense of Menshikov's inflated ego and love of luxury. Particularly noteworthy are the restored bedrooms: the walls and ceilings are completely covered with handcrafted ceramic tiles. It's said that Peter had them sent home from Delft for himself, but that Menshikov liked them and appropriated them. After Menshikov's exile to Siberia in 1727, his palace was turned over to a military training school and was significantly altered over the years. In June 1917 it served as the site of the First Congress of Russian Soviets. The Menshikov Palace is today a branch of the Hermitage Museum. In addition to the restored living quarters of the Menshikov family, there's an exhibit devoted to early-18th-century Russian culture. ⊠*15 Universitetskaya nab., Vasilievsky Island* ☏*812/323–1112* 🎟*200R, includes guided tour; 700R for multi-access ticket to State Hermitage Museum; 1,500R for English- or French-guided tour for up to 15 people: order by phone 1–2 days in advance* 🕙*Tues.–Sun. 10:30–4:30* Ⓜ*Vasileostrovskaya.*

⑯ Most Leytenanta Shmidta *(Lieu-tenant Schmidt Bridge,* **Мост Лейтенанта Шмидта***).* Built between 1842 and 1850 this was the first stationary bridge to connect Vasilievsky Island with the left bank of the Neva; it was renamed in honor of the naval officer who was a leader of the Black Sea Fleet mutiny during the 1905–07 Revolution. It has been renamed Blagoveschensky Bridge but it is still mainly known by its old name. ✉ *Vasilievsky Island* Ⓜ *Vasileostrovskaya.*

> ### BIGGER THAN IT SEEMS
>
> St. Petersburg, thanks to its intimate historic center, is thought of as a small city. But by population it is Europe's fourth largest city after Moscow, London, and Paris. At approximately 4.6 million people, St. Petersburg is bigger than Los Angeles and Detroit combined.

⑱ Russian Academy of Sciences *(Rossiiskaya Akademiya Nauk,* **Российская Академия Наук***).* Erected on strictly classical lines between 1783 and 1789, this structure, the original building of the Russian Academy of Sciences, is considered Giacomo Quarenghi's grandest design, with an eight-column portico, a pediment, and a double staircase. The administrative offices of the academy, founded in 1724 by Peter the Great, were transferred to Moscow in 1934. This building, which stands next to the Chamber of Art, now houses the St. Petersburg branch of the Russian Academy of Sciences and is not open to the public. ✉ *Universitetskaya nab., Vasilievsky Island* Ⓜ *Vasileostrovskaya.*

㉗ St. Nicholas Cathedral *(Nikolsky Sobor,* **Никольский Собор***).* This turquoise-and-white extravaganza of a Russian baroque cathedral was designed by S. I. Chevakinsky, a pupil of Bartolomeo Francesco Rastrelli. It's a theatrical showpiece, and its artistic inspiration was in part derived from the 18th-century Italian prints of the Bibiena brothers, known for their opera and theater designs. The church's wedding-cake silhouette, marked by a forest of white Corinthian pilasters and columns, closes ulitsa Glinka and makes the area a natural pole of attraction if you find yourself in the vicinity. Canals and green spaces surround the cathedral, which is also flanked by an elegant campanile. Inside are a lower church (low, dark, and warm for the winter) and an upper church (high, airy, and cool for the summer), typical of Russian Orthodox sanctuaries. The interior is no less picturesque than the outside. This is one of the few Orthodox churches that stayed open under Soviet power. It's also of special significance to the Russian navy; as such, the cathedral held the memorial service in honor of those who died aboard the *Kursk* nuclear submarine, which sank in 2000. If you go during a service, you'll likely hear the beautiful choir. ✉ *1/3 Nikolskaya Pl., Admiralteisky* ☎ *812/714–6926* ☉ *Daily, usually 6:30 AM–7:30 PM; morning services at 7 and 9 AM, vespers at 6 PM* Ⓜ *Sennaya Ploshchad.*

⑫ St. Petersburg State University *(Sankt-Peterburgskii Gosudarstvenny Universitet,* **Санкт-Петербургский Государственный Университет***).* In 1819 Tsar Alexander I founded this university, today one of Russia's leading institutions of higher learning, with an enrollment of more than 20,000. Its campuses date from the time of Peter the Great. The bright-red baroque building on the right (if you're walking west along the embankment) is the **Twelve Colleges Building,** named for the governmental administrative bodies established during Peter's reign. The building, which was designed by Domenico Trezzini and completed in 1741, 16 years after Peter's death, was transferred to the university at the time of its establishment and today houses the university library and administrative offices. It's not officially open to the public, but no one will stop you from looking around.

The next building in the university complex is the **Rector's Wing,** another red building in the yard of the Twelve Colleges Building, where a plaque on the outside wall attests that the great Russian poet Alexander Blok (d. 1921) was born here in 1880. The third building along the embankment is a former **palace** built for Peter II (1715–30), Peter the Great's grandson, who lived and ruled only briefly. Completed in 1761, the building was later given to the university. The palace is connected to the Twelve Colleges Building via a gate and its facade faces the Neva River. It's a three-story rectangular building with two-story wings. The three blocks together with the palace form a large inner courtyard. The palace houses one of the University's most prestigious departments of philology where dozens of foreign languages are taught. ⊠*7 Universitetskaya nab., Vasilievsky Island* Ⓜ *Vasileostrovskaya.*

㉑ **Senate and Synod** *(Senat i Synod,* **Сенат и Синод***).* Before the Revolution of 1917, this long, light-yellow building, built along classical lines, housed Russia's highest judicial and administrative bodies, the Senate and the Synod. It was designed by Carlo Rossi and erected between 1829 and 1834. In Soviet times the building housed state historical archives and was closed to the public. In need of serious repairs and deemed an unsafe home for the valuable collection of documents, Russian authorities decided to move the Russian Constitutional Court from Moscow to St. Petersburg and to house it in this building instead. At the end of 2006 the state historical archives were moved to their new building at Zanevsky prospekt 36. It took 10 months to transport 6.5 million archive files to the new location. The repairs of Senat and Synod should be complete by February of 2008, and in March of 2008 the Constitutional Court will make the move to St. Petersburg. ⊠*Dekabristov Pl., Admiralteisky* Ⓜ *Sennaya Ploshchad.*

㉕ **Siniy most** *(Blue Bridge,* **Синий мост***).* This bridge spanning the Moika River is so wide (328 feet) and stubby that it seems not to be a bridge at all but rather a sort of quaint raised footpath on St. Isaac's Square. It's named for the color of the paint on its underside. ⊠*Admiralteisky* Ⓜ *Sennaya Ploshchad.*

❽ **Strelka** (**Стрелка**). The Strelka ("arrow" or "spit") affords a dazzling view of both the Winter Palace and the Peter and Paul Fortress. This bit of land also reveals the city's triumphant rise from a watery outpost to an elegant metropolis. Seen against the backdrop of the Neva, the brightly colored houses lining the embankment seem like children's toys—the building blocks of a bygone aristocracy. They stand at the water's edge, seemingly supported not by the land beneath them but by the panorama of the city behind them. Gazing at this architectural wonder is a great way to appreciate the scope of Peter the Great's vision for his country. The view is also revealing because it makes clear how careful the city's founders were to build their city not despite the Neva but around and with it. The river's natural ebb and flow accord perfectly with the monumental architecture lining its course. The Strelka is very popular with wedding couples that traditionally come to visit the sight on their wedding day and often break a bottle of champagne on the ground here. It is a very romantic spot, especially in summer. ⊠ *Vasilevsky Island, at the north end of Dvortsovy Most (Palace Bridge), Vasilievsky Island* Ⓜ *Vasileostrovskaya.*

> ## NABOKOV
>
> Vladimir Nabokov was born in St. Petersburg to a rich noble family. Though he loved St. Petersburg, the Nabokovs fled Russia soon after the Bolshevik Revolution and would never return. In 1940 they left for the United States, where he wrote *Lolita* in English. Never forgetting his roots, he once said of himself, "I am an American writer, born in Russia, educated in England, where I studied French literature before moving for 15 years to Germany . . . My head speaks English, my heart speaks Russian, and my ear speaks French."

❷❻ **Vladimir Nabokov Museum-Apartment** *(Musei Kvartira Vladimira Nabokova,* **Музей-квартира Владимира Набокова***)*. Vladimir Nabokov (1899–1977), author of the novel *Lolita,* was born and lived in this apartment until his 18th year. Judging from Nabokov's novels, in which the author often describes his building in detail or at least mentions it, one can say that the writer always kept warm memories about his first home. When in exile, Nabokov lived in hotels or rented apartments in different cities but never had his own house. When asked why he didn't want to buy his own, he would answer, "I already have one in St. Petersburg." Although the museum has not restored interiors of the writer's apartment, it presents family photos; the writer's drawings and various editions of his books; some of his belongings; and his collection of butterflies, which was previously kept at Harvard University. All these exhibits are in one room on the first floor. The museum is very close to the Manège. ⊠ *47 ul. Bolshaya Morskaya, Admiralteisky* ☏ *812/315–4713* 💰 *100R* 🕙 *Weekdays Tues.–Fri. 11–6, weekends 12–5* Ⓜ *Sennaya Ploshchad.*

❷❽ **Yusupov Palace** *(Yusupovsky Dvorets,* **Юсуповский Дворец***)*. On the
★ cold night of December 17, 1916, this elegant yellow palace, which belonged to one of Russia's wealthiest families, the Yusupovs, became the setting for one of history's most melodramatic murders. Prince Yusupov and others loyal to the tsar spent several frustrating and frightening hours trying to kill Grigory Rasputin (1872–1916), who had strongly influenced the tsarina, who in turn influenced the tsar, during the tumultuous years leading up to the Bolshevik Revolution. On display in the palace, which is set on the bank of the Moika River, are the rooms in which Rasputin was (or began to be) killed, as well as

CLOSE UP

Rasputin: Faith Healer or Antichrist?

Neither a monk nor a priest as commonly believed, Rasputin was a wandering peasant who eventually came to exert great power over Nicholas II, the last Tsar of Imperial Russia. The royal family came under his spell when, claiming to have visions of the future and strange healing powers, they allowed him to see Nicholas's young son, Alexei. Alexei suffered from hemophilia, but when Rasputin prayed over the child, the hemorrhaging mysteriously stopped. The tsarina, Alexandra, soon came to believe that without Rasputin, her son would die. He became a regular palace visitor, though his presence was not always welcome. He was accused of scandalous misdeeds, including rape, and of having too much political control over the royal family. A number of people eventually tired of Rasputin's influence and conspired to murder him. On one cold December night in 1916, the mad healer was lured to the palace of Prince Felix Yusupov, where he was fed cakes and drinks laced with cyanide. To the horror of the conspirators, however, Rasputin was unaffected by their poisons. In desperation, they shot him several times and beat him before dumping him into the icy waters of the Neva River. His body was later found and autopsied; the results purportedly showed that he died of hypothermia, not cyanide or gunshot wounds.

a waxworks exhibit of Rasputin and Prince Yusupov (who was forced to flee the country when Rasputin's murder was uncovered). They are visible only on an organized tour given once daily in the late afternoon. Another organized tour (given several times daily during the afternoon) takes you through the former reception rooms of the second floor. As for the scene where the final acts of the drama were played out—the palace's underground tunnel—it is ostensibly off-limits, but you may be able to view the tunnel if you can avail yourself of the bathroom facilities on the lower level of the mansion. It's essential that you phone ahead at least a week in advance to arrange an English-language tour.

On a lighter note, the showpiece of the palace remains the jewel-like rococo theater, whose stage was once graced by Liszt and Chopin; today, concerts are still presented here, as well as in the palace's august and elegant White-Columns Room (concert tickets usually have to be purchased just before performance time). ✉ *94 nab. Moika, Admiralteisky* ☎ *812/314–9883, 812/314–8893 tours* 💶 *400R, extra 150R includes tour in Russian to Rasputin Rooms* ⊙ *Daily 10:45–5, tour in Russian Mon. 1:45. Closed 1st Wed. of month* Ⓜ *Sennaya Ploshchad.*

❿ Zoological Museum *(Zoologichesky Muzey,* Зоологический Музей*).*
☺ The prize of this zoological museum's unusual collection, which contains more than 40,000 species, is a stuffed mammoth recovered from Siberia in 1901. The museum also has impressive skeletons of whales and large fish, but no dinosaur fossils. The other stuffed animals, posed in natural compositions, run the gamut of world fauna: tigers, foxes, bears, goats, and many kinds of birds. A few families of penguins seem to proudly pose with their countless funny nestlings on a piece of artifi-

cial ice; a moose walks along a fading fall forest. The museum also has a large collection of butterflies and other insects. ⊠*1 Universitetskaya nab., Vasilievsky Island* ☎*812/328–0112* 💳*150R* ⊘ *Wed.–Mon. 11–6, kassa open until 4:50* Ⓜ*Vasileostrovskaya.*

THE PETROGRAD SIDE ПЕТРОГРАДСКАЯ СТОРОНА

St. Petersburg was born in the battles of the Northern Wars with Sweden, and it was in this area, on Hare Island (Zayachy Ostrov), that it all began: in 1703 Peter laid the foundation of the first fortress to protect the mainland and to secure Russia's outlet to the sea. Ever since, the small hexagonal island forms, as it were, the hub around which the city revolves. The showpiece of the island is the magnificent Peter and Paul Fortress, the starting point for any tour of this section of the city, which actually consists of a series of islands, and is commonly referred to as the Petrograd Side (Petrogradskaya Storona). Hare Island and the fortress are almost directly across the Neva from the Winter Palace. Cut off from the north by the moatlike Kronverk Canal, the island is connected by a footbridge to Trinity Square (Troitskaya Ploshchad, sometimes still referred to by its Soviet name, Revolution Square) on Petrograd Island (Petrogradsky Ostrov). Along with its famous monuments, this part of the city is also one of its earliest residential areas, and Troitskaya Ploshchad, named for the church that once stood here (demolished in 1934), is the city's oldest square.

TIMING   Simply walking around the sights on the Petrograd Side requires two or three hours. The main attraction, the Peter and Paul Fortress, can easily eat up an afternoon. Note that the cathedral within the fortress is closed on Wednesday.

MAIN ATTRACTIONS

㉞ *Avrora* (**Аврора**). This historic cruiser is permanently moored in front
☺ of the **Nakhimov Academy of Naval Officers.** Launched in 1903, it fought in the 1904–05 Russo-Japanese War as well as in World War II, but it's best known for its role in the Bolshevik Revolution. At 9:40 PM on November 7, 1917, the cruiser fired the shot signaling the storming of the Winter Palace. The revolution it launched brought itself under fire in the end. A cherished relic in the Soviet era—it was scuttled during the siege of Leningrad to keep it from being hit by a German shell, and resurfaced later—the *Avrora* was carefully restored in the 1980s and opened as a museum. The cruiser is a favorite of families, and on weekends you may encounter long lines. On display are the crew's quarters and the radio room used to broadcast Lenin's victory address. ⊠*4 Petrogradskaya nab., Petrograd Side* ☎*812/230–8440* 💳*Free; tours usually 200R per person, price depends on group size* ⊘ *Tues.–Thurs. and weekends 10:30–4, last tour at 3* Ⓜ*Gorkovskaya.*

㉙ **Peter and Paul Fortress** *(Petropavlovskaya Krepost,* **Петропавловская**
FodorsChoice **Крепость**). The first building in Sankt-Piter-Burkh, as the city was then
★ called, the fortress was erected in just one year, between 1703 and 1704, during the Great Northern War against Sweden. It was never used for its intended purpose, however, as the Russian line of defense

quickly moved farther north, and, in fact, the war was won before the fortress was mobilized. Instead, the fortress served mainly as a political prison, primarily under the tsars. The date on which construction began on the fortress is celebrated as the birth of St. Petersburg.

Cross the footbridge and enter the fortress through **St. John's Gate** (Ioannovskyie Vorota), the main entrance to the outer fortifications. Once inside, you'll need to stop at the ticket office, which is inside the outer fortification wall on the right.

Entrance to the inner fortress is through **St. Peter's Gate** (Petrovskiye Vorota). Designed by the Swiss architect Domenico Trezzini, it was built from 1717 to 1718. After you

> ## THE BURIAL PLACE OF TSARS
>
> Beginning with Peter the Great, the Cathedral of Saints Peter and Paul is the final resting spot of nearly all the tsars. Nicholas II, who was executed with his family in Yekaterinburg (Siberia) in 1918, was one notable exception. In 1998, what were thought to be the remains of Nicholas II and his family were found and buried here, but in July 2007 the remains of two more people, believed to be the tsarevich Alexei and his sister Maria, were found in Yekaterinburg. Experts are currently working on identifying the remains.

pass through St. Peter's Gate, the first building to your right is the **Artilleriisky Arsenal**, where weaponry was stored. Just to your left is the **Engineer's House** (Inzhenerny Dom), which was built from 1748 to 1749. It's now a branch of the Museum of the History of St. Petersburg (as are all exhibits in the fortress) and presents displays about the city's prerevolutionary history.

As you continue to walk down the main center lane, away from St. Peter's Gate, you soon come to the main attraction of the fortress, the **Cathedral of Saints Peter and Paul** (Petropavlovsky Sobor). Constructed between 1712 and 1733 on the site of an earlier wooden church, it was designed by Domenico Trezzini and later embellished by Bartolomeo Rastrelli. It's highly unusual for a Russian Orthodox church. Instead of the characteristic bulbous domes, it's adorned by a single, slender, gilded spire whose height (400 feet) made the church for more than two centuries the city's tallest building. The spire is identical to that of the Admiralty across the river, except that it's crowned by an angel bearing a golden cross. The spire remained the city's highest structure—in accordance with Peter the Great's decree—until 1962, when a television tower was erected (greatly marring the harmony of the city's skyline).

The interior of the cathedral is also atypical. The baroque iconostasis, designed by Ivan Zarudny and built in the 1720s, is adorned by freestanding statues. Another uncommon feature is the pulpit. According to legend, it was used only once, in 1901, to excommunicate Leo Tolstoy from the Russian Orthodox Church for his denouncement of the institution. You can exit the cathedral through the passageway to the left of the iconostasis. This leads to the adjoining **Grand Ducal Crypt**

(Usypalnitsa), built between 1896 and 1908. You can identify Peter the Great's tomb by the tsar's bust on the railing on the far right facing the iconostasis.

As you leave the cathedral, note the small classical structure to your right. This is the **Boathouse** (Botny Domik), built between 1762 and 1766 to house Peter the Great's boyhood boat. The boat has since been moved to the Naval Museum on Vasilievsky Island, and the building is not open to the public.

The long pink-and-white building to your left as you exit the cathedral is the **Commandant's House** (Komendantsky Dom), erected between 1743 and 1746. It once housed the fortress's administration and doubled as a courtroom for political prisoners. The Decembrist revolutionaries were tried here in 1826. The room where the trial took place forms part of the ongoing exhibits, which deal with the history of St. Petersburg from its founding to 1917. Across the cobblestone yard, opposite the entrance to the cathedral, stands the **Mint** (Monetny Dvor), which was first built in 1716; the current structure, however, was erected between 1798 and 1806. The mint is still in operation, producing coins, medals, military decorations, and *znachki,* or Russian souvenir pins. The coins that were taken along on Soviet space missions were made here.

Take the pathway to the left of the Commandant's House (as you're facing it), and you'll be headed right for **Neva Gate** (Nevskiye Vorota), built in 1730 and reconstructed in 1787. As you walk through its passageway, note the plaques on the inside walls marking flood levels of the Neva. The most recent, from 1975, shows the river more than 9 feet above normal. The gate leads out to the **Commandant's Pier** (Komendantskaya Pristan). Up above to the right is the **Signal Cannon** (Signalnaya Pushka), fired every day at noon. From this side you get a splendid view of St. Petersburg. You may want to step down to the sandy beach, where even in winter hearty swimmers enjoy the Neva's arctic waters. In summer the beach is lined with sunbathers, standing up or leaning against the fortification wall.

As you return to the fortress through the Neva Gate, you'll be following the footsteps of prisoners who passed through this gate on the way to their executions. Several of the fortress's bastions, concentrated at its far western end, were put to use over the years mainly as political prisons. One of them, **Trubetskoi Bastion,** is open to the public as a museum. Aside from a few exhibits of prison garb, the only items on display are the cells themselves, restored to their chilling, prerevolutionary appearance. The first prisoner confined in its dungeons was Peter the Great's own son, Alexei, who was tortured to death in 1718 for treason, allegedly under the tsar's supervision. The prison was enlarged in 1872, when an adjacent one, Alexeivsky Bastion, which held such famous figures as the writers Fyodor Dostoyevsky and Nikolai Chernyshevsky, became overcrowded with dissidents opposed to the tsarist regime. A partial chronology of revolutionaries held here includes some of the People's Will terrorists, who killed Alexander II in 1881; Lenin's elder brother Alexander, who attempted to murder Alexander III (and was executed for his role in the plot); and Leon Trotsky and Maxim Gorky, after taking part in the 1905 revolution. The Bolsheviks themselves imprisoned people here for a short period, starting with members of the Provisional Government who were arrested and "detained for their own safety" for a few days, as well as sailors who mutinied against the Communist regime in Kronstadt in 1921. They were apparently the last to be held here, and in 1925 a memorial museum (to the prerevolutionary prisoners) was opened instead. Some casements close to the Neva Gate have been converted into a printing workshop (**pechatnya**), where you can buy good-quality graphic art in a broad range of prices. Original late-19th-century presses are used to create lithographs, etchings, and linocuts depicting, most often, urban St. Petersburg landscapes, which make nice alternatives to the usual souvenirs. In the basement, the original foundations were excavated; different layers of the history of the fortress can thus be seen. ⊠3 *Petropavlovskaya Krepost, Petrograd Side* ☎812/230–6431, 232–9454 excursions 🖼*Cathedral 150R, cathedral and other sights and exhibitions 250R, audio guide in English 250R (purchase guide at the Fortress's new Information Center located at Ioanovsky Ravelin)* ⊘ *Thurs.–Tues. 11–6, kassa open until 5 Thurs.–Mon., until 4 on Tues. Cathedral of Sts. Peter and Paul closed Wed., fortress closed last Tues. of month* Ⓜ *Gorkovskaya.*

ALSO WORTH SEEING

㉚ Artillery Museum *(Artilleriysky Muzey,* **Артиллерийский Музей***).* Formerly the city's arsenal, this building was turned over to the Artillery Museum in 1872. You can't miss it—just look for the hundreds of pieces of artillery on the grounds outside. The museum itself dates from the days of Peter the Great, who sought to present the entire history of weaponry, with a special emphasis on Russia. Today the Artillery Museum is St. Petersburg's main army museum. Like the Naval Museum in the old Stock Exchange, it still has exhibits with a distinctly Soviet feel—if you're interested in circuit boards inside ballistic missiles, for example, this is the place to come. It also contains plenty of military curiosities both modern and ancient. ⊠7 *Alexandrovsky Park, Petrograd Side* ☎812/232–0296 🖼*300R* ⊘ *Wed.–Sun. 11–5, kassa open until 5. Closed last Thurs. of month* Ⓜ *Gorkovskaya.*

NEED A BREAK? The **Evropa Restaurant** (⊠ *3 nab. Mytninskaya, Petrograd Side* ☎ *812/230– 9462 or 812/972–3447* Ⓜ *Gorkovskaya*) **is on a ship permanently moored (the third in the row) in the Kronverk Canal, just south of the Artillery Museum. Below deck is a snug bar where you can enjoy a cup of strong coffee, a pastry, or even a shot of cognac. The restaurant on the second floor offers three different halls, two of which have magnificent views of the Hermitage Museum over the Neva River.**

Botanical Gardens *(Botanichesky Sad,* **Ботанический Сад***).* Founded as an apothecary garden for Peter the Great, the grounds here display millions—literally—of different forms of plant life. The gardens are near the cruiser *Avrora.* ⊠2 *ul. Professora Popova, Petrograd Side*

☎*812/234–1764* 💰*140R* ⊙*Hothouses Sat.–Thurs. 11–4; grounds mid-May–Sept., daily 10–6* Ⓜ*Petrogradskaya.*

㉜ Mosque (*Mechet,* **Мечеть***).* Built between 1910 and 1914 to serve St. Petersburg's Muslim community, the Mosque was designed after the Gur Emir in Samarkand, Uzbekistan, where Tamerlane, the 14th-century conqueror, is buried. The huge dome is flanked by two soaring minarets, and covered with sky-blue ceramics. In the style of St. Petersburg's northern architecture, the walls of the mosque are lined with rough, dark-gray granite. The inside columns, which support the arches under the dome, are faced with green marble. In the center of the praying hall is a huge chandelier upon which sayings from the Koran are engraved. It's open only during services. ✉*7 Kronversky pr., Petrograd Side* ☎*812/233–9819* ⊙*Services daily at 2:20* Ⓜ*Gorkovskaya.*

㉝ Peter the Great's Cottage (*Domik Petra Pervovo,* **Домик Петра Первого***).* Built in just three days in May 1703, this cottage was home to Peter the Great during construction of the Peter and Paul Fortress. It's made of wooden logs painted to resemble bricks. The stone structure enclosing the cottage was erected in 1784 by Catherine the Great to protect it from the elements. Inside, 18th-century furniture is on display, arranged as it might have been in Peter's day, along with a few of Peter's personal effects. The cottage consists of just three rooms, whose ceilings are surprisingly low—considering that Peter the Great was nearly 7 feet tall. In the courtyard in front of the cottage stands a bronze bust of the tsar. The large stone sculptures of the Shi-Tsza (Lion-Frogs) flanking the stairwell leading down the embankment side were brought to Russia from Manchuria in 1907. ✉*6 Petrovskaya nab., Petrograd Side* ☎*812/232–4576, 812/314–0374 tours (call ahead to schedule a tour)* 💰*200R* ⊙ *Wed.–Sun. 10–6, Mon. 10–5. Closed last Mon. of month* Ⓜ*Gorkovskaya.*

㉛ Russian Political History Museum (*Gosudarstvenny Muzey Politicheskoi Istorii Rossii,* **Государственный Музей Политической Истории России***).* "From Sublime to Ridiculous," the most popular permanent display at this museum, traces the history of Russia in the 20th century through paintings, posters, flags, and porcelain. Socialist realism is featured prominently in the collections. There are always several theme exhibitions on political figures, spies, and controversial historical personages such as Rasputin. The elegant house itself, which was built in the art nouveau style in 1905 by Alexander Goguen, is the former mansion of Mathilda Kshesinskaya, a famous ballerina and the mistress of the last Russian tsar, Nicholas II, before he married Alexandra. She left Russia in 1917 for Paris, where she married a longtime lover, Andrei Vladimirovich, another Romanov. One of Kshesinskaya's pupils was the great English ballerina Margot Fonteyn. The mansion served as Bolshevik committee headquarters in the months leading up to the October Revolution (an exhibit at the museum that reconstructs Lenin's study is a nod to this period). In 1957 it was linked to the adjoining town house by a rather nondescript central wing and turned into the Museum of the Great October Socialist Revolution; in 1991 it was given its current name. All that is left of the original interiors is the reception hall. Call in advance to arrange a guided tour. ✉*2/4 ul. Kuybysheva, Petrograd Side* ☎*812/233–7052* ✉*150R; 200R per person with Russian-speaking guide; 700R with English-speaking guide, per group of up to five people or 1,300R per group of 5–15 people* 🕑*Fri.–Wed. 10–6, kassa open until 5. Closed last Mon. of month* Ⓜ*Gorkovskaya.*

ʼPER NEVSKY PROSPEKT & VLADIMIRSKAYA (LOWER NEVSKY ʼOSPEKT) НЕВСКИЙ ПРОСПЕКТ & ВЛАДИМИРСКАЯ

"There is nothing finer than Nevsky prospekt, not in St. Petersburg at any rate, for in St. Petersburg it is everything . . ." wrote the great Russian author Nikolai Gogol more than 150 years ago. Today Nevsky prospekt may not be as resplendent as it was in the 1830s, when noblemen and ladies strolled along the elegant avenue or paraded by in horse-drawn carriages, but it's still the main thoroughfare, and remains the pulse of the city. Today, Nevsky is a retail center, complete with souvenir shops, clubs, neon lights, and young hipsters sporting some outrageous clothes.

TIMING If you want to just see the sights on Nevsky prospekt, you need only plan for a few hours of walking. The main attractions you will most likely want to visit are Kazan Cathedral, Alexander Nevsky Lavra, and Nevsky prospekt. If you want to do some shopping then you may spend another couple of hours at Gostiny Dvor department store. Most of the souvenir shops are on and around Nevsky prospekt.

MAIN ATTRACTIONS

㊱ **Alexander Nevsky Lavra (Александро-Невская Лавра)**. The word *lavra* ʼdorʼsChoice in Russian is reserved for a monastery of the highest order, of which ★ there are just four in all of Russia and Ukraine. Named in honor of St. Alexander Nevsky, this monastery was founded in 1710 by Peter the Great and given lavra status in 1797. Prince Alexander of Novgorod (1220–63), the great military commander, became a national hero and saint because he halted the relentless eastward drive for Russian territory by the Germans and the Swedes. Peter chose this site for the monastery, thinking that it was the same place where the prince had fought the battle in 1240 that earned him the title Alexander of the Neva (Nevsky); actually, the famous battle took place some 20 km (12 mi) away. Alexander Nevsky had been buried in Vladimir, but in 1724, on Peter's orders, his remains were transferred to the monastery that was founded in his honor.

Entrance to the monastery is through the archway of the elegant **Gate Church** (Tserkovnyye Vorota), built by Ivan Starov between 1783 and 1785. The walled pathway is flanked by two cemeteries—together known as the Necropolis of Masters of Arts—whose entrances are a short walk down the path. To the left lies the older **Lazarus Cemetery** (Lazarevskoye kladbische). The list of famous people buried here reads like a who's who of St. Petersburg architects and includes Quarenghi, Rossi, de Thomon, and Voronikhin. The cemetery also contains the tombstone of the father of Russian science, Mikhail Lomonosov. The **Tikhvinskoye kladbische** on the opposite side, is the final resting place of several of St. Petersburg's great literary and musical figures. The grave of Fyodor Dostoyevsky, in the northwestern corner, is easily identified by the tombstone's sculpture, which portrays the writer with his flowing beard. Continuing along the walled path you'll soon reach the composers' corner, where Rimsky-Korsakov, Mussorgsky, Borodin, and Tchaikovsky are buried. The compound includes an exhibition hall with temporary exhibits of "urban sculpture."

After this look at St. Petersburg's cultural legacy, return to the path and cross the bridge spanning the quaint **Monastyrka River.** As you enter the monastery grounds, the **Church of the Annunciation** (Tserkov Blagovescheniya), under renovation at this writing, greets you on your left. The red-and-white rectangular church was designed by Domenico Trezzini and built between 1717 and 1722. It now houses the Museum of City Sculpture (open daily 9:30–1 and 2–5), which contains models of St. Petersburg's architectural masterpieces as well as gravestones and other fine examples of memorial sculpture. Also in the church are several graves of 18th-century statesmen. The great soldier Generalissimo Alexander Suvorov, who led the Russian army to numerous victories during the Russo-Turkish War (1768–74), is buried here under a simple marble slab that he purportedly designed himself. It reads simply: "Here lies Suvorov." Opposite the church, a shop sells religious items and souvenirs.

Outside the church and continuing along the same path, you'll pass a millennial monument celebrating 2,000 years of Christianity on your right, before reaching the monastery's main cathedral, the **Trinity Cathedral** (Troitsky Sobor), which was one of the few churches in St. Petersburg allowed to function during the Soviet era. Designed by Ivan Starov and completed at the end of the 18th century, it stands out among the monastery's predominantly baroque architecture for its monumental classical design. Services are held here daily, and the church is open to the public from 6 AM until the end of the evening service around 8 PM. The magnificent interior, with its stunning gilded iconostasis, is worth a visit. The large central dome, adorned by frescoes designed by the great architect Quarenghi, seems to soar toward the heavens. The church houses the main relics of Alexander Nevsky.

As you leave the church, walk down the steps and go through the gate on the right. A door on the left bears a simple inscription, written by hand: SVEZHY KHLEB (fresh bread). Here you can buy delicious bread baked on the premises. After the gate comes a courtyard and, at the back of the church, a gate to yet another burial ground: **St. Nicholas Cemetery** (Nikolskoye Kladbishche), opened in 1863 and one of the most prestigious burial grounds of the time; it's open daily 9–8 (until 7 in winter). In 1927 the cemetery was closed and the remains of prominent people buried here, including novelist Goncharov and composer Rubinstein, were transferred over the course of several years to the Volkovskoye Cemetery and the Necropolis of Masters of Arts. This pilferage of the tombs went on until the 1940s, by which time valuable funeral monuments had been irretrievably lost. As you reach the steps of the little yellow-and-white church in the center (which gave

White Nights

St. Petersburg is located at 59 degrees north latitude, roughly the same latitude as Oslo, Norway; Stockholm, Sweden; and Anchorage, Alaska. Due to this northerly position, the summer months receive many more hours of sunlight, especially in June and July. Known as White Nights, the sun's short trip around this part of the earth creates an ethereal glow of twilight into the wee hours. "On such nights, it's hard to fall asleep because it's too light and because any dream will be inferior to this reality. Where a man doesn't cast a shadow, like water," wrote poet Joseph Brodsky. If you are visiting St. Petersburg during this time, you should partake in the many festivals, such as the Mariinsky Theatre's Stars of the White Nights, and spend at least one late night outdoors. Take

a walk around the historic center, by Peter and Paul Fortress, St. Isaac's Cathedral, and the State Hermitage Museum which all face the Neva. Stroll along the banks of the river until you come across a bridge such as Dvortsovy most (Palace Bridge) next to the Hermitage and stop to watch the ships pass through the open bridge. Each bridge has its own time schedule but they begin to open at approximately 1 AM and close at about 5 AM. If you don't want to stay out all night, be sure to stay on the side of the river that your hotel is on. However, getting trapped on the other side of the city is rather romantic and you'll see couples kissing on the embankment while "waiting" for the bridges to close.

its name to the graveyard), turn right and walk to a derelict chapel of yellow brick, which has been turned into a makeshift **monument to Nicholas II.** Photocopies stand in for photographs of the Imperial family; pro-monarchy white, yellow, and black flags hang from the ceilings; and passionate adherents have added primitive frescoes to the scene. Nearby, in front of Trinity Cathedral, is yet another final resting place on the lavra's grounds—the **Communist Burial Ground** (Kommunisticheskaya Ploshchadka), where, starting in 1919, defenders of Petrograd, victims of the Kronshtadt rebellion, old Bolsheviks, and prominent scientists were buried. The last to receive that honor were people who took part in the siege of Leningrad.

Entrance to the monastery grounds is free, although you are asked to make a donation. You must purchase a ticket for the two cemeteries of the Necropolis of Masters of Arts and the museum, and (as with most Russian museums) it costs extra to take photos or use a video camera. There are ticket kiosks outside the two paying cemeteries, after the gate, and inside the Tikhvin Cemetery, on the right side. ⊠ *1 Pl. Alexandra Nevskovo, Vladimirskaya* ☎ *812/274–1612* ⊕ *lavra.spb.ru* 🎫 *60R donation, Museum of City Sculpture 30R* ☉ *Fri.–Wed. 9:30– 5:30* Ⓜ *Ploshchad Alexandra Nevskovo.*

㊳ Anichkov most *(Anichkov bridge,* **Аничков мост***).* Each corner of this beautiful bridge spanning the Fontanka River (the name means "fountain") bears an exquisite equestrian statue designed by Peter Klodt and erected in 1841; each bronze sculpture depicts a phase of horse taming.

Taken down and buried during World War II, the beautiful monuments were restored to their positions in 1945. The bridge was named for Colonel Mikhail Anichkov, whose regiment had built the first wooden drawbridge here. At that time, early in the 18th century, the bridge marked the city limits, and the job of its night guards was much the same as that of today's border guards: to carefully screen those entering the city. As you cross the bridge, pause for a moment to look back at No. 41, on the corner of Nevsky and the Fontanka. This was formerly the splendiferous **Palace of Prince Beloselsky-Belozersky**—a highly ornate, neobaroque pile designed in 1848 by Andrei Stackenschneider, who wanted to replicate Rastrelli's Stroganovsky Dvorets. The facade of blazing red stonework and whipped-cream stucco trim remains the most eye-knocking in St. Petersburg. The lavish building, once opulent inside and out, housed the local Communist Party headquarters during the Soviet era. Today it is the setting for classical music concerts. The interiors have been largely destroyed and are no longer as magnificent as the facades.

44 **Gostinny Dvor** (**Гостиный Двор**). Taking up an entire city block, this is St. Petersburg's answer to the GUM department store in Moscow. Initially constructed by Rastrelli in 1757, it was not completed until 1785, by Vallin de la Mothe, who was responsible for the facade with its two tiers of arches. At the time the structure was erected, traveling merchants were routinely put up in guesthouses (called *gostinny dvor*), which, like this one, doubled as places for doing business. This arcade was completely rebuilt in the 19th century, by which time it housed some 200 general-purpose shops that were far less elegant than those in other parts of the Nevsky. It remained a functional bazaar until alterations in the 1950s and 1960s connected most of its separate shops into St. Petersburg's largest department store. Today Gostinny Dvor houses fashionable boutiques, and you can also find currency-exchange points and ATMs here. Virtually across the street, at 48 Nevsky prospekt, is the city's other major "department store," also an arcade, called **Passazh**, built in 1848. ✉ *35 Nevsky pr., City Center* ☎ *812/710–5408* ☉ *Daily 10–10* Ⓜ *Gostinny Dvor.*

48 **Kazan Cathedral** *(Kazansky Sobor,* **Казанский Собор***)*. After a visit to Rome, Tsar Paul I (1754–1801) commissioned this magnificent cathedral, wishing to copy—and perhaps present the Orthodox rival to—that city's St. Peter's. It was erected between 1801 and 1811 from a design by Andrei Voronikhin. You approach the huge cathedral through a monumental, semicircular colonnade. Inside and out, the church abounds with sculpture and decoration. On the prospekt side the frontage holds statues of St. John the Baptist and the apostle Andrew as well as such sanctified Russian heroes as Grand Prince Vladimir (who advanced the Christianization of Russia) and Alexander Nevsky. Note the enormous bronze front doors—exact copies of Ghiberti's Gates of Paradise in Florence's Baptistery.

In 1932 the cathedral, which was closed right after the revolution, was turned into the Museum of Religion and Atheism, with emphasis on the latter. The history of religion was presented from the Marxist point of view, essentially as an ossified archaeological artifact. The museum has since moved to 14 Pochtamtskaya ulitsa, not far from St. Isaac's Cathedral and opposite the main post office (the *pochtamt*). Kazan Cathedral is once again a place of worship.

At each end of the square that forms the cathedral's front lawn are statues of a military leader—at one end, one of Mikhail Barclay de Tolly, at the other, Mikhail Kutuzov. They reflect the value placed in the 19th century on the cathedral as a place of military tribute, especially following Napoléon's invasion in 1812. Kutuzov is buried in the cathedral's northern chapel, where he's supposed to have prayed before taking command of the Russian forces. ⊠ *2 Kazanskaya Pl., City Center* ☎ *812/314–4663* ⊙ *Open daily 8:30–8; services weekdays at 10* AM *and 6* PM, *weekends at 7 and 10* AM *and 6* PM Ⓜ *Nevsky Prospekt.*

3

❸❺ **Nevsky prospekt** (Невский проспект). St. Petersburg's Champs-Élysées,
★ Nevsky prospekt was laid out in 1710, making it one of the city's first streets. Just short of 5 km (3 mi) long, beginning and ending at different bends of the Neva River, St. Petersburg's most famous street starts at the foot of the Admiralty building and runs in a perfectly straight line to the Moscow station, where it curves slightly before ending a short distance farther at the Alexander Nevsky Lavra. Because St. Petersburg was once part of the larger lands of Novgorod, the road linking the city to the principality was known as Great Novgorod Road; it was an important route for trade and transportation. By the time Peter the Great built the first Admiralty, however, another major road clearly was needed to connect the Admiralty directly to the shipping hub. Originally this new street was called the Great Perspective Road; later it was called the Nevskaya Perspektiva, and finally Nevsky prospekt.

On the last few blocks of Nevsky prospekt as you head toward the Neva are some buildings of historic importance. No. 18, on the right-hand side, was once a private dwelling before becoming a café called Wulf and Beranger; it's now called **Literary Café.** It was reportedly here that Pushkin ate his last meal before setting off for his fatal duel. **Chicherin's House,** at No. 15, was one of Empress Elizabeth's palaces before it became the Nobles' Assembly and, in 1919, the House of Arts. Farther down, at No. 14, is one of the rare buildings on Nevsky prospekt built *after* the Bolshevik Revolution. The blue sign on the facade dates from World War II and the siege of Leningrad; it warns pedestrians that during air raids the other side of the street is safer. The city was once covered with similar warnings; this one was left in place as a memorial, and on Victory Day (May 9 in Russia) survivors of the siege lay flowers here. ⊠ *City Center* Ⓜ *Nevsky Prospekt, Gostinny Dvor, Mayakovskaya, Ploschad Vosstaniya, or Ploschad Alexandra Nevskovo.*

ALSO WORTH SEEING

❹❶ **Alexander Pushkin Drama Theater** (*[Pushkinsky] Alexandrinskyi Teatr,* Александринский [Пушкинский] Театр). The most imposing building on Ploshchad Ostrovskovo (also referred to as Alexandrinskaya Ploshchad) is this theater built in classical style between 1828 and

1832. Six Corinthian columns adorn the Nevsky facade. Apollo's chariot dominates the building, with statues of the muses Terpischore and Melpomene to keep him company. In the small garden in front of the theater stands the **Catherine Monument,** which shows the empress towering above the principal personalities of her famous reign. Depicted on the pedestal are Grigory Potemkin, Generalissimo Alexander Suvorov, the poet Gavril Derzhavin, and others. Among the bronze figures is Princess Dashkova, who conspired against her own sister's lover—who just happened to be Catherine's husband, Peter III—to help the empress assume the throne. ✉*2 Pl. Ostrovskovo, City Center* ☎*812/312–1545 or 812/710–4103* Ⓜ*Gostinny Dvor or Nevsky Prospekt.*

The **St. Petersburg Tourist Information Center** (*Gorodskoi Turistichesky Tsentr Informatsii ot Soveta po Turismu* ✉*14/52 ul. Sadovaya, City Center* ☎*812/310–2822, 812/310–2231 for information in English* Ⓜ*Nevsky Prospekt*) is at the corner of Nevsky prospect. It's open weekdays 10–7.

㊴ Anichkov Palace *(Anichkov Dvorets,* **Аничков Дворец***).* This palace, which was named for the colonel whose regiment constructed the nearby Anichkov Most, was built by Empress Elizabeth for her lover, Alexei Razumovsky, between 1741 and 1750. As if to continue the tradition, Catherine the Great later gave it to one of her many favorites, Grigory Potemkin. An able statesman and army officer, Potemkin is famous for his attempts to deceive Catherine about conditions in the Russian south. He had fake villages put up for her to view as she passed by during her 1787 tour of the area. The term "Potemkin village" has come to mean any impressive facade that hides an ugly interior.

The palace's neoclassical ensemble was originally designed by Mikhail Zemtsov and completed by Bartolomeo Francesco Rastrelli; it has undergone numerous changes, and little now remains of the elaborate baroque facade. The shady garden has two pavilions—the pearls of Carlo Rossi's architecture. This was once a suburban area, which explains why the main entrance faces the Fontanka rather than Nevsky, where there's only a side entrance. Today, its role as a Youth Palace (once the Pioneer Palace), a kind of recreation center, combined with the fact that it hosts the occasional business conference makes for a strange mix. ✉*Nevsky pr., City Center* Ⓜ*Nevsky Prospekt.*

⓲ Anna Akhmatova Literary Museum *(Muzey Anny Akhmatovoy,* **Музей Анны Ахматовой***).* This museum occupies the former palace of Count Sheremetyev and is accessible either from 53 Liteiny prospekt or from the Fontanka embankment, through the palace hall and the garden. The famous St. Petersburg poet lived for many years in a communal apartment in a wing of the palace. She was born in 1888 in Odessa and was published for the first time in 1910. Akhmatova did not leave Petrograd after the October Revolution, but remained silent between 1923 and 1940. She died in 1966 and is remembered as one of the greatest successors to Pushkin. Her museum is also the venue for occasional poetry readings, other literary events, and temporary exhibitions—in short, a slice of the old-style Russian intelligentsia. Tours are available in Russian only. ✉*34 nab. Fontanki or 53 Liteiny pr., City Center* ☎*812/272–2211 or 812/272–5895* ⊕*www.akhmatova.spb.ru* ✉*100R, guided tour 200R for groups up to 10 people (admission fee not included)* ⊗*Tues.–Sun. 10:30–6, kassa open until 5:30* Ⓜ*Nevsky Prospekt.*

45 **Armenian Church** *(Armyanskaya Tserkov,* **Армянская Церковь***).* A fine example of the early-classical style, this blue-and-white church set back from the street was built by Yuri Velten between 1771 and 1780. It's known as "the blue pearl of Nevsky prospekt." This is a quiet, soothing spot to catch your breath before you head back out onto the main Nevsky thorough-fare. ✉*Nevsky pr., between Nos. 40 and 42, City Center* ☎*812/570–4108* ⊗*Daily 9–9* Ⓜ*Nevsky Prospekt.*

> ### THE SONG OF GRIEF
>
> One of Anna Akhmatova's most famous poems is "Requiem," which she wrote at the end of the 1930s when her son, historian Lev Gumilev, spent many years imprisoned during Stalin's Terror. Akhmatova was asked to describe what was happening by another woman waiting in the visitors' line at the prison. She did just that in the haunting lines: "This happened when only the dead wore smiles—/ they rejoiced at being safe from harm. / And Leningrad dangled from its jails / like some unnecessary arm."

NEED A BREAK? **The Grand Hotel Europe (** ✉*1/7 Mikhailovskaya ul., City Center* ☎*812/329–6000* Ⓜ *Nevsky Prospekt***)** has a lovely mezzanine café, where you can enjoy a pot of tea or a glass of champagne, served with bowls of strawberries. Take a peek at the art nouveau lobby, replete with stained-glass windows and antique furnishings.

46 **Church of St. Catherine** *(Tserkov Svyatoi Yekateriny,* **Церковь Святой Екатерины***).* Built between 1763 and 1783 by Vallin de la Mothe and Antonio Rinaldi, this Catholic church incorporates the baroque and classical styles that were converging at the time in Russia. The grave of Stanislaw Poniatowski, the last king of Poland and yet another lover of Catherine the Great, is here. As with so many churches in the city, services stopped here during the Soviet period, but St. Catherine's is once again fully operational. The small square outside is a favorite haunt of St. Petersburg's street artists. ✉*34 Nevsky pr., City Center* ☎*812/571–5795* ⊗*Daily 8–8* Ⓜ*Nevsky Prospekt.*

47 **City Duma** *(Gorodskaya Duma,* **Городская Дума***).* This building with a notable red-and-white tower served as the city hall under the tsars. Its clock tower, meant to resemble those in European cities, was erected by Ferrari between 1799 and 1804. It was originally equipped with signaling devices that sent messages between the Winter Palace and the royal summer residences. ✉*1 ul. Dumskaya, City Center* Ⓜ*Nevsky Prospekt.*

40 **Dom Knigi** *(House of Books,* **Дом Книги***).* This is where you'll find Petersburgers in a favorite pursuit: perusing and buying books. The city's largest bookstore still goes by its generic Soviet name. You may be pleasantly surprised by the prices for classic Russian literature in the original language. Some English-language books are also sold. The store has several branches around the city. ✉ *62 Nevsky pr., City Center* ☎ *812/570–6546* ◷ *Daily 9* AM*–10* PM Ⓜ *Gostiny Dvor.*

⑲ F. M. Dostoyevsky Literary-Memorial Museum *(Literaturno Memorialnyi Muzey Fyodora Dostoyevskovo,* Литературно-мемориальный Музей Ф.М. Достоевского). Here, at the last place in which he lived, Fyodor Dostoyevsky (1821–81) wrote *The Brothers Karamazov.* Dostoyevsky preferred to live in the part of the city inhabited by the ordinary people who populated his novels. He always insisted that the windows of his workroom overlook a church, as they do in this simple little house that has been remodeled to look as it did at the time Dostoyevsky and his family lived here. Perhaps the most interesting section of the museum deals with the writer's stay in prison in the Peter and Paul Fortress, and his commuted execution. ✉ *5/2 Kuznechny per., Vladimirskaya* ☎ *812/571–4031* ⊕ *www.md.spb.ru* ✍ *120R, 1,000R for English-guided tour for groups of up to 20 people. Call ahead to book tour.* ◷ *Tues.–Sun. 11–6, kassa open until 5* Ⓜ *Dostoyevskaya or Vladimirskaya.*

NEED A BREAK?
Abrikosov (✉ *40 Nevsky pr., City Center* ☎ *812/312-2457* Ⓜ *Nevsky Prospekt*), a German venture with a restaurant and a coffee bar, is a soothing place to take a break with a good view of Nevsky prospekt. Coffee, ice cream, and scrumptious cakes are available in the restaurant section, a no-smoking environment.

Zhyly-Byly (✉ *52 Nevsky pr., City Center* ☎ *812/314-6230* Ⓜ *Nevsky Prospekt*) takes its name from the phrase used to open every Russian folktale (something like "Once upon a time"), and the clean, cool interior displays a smattering of folk-related objects. It's open around the clock, and serves mainly excellent salads, as well as pastries, and the most delicious and beautiful cakes. Most surprising is its lengthy wine list.

⑭ Lutheran Church *(Lyuteranskaya Tserkov,* Лютеранская Церковь). Designed by Alexander Bryullov in 1833 to replace an older church that had become too small, this church follows the Romanesque tradition of rounded arches and simple towers. It suffered the same fate as the giant Cathedral of Christ Our Savior in Moscow: during the years in which religion was repressed, the church was converted into a municipal swimming pool. Now, the upper floor is once again a church full of light. Farther down, at No. 20, is the **Dutch Church** (currently a library), yet another reminder of the many denominations that once peacefully coexisted in old St. Petersburg. ✉ *22–24 Nevsky pr., City Center* ☎ *812/717–2423* ◷ *Services Sun. at 10:30* AM *and 6* PM Ⓜ *Nevsky Prospekt.*

㉞ Ploshchad Vosstaniya *(Insurrection Square,* Площадь Восстания). Originally called Znamenskaya Ploshchad (Square of the Sign) after a church of the same name that stood on it, the plaza was the site of many revolutionary speeches and armed clashes with military and police forces—hence its second name. Like Decembrists' Square, the plaza has reverted to its original name, though people still generally call it Insurrection Square (the metro station of the same name hasn't changed). The busy Moscow railroad station is here, and this part of Nevsky prospekt is lined with almost every imaginable kind of shop, from fruit markets to art salons to bookstores—although as with elsewhere in the city, some of this area is being cleaned up and put on a semiofficial footing. A stroll here is not a casual affair, for Nevsky is almost always teeming with bustling crowds of shoppers and street artists. Budding entrepreneurs, who sell their wares on the sidewalk on folding tables, further obstruct pedestrian traffic. Here you will also see an increasingly rare sight, the old men of the Great Patriotic War (the Russian name for World War II), still proudly wearing their medals. ⊠*Vladimirskaya* Ⓜ*Ploshchad Vosstaniya.*

⑳ Rimsky-Korsakov Museum *(Muzei Rimskovo-Korsakova,* **Музей Римского-Корсакова***).* Classical concerts are held twice a week in the small concert hall of the composer's former home. On display are many of his personal effects. To get to this small museum from Insurrection Square go south and west to Vladimirsky, then to Zagorodny prospekt. ⊠*28 Zagorodny pr., Apt. 39, Vladimirskaya* ☎*812/713–3208* 🎟*75R* ☉ *Wed.–Sun. 11–6. Closed last Fri. of month* Ⓜ*Dostoyevskaya.*

㊷ Russian National Library *(Rossiiskaya Natsionalnaya Biblioteka,* **Российская Национальная Библиотека***).* Opened in 1814 as the Imperial Public Library, this was Russia's first public library, and today it's still known fondly as the "Publichka." It holds more than 20 million books and claims to have a copy of every book ever printed in Russia. Among its treasures are Voltaire's personal library and the only copy of *Chasovnik* (1565), the second book printed in Russia. The building comprises three sections. The main section, on the corner of Nevsky prospekt and Sadovaya ulitsa, was designed by Yegor Sokolov and built between 1796 and 1801. Another wing, built between 1828 and 1832, was designed by Carlo Rossi as an integral part of Ploshchad Ostrovskovo. True to the building's purpose, the facade is adorned with statues of philosophers and poets, including Homer and Virgil, and the Roman goddess of wisdom, Minerva. You can see the facilities if you bring your passport and ask very nicely. Using the library requires a passport, registration note, and two photos. ⊠*18 Sadovaya ul., City Center* ☎*812/310–7137* ☉ *Weekdays 9–9, weekends 11–7. Closed last Tues. of month* Ⓜ*Nevsky Prospekt.*

㊿ Smolnyi (**Смольный**). Confusion abounds when you mention the
★ Smolny, for you can mean either the beautiful baroque church and convent or the classically designed institute that went down in history as the Bolshevik headquarters in the Revolution of 1917. The two architectural complexes are right next door to each other, on the Neva's left bank. Construction of the Smolny convent and cathedral began under Elizabeth I and continued during the reign of Catherine the Great, who established a school for the daughters of the nobility within its walls. The centerpiece of the convent is the magnificent five-dome **Cathedral**

of the Resurrection, which was designed by Bartolomeo Rastrelli and which is, some historians say, his greatest creation. At first glance, the highly ornate blue-and-white cathedral seems to have leaped off the pages of a fairy tale. Its five white onion domes, crowned with gilded globes supporting crosses of gold, convey a sense of magic and power. Begun by Rastrelli in 1748, the cathedral was not completed until the 1830s, by the architect Vasily Stasov. Though under renovation it's now open to the public, but few traces of the original interior have survived. It's currently used for concerts, notably of Russian sacred music, and rather insignificant exhibits. The cathedral tower affords beautiful views of the city. ⊠*3/1 Pl. Rastrelli, Liteiny/Smolny* ☎*812/710–3143 guided tours, 812/577–1421 box office* 🎟*Cathedral 200R, cathedral tower 100R* ⊘*Thur.–Tues. 10–5* Ⓜ*Chernyshevskaya.*

Piskaryevskoye   Cemetery   *(Piskaryevskoye   Kladbische,* **Пискаревское кладбище**)*.* The extent of this city's suffering during the 900-day siege by the Nazis between 1941 and 1944 becomes clear after a visit to the sobering Piskaryevskoye Cemetery. Located on the northeastern outskirts of the city, the field here was used, out of necessity, as a mass burial ground for the hundreds of thousands of World War II victims, some of whom died from the shelling, but most of whom died from cold and starvation. The numbingly endless rows of common graves carry simple slabs indicating the year in which those below them died. In all, nearly 500,000 people are buried here. The cemetery, with its memorial monuments and an eternal flame, serves as a deeply moving historical marker. The granite pavilions at the entrance house a small museum with photographs and memoirs documenting the siege. To visit the cemetery go to Lesnaya stop, then follow the crowd and take the free shuttle, Bus 80, to Ploshchad Muzhestva metro station (which the transit authority has been promising to reconnect to the line for years); from there, walk back 20 yards to the other side of the avenue and take Bus 123 to the cemetery. On the way back, Bus 123 will leave you at the exact same bus stop where you will board Bus 80 to Lesnaya. ⊠*74 Nepokorennykh, Vyborg Side* ☎*812/247–5716* 🎟*Free* ⊘*Daily 10–6* Ⓜ*Ploschad Muzhestva via shuttle from Lesnaya.*

㉔ Smolnyi Institut (**Смольный Институт**). The institute, just south of the Cathedral of the Resurrection at Smolny, is a far different structure. Giacomo Quarenghi designed the neoclassical building between 1806 and 1808 in the style of an imposing country manor. The Smolnyi Institute will long be remembered by the Russian people as the site where Lenin and his associates planned the overthrow of the Kerensky government in October 1917. Lenin lived at the Smolnyi for 124 days. The rooms in which he resided and worked are now a memorial museum; to visit the museum you must call for an appointment at least a day in advance and you must bring your passport. Today the rest of the building houses the offices of the governor of St. Petersburg and can be visited only by special request. ⊠*1 Proletarskoy Diktatury, Liteiny/Smolny* ☎*812/576–7461* 🎟*Museum 1,500R for groups of up* *to 10 people, 3,000R for groups of more than 10 people* ⏲*Museum weekdays 10–5 by appointment* Ⓜ*Chernyshevskaya.*

(50) **Stroganov Palace** *(Stroganovsky Dvorets,* **Строгановский Дворец***).* Even by the regal standards of Russia's aristocratic past, the Stroganovs were the richest of the rich, so it's not surprising that their palace, completed in 1754, is an outstanding example of the Russian baroque and one of Rastrelli's finest achievements. Above the archway of the entrance facing Nevsky prospekt is the family coat of arms: two sables holding a shield with a bear's head above. It symbolizes the Stroganovs' source of wealth—vast holdings of land, with all its resources, including furs—in Siberia. This was, by the way, the birthplace of beef Stroganoff, and it's therefore fitting that the palace courtyard is now the site of the Stroganoff Yard restaurant. The palace, a branch of the State Museum of Russian Art, is open to the public. It houses temporary exhibits, plus a permanent exhibit of exquisite Russian porcelain. ✉*17 Nevsky pr., City Center* ☎*812/571–8238* *300R* ⏲*Mon. 10–4, Wed.–Sun. 10–5:30* Ⓜ*Nevsky Prospekt.*

3

(53) **Taurida Palace** *(Tavrichesky Dvorets,* **Таврический Дворец**). Built between 1783 and 1789 on the orders of Catherine the Great for her court favorite, Count Grigory Potemkin, the palace is one of St. Petersburg's most magnificent buildings. Potemkin had been given the title of the Prince of Taurida for his annexation of the Crimea (ancient Taurida) to Russia. The Taurida Palace is a splendid example of neoclassicism, the main trend in Russian architecture in the late 18th century. The luxurious interior contrasts with the palace's modest exterior. The palace was inhabited for a long period after Potemkin's death, but in 1906 it was partially rebuilt for the State Duma, Russia's parliament. During the February Revolution of 1917 the Taurida Palace became a center of revolutionary events. Today the palace is used for international conferences and meetings; it also houses the Interparliamentary Assembly of the Commonwealth of Independent States (CIS). It's not open to the public. ✉*47 Shpalernaya ul., Liteiny/Smolny* Ⓜ*Chernyshevskaya.*

Zodchevo Rossi Ulitsa (**Улица Зодчего Росси**). This thoroughfare, once world famous as "Theater Street" (because it meets with the Alexandrinsky Theater), has extraordinary proportions: it's bounded by two buildings of exactly the same height, its width (72 feet) equals the height of the buildings, and its length is exactly 10 times its width. It reminds one of a big dancing hall without a roof. A complete view unfolds only at the end of the street, where it meets Lomonosov Ploshchad. The perfect symmetry is reinforced by the identical facades of the two buildings, which are painted the same subdued yellow and decorated with impressive white pillars. One of the buildings here is the legendary **Vaganova Ballet School** (founded in 1738), whose pupils included Karsavina as well as Pavlova, Nijinsky, Ulanova, Baryshnikov, and Nureyev. ✉*City Center* Ⓜ*Nevsky Prospekt.*

OFF THE BEATEN PATH

TsPKiO (**ЦПКиО**). The commonly used acronym of this park stands for "Central Park of Culture and Leisure named after Kirov." It covers most of Yelagin Ostrov, an island named after its 18th-century aristocratic owner. Within the park are an open-air theater, boating stations, a beach, and Yelagin Palace, designed by Carlo Rossi in the 18th century for Alexander I, who then presented it to his mother, Catherine the Great. The palace contains several fine rooms, including the Porcelain Room, beautifully decorated with painted stucco by Antonio Vighi, and the Oval Hall. If you walk along Primorsky prospekt for about 1 km (½ mi) to the *strelka* (spit), you can catch a view of the sunset over the Gulf of Finland. To reach the park, which is popular

year-round with city residents, head south from the Staraya Derevnya metro station along Lipovaya alleya. As you reach the embankment, you'll see a bridge to the island. ✉ *4 Yelagin Ostrov, Vyborg Side* ☎ *812/430–0911* ✉ *Free, 30R on weekends and holidays* ⊙ *Park daily 6* AM*–midnight, palace Wed.–Sun. 11–5* Ⓜ *Staraya Derevnya.*

㊸ Yeliseyevsky Food Emporium (Елисеевский Магазин). Officially called Gastronome No. 1 under the Communists, this famous store directly across the street from the Catherine Monument is known once again by its original name. Built at the turn of the 20th century for the immensely successful grocer Yeliseyev, the store is decorated in the style of early art nouveau. The interior, with its colorful stained-glass windows, gilded ceilings, and brass chandeliers, is worth a look. Before the revolution Yeliseyevsky specialized in imported delicacies, and after several lean decades, goods again overflow its shelves—this is a particularly good place to find wines and spirits from all over the former Soviet Union. ✉ *56 Nevsky pr., at Malaya Sadovaya, City Center* ☎ *812/312–1865* ⊙ *Weekdays 10–9, weekends 11–9* Ⓜ *Nevsky Prospekt.*

FROM THE SQUARE OF THE ARTS TO THE FIELD OF MARS
ОТ ПЛОЩАДИ ИСКУССТВ ДО МАРСОВА ПОЛЯ

This area introduces you to some of St. Petersburg's prettiest inner streets, squares, and gardens, starting at Ploshchad Iskusstv (Square of the Arts). Along the route are several squares and buildings of historic interest: it was in this part of the city that several extremely important events in Russian history took place, including the murder of tsars Paul I, who was assassinated in the Engineer's Castle by nobles opposed to his rule, and Alexander II, killed when a handmade bomb was lobbed at him by revolutionary terrorists as he was riding in a carriage along Kanal Griboyedova.

TIMING   Touring this section of the City Center might take between two and three hours, unless you want to linger at the State Museum of Russian Art, in which case you might want to plan an entire day here. Outdoor attractions, such as the Summer Garden, are worth visiting at any time of the year. Note that the Neva is very close here and that it's windy year-round.

MAIN ATTRACTIONS

59 **Church of the Savior on Spilled Blood** *(Khram Spasa na Krovi,*
★ **Храм Спаса на Крови***).* The highly ornate, old-Russian style of this colorful church seems more befitting to Moscow than St. Petersburg, where the architecture is generally more subdued and subtle; indeed, the architect, Alfred Parland, was consciously aiming to copy Moscow's St. Basil's. The drama of the circumstances leading to the church's inception more than matches the frenzy of its design, however. It was commissioned by Alexander III to memorialize the shocking death of his father, Alexander II, who was killed on the site in 1881 by a terrorist's bomb.

The church opened in 1907 but was closed by Stalin in the 1930s. It suffered damage over time, especially throughout World War II, but underwent meticulous reconstruction for decades (painstaking attempts were made to replace all original components with identically matched materials) and finally reopened at the end of the 20th century. The interior is as extravagant as the exterior, with glittering stretches of mosaic from floor to ceiling (70,000 square feet in total). Stone carvings and gold leaf adorn the walls, the floors are made of pink Italian marble, and the remarkable altar is constructed entirely of semiprecious gems and supported by four jasper columns. Blinded by all this splendor, you could easily overlook the painted scenes of martyrdom, including one that draws a parallel between the tsar's death and the crucifixion of Christ. Across the road there's an exhibit that takes a compelling look at the life of Alexander II. ⊠ *2a Kanal Griboyedova, City Center* ☎ *812/315–1636* 🖃 *300R* 🕑 *Thurs.–Tues. 11–6* Ⓜ *Nevsky Prospekt.*

64 **Mikhailovsky (Inzhenernyi) Castle** *(Mikhailovsky Zamok,* **Инженерный Замок***).* This orange-hued building belonged to one of Russia's stranger and more pitiful leaders. Paul I grew up in the shadow of his powerful mother, Catherine the Great, whom he despised; no doubt correctly, he held her responsible for his father's death. By the time Paul became tsar, he lived in terror that he, too, would be murdered. He claimed that, shortly after ascending the throne, he was visited in a dream by the Archangel Michael, who instructed him to build a church on the site of his birthplace hence the name of this landmark: Mikhailovsky Castle. Paul then proceeded to erect not just a church but a castle, which he tried to make into an impenetrable fortress. Out of spite toward his mother, he took stones and other materials from castles that she had built. The Fontanka and Moika rivers cut off access from the north and east; and for protection everywhere else, he installed secret passages, moats with drawbridges, and earthen ramparts. All of Paul's intricate planning, however, came to naught. On March 24, 1801, a month after he began living there, he was murdered—suffocated with a pillow in his bed. Historians speculate that his own son Alexander I knew that such a plot was under way and may even have participated. After Paul's death, the castle stood empty for 20 years, then was turned over to the Military Engineering Academy. One of the school's pupils was Fyodor Dostoyevsky, who may have absorbed something of the castle while he studied here: as a novelist he was preoccupied with themes of murder and greed. The castle is now part of the State Museum of Russian Art; it houses temporary exhibits from the museum, plus an exhibit on the history of the castle. ⊠*2 Sadovaya ul., City Center* ☎*812/570–5112* ⊕*www.rusmuseum.ru* ✉*300R, 2,000R for group tour in Russian* ☉*Mon. 10–4, Wed.–Sun. 10–5; tours weekends at 2 and 4* Ⓜ*Nevsky Prospekt.*

54 **Ethnography Museum** *(Etnograficheskii Muzey,* Этнографический Музей*)*. This museum contains a fascinating collection of applied art, national costumes, weapons, and many sociological displays about peoples of the 19th and 20th centuries, including the various ethnic groups of the former Soviet Union. On Sunday the museum offers very interesting Russian crafts workshops where you can learn to paint on wood or clay, model something out of clay or birch bark, or make a folk doll. These activities can be particularly interesting for children. ⊠*4/1 Inzhener-naya ul., City Center* ☎*812/570–5421* ✉*300R, 450R for crafts workshop* ☉*Museum Tues.–Sun. 11–6, kassa open until 5. Closed last Fri. of month. Crafts workshop Sun. 11–5* Ⓜ*Nevsky Prospekt.*

57 **Shostakovich Philharmonia** (Филармония имени Шостаковича). Once part of the private Nobles' Club, the Philharmonia, or Philharmonia Hall, is now home to the **St. Petersburg Philharmonic.** Its main concert hall, the Bolshoi Zal, with its impressive marble columns, has been the site of many celebrated performances, including in 1893 the first presentation of Tchaikovsky's Sixth (*Pathétique*) Symphony, his final masterpiece, with the composer conducting. (He died nine days later.) More recently, in 1942, when Leningrad was completely blockaded, Dmitri Shostakovich's Seventh (*Leningrad*) Symphony premiered here, an event broadcast in the same spirit of defiance against the Germans in which it was written. Later the concert hall was officially named for this composer. A smaller hall, the **Maly Zal** (*Glinka Hall* ⊠*30 Nevsky pr., City Center* ☎*812/579–8333*), around the corner, is also part of the complex. ⊠*2 Milkhailovskaya ul., City Center* ☎*812/710–4257 kassa, 812/710–4290 directory service* Ⓜ*Nevsky Prospekt.*

58 **State Museum of Russian Art** *(Gosudarstvenny Russky Muzey,* Государственный Русский Музей*)*. In 1898 Nicholas II turned the stupendously majestic neoclassical **Mikhailovsky Palace** (Mikhailovsky Dvorets) into a museum that has become one of the country's most important art galleries. He did so in tribute to his father, Alexander III, who had a special regard for Russian art and regretted, after seeing Moscow's Tretyakov Gallery, that St. Petersburg had nothing like it.

Fodor'sChoice
★

The collection at the museum, which is sometimes just referred to as the Russian Museum, is four times greater than Moscow's Tretyakov Gallery, with scores of masterpieces on display. Outstanding icons include the 14th-century *Boris and Gleb* and the 15th-century *Angel Miracle of St. George*. Both 17th- and 18th-century paintings are also well represented, especially with portraiture. One of the most famous 18th-century works here is Ivan Nikitin's *The Field Hetman.* By far the most important cache, however, comprises 19th-century works—huge canvases by Repin, many fine portraits by Serov (his beautiful *Countess Orlova* and the equally beautiful, utterly different portrait of the dancer Ida Rubinstein), and Mikhail Vrubel's strange, disturbing *Demon Cast Down.* For many years much of this work was unknown in the West, and it's fascinating to see the stylistic parallels and the incorporation of outside influences into a Russian framework. Painters of the World of Art movement—Bakst, Benois, and Somov—are also here. There are several examples of 20th-century art, with works by Kandinsky and Kazimir Malevich. Natan Altman's

HEROIC MUSIC

During Hitler's siege of Leningrad conductor Karl Eliasberg managed to put an orchestra together for the premiere of Dmitri Shostakovich's Seventh Symphony Leningrad, despite some of the musicians being too weak from starvation to hold their instruments. The performance went on as scheduled at the Philharmonic on August 9, 1942—the day which Hitler had predicted would mark the success of the German siege. Batteries of loudspeakers were arranged outside the hall for everyone to hear and, in defiance, at the edge of the city so it could be heard across German lines.

striking portrait of the poet Anna Akhmatova is in Room 77. The museum usually has at least one excellent special exhibit in place, and there's a treasure gallery here as well (guided tours only; you need a special ticket that you can get before noon). The Marble Palace, Engineer's Castle, and Stroganov Palace are all branches of the museum.

The square in front of the palace was originally named Mikhailovsky Ploshchad for Grand Duke Mikhail Pavlovich (1798–1849), the younger brother of Alexander I and Nicholas I and resident of the palace. The square's appearance is the work of Carlo Rossi, who designed the facade of each building encircling it as well as the Mikhailovsky Palace. Each structure, as well as the plaza itself, was made to complement Mikhail's residence on its north side. The palace, which was built between 1819 and 1825, comprises a principal house and two service wings. The central portico, with eight Corinthian columns, faces a large courtyard now enclosed by a fine art nouveau railing, a late (1903) addition. The statue of Alexander Pushkin in the center of the plaza was designed by Mikhail Anikushin and erected in 1957. ⊠ *4/2 Inzhenernaya ul., City Center* ☎ *812/595–4248* ⊕ *www.rusmuseum.ru* ⊠ *300R* ☉ *Mon. 10–5, Wed.–Sun. 10–6, kassa open until 1 hr before closing* Ⓜ *Nevsky Prospekt.*

63 ★ **Summer Garden** *(Letny Sad,* Летний Сад*).* Inspired by Versailles, the Summer Garden was one of Peter the Great's passions. When first laid out in 1704, it was given the regular, geometric style made famous by Louis XIV's gardener, Andre Le Nôtre, and decorated with statues and sculptures as well as with imported trees and plants. Grottoes, pavilions, ponds, fountains, and intricate walkways were placed throughout, and the grounds are bordered on all sides by rivers and canals. In

1777, however, disastrous floods did so much damage (entirely destroying the system of fountains) that the Imperial family stopped using the garden for entertaining. When they decamped for environs farther afield, they left the Summer Garden for use by the upper classes. Today it's a popular park accessible to everyone, but you'll have to imagine the first formal garden, for it's no longer there. The graceful wrought-iron fence that marks the entrance to the garden was designed in 1779 by Yuri Felten; it's supported by pink granite pillars decorated with vases and urns.

Just inside this southeastern corner is Peter's original **Summer Palace,** Letny Dvorets. Designed by Domenico Trezzini and completed in 1714, the two-story building is quite simple, as most of Peter's dwellings were. The walls are of stucco-cover brick, painted primrose yellow. Open since 1934 as a museum, it has survived without major alteration. Two other attractive buildings nearby are the **Coffee House** (Kofeinyi Domik) built by Carlo Rossi in 1826 and the **Tea House** (Tchainyi Domik) built by L. I. Charlemagne in 1827), neither of which, alas, serves the beverage for which it is named.

As you walk through the park, take a look at some of its more than 80 statues. *Peace and Abundance,* sculpted in 1722 by Pietro Baratta, is an allegorical depiction of Russia's victory in the war with Sweden. Another statue, just off the main alley, is of Ivan Krylov, a writer known as "Russia's La Fontaine." Peter Klodt, who also did the Anichkov Bridge horse statues, designed this sculpture, which was unveiled in 1855. Scenes from Krylov's fables, including his version of "The Fox and the Grapes," appear on the pedestal. As in many other parks and public places, the sculptures are protected from the harsh weather by wooden covers from early fall to late spring. There's a small admission fee (15R) to the park on weekends in summer. ⊠ *City Center* Ⓜ *Chernyshevskaya or Nevsky Prospekt.*

ALSO WORTH SEEING

NEED A BREAK?

No. 5 Ploshchad Iskusstv had a famous café–cum–art salon, the Stray Dog, in its basement from 1911 to 1915. A diverse group of painters, writers, and musicians—including the poets Anna Akhmatova, Nikolai Gumilev, and Osip Mandelstam—used it as a creative meeting point. The restaurant is now open again under the same name, **Podval Brodyachei Sobaki** (⊠ *5 Pl. Iskusstv, City Center* ☎ *812/312-8047* Ⓜ *Nevsky Prospekt*). It valiantly tries to recreate some of the original "arty" ethos.

❻❶ Marble Palace *(Mramorny Dvorets,* Мраморный Дворец). One of Catherine the Great's favorite palaces, this was designed for Count Grigory Orlov, one of the empress's more famous amours, by Arnoldo Rinaldi and built between 1768 and 1785. However, Count Orlov never lived in the palace because he died two years before the end of its construction. Later the palace belonged to members of the Russian royal family. Its name derives from its pale pink-purple marble facing. From 1937 to 1991 it housed the Lenin Museum; in the courtyard was the armored automobile from which he made his revolutionary speech

3

at the Finland station. Today, instead of Lenin's automobile you can see an equestrian statue of Tsar Alexander III first erected in 1909 on Znamenskaya Ploshchad (by the Moscow station). The statue survived under the Soviets, hidden in the State Museum of Russian Art's courtyard. The palace now belongs to that noted museum and houses three main collections: on the second floor are pieces by foreign artists who worked in Russia in the 18th and early 19th centuries, as well as a collection of contemporary art by 33 artists (including Rauschenberg, Lichtenstein, and Warhol), donated to the museum by the noted German collectors Peter and Irene Ludwig.

You may also wish to have a look at the Marble Hall, covered with lazurite and marbles from the Urals, northern Russia, and Italy; enjoy the superb views of the Peter and Paul Fortress and the Engineer's Castle; check out the curious *Peter the Great as a Child, Saved by His Mother from the Fury of the Streltsy* by Steuben; and then head to the third floor. The gallery here is called "a museum in the museum"; it houses paintings and drawings by such avant-garde Constructivists as Puni, Altman, Tatlin, Malevich, and Matiushin, put together between 1918 and 1922 for the Museum of Fine Arts, which belongs to the palace and is included in the admission price. The Constructivists' work, which developed on a par with that of the French Cubists in the early 20th century, was deemed unacceptable under the Soviets and was kept in storage until perestroika. A separate ticket (100R) is required for a guided tour of Grand Duke Konstantin Konstantinovich Romanov's private quarters (groups of 10 people maximum). This grand duke (1858–1915), uncle of the last Russian tsar, was also known as a writer and was head of Emperor's Academy of Science. He was the last owner of Marble Palace. ⊠*5/1 Millionaya ul., City Center* ☎*812/312–9054 or 812/312–9196* ⊕*www.rusmuseum.ru* 🎟️*300R* 🕐*Mon. 10–5, Wed.–Sun. 10–6, kassa open until 1 hr before closing* Ⓜ*Chernyshevskaya or Nevsky Prospekt.*

🟤 **Field of Mars** *(Marsovo Pole,* **Марсово Поле***).* The site was once a marsh, from which both the Mya and the Krikusha rivers began. Peter the Great had it drained (and the rivers linked by a canal), and the space was subsequently used for parades and public occasions. The field acquired its current name around 1800, when it began to be used primarily for military exercises. Shortly after 1917 it was turned into a burial ground for Red Army victims of the revolution and ensuing civil war. The massive granite **Monument to Revolutionary Fighters** was unveiled here on November 7, 1919, with an eternal flame lit 40 years later, on the revolution's anniversary. Keep an eye out for newlyweds, who come here (among other famous city landmarks) immediately after their weddings for good luck. ⊠*City Center* Ⓜ*Chernyshevskaya or Nevsky Prospekt.*

🟤 **Mussorgsky Theater of Opera and Ballet** (**Театр Оперы и Балета имени Мусоргского**). This historic theater built in 1833 is also known as the Maly, or Little Theater, the name given it during the Communist era, but a nomenclature that makes the theater itself bridle. Before the revolution it was the Mikhailovsky Theater, but French companies performed here so often that it was more commonly referred to as the French Theater. After the Mariinsky (formerly the Kirov), this is St. Petersburg's second-most important theater. ⊠*1 Pl. Iskusstv, City Center* ☎*812/595–4305 or 812/595–4284* Ⓜ*Nevsky Prospekt.*

❺❻ Square of the Arts*(Ploshchad Iskusstu).*The magnificent State Museum of Russian Art is at the far end of this square. If you stand in front of the museum and turn to survey the entire square, the first building on your right, with old-fashioned lanterns adorning its doorways, is the Mussorgsky Theater of Opera and Ballet. Next door, at No. 3, is the Isaac Brodsky Museum. Bordering the square's south side, on Mikhailovskaya ulitsa's east corner, is the former Nobles' Club, now the Shostakovich Philharmonia, home to the St. Petersburg Philharmonic. The buildings on the square's remaining side are former residences and school buildings. ⊠*City Center* Ⓜ*Chernyshevskaya or Nevsky Prospekt.*

❶❼ St. Petersburg Circus *(Tsirk Sankt-Peterburga,* Цирк Санкт-Петербурга*).* Though perhaps not as famous as the Moscow Circus, the St. Petersburg Circus, dating from 1867, remains a popular treat for children. Avid young circus fans get a kick out of its adjacent **Circus Art Museum** as well, with displays about the world of the circus. ⊠*3 nab. Fontanki, City Center* ☎*812/570–5198 circus, 812/313–4413 museum* ◔*Performances Fri. 7* PM, *Sat. 3 and 7* PM, *Sun. 1 and 5* PM; *museum weekdays noon–5* ▣*100R–400R* Ⓜ*Chernyshevskaya or Nevsky Prospekt.*

❻❷ Suvorovskaya Ploshchad *(Suvorov Square,* Суворовская Площадь*).* In the middle of this square stands a statue of the military commander Alexander Suvorov, cast as Mars, god of war. Appropriately enough, when first unveiled in 1801, the statue stood in the Field of Mars, but in 1818 it was moved to its current location. ⊠*City Center* Ⓜ*Chernyshevskaya or Nevsky Prospekt.*

WHERE TO EAT

The new restaurants and cafés of the burgeoning scene stand in sharp contrast to the traditional, sometimes uninspired, Russian-style eateries of the former Soviet Union. Although it's certainly worth experiencing Russian-style dining, know that you have plenty of options.

Hotels often house excellent restaurants and foreign chefs which have become an integral part of the city's culinary scene. At the restaurants of the Grand Hotel Europe, the Astoria and the Radisson SAS Royal you will find top-notch service, food, and often good views. Most leading hotels and finer restaurants offer tempting three-course or generous buffet business lunches for 250R–370R. They are normally advertised or reviewed in dining sections of the *St. Petersburg Times* and *St. Petersburg In Your Pocket,* and are worth checking out.

Homey and jovial budget eateries serving quick, substantial, and good meals for under 250R have mushroomed around the city. Stands sell ing Russian *blini*, the hearty Russian cousin of the French crepe, are everywhere and make a great pit stop.

It's not necessary to plan ahead if you want to land a table in a nice establishment on weekdays, but it's generally a good idea to reserve ahead for weekend dining. Ask your hotel or tour guide for help making a reservation. Note that few restaurants in St. Petersburg have no-smoking sections; in fact, some places have cigarettes listed on the menu. Most restaurants stop serving food around 11 PM or midnight, although more and more 24-hour cafés are opening.

3

WHAT IT COSTS IN RUSSIAN RUBLES					
	¢	$	$$	$$$	$$$$
T DINNER	under 250R	250R–450R	451R–650R	651R–850R	over 850R

Prices are per person for a main course at dinner.

CITY CENTER: PALACE SQUARE & THE HERMITAGE

AMERICAN

$$$ ✕**Tinkoff.** The crowded, loftlike Tinkoff was St. Petersburg's first microbrewery. Trendy people come to enjoy beer and tasty comfort food in a relaxed, almost clublike dining room. Frequent Western jazz, lounge, and cool pop acts appear at Tinkoff, but when they're here the cover price can be very high, usually around 1,500R. There's a sushi bar, too, with combos starting from 250R, but you're better off sticking with the beer and burgers. ⊠*7 Kazanskaya ul., City Center* ☎*812/718–5566* ⊕*www.tinkoff.ru* ⊟*DC, MC, V* Ⓜ*Nevsky Prospekt.*

ARMENIAN

$ ✕**Kilikia.** A haven for the local Armenian diaspora, Kilikia, named after the Armenian region in Turkey, has a strong reputation for its ethnic cuisine. Sizzling beef stew is a hit, and expertly cooked kebabs are available in tempting variety. There are six halls in this sprawling, dimly lit eatery but seating only expands to them as space is needed. The seemingly endless menu may confuse the noninitiated, but the staff are competent and are a great help with orientation. Budget travelers will be thrilled by Kilikia's business lunch at only 100R. ⊠*26/40 Gorokhovaya ul., City Center* ☎*812/327–2208* ⊟*MC, V* Ⓜ*Sennaya Ploshchad.*

CAFÉS

¢ ✕**Coffeehouse.** After settling a legal dispute about the use of its trademark, Starbucks finally opened its first outlet in Russia in 2007. But by then, Starbucks clones had sprung up on seemingly every corner, and in St. Petersburg the market leader is Coffeehouse. Unlike Starbucks, you can grab a business lunch here for 250R which includes a salad, sandwich, and coffee or tea. They also serve the full range of not-always-expertly-made coffee variations. ⊠*7/9 Nevsky pr., City Center* ☎*812/570–4774* ⊕*www.coffeehouse.ru* ⊟*MC, V* Ⓜ*Nevsky Prospekt* ⊠*17 Kanal Griboedova, City Center* ☎*812/570–6533*

Where to Eat in
St. Petersburg

PETROGRAD
SIDE

Lenina ul.

Maly pr.

Zelenina ul.

Krasnogo kursanta ul.

Chkalovsky pr.

Dobrolyubova

Bolshoy pr.

Kronverksky pr.

Kamennostroisky pr.

Skorochodova ul.

Mira ul.

Gorkovskaya

Alexandrovsky
Park

Kronverk Canal

Peter and Paul
Fortress

Troitskaya
Pl.

Petrovskaya nab.

Troitsky
most

Pirogovskaya nab.

Bolshaya Nevka

Petrogradskaya nab.

Kuybysheva nab.

Svobody
most

Vyborgskay

Smirnov ul.

Bolshoy Sampsonievsky

Finlyan
Sta

Le
Plosh

Liteir
mos

Sportivnaya

Malaya

Neva

nab.

Makarova

Vasilievsky

VASILIEVSKY
ISLAND

Sredny pr.

4-5 linya

Sverdovskaya l.

Bolshoy pr.

Universitetskaya

most
Leytenanta
Shmidta

Neva

Angliyskaya nab.

Truda ul.

Pisareva ul.

Maklina

Mend l.

nab.

Stock
Exchange

Birzhevoy
most

Marble
Palace

Engineer's
Castle

Sadovaya ul.

Moskhovaya ul.

Liteiny pr.

Nekr

Dvortsovy
most

Dvortsovaya nab.

State Hermitage
Museum

Winter
Palace

Armiralteistvo

Admiralteysky pr.

Nevsky pr.

Ethnography
Museum

Pl.
Iskusstv

Gostinny Dvor/
Nevsky Prospekt

Z. Rossi
ulitsa

Vladimirsky pr.

Dostoyevsko
Vladimirska

Kazan
Cathedral

Lomonosova

Lomonosov
Pl.

Ligov
Prosp

Konnogvardeyskiy
bulvar

reka

Moika

Gorokhovaya ul.

Kazanskaya ul.

Griboyedov
Canal

Sadovaya

ul.

Dekabristov ul.

Voznesensky pr.

Sadovaya

Sennaya Pl./
Sadovaya

Rimskogo-Korsakova

St. Nicholas
Cathedral

Turgenyeva
ploshchad

reka fontanka

reka fontanka

Pushkinskaya

Vitebsky
Station

Zvenigorodnaya ul.

Zagorodny pr.

Ruzovskaya ul.

Ligovsky

Tekhnologichesky
Institut

Lermontovsky pr.

Voznesensky pr.

Yegorova ul.

Moskovsky pr.

Klinsky

Malodetskoselsky

Obvodniy Canal

Ogorodnikova

Kurlyandskaya ul.

Borovaya ul.

3

Map labels:

Mineralnaya ul.

Zhukova ul.

VYBORG SIDE

Arsenalnaya ul.

Kondratyevsky pr.

Sverdlovskaya nab.

...shchad ...ina

Komsomola ul.

...nalnaya nab.

Neva

Shpalernaya ul.

Taurida Palace

...skogo ul.

Tavrichesky Park

...shevskaya

...altykova-Shchedrina ul.

Tavricheskaya ul.

Tulskaya ul.

LITEINY

SMOLNY

Suvorovski pr.

48

47

Grechesky pr.

8 Sovetskaya ul.

Moiseyenko ul.

Novgoradskaya ul.

...ad ...iyd/ ...vskaya

45

Mytninskaya ul.

Bakunina

Neva

43

44

Stary

VLADIMIRSKAYA

Nevsky pr.

49 A. Nevsky Pl.

Ploshchad Aleksandra Nevskovo M

Alexander Nevsky Lavra

50

KEY

M *Metro stops*

☐*MC, V* Ⓜ*Nevsky Prospekt* ✉*3 Malaya Sadovya, City Center* ☎*812/314–3610* ☐*MC, V* Ⓜ*Nevsky Prospekt.*

$ ✕ **James Cook.** Upon entering James Cook you have a choice: turn right for the pub with a decent menu or left to a coffee and cake shop. Choose from 40 kinds of coffee, elite teas, various coffee cocktails, and desserts. The breakfast deal at the coffee shop is one of the best in town: 125R will buy you a hot dish plus coffee or tea, toast, and a choice of yogurt or fruit salad. There is a second James Cook Pub at 45 Kamenoostrovsky prospekt on the Petrograd Side. ✉*2 Shvedsky per., City Center* ☎*812/312–3200* ☐*DC, MC, V* Ⓜ*Nevsky Prospekt.*

¢   ✕ **Shokoladnitsa.** A Moscow invader giving Coffeehouse a serious run for its money, this coffee joint is classier and a tad pricier, but the food options are a rung above the competitors. They have everything from sandwiches and quiches to cakes, tarts, and ice cream. This location, on the second floor of the newly refurbished Dom Knigi offers a New York City vibe and is one of the best people-watching spots in St. Petersburg. ✉*62 Nevsky pr., City Center* ⊕*www.shoko.ru* ☐*MC, V* Ⓜ*Nevsky Prospekt.*

¢   ✕ **Teremok.** Don't be intimidated by the café's spartan setting. Teremok's
★   owners penny-pinch only on furnishings and presentation. Cooked in front of your eyes, their famous blini—priced at 40R–100R—are deservedly rated the best in town. Stuffed with mushrooms, ham, pork, grilled chicken, cream, honey, and a dozen other fillings, the blini, rich in flavor and never over- or underdone, taste just as if a Russian mom cooked them. A single blini is so rich and hefty, it may leave you stuffed. Be conservative when you order unless you are absolutely starving. Aside from this café, Teremok encompasses a chain of 15 street stands. ✉*60 Nevsky pr., City Center* ☎*No phone* Ⓜ*Nevsky Prospekt*

FRENCH

$$$$ ✕ **Bellevue.** Head and shoulders above any other restaurant in St. Petersburg—literally, thanks to its breathtaking, 360-degree panorama from atop the Kempinski Hotel Moika 22—Bellevue is very expensive but worth every kopek. Chef Philippe Boussert has conjured up a modern French seafood-heavy menu with Asian influences. Appetizers such as grilled tuna cubes on a mustard sauce with roasted sesame seeds and a bed of marinated Chinese cabbage (890R) and a smoked salmon rose with black-caviar cream (950R) come highly recommended. Bellevue welcomes diners who are not guests as well as those who just want to stop in for coffee to check out the unrivaled view. ✉*Kempinski Hotel Moika 22, 22 nab. reki Moika, City Center* ☎*812/335–911* ✎*moika@kempinski.com* ⊕*www.kempinski-st-petersburg.com* ☐*AE, DC, MC, V* Ⓜ*Nevsky Prospekt.*

$$$$
Fodor'sChoice
★
✕**Palkin.** The Premiere Casino's grand restaurant evokes the name of a legendary restaurant established on this spot in 1785. The interior is formal and elegant and you'll be treated like royalty the moment you enter, although the place has become a bit worn around the edges since its Yeltsin-era heyday. Look for poularde with morel sauce, venison with pine nuts marmalade, fillet of turbot served with pistachio nuts and curry sauce, and salad of smoked salmon with fresh oysters and beluga caviar. It's worth a visit for the window seats alone which look out onto bustling Nevsky prospekt. ⊠*47 Nevsky pr., at Vladirmirsky pr., City Center* ☎*812/703–5371* ⊕*www.palkin.ru* ⚭*Reservations essential* ⊟*AE, MC, V* Ⓜ*Mayakovskaya or Nevsky Prospekt.*

GREEK

$
✕**Oliva.** The size of this Greek taverna, seating more than 150 people, illustrates the confidence of its cooks, and the venue is almost always full. Feta cheese is delivered directly from Greece, and the house specialties get high marks in the city. Try *mussaka* (minced meat baked with potatoes and spices) and kefal fish baked with tarragon. With friendly multilingual servers, it's a great place for lunch, groups, and fans of live Greek folk music (on most nights). ⊠*31 Bolshaya Morskaya ul., City Center* ☎*812/314–6563* ⊕*www.tavernaoliva.ru* ⊟*MC, V* Ⓜ*Nevsky Prospekt.*

INDIAN

$$
✕**Tandoor.** One of the best ethnic restaurants in town, Tandoor has a great location across the street from St. Isaac's Cathedral. Every meal is a gastronomic delight and you can trust finding your Indian favorites here. Waiters, dressed in ethnic costumes and soft embroidered shoes, move soundlessly in this comfortable and quiet little place. Tandoor is inexpensive, at least by Russian standards, and the food is well worth it. The restaurant also serves a generous business lunch for 325R. ⊠*2 Voznesensky pr., City Center* ☎*812/312–3886* ⊕*www.tandoor.restaurant.ru* ⊟*AE, DC, MC, V* Ⓜ*Sennaya Ploshchad.*

INDONESIAN

$$
✕**Sukawati.** The first Indonesian restaurant in Russia, Sukawati has a trendy interior and good, reliable cuisine. The coexistence of Indonesian and Japanese dishes on the menu is bizarre, but if quality is the issue, nobody is complaining. If you feel like a big meal, order one of the rice platters as well as the renowned Indonesian dessert, *gendar bali* (a warm black-rice pudding served with coconut cream, fruit, and vanilla ice cream). The Herculean four-course business lunch (175R) includes a drink and a dessert. ⊠*8 Kazanskaya ul., City Center* ☎*812/312–0540* ⊕*www.sukawati.ru* ⊟*MC, V* Ⓜ*Nevsky Prospekt.*

ITALIAN

$$$$
★
✕**Il Grappolo.** One of the city's best Italian restaurants, the comfortable, elegant Grappolo is a culinary treat, a place for people who know and appreciate good food. The chef and owners are knowledgeable and use only the best ingredients available—like true buffalo mozzarella, which makes the delicious Caprese salad a house specialty. The menu includes fresh arugula salad, mushroom risotto, veal with mushroom sauce (or

just about anything with porcini mushrooms), and an excellent tiramisu. Downstairs at the sister wine bar, Probka, you can order wines by the glass from the well-chosen list and eat an authentic Caesar salad. ⊠*5 ul. Belinskogo, City Center* ☎*812/273–4904* ⊕*www.probka.org* ▱*AE, DC, MC, V* Ⓜ*Gostiny Dvor.*

$ ✕**Da Albertone.** Get your cheap and scrumptious pizza here. This cheerful pizzeria serves more than 40 kinds of pizza prepared by Italian cooks who are very good at what they do. Although clearly not a gastronomic palace, Da Albertone has a diverse choice of traditional dishes. Though it's busy, the service is friendly and prompt. The children's playroom is an added draw for families. ⊠*23 Millionnaya ul., City Center* ☎*812/315–8673* ⊕*www.daalbertone.ru* ▱*AE, MC, V* Ⓜ*Nevsky Prospekt.*

RUSSIAN

$$$$ ✕**L'Europe.** This elegant restaurant in the Grand Hotel Europe serves
Fodor'sChoice fine Russian and Continental cuisine. The breathtaking interior—com-
★ plete with an art nouveau stained-glass roof, shining parquet floors, and private balconies—is fit for a tsar, as are the prices. The menu is mouthwatering, with some dishes inspired by authentic royal recipes. Try the venison marinated in vodka and juniper berries, or the lobster, sturgeon, and salmon *à la Russe*. The popular Sunday champagne-and-caviar brunch (2,900R) is the place to see and be seen among the city's high-rollers. Reserve well ahead, particularly in summer. ⊠*Grand Hotel Europe, 1/7 Mikhailovskaya ul., City Center* ☎*812/ 329–6630* ⊕*www.grandhoteleurope.com* ⚘*Reservations essential Jacket and tie* ▱*AE, DC, MC, V* Ⓜ*Nevsky Prospekt or Gostinny Dvor.*

$$$$ ✕**Onegin.** Chic or pretentious, it's your call, but Onegin exemplifies the latest in St. Petersburg's dining and social scene, with the restaurant turning into an exclusive dance club late at night. The duck, fish, and arugula salad (a rare find in this city) are flavorful, but pricey, as are most of the dishes. The design of this underground refuge is a modern twist on Imperial St. Petersburg style, down to the ceiling reliefs finessed by the artisans who keep the Hermitage's baroque details looking spectacular. It all feels like a private party at an aristocratic Russian's home. ⊠*11 Sadovaya ul., City Center* ☎*812/571–8384* ▱*AE, MC, V* Ⓜ*Gostinny Dvor.*

$$$$ ✕**Taleon.** An opulent mansion houses an ultra-exclusive restaurant, pri-
Fodor'sChoice vate club, and casino, all connected with the Yeliseyev Palace Hotel.
★ You'll find the usual array of fun for the bodyguard-protected high-society set—gambling, cigars, cognac—in a glittering setting, with marble fireplaces and gilded ceilings. The Russian and European menus are full of hearty, classic options, including caviar, oven-baked partridge in coriander sauce, veal cutlet with sage sauce, and carré d'agneau (rack of lamb) in rosemary sauce. The Sunday brunch (2,200R) includes black and red caviar as well as lobster and champagne. Be sure to tour the casino, with its lush cigar lounge with walnut-covered walls and leather sofas. ⊠*59 nab. Moika, City Center* ☎*812/324–9911 or 812/324–9944* ⊕*www.taleon.ru* ⚘*Reservations essential Jacket and tie* ▱*AE, DC, MC, V* Ⓜ*Nevsky Prospekt.*

3

$$ ✕**Hermitage Restaurant.** Although it differs greatly in style from the Hermitage's General Staff Building in which it's housed, this modern, stylish restaurant maintains subtle connections to the museum—for example, the green throughout the museum appears everywhere here, from the fresh apple juice to the staff uniforms. Each dining "hall" is different: the Music Salon hosts live music, while the Cameo Room is romantic with amber lamps and tables for two. Paintings by local artists line the walls of the hall connecting these dining rooms. There are two menus—one European, one Russian—with many reasonably priced options. Try any of the salads, soups, or blini. ⊠ *General Staff Bldg., 6–8 Dvortsovaya Pl., City Center* ☎ *812/314–4772* ⊟ *AE, DC, MC, V* Ⓜ *Nevsky Prospekt.*

¢ ✕**Chainaya Lozhka.** Distinguishable by its white and orange teaspoon logo, this is an extremely cheap and cheerful counter-service blini chain with locations all over downtown. You may be put off by the plastic cutlery and the lackadaisical service but the blini are authentic and filling, and at about 45R per, they're a great deal when you are in a hurry. ⊠ *42 Sadovaya ul., City Center* ☎ *812/310–1315* ⊕ *www. teaspoon.ru* ⊟ *No credit cards* Ⓜ *Sadovaya* ⊠ *44 Nevsky pr., City Center* ☎ *812/571–4657* Ⓜ *Gostinny Dvor.*

ADMIRALTEISKY

CAFÉS

¢ ✕**Pirozhkovaya Stolle.** The two branches on the same street combine the best of the old and new: the fashionable surroundings are comfortable, clean, and spacious, while the kitchen turns out fresh pirogi. Choose from sweet or savory fillings, including fish, vegetables, and fruits. The apricot is a must and the salmon is a dream, but they are all mini-masterpieces. ⊠ *19 ul. Dekabristov, Admiralteisky* ☎ *812/315–2383* ⊕ *www. stolle.ru* Ⓜ *Sennaya Ploshchad* ⊠ *33 ul. Dekabristov, Admiralteisky* ☎ *812/714–2571* ⊟ *No credit cards* Ⓜ *Sennaya Ploshchad.*

> **WORD OF MOUTH**
>
> "As for the restaurants and cafés, I did like very much small cozy cafés nearby our hotel—Stolle (it's a wonderful pie café) it was around $10 per person to have lunch. There is also a nice place, called Pushka Inn. I had the best Borscht and beef Stroganoff there." —Sturbun

CONTINENTAL

$$$$ ✕**Dvoryanskoye Gnezdo.** At the Noble Nest, tucked away in the gar-
★ den pavilion of the Yusupov Palace, formal attire matches the service, decor, and Continental food. There are two set menus: the "Turgenev" is very Russian, and the "Nobleman" has more of a French touch. Try the fillet of venison, baked pheasant, or a selection from the small vegetarian menu. The wine list is extensive and includes Lafite, Latour, and Margaux at extraordinary prices, but there are some more reasonable choices. With the Mariinsky Theatre just around the corner, the restaurant attracts a post-theater crowd as well as foreign dignitaries and businesspeople (an expense account helps). ⊠ *21 ul. Dekabristov,*

Admiralteisky ☎812/3120911 *or* 812/310–3205 ⊕*www.dvgnezdo.
ru* ⚓*Reservations essential Jacket and tie* ⊟*AE, DC, MC, V* Ⓜ*Sadovaya or Sennaya Ploshchad.*

$$$$ ✕**Za Stsenoi.** Just steps from the Mariinsky Theatre, with windows
overlooking the pretty Kryukova Canal, "Backstage" has a dramatic
setting. Its floorboards were taken from the old Mariinsky stage, and
the exposed-brick walls are bedecked with ornate mirrors and theater props. The menu fuses French and Russian influences. Venison
carpaccio and crème lobster soup with cognac make good overtures
for beluga fillet baked with mushrooms and béchamel sauce or grilled
salmon with caviar sauce. A great choice for a post-theater dinner, but
be sure to plan ahead as it fills up quickly. You can read the full menu
and make a reservation at the Mariinsky Theatre Web site (⊕*www.
mariinsky.ru*). ⊠*18/10 Teatralnaya Pl., Admiralteisky* ☎812/327–
0521 ⚓*Reservations essential* ⊟*AE, DC, MC, V* Ⓜ*Sadovaya or
Sennaya Ploshchad.*

ISRAELI

$ ✕**LeChaim.** This spacious, and welcoming kosher restaurant has been
a hit with cosmopolitans and a nonreligious crowd since it opened. In
a spacious basement of the St. Petersburg Great Choral Synagogue,
LeChaim serves generous portions of Jewish cuisine at modest prices.
Try chicken schnitzel or trout fillet wrapped in grape leaves. The restaurant can be difficult to find since its doorway is discreetly marked. It is
often booked out for weddings and other celebrations that take place
in the synagogue so call ahead. ⊠*2 Lermontovsky pr., Admiralteisky*
☎812/972–2774 ⊕*www.lehaim-spb.ru* ⊟*No credit cards* Ⓜ*Sennaya
Ploschad, Sadovaya.*

MIDDLE EASTERN

$$$$ ✕**Caravan.** The stuffed camel, Turkish carpets, and food cooking in the
middle of the room leave you in little doubt as to the theme of this spacious restaurant, a leading contender for the best Mideastern eatery in
town. You can lounge in separate booths at one end of the restaurant,
or sit at the more orthodox chairs and tables nearer the entrance. The
kutab, a lightly fried pocket filled with shrimp, pumpkin, or cheese,
makes a good starter. From there move on to any of the more than 30
varieties of kebabs. ⊠*46 Voznesensky pr., Admiralteisky* ☎812/310–
5678 ⊟*AE, DC, MC, V* Ⓜ*Sadovaya or Tekhnologichesky Institut.*

RUSSIAN

$$$$ ✕**Canvas.** Canvas, on the first floor of the St. Petersburg Renaissance
★   Baltic Hotel, is a cozy little restaurant that juxtaposes traditional Russian ingredients with a European approach and artistic presentation.
A perfect example is beetroot jelly with herring fillet and Laredo apple
served on toasted black bread with potatoes and dill-mustard sauce.
Try sturgeon roulade with spinach and the excellent game *solyanka*
(meat stew) made with bear, elk, or wild-boar meat. Dinner can also
be served on the hotel's sixth-floor terrace, where the shiny golden
cupola of St. Isaac's Cathedral, set against charming crumbling roof-
tops, makes for an wonderful view. Canvas offers an excellent three-

course business lunch at 375R. ⊠*4 Pochtamtskaya ul., Admiralteisky* ☎*812/380–4000* ⊟*AE, DC, MC, V* Ⓜ*Sadovaya.*

$$$ ✕**1913.** With its name, this exclusive restaurant recalls Russia's best year in history. Low-key, comfortable elegance combines with a giant menu and giant portions. It's a cozier alternative to the stuffier, more touristy dining options, and it's convenient to the Mariinsky Theatre. The menu's traditional Russian cuisine emphasizes game and fish, plus there are European dishes. Try the mushroom soup or borscht for a starter, followed by sturgeon or salmon. ⊠*13/2 Voznesensky pr., Admiralteisky* ☎*812/315–5148* ⊕*www.restaurant-1913.spb.ru* ⚑*Reservations essential* ⊟*AE, DC, MC, V* Ⓜ*Sadovaya or Sennaya Ploshchad.*

VASILIEVSKY ISLAND

CAFÉS

¢ ✕**Pirozhkovaya Stolle.** This spot combines the best of the old and new: the fashionable surroundings are comfortable, clean, and spacious, while the kitchen turns out fresh pierogi. *See* the full review *in* the Admiralteisky neighborhood. ⊠*50 1st liniya, Vasilievsky Island* ☎*812/328–7860* ⊕*www.stolle.ru* ⊟*No credit cards* Ⓜ*Vasileostrovskaya.*

CONTINENTAL

$$$$ ✕**Staraya Tamozhnya.** Considered for many years the best restaurant
★ in St. Petersburg, the Old Customs House has been surpassed, but it's still pretty impressive and a good time. It remains classy without being snobbish, with the open brickwork walls and immaculately presented tables. Much of the food is exquisitely prepared like the salmon with coconut sauce and the roast veal with figs and a pumpkin-morel puree. The wine list is excellent and the service is top-notch and friendly. ⊠*1 Tamozhenny per., Vasilievsky Island* ☎*812/327–8980* ⚑*Reservations essential* ⊟*AE, MC, V* Ⓜ*Nevsky Prospekt or Vasileostrovskaya.*

RUSSIAN

$$$$ ✕**New Island.** In summer this ship-turned-restaurant has a stunning
★ view as it sails along the Neva River, past the rows of colorful palaces lining its banks. New Island sets sail promptly at 2, 6, 8, and 10:30 PM. In winter, when the river is frozen, lights adorn the ship, and it remains docked in the harbor (and prices go down significantly). Inside, all is simple but refined, including the menu. Try the duck carpaccio as a starter, the fried fillet of trout with almonds and the various blini are also good. The wine list is extensive and pricey. ⊠*Universitetskaya nab., between Lieutenant Schmidt (recently renamed Blagovyeshchensky most) and Palace bridges, Vasilievsky Island* ☎*812/320–2100* ⚑*Reservations essential* ⊟*AE, MC, V* Ⓜ*Vasileostrovskaya.*

$-$$ ✕**Restoran.** Spacious, with soft lighting and earth tones, Restoran (lit-
Fodor'sChoice erally "Restaurant") is at once stylish and traditional, and it bustles
★ with tour groups and locals who know the *Russkiy stol* (Russian table) is the real thing—and a real bargain at 350R. It's an all-you-can-eat smorgasbord of Russian *zakuski*, or small dishes: soups, salads (such as tuna), and pickled treats like garlic, green tomatoes, and cucumbers.

The main courses are as minimalist as the decor; try the simple veal with broccoli and cauliflower in a cheese sauce. For dessert, return to the Russian table for teas, cakes, and other Russian delights. ⊠*2 Tamozhenny per., Vasilievsky Island* ☎*812/327–8979* ⚐*Reservations essential* ▭*AE, DC, MC, V* Ⓜ*Vasileostrovskaya.*

VLADIMIRSKAYA (LOWER NEVSKY PROSPEKT)

CAFÉS

$　✕**Che.** A trendy 24-hour café, Che is a popular stop for many clubbers. It has live music in the evenings, good coffee and tea, and even better desserts. ⊠*3 Poltavskaya ul., Vladimirskaya* ☎*812/716–7608* ⊕*www.cafeclubche.ru* ▭*No credit cards* Ⓜ*Ploshchad Vosstania.*

¢　✕**Teremok.** Cooked in front of your eyes, their famous blini—priced at
★ 40R–100R—are deservedly rated the best in town. *See* the full review *in* the City Center neighborhood. ⊠*93 Nevsky pr., Vladimirskaya* ☎*812/277–0881* Ⓜ*Ploshchad Vosstania*

FRENCH

$$$　✕**Bistro Garçon.** This comfortable, Parisian-style bistro on Nevsky prospekt may not have the timeworn quality of the real thing, but from the first bite of baguette, it doesn't matter—the food is the real deal here. The menu changes seasonally but you can always expect delicious onion soup, mussels, salad Roquefort, quiche, and crème brûlée. Fresh oysters are flown in from Cancale, France, on Monday and Thursday. With omelets starting at 100R, real croissants for 120R, and good coffee, this is one of the best places for breakfast in the city (it opens at 9 AM). The excellent Boulangerie Garçon is virtually next door, at 103 Nevsky prospekt. ⊠*95 Nevsky pr., Vladimirskaya* ☎*812/717–2467* ▭*AE, MC, V* Ⓜ*Ploshchad Vosstania.*

GEORGIAN

$$$$　✕**Bagrationi.** The dining room may be a little sterile and the live music droning, but they take their Georgian cooking seriously here. Everything is prepared fresh and very slowly, but it's worth the wait. Start with the *adjarsky khachapuri,* a Georgian calzone topped with egg. The fish and the *shashlyk* (grilled kebabs) are sure bets. Ask for the *tkemali* (plum) sauce with your meat. The dishes are heavy, but you can order half-portions, which will do less damage to your heart and wallet. Bagrationi also owns the simple next-door café, which serves many of the same dishes at one-third the price and half the wait. ⊠*2 Pl. Alexandra Nevskogo, at ul. Chaikovskovo, Vladimirskaya* ☎*812/333–2260* ⚐*Reservations essential* ▭*MC, V* Ⓜ*Chernyshevskaya.*

ITALIAN

$$　✕**Macaroni.** A sister restaurant of the excellent Il Grappolo (City Center), this trattoria serves simple Italian fare with an emphasis on fresh ingredients. The risotto primavera, pastas, pizzas, and salads are delicious and reasonably priced. The plush booths and muted shades of red, orange, brown, and green give this trattoria a unique look that sets it apart from other restaurants in the city. All and all, Macaroni is a comfortable, casual break from the hectic city. A 20% discount

is offered for weekday dining between noon and 5 PM. ✉*23 ul. Rubinshteina, Vladimirskaya* ☎*812/572–2849* ⊟*No credit cards* Ⓜ*Dostoevskaya, Vladimir-skaya, or Mayakovskaya.*

$ ✕**Marcelli's.** This friendly, unpretentious spot is a great place for a long, inexpensive lunch of pasta and salad or as a rendevous point for a late-night tryst (it's open until midnight). Enjoy the Caeser salad or the satisfying mushroom tortellini with sun-dried tomatoes in

> **WITHDRAWAL SYMPTOMS?**
>
> St. Petersburg is now fully stocked with Western fast-food outlets on and around Nevsky prospekt and other main areas if you need a fix. Familiar names include McDonald's, of course, Subway, Carl's Jr., Pizza Hut, Sbarro, and KFC (in partnership with a Russian company, Rostiks).

a dining room decorated with Italian knickknacks and bare wooden tables. For an un-Russian shopping experience, you can shop at the retail counter for imported cheeses, cold meats, and coffees. ✉*15 Vosstaniya ul., Vladimirskaya* ☎*812/702–8010* ⊕*www.marcellis.ru* ⊟*MC, V* Ⓜ*Ploshchad Vosstaniya.*

RUSSIAN

$$$$ ✕**Mechta Molokhovets.** A refined restaurant with prerevolutionary flair,
Fodor'sChoice "Molokhovets' Dream" has a tantalizing menu based entirely on a
★ famous 19th-century cookbook *A Gift to Young Housewives* by the Russian Mrs. Beaton, Yelena Molokhovets. Cooking is state-of-the-art here and you pay for it with entrées starting at a whopping 3,000R. Try venison fillet accompanied by baked pears filled with cranberries and soaked in chanterelle sauce, foie gras with hot saffron sauce and iced apples, or pike-perch soaked in a piquant sauce made with red caviar. The restaurant's solid waiters show reverence to the guests, serving them in a pleasant ceremonial, but not at all artificial, manner. With only six tables, it's an intimate dining experience. ✉*23/10 Kovensky per., Vladimirskaya* ☎*812/929–2247* ⊕*www.molokhovets.ru* ⚑*Reservations essential* ⊟*MC, V* Ⓜ*Ploshchad Vosstania.*

¢ ✕**Bliny Domik.** This homey, pocket-size place is all about blini. Everything served here is tasty, filling, and inexpensive—try the mushroom soup, followed by pork, cheese, or jam blini. *Blinchiki* are also available; they differ from blini in that they are wrapped around fillings and sometimes fried. Bliny Domik is no longer the secret it once was, but that only means it's even more foreigner-friendly. You sit at communal picnic tables, giving you a chance to meet other travelers and strike up conversations. ✉*8 Kolokolnaya ul., Vladimirskaya* ☎*812/315–9915 or 812/315–5345* ⊕*www.blinka.allcafe.info/menu* ⊟*AE, MC, V* Ⓜ*Vladimirskaya.*

¢ ✕**Chainaya Lozhka.** Distinguishable by its white and orange teaspoon logo, this is an extremely cheap and cheerful counter-service blini chain with locations all over downtown. *See the full review in the City Center neighborhood.* ✉*44 Ligovsky pr., Vladimirskaya* ☎*812/764–6433* ⊕*www.teaspoon.ru* Ⓜ*Ploschad Aleksandra Nevskovo.*

¢ ✕**Pirozhkovaya Mr. Baker.** With a choice of two dozen expertly cooked rich and filling pies priced between 40R and 80R apiece, this place is a budget traveler's dream. Fish and mushroom pies are particular favorites. Accompanied by traditional Russian soups served in hearty portions, the meal provides a substantial refuel. ⊠*33 ul. Vosstania, Vladimirskaya* ☎*812/279–6410* ⊟*No credit cards* Ⓜ*Ploshchad Vosstania.*

PETROGRAD SIDE

CHINESE

$$ ✕**Akvarium.** Chinese restaurants are easy to find all over the city, but this spacious, sophisticated spot, not far from the Peter and Paul Fortress and right next to the famed LenFilm movie studio, is particularly worth seeking out. Start with the meat-and-vegetable rolls in bean paper, or the wonton soup, which is pricey but full of flavor. Any of the dishes cooked in clay pots, such as the five-spice pork in garlic sauce or the duck, are good choices. The back of the menu has a curious "food tonic menu"—one for men, one for women—that's touted as being "good for health." ⊠*10 Kamennoostrovsky pr., Petrograd Side* ☎*812/326–8286* ⊟*MC, V* Ⓜ*Gorkovskaya.*

ECLECTIC

$$$$ ✕**Aquarel.** With three stories of floor-to-ceiling windows overlooking Vasilievsky Island's Rostral Columns and Stock Exchange, this flashy restaurant-boat docked on the Neva River has great views. There are two restaurants here, Aquarel and Aquarelissimo, and a disco on the top deck. The former combines European and Asian cuisines. Try the terrine of foie gras with cognac-scented winter fruits, Thai lobster hot pot, or Asian brined veal chops. The latter, on the third floor, serves modern Italian and Mediterranean cuisine. The tapas menu is a tempting option, while pasta papardelle and *vitello tonnato* (fillet of veal and fresh bluefin tuna) are among the restaurant's signature dishes. ⊠*Near Birzhevoy most, Petrograd Side* ☎*812/320–8600* ⊟*MC, V* Ⓜ*Sportivnaya.*

$$$ ✕**Bessonnitsa.** At the classy "Insomnia," innovative chefs creatively interpret European and Asian dishes. Veal fillet is served with fried grapefruit and blackberry sauce. The Vietnamese noodle soup Fo Bo arrives sizzling hot, leaving you to put the finishing touches on it by dropping in thin slices of raw meat. Pasta farfalle with mushrooms and cedar nuts is fresh and aromatic. Consider carrot cutlets and the French omelet for breakfast. Beige linen, terra-cotta lamps, and chocolate-color walls make up the comfortable interior that overlooks the Winter Palace. ⊠*3 Mytninskaya nab., Petrograd Side* ☎*812/973–3577* ⌂*Reservations essential* ⊟*MC, V* Ⓜ*Sportivnaya.*

FRENCH

$ ✕**Jean Jacques Rousseau.** This hidden-away gem is full of character and worth seeking out for its authentic bistro ambience even if the food is more peasant than haute cuisine. Mirrored walls, red and mahogany furnishings, attentive servers, and tables topped with paper for doodling are all part of the charm. With seating for only 25 people, it is

Vodka: A Taste of Russia

The national drink is an inseparable part of Russian social life. Vodka is drunk everywhere, with the intention of breaking down inhibitions and producing a state of conviviality Russians refer to as *dusha-dushe* (soul-to-soul). When a Russian taps his throat, beware: it's impossible to refuse this invitation to friendship. If you have a cold, sore throat, or any such minor ailment, don't be surprised if someone prescribes a shot of vodka—even for a hangover. Russians' belief in the curative and preventative powers of this drink is almost limitless.

There are hundreds of brands of vodka in Russia, as a glance into any store will show. Some of these are rough and best left alone; two of the best are Flagman and Russky Standart, although there are many acceptable cheaper brands. Alcohol counterfeiting, which can lead to alcohol poisoning, is a big problem, so you should always purchase vodka from a reputable-looking store, and never from a kiosk.

When you're drinking vodka, there is some etiquette involved. In North America and Great Britain, vodka is generally associated with cocktails and martinis. In Russia, mixing vodka with anything else is considered a waste, unless the mixer is beer, which produces a fearsome beverage known as *yorsh*. Vodka is meant to be gulped down in one go, not sipped. Since this can give you a bit of a kick, Russians always have some *zakuski,* or snacks (including pickles, herring, boiled potatoes, and black bread) to chase the shot. You may witness something called the "vodka procedure," which, if you want to try it yourself, goes roughly as follows. Prepare a forkful of food or chunk of bread. Inhale and exhale quickly, bringing the food to your nose. Breathe in and tip the vodka down your throat. Now breathe out again, and eat your food.

Vodka shots (unlike beer and wine) are downed collectively, and always preceded by a toast. You'll score points if you propose toasts—it doesn't matter if they are in English, particularly if you wax long and eloquent. Drinking before a toast is considered a faux pas of the first order. Although you're expected to gulp down the first couple of shots, no one will mind if you take it a little easier after that—saying *choot'-choot', pozhaluista* (just a little, please) is a polite way of asking for a smaller refill. Vodka is also considered predominantly a man's drink, so it's more acceptable for women to take things easier.

If all this sounds like an ordeal, rest assured that vodka drinking can be an extremely pleasurable experience, involving good food, great company, and a unique sense of mild inebriation that can last for hours. It's a memorable taste of Russia in more ways than one.

advisable to come early or call ahead to enjoy fine wines (about 150R per glass) with classics like onion soup, steak and bordelaise sauce, and crème brûlée. It also offers one of the best Continental breakfast menus in the city, served until 1 PM. ⊠2 *Gatchinskaya ul., Peterograd Side* ☎812/232–9981 ⊟*MC, V* Ⓜ*Chkalovskaya or Petrogradskaya.*

GEORGIAN

$ ✕**Tbliso.** A lot of thought was put in to the task of refurbishing this busy and authentic Georgian restaurant which evokes the atmosphere of old Tblisi, the capital of Russia's southern neighbor. There may be political tensions between the nations these days, but Russians' love affair with Georgian cuisine, from salads such as *lobio* (bean salad) and grilled meat and fish *shashlyks* (shish kebabs) to wonderful breads such as *lavash* (flat bread) and *khatchapuri* (cheese-filled bread), remains passionate. Tbliso satisfies this passion and then some with servers in national costume and a Georgian choir that serenades diners. If you visit only one Georgian restaurant in St. Petersburg, make it this one. ✉ *10 Sytninskaya ul., Petrograd Side* ☎ *812/232–9391* ═ *MC, V* Ⓜ *Petrogradskaya or Gorkovskaya.*

RUSSIAN

$$ ✕**Chekhov.** Step into an early-20th-century Russian country home at this small family restaurant. Wicker furniture, handwoven napkins, and a birdcage with canaries and finches are some of the charms hidden at this shady backstreet spot. The menu lovingly re-creates Russian recipes of yesteryear, such as grilled quail with fresh dill resting on sweet baked apple halves stuffed with a mixture of cowberries (lingonberries), pine nuts, and rhubarb; stuffed trout with blini and potatoes; and, as an alternative to vodka, a range of fruit liqueurs that will transport you to the world of Chekhov's *The Cherry Orchard.* ✉ *4 Petropavlovskaya ul., Petrograd Side* ☎ *812/347–6045* ☜ *Reservations essential* ═ *MC, V* Ⓜ *Petrogradskaya.*

KIROV ISLANDS

RUSSIAN

$$ ✕**Russkaya Rybalka.** The gimmick at "Russian Fishing" is that you catch your own dinner. It's set in a charming wooden house overlooking a lake full of trout, sturgeon, and beluga sterlet. Tackle, bait, and expert advice are provided, and your catch is prepared before you on the grill. It even operates during winter when everything else is frozen solid—the restaurant literally breaks up the ice in the lake so it's still fishable. There are several other options on the menu as well, including a baked eggplant dish that is quite good. ✉ *Primorsky Park Pobedy, 11 Yuzhnaya doroga, Kirov Islands* ☎ *812/323–9813* ⊕ *www.russian-fishing.ru* ═ *No credit cards* Ⓜ *Krestovsky Ostrov.*

WHERE TO STAY

The city's capacity for overnight visitors is small, but growing. By 2010 St. Petersburg plans to have added dozens of new hotels. What the city especially lacks are two- and three-star hotels, which would be a welcome alternative to the predominance of expensive ones, although mid-range hotels are opening all the time.

On an organized tour, you're likely to land in one of the old Intourist standbys, which used to belong to the Soviet tourist agency that enjoyed a monopoly. Most U.S. and British tour operators take advantage of the discounted rates at the Moskva, the Pribaltiyskaya, or the St. Petersburg. The main reason to choose one of these hotels is their lower rates; note that many of them are not convenient to the major attractions. Almost all of the hotels with Web sites have online booking facilities, though you should confirm via phone.

An expanding number of realty agents can organize a suitable and safe apartment rental, usually in the center of the city. The prices for such apartments usually run the level of three-star hotels, but they often have much more space. Another budget stay option is the mini-hotel; they are as close as Russia gets to bed-and-breakfasts.

WHAT IT COSTS IN RUSSIAN RUBLES					
	¢	$	$$	$$$	$$$$
For 2 People	under 2,500R	2,500R–5,000R	5,001R–7,500R	7,501R–10,000R	over 10,000R

Prices are for a standard double room in high season, excluding taxes and service charge.

CITY CENTER (PALACE SQUARE, THE HERMITAGE)

$$$$
Fodor's Choice
★
Grand Hotel Europe. Combining the elegance of prerevolutionary St. Petersburg with every modern amenity, this luxurious 1875 vies for the unofficial title of finest accommodation in town. Behind the stunning baroque facade lies an art nouveau interior, complete with stained-glass windows and antique furnishings. Pleasing shades of mauve, cream, and gold decorate the stylish and comfortable rooms. The Russian staff upholds European standards but since its 1990s renaissance the Grand Hotel Europe has become worn around the edges and acquired a vaguely sinister ambience. Nevsky prospekt, the Hermitage, and Ploshchad Iskusstv are all within walking distance. If money is no object, this is the place to stay. **Pros:** elegant interiors; prime location; historic building. **Cons:** with the average room going for 24,050R, a stay here is well beyond most budgets; a bit frayed about the edges. ✉ 1/7 Mikhailovskaya ul., City Center 191011 ☎ 812/329–6000 ⊕ www.grand-hotel-europe.com 🛏 212 rooms, 65 suites ⌂ In-hotel: 5 restaurants, room service, bar, gym, laundry service, public Internet, no-smoking rooms ☐ AE, MC, V Ⓜ Nevsky Prospekt or Gostinny Dvor.

$$$$
Kempinski Hotel Moika 22. This new hotel has successfully wrested the unofficial title of "St. Petersburg's best five-star hotel" from its rival the Grand Hotel Europe by providing more personal service. The hotel retained the pretty 1853 facade of the palace in which it was built while constructing a modern hotel inside. There are romantic views of the Winter Palace and two spectacular atria flood the building with light. The rooms have a subtle maritime look with navy, cream, and polished-wood detailing. You'll also find a French restaurant, a cozy tea room, a tony lounge, and a wellness center with skyline views within. **Pros:** unbeatable views; unpretentious personal service; next to the Hermitage. **Cons:** limited business services; some rooms overlook

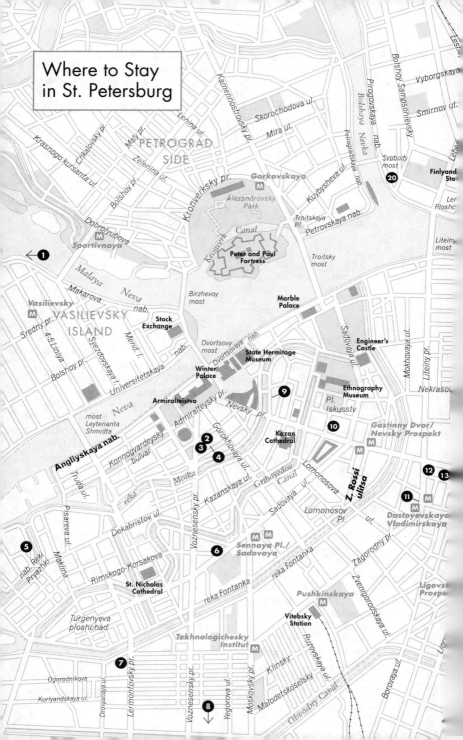

Where to Stay in St. Petersburg

PETROGRAD SIDE

Chkalovskaya pr.
Krasnogo kursanta ul.
Maly pr.
Lenina ul.
Zelenina ul.
Bolshoy pr.
Kamennostroisky pr.
Skorochodova ul.
Mira ul.
Bolshaya Pirogovskaya
Petrogradskaya nab.
Bolshoy Sampsonievsky
Vyborgskaya
Smirnov ul.

Dobrolyubova
Kronverksky pr.
Gorkovskaya
Kuybysheva ul.
Svobody most
20
Finlyand Sta

Sportivnaya

Alexándrovsky Park
Kronverk Canal
Troitskaya Pl.
Petrovskaya nab.
Ler Ploshc

Malaya Neva nab.
Makarova
Kronverk
Peter and Paul Fortress
Troitsky most
Liteiny most

1

Vasilievsky
VASILIEVSKY ISLAND
Sredny pr.
4-5 Liniya
Svezdovskaya l.
Mend. l.
Bolshoy pr.
Universitetskaya nab.

Birzhevoy most
Stock Exchange
Marble Palace

Dvortsovy most
Dvortsovaya nab.
State Hermitage Museum
Engineer's Castle
Sadovaya ul.
Mokhovaya ul.

Neva most Leytenanta Shmidta
Winter Palace
Ethnography Museum
Pl. Iskusstv
Nekraso

Armiralteistvo
Nevsky pr.
9

Angliyskaya nab.
Admiralteysky pr.
Gorokhovaya ul.
Kazan Cathedral
10
Gostinny Dvor/ Nevsky Prospekt

Truda ul.
Konnogvardeysky bulvar
reka Moika
2
3
4
Kazanskaya ul.
Griboyedov Canal
Lomonosova ul.
Z. Rossi ulitsa
12 **13**

Pisareva ul.
Voznesensky pr.
Sadovaya ul.
Lomonosov Pl.
11
Dostoyevskaya Vladimirskaya

Dekabristov ul.
5
reka Fontanka
Zagorodny pr.
Zvenigorodskaya ul.
Ligovsk Prospe

nab. Reki Pryazhki
Maklina
Rimskogo-Korsakova
6
Sennaya Pl./ Sadovaya
reka Fontanka
Pushkinskaya
St. Nicholas Cathedral
reka Fontanka
Vitebsky Station

Turgenyeva ploshchad
Tekhnologichesky Institut

Ogorodnikova
Lermontovsky pr.
7
Drovyanaya
Klinsky
Moskovsky pr.
Ruzovskaya ul.
Borovaya ul.
Lor

Kurlyandskaya ul.
Voznesensky pr.
Yegorova ul.
8
Malodetskoselsky
Obvodny Canal

3

Mineralnaya ul.

Zhukova ul.

**VYBORG
SIDE**

Arsenalnaya ul.

Kondratyevsky pr.

Sverdlovskaya nab.

**Ploshchad
Lenina**

Komsomola ul.

rsenalnaya nab.

Neva

Shpalernaya ul.

**Taurida
Palace**

kovskogo ul.

*Tavrichesky
Park*

Tavricheskaya ul.

rnyshevskaya

Saltykova-Shchedrina ul.

Tulskaya ul.

**LITEINY
SMOLNY** **18**

Suvorovski pr.

Grechesky pr.

8 Sovetskaya ul.

Moiseyenko ul.

Novgorodskaya ul.

vskogo
l.

17

Mytninskaya ul.

14

Bakunina

**Ploshchad
Vosstaniya/
Mayakovskaya**

Stary

vsky
ation

VLADIMIRSKAYA

Nevsky pr.

*A. Nevsky
Pl.*

16

**Ploshchad
Aleksandra Nevskovo**

**Alexander
Nevsky Lavra**

15

19

KEY

M *Metro stops*

busy restaurant; no gym or pool. ✉*22 nab. reki Moika, City Center* ☎*812/335–9111* ⊕*www.kempinski-st-petersburg.com* ↩*174 rooms, 23 suites* ⌂*In-hotel: 2 restaurants, bar, concierge, laundry service, parking (no fee)* ▭*AE, DC, MC, V* Ⓜ*Nevsky Prospekt.*

ADMIRALTEISKY

$$$$ 🏨**Ambassador.** This nine-story hotel opened in 2005 next to Yusupovsky Garden. The over the top entrance hall in Vegas-style white and cream has marble floors, leather sofas, and sparkling Czech glass chandeliers. The focus of the interior is the atrium that houses the Ambassador restaurant and allows romantic views of the city. Guest rooms are furnished with light-brown alder-tree furniture, plasma TV sets, and high-standard bath facilities. ■TIP➔**There are also rooms equipped for disabled guests.** The restaurant on an upper floor offers not only exquisite cuisine but also a panoramic view of St. Petersburg. **Pros:** modern building; quiet location; stylish interiors. **Cons:** soulless building; not quite central locaton: a 7-minute walk to the metro and a 20-minute walk to sights; over-the-top interiors. ✉*5– 7 pr. Rimskovo-Korsakova, Admiralteisky 190068* ☎*812/331–8844* ⊕*www.ambassador-hotel.ru* ↩*255 rooms* ⌂*In-room: safe. In-hotel: 2 restaurants, bar, pool, gym, laundry service, public Wi-Fi, parking (no fee)* ▭*AE, DC, MC, V* Ⓜ*Sadovaya or Sennaya.*

> ### THE ASTORIA AND HITLER
>
> Legend has it that Adolf Hitler, on giving the order to lay siege to Leningrad in September 1941, claimed he'd be celebrating New Year's in the Astoria Hotel. The fact that Leningraders held back the Nazis, at the cost of hundreds of thousands of lives, until 1944 and Hitler never got his party in the hotel, is a source of great local pride.

$$$$ 🏨**Astoria.** The Astoria is actually two hotels: it connects with the older,
Fodor'sChoice   slightly less luxurious Angleterre, whose enduring "fame" is thanks
★   to the beloved poet Sergei Yesenin's suicide there in 1925. Built in art nouveau style between 1910 and 1912, the Astoria was one of St. Petersburg's most renowned hotels before the Revolution of 1917; despite protests by residents, the original internal structure was gutted and rebuilt in the early 1990s during the renovation that connected it to the Angleterre. Nevertheless, it's a magnificent hotel in downtown St. Petersburg, near the Hermitage. Antiques retrieved from various museums decorate the splendid interior. The restaurant Borsalino at the Angleterre ($$$$) affords memorable views of St. Isaac's Cathedral. **Pros:** amazing location; classy dining; stylish rooms. **Cons:** odd-shape rooms; busy with tour groups; security checks when a VIP stays here. ✉*39 Bolshaya Morskaya ul., Admiralteisky 190000* ☎*812/313–5757* ⊕*www.hotel-astoria.ru* ↩*223 rooms in Astoria, 213 rooms in Angleterre* ⌂*In-hotel: 2 restaurants, bar, pool, gym* ▭*AE, MC, V* Ⓜ*Sennaya Ploshchad or Sadovaya.*

$$ 🏨**Casa Leto.** Next to the Hermitage and St. Isaac's Cathedral, Casa Leto has a mere five rooms. With high ceilings, stucco work, and neutral tones, rooms are spare, but larger than average for the city.

Complimentary extras include breakfast, light refreshments, local telephone calls (and international to most destinations), and high-speed Internet. The staff can organize tickets to performances and tours beyond the usual, such as mushroom picking, ice fishing, or visiting the vaults of the Hermitage. **Pros:** personal service; stylish rooms; attention to detail. **Cons:** on a busy street; shares a building with a sushi joint and hair salon; possible disruption from a planned expansion in 2008. ⊠*34 ul. Bolshaya Morskaya, Admiralteiskyr 190000* ☎*812/314–6622 or 812/600–1096* ⊕*www.casaleto.com* ⇗*5 rooms* ⌂*In-room: Wi-Fi. In-hotel: airport shuttle* ⊟*AE, DC, MC, V* ⊺⊚*BP* Ⓜ*Sadovaya or Sennaya.*

¢ 🖼 **Matisov Domik.** If you're looking for homey accommodations, consider this small, quiet hotel, a cozy blue cottage with a tiled roof. Most of the rooms overlook the Pryazhka River and the small, pleasant yard with maple and chestnut trees, flowers, and benches. Though the halls are narrow, the pleasant pastel colors, wood paneling, and smiling staff are welcoming. Continental breakfast is included. **Pros:** ten minutes from the Mariinsky Theatre; shuttle buses provided; pleasant leafy location. **Cons:** far from metro stations; rooms have thin walls, especially on third floor; no air-conditioning. ⊠*3/1 nab. Reki Pryazhki, Admiralteisky 190121* ☎*812/495–0242 or 812/495–0374* ⊕*www. matisov.spb.ru* ⇗*46 rooms, 2 suites, 7 apartments* ⌂*In-room: no a/ c, refrigerator. In-hotel: public Internet, airport shuttle, parking (no fee)* ⊟*MC, V* ⊺⊚*CP.*

VASILIEVSKY ISLAND

$$$ 🖼 **Park Inn Pribaltiyskaya.** This huge '70s-era skyscraper is frequently booked by tourist groups and international conferences. The modest furnishings in the clean rooms are adequate and much effort has been put into freshening up the look of the hotel and providing more comprehensive services in its out-of-the-way location. The views of the Gulf of Finland from rooms on the western side of the hotel are phenomenal, especially at sunset, but otherwise the location on the western tip of Vasilievsky Island is a drawback. The predominantly residential area has a combination of endless Soviet-era high-rises and modern elite apartment buildings, but few shops and restaurants. Breakfast is included. **Pros:** self-contained services; open-air location. **Cons:** enormous Soviet-era monster; windswept location; far from the metro and a good 20-minute drive from downtown St. Petersburg. ⊠*14 ul. Korablestroitelei, Vasilievsky Island 199226* ☎*812/356–0158 or 812/356–3001* ⇗*1,180 rooms, 20 suites* ⌂*In-hotel: 11 restaurants, room service, bars, pool, laundry facilities, laundry service, public Wi-Fi, parking (fee)* ⊟*AE, DC, MC, V* ⊺⊚*BP* Ⓜ*Vasileostrovskaya, accessible from hotel by bus.*

VLADIMIRSKAYA (LOWER NEVSKY PROSPEKT)

$$$$ 🖼 **Corinthia Nevsky Palace Hotel.** This spacious and light-filled hotel is a complete reconstruction of two 19th-century buildings. The main building, facing Nevsky prospekt, was built in 1861 in neoclassic style

and belonged to the actors' dynasty of the Samoilovs. A museum within the hotel honors the family. Behind the historical facade, huge glass doors reveal the most modern of interiors, full of glass but devoid of character. The central location means no time lost in the city's traffic jams. The hotel is also known for its fine restaurant complex, which serves just about any cuisine you might crave. The hotel's high prices lower if it is not full. **Pros:** on busy Nevsky prospekt; full business services; ruthless efficiency. **Cons:** on crowded and loud Nevsky prospekt; full of business travelers; ruthless efficiency. ✉ *57 Nevsky pr., City Center, 191025* ☎ *812/380–2001* ⊕ *www.corinthia.ru* 🛏 *283 rooms, 22 suites* ⚬ *In-hotel: 4 restaurants, bar, gym, laundry facilities, public Internet, parking (no fee)* ⊟ *AE, DC, MC, V* Ⓜ *Mayakovskaya.*

$$$$
★ 🏨 **Radisson SAS Royal.** Originally built in 1765, this grand historic structure first became a hotel in 1879; the writer Anton Chekhov stayed here during his first visit to the city. In Soviet times the building housed Café Saigon, the noted hangout for city dissidents and rock-and-rollers. Once again it's a sumptuous hotel, with antique reproductions, soft cream walls and navy carpets in the guest rooms, and heated floors in the bathrooms. On the corner of Nevsky prospekt and Vladimirsky prospekt, it's in the heart of St. Petersburg. The hotel can also offer visa support (via previous fax arrangements). Check the Web site for special rates. Guide dogs for blind guests are allowed. **Pros:** interiors have character; Scandinavian efficiency; centrally located. **Cons:** on Vladimirsky prospekt side, rooms can be dark; on Nevsky prospekt side, noisy; a bit of a warren. ✉ *49/2 Nevsky pr., City Center 191025* ☎ *812/322–5000* ⊕ *www.radisson.com* 🛏 *147 rooms, 17 suites* ⚬ *In-room: safe, ethernet. In-hotel: restaurant, room service, bar, gym, laundry service* ⊟ *AE, DC, MC, V* Ⓜ *Mayakovskaya.*

$$$ 🏨 **Dostoyevsky.** This modern hotel, named after famed writer Fyodor Dostoyevsky, who used to live close by, presents the new standard among St. Petersburg three-star hotels. Directly in the trade and hotel complex of Vladimirsky Passage (with 200 shops), the decor combines classic style with modern comfort. Rooms have heated floors and Internet access. Some are equipped for hosting disabled travelers. A 24-hour supermarket and currency exchange in the complex can save you precious time. Breakfast is included. **Pros:** part of a busy mall; next to a metro station; stylish restaurants nearby. **Cons:** part of a cheesy mall; next to a traffic-clogged intersection; overpriced restaurants nearby. ✉ *19 Vladimirsky pr., City Center 191002* ☎ *812/331–3200* 🛏 *207 rooms* ⚬ *In-hotel: restaurant, bar, pool, gym, laundry service, public Wi-Fi, parking (no fee)* ⊟ *AE, DC, MC, V* ⍟ *BP* Ⓜ *Vladimirskaya or Dostoyevskaya.*

$$ 🏨 **Moskva.** The main attraction here is location: this enormous, visibly aging hotel is literally on top of the metro and faces the entrance to the 18th-century Alexander Nevsky Lavra, which is at one end of Nevsky prospekt, but still in the center of town. The Moskva has recently upgraded rooms, replacing carpets, adding new curtains, and so on, and is trying sincerely to shake off a reputation for lackluster service. Though the rooms are hardly sophisticated, they are neat and clean, as are the public areas with their flowers and greenery. This is a popular

option for tour groups. **Pros:** location, location, location. **Con:** service is not yet up to par. ⊠*2 Pl. Alexandra Nevskogo, City Center 193317* ☎*812/274–0022 or 812/274–4001* ⊕*www.hotel-moscow.ru* ↝*770 rooms* ☝*In-hotel: 2 restaurants, bars, laundry service, public Internet, parking (fee)* ▭*AE, DC, MC, V* Ⓜ*Ploshchad Alexandra Nevskovo.*

$$ ⌂**Oktyabrskaya.** It's hard to miss this Soviet-era monolith in the city center. Directly opposite the Moscow station, the Oktyabrskaya hits you right between the eyes with its huge sign, LENINGRAD–GOROD GEROI (Leningrad–Hero City), set on top. The location, near Nevsky prospekt, is great. The hotel opened in 1851 in conjunction with Russia's first railroad between the then capital of St. Petersburg and Moscow. In those times it was known as one of the city's best hotels. The hotel no longer has that reputation but has undergone extensive renovations and has added dark-wood furniture and cream accents in the rooms. There's an annex across the street and breakfast is included in the room rate. **Pros:** next to main railway station; in the heart of shopping district; surrounded by restaurants. **Cons:** huge and impersonal; on a noisy intersection; surrounded by litter-strewn streets. ⊠*10 Ligovsky pr., City Center 193036* ☎*812/717–6330* ⊕*www.hoteloktiabrskaya.ru* ↝*555 rooms in main hotel, 108 rooms in annex* ☝*In-room: no a/c, dial-up. In-hotel: restaurant, bars* ▭*AE, DC, MC, V* ⍟*BP* Ⓜ*Ploshchad Vosstaniya.*

¢ ⌂**St. Petersburg International Hostel.** One of the first projects to freshen up the entrepreneurial landscape of the city, this joint Russian-American enterprise was launched in the early '90s. The converted dormitory has rooms holding three to five beds; breakfast and linens are included. The staff is friendly, and the location near the Moscow station is excellent. An in-house Sindbad Travel caters to budget travelers and is the starting point of walking tours. There's a curfew from 1 AM to 8 AM. The hostel fills up quickly in summer. **Pros:** professional services for independent travelers; travel agency with visa support; friendly atmosphere. **Cons:** located on a small street that is difficult to find; often fully booked; small rooms. ⊠*28 3rd Sovietskaya ul., City Center* ✉*Box 8, SF-53501, Lappeenranta, Finland* ☎*812/329–8018* ⊕*www.ryh.ru* ↝*55 beds with shared bath* ▭*No credit cards* Ⓜ*Ploshchad Vosstaniya or Mayakovskaya.*

ITEINY/SMOLNY

$$$$ ⌂**Grand Emerald Hotel.** A dark-glass exterior with a modern turret fronts this luxurious, high-tech hotel built in 2003. Inside, marble floors and chandeliers made of Swarovski crystal decorate the elegant public spaces. The airy atrium café has wicker chairs, old-fashioned

street lamps, and plenty of natural light. Italian wood furniture fills the bright, spacious guest rooms, some of which have parquet floors. Most rooms overlook one the city's oldest streets—Suvorovsky prospekt—or offer an enchanting view into the atrium. Some standard rooms have a bay window where comfortable arm chairs and coffee tables are arranged. Bathrobes, towels, slippers, and amenities are at the guests' disposal. Breakfast and tax are included in the room price. **Pros:** strenuous efforts at luxury service; large rooms; modern building. **Cons:** 20-minute walk from downtown; no metro nearby; anonymous district. ⊠ *18 Suvorovsky pr., City Center 193036* 📠 *812/740–5000* ⊕ *www.grandhotelemerald.com* ⚲ *59 rooms, 34 suites* ⌂ *In-room: safe. In-hotel: restaurant, room service, bar, gym, spa, laundry service, public Wi-Fi, airport shuttle, no-smoking rooms* ⊟ *AE, MC, V* ⦾ *BP* Ⓜ *Ploschad Vosstaniya or Chernyshevskaya.*

VESYOLYI POSYOLOK

$$ ⊡ **Deson-Ladoga.** This three-star hotel, built in the 1960s and renovated in the 1990s, sits on the right bank of the Neva. The location may look slightly inconvenient compared to the centrally located hotels, but it's a five-minute walk from a metro station. The hotel specializes in hosting foreign tourists, most often from Scandinavia and Europe. The personnel of the hotel speak English and are particularly attuned to the needs of foreign guests. The rooms are modest, but fresh and comfortable, with light colors and dark-brown furniture. The lobby, which also houses a souvenir shop, is small but cozy. The price includes a Swedish breakfast and sauna. The restaurant serves European and Chinese food. **Pros:** handy for the Ice Palace; quiet neighborhood; suits both business and tourist travelers. **Cons:** impersonal; far from city center; overpriced. ⊠ *26 Shaumyana pr., Vesyolyi Posyolok 195213* 📠 *812/528–5393* ⚲ *101 rooms* ⌂ *In-room: no a/c. In-hotel: restaurant, bar, public Internet, parking (no fee), no-smoking rooms* ⊟ *AE, DC, MC, V* ⦾ *BP* Ⓜ *Novocherkasskaya.*

$ ⊡ **Okhtinskaya-Victoria.** You get a nice view of Smolny cathedral across
★ the river from some of the rooms here, and though St. Petersburg's main attractions and the metro are some distance away, a hotel shuttle bus runs to Nevsky prospekt. A controversial new skyscraper to serve as the HQ of energy monopoly Gazprom is proposed to be built nearby. Service at this modern hotel is unusually friendly, and the reasonable rates include breakfast. Marble and chrome adorn the interior, and the public areas are cheery and bright. Imported furnishings and pretty flowered wallpaper decorate the clean rooms. Most have balconies, but only suites have full bathtubs. **Pros:** cheaper than most hotels; good views; Nevsky shuttle bus. **Cons:** Gazprom tower development could become a nuisance; cheap-looking fixtures; scary to get to late at night. ⊠ *4 Bolsheokhtinsky pr., Okhta 195027* 📠 *812/227–4438 or 812/227–3767* ⊕ *www.okhtinskaya.spb.ru* ⚲ *204 rooms* ⌂ *In-hotel: 2 restaurants, bars* ⊟ *AE, DC, MC, V* ⦾ *BP* Ⓜ *Novocherkasskaya, accessible from hotel by bus.*

VYBORG SIDE

$ ⬚ **St. Petersburg.** Although this is not the luxury hotel it once was, if you
Fodor'sChoice can land a waterfront room, the St. Petersburg is the place to stay for
★ ultimate White Nights vistas. If you can't get a room facing the Neva
River and the waterfront architecture, you'll likely have a depressing city
view for only slightly less. The Finnish-decorated interior is faded and
the furnishings are worn, but the rooms and public areas are clean. The
Congress Hall makes the hotel popular with international conference
planners. The Finland station and metro are within walking distance,
but the route is unpleasant and takes you along a busy highway. Swedish breakfast is included. **Pros:** phenomenal White Nights views; cruiser
Avrora nearby; new middle-class residential buildings have spruced up
the area. **Cons:** dingy winter views; cut off by open bridges in summer;
surrounding area is becoming gentrified and expensive. ✉ *5/2 Pirogovskaya nab., Vyborg Side 194044* ☎ *812/380–1919* ⊕ *www.hotel-spb.ru*
🛏 *410 rooms* ⟁ *In-room: no a/c, dial-up. In-hotel: 2 restaurants, bars*
🖃 *AE, DC, MC, V* ⛟ *BP* Ⓜ *Ploshchad Lenina.*

SOUTHERN SUBURBS

$$$ ⬚ **Park Inn Pulkovskaya.** The attractive, Scandinavian-design interior of
this hotel is in decent condition, thanks to renovations for the city's 300th-
anniversary celebrations in 2003 and more recent upgrades by its new
Western management. Far from the city center, the hotel is convenient to
the airport and handy for travelers who wish to visit the Imperial palaces
of Pushkin, Pavlovsk, and Peterhof. The metro is a 10-minute walk away,
and the ride into town takes 20 minutes. The surrounding residential area
has plenty of shops and a few restaurants. The views from the rooms—of
gloomy high-rises and smokestacks or of the severe, very Soviet Victory
Square monument—can be depressing. Breakfast is included. **Pros:** quiet
residential surroundings; Victory Square museum nearby; en route to the
airport. **Cons:** on a busy intersection; next to Victory Square monument
eyesore; miles from the city center. ✉ *1 Pobedy Pl., Southern Suburbs
196240* ☎ *812/140–3900* ⊕ *www.pulkovskaya.ru* 🛏 *840 rooms, 17
suites* ⟁ *In-room: dial-up. In-hotel: 4 restaurants, bars, pools, some pets
allowed* 🖃 *AE, DC, MC, V* ⛟ *BP* Ⓜ *Moskovskaya.*

$$ ⬚ **Azimut–Hotel St. Petersburg Sovietskaya.** The recent renovation has
done much to improve the once-decaying interiors of this 1960s con-
crete-and-steel monstrosity in an unattractive section of downtown.
Although the location allows for some good views of St. Petersburg's
canals and sights, it's still a long walk to just about anywhere, including
the metro. A currency-exchange office, taxi and transfer service, and
visa support are all available. The room rate includes a Swedish breakfast, and if you book through the Web site you can get a discount. **Pros:**
good value; genuine efforts made to improve service; suits the business
traveler. **Cons:** looks awful from the outside; obscure part of town;
service may falter. ✉ *43/1 Lermontovsky pr., Vladimirskaya 190103*
☎ *812/740–2640* ⊕ *www.azimuthotels.ru* 🛏 *1,000 rooms* ⟁ *In-room:
no a/c (some), safe (some), dial-up (some). In-hotel: 2 restaurants, bars*
🖃 *AE, MC, V* ⛟ *BP* Ⓜ *Baltiyskaya.*

CLOSE UP

St. Petersburg's Mini-Hotels

During the Bolshevik Revolution many of the city center's lavish mansions where appropriated from their owners and divided into communal apartments. Though some residents still live in these apartments, many have moved to private residences in the suburbs. This created an opportunity to dent St. Petersburg's chronic lack of hotels, and entrepreneurs transformed the former mansions–turned–apartments into "mini-hotels."

Much nicer in this reincarnation, these small guesthouses offer an intimate, reasonably priced alternative to the city's major hotels.

¢–$ Central Inn (✉ *2 ul. Yakubovicha, Apt 14* ☎ *812/571–4516* ⊕ *www.central-inn.ru* ↩ *14 rooms*) is in a prime location next to St. Isaac's Cathedral and has a small gym and a sauna.

$–$$ Comfort Hotel (✉ *25 ul. Bolshaya Morskaya* ☎ *812/570–6700* ⊕ *www.comfort-hotel.ru* ↩ *14 rooms*) is close to the Admiralty with plenty of good restaurants nearby. Single rooms are a great value but the doubles are a bit overpriced and Bolshaya Morskaya can be noisy.

$ Herzen House (✉ *25 ul. Bolshaya Morskaya* ☎ *812/571–5098* ⊕ *www.herzenhotel.spb.ru* ↩ *20 rooms*) is located within the same building as the Comfort Hotel and has rooms with air-conditioning.

¢ Nevsky Inn 1 (✉ *2 Kirpichny per., Apt 19* ☎ *812/972–6873* ⊕ *www.nevskyinn.ru* ↩ *7 rooms*) is small, inexpensive, and friendly. Watch out if you're carrying heavy luggage, there's a steep climb to the fourth floor.

$ Nevsky Inn 2 (✉ *9 ul. Malaya Morskaya, Apt 3* ☎ *812/312–2686* ⊕ *www.nevskyinn.ru* ↩ *4 rooms*) has relatively large rooms with sofas and air-conditioning. However, the windows face a noisy street and the kitchen is very small.

$ Old Vienna (✉ *13 ul. Malaya Morskaya, entrance on Gorokhovaya ul.* ☎ *812/312–9339* ⊕ *www.vena.old-spb.ru* ↩ *14 rooms*), with its stylish art nouveau interior, sauna, and DVD players in the rooms is a step above most mini-hotels. It's a bit hard to find, though, on the third floor of the building.

$ Rachmaninov Yard (✉ *5 Kazanskaya ul.* ☎ *812/571–7618* ⊕ *www.hotelrachmaninov.com* ↩ *25 rooms*) has views of Kazan Cathedral and busy Nevsky prospekt, and is furnished with antiques. Herzen University is nearby.

$ Residence by the Admiralty (✉ *8 Gorokhovaya ul.* ☎ *812/312–7377* ⊕ *www.residencehotels.ru* ↩ *4 rooms*) is popular with Russians and has a business hotel feel. There are two other mini-hotels within the Residence group as well.

APARTMENTS

City Realty. This American-owned company will find whatever type of accommodation you're looking for, be it a mini-hotel or B&B or a selection of central apartments, which it normally owns. It's better to make a reservation a week or two in advance in order to choose from a wider range of apartments. Prices vary but are competitive with hotel rates, and City Realty also offers visa support and registration. **Pros:** can choose your own apartment; personalized service;

downtown locations. **Cons:** overpriced; no services; feels like staying in a stranger's house. ✉ *35 ul. Bolshaya Morskaya, City Center* ☎ *812/312-7842* ⊕ *www.cityrealtyrussia.com* ⊘ *Weekdays 9:30–6:30* Ⓜ *Nevsky Prospekt.*

NIGHTLIFE & THE ARTS

Your best source for information about what's going on is the *St. Petersburg Times* (⊕ *www.sptimes.ru*), a free, local, independent English-language newspaper. It comes out on Tuesday and Friday and can be found at Western airline offices, bars, clubs, hotels, cafés, and other places generally patronized by foreigners or students. The Friday edition has a calendar of events in the All About Town section, with theater and concert listings, and a restaurant column.

THE ARTS

St. Petersburg's cultural life is one of its top attractions. Except for the most renowned theaters, tickets are easily available and inexpensive. You can buy them at the box offices of the theaters themselves, at *teatralnaya kassa* (theater kiosks) throughout the city—Central Box Office No. 1 is at 42 Nevsky prospekt (☎ *812/571-3183*) and is open daily from 11 to 7—and at service bureaus in hotels, most of which post performance listings in their main lobby. Note that many venues controversially continue to charge different prices for Russians and foreigners. ■ TIP→ **If you know a local resident, they can help you to get a ticket at a local price—as much as five times cheaper—albeit involving a bit of deception.**

The Mariinsky Theatre sells tickets online through its Web site (⊕ *www. mariinsky.ru*), or at the theater itself, not through other agencies.

Bear in mind that theater tickets purchased through hotels are the priciest of all, as most hotels tend to charge a markup on the foreigner price. All in all, your best option is to go in person to the theater concerned and buy the ticket there.

Most major theaters close down between mid-July and early August and start up again in mid-September or early October. However, summer is also the time for touring companies from other regions in Russia to come to town, so it's a rare day that there are no shows on at all. Sumptuous balls are thrown in the most famous palaces and concert halls in winter; one such event is the Temirkanov Ball on New Year's Eve.

FESTIVALS

St. Petersburg's premier arts event is the Mariinsky Theatre's **Stars of the White Nights** (☎ *812/714-4344* ⊕ *www.mariinsky.ru*), which stretches from the end of May until the middle of July or longer. The event's founder and driving force is Mariinsky's indefatigable artistic director Valery Gergiev, who puts on a pantheon of international stars and orchestras that any other Russian festival can only dream of inviting.

It helps that Gergiev, a principal guest conductor with the New York's Metropolitan Opera and the London Symphony Orchestra, is a regular with the world's most acclaimed orchestras. The festival interweaves opera, ballet, symphonic, and chamber music in almost equal proportions and provides a rare opportunity to see the Mariinsky's most renowned soloists—who spend most of their time between La Scala, Opera Bastille, and the Met—perform on home soil. Don't miss mezzo-soprano Olga Borodina, tenor Vladimir Galuzin, bass Ildar Abdrazakov, baritone Nikolai Putilin, and soprano Anna Netrebko. Prices soar during the festival and may reach 4,000R or more. Price policy ranges wildly at the Mariinsky, sometimes not following any apparent logic.

Another attractive event is the **Musical Olympus** (⊕ *www.musicalolympus.ru*) festival organized by acclaimed Russian pianist Irina Nikitina at the Philharmonic in May and June. The festival assembles winners and laureates of each year's most respected musical contests from all over the globe. Each musician is handpicked by Nikitina herself or members of the festival's honorary committee, ranging from Placido Domingo to Claudio Abbado. What is especially precious about this festival is that the audiences get to see the rising talent immediately after they have claimed the fame but haven't yet been booked for years to come.

The Arts Square Winter Festival (⊕ *www.artsquarewinterfest.ru*), brainchild of Yury Temirkanov, artistic director of the St. Petersburg Philharmonic, runs between Western Christmas (December 25) and Russian Orthodox Christmas (January 7) and showcases classical concerts and ballets with top-notch international stars. A reliable program is available from its Web site. The State Russian Museum, located across Arts Square from the Philharmonic, organizes special exhibitions and hosts receptions for the festival, which culminates on New Year's Eve with a luxurious ball in Yusupov Palace.

The **Palaces of St. Petersburg** (☎ *812/572–2226* ⊕ *www.palacefest.spb.ru*) festival presents an impressive series of classical concerts in more than two dozen magnificent palaces and mansions year-round. Remarkably enough, in the heyday of Imperial Russia, the social season, with its grand balls, masquerades, and concerts, occurred in winter. White nights or not, during the stuffy summers the pillars of high society abandoned the heat and dust of the city to enjoy a relaxing escape in their country estates and summer residences. A century later, St. Petersburg is trying to restore the glories of the past.

Also of interest is the city's **Early Music Festival** (⊕ *www.earlymusic.ru*), which attracts international soloists and ensembles; it's usually held late September through early October. Every fall, vibrant performances of its refined ensembles evoke, embody, and revive the long-lost noble spirit of St. Petersburg.

ART GALLERIES

St. Petersburg may have one of the world's great museums, but it's not known for its contemporary art. The paradox of St. Petersburg is that although originally designed as a cosmopolitan metropolis, it has evolved into a place remarkably resistant to foreign influences. Reclusive and trapped in endless reflection, the city makes it difficult for young, experimental, and unorthodox artists to get exposure, let alone recognition. That said, the Iron Curtain played a weird trick with modern Russian artists. When the borders fell, they were so eager to catch up with what they had been missing that many of them somehow lost their own ideas, direction, and identity in the process. A new work of art is generally judged according to whether it fits in with the city's venerable artistic traditions. The issue is taken so seriously that the installation of every new monument, especially in the city center, provokes a massive debate. There's a history of modern artworks being removed because of public protests and pressure from cultural circles. The temptation to preserve the historical center in its original state is so strong that contemporary sculpture is largely absent from the streets of St. Petersburg.

> ### A NOTE ABOUT FESTIVALS
>
> The English use of the word "festival" usually denotes a special season or bonanza of events such as the Cannes Film Festival. But in Russia the word, which is the same in Russian, is often attached to random or run-of-the-mill presentations or even to a single performance in order to generate interest. It is worth checking ahead to verify that the event is worthwhile.

However, there is a growing contemporary art scene with galleries showcasing the work of a range of artists in many styles. If you buy any artwork in St. Petersburg other than a standard souvenir, ask the shop to provide you with the necessary documentation to let you take it out of the country. Anything more than 100 years old or of significant cultural value cannot leave the country. Art stores and antiques shops should be able to handle the paperwork, but if you're in any doubt, take the item to the **Board for the Preservation of Cultural Valuables** (*Upravlenie po sokhraneniu kulturnikh tsennostei* ✉ *17 Malaya Morskaya ul., City Center* ☎ *812/571–5196* Ⓜ *Nevsky Prospekt*) for assessment and to receive the relevant certificate. This can cost anywhere from 400R to 1,000R, depending on the item and how quickly you need the paperwork to be processed.

Borey. On display here are the works of avant-garde and academic artists, including paintings, graphics, and applied art. ✉ *58 Liteiny pr., Liteiny/Smolny* ☎ *812/273–3693* Ⓜ *Mayakovskaya.*

Exhibition Center of the St. Petersburg Artists Union. There's an exhibition hall on the ground floor, and art by theatrical artists for sale upstairs. ✉ *38 Bolshaya Morskaya, City Center* ☎ *812/315–7414* Ⓜ *Nevsky Prospekt or Gostinny Dvor.*

Guild of Masters. You'll find paintings, graphics, applied art, and various jewelry items here. ✉ *82 Nevsky pr., City Center* ☎ *812/279–0979* Ⓜ *Nevsky Prospekt or Gostinny Dvor.*

Lion's Bridge. Soviet art with an emphasis on social realism is represented here, with most works dating from 1920 to1970. You'll find masterpieces of propaganda art, landscapes, still lifes, and some examples of Soviet impressionism. ✉ *96 Kanal Griboedova, Admiralteisky* ☎ *812/31–0795 or 812/380–7458* ⊕ *www.lionsbridge.ru* Ⓜ *Sadovaya/Sennaya Ploshchad.*

Marina Gysich's Private Art Gallery. One of the best small galleries in St. Petersburg, Marina Gysich hosts local and national Russian artists and exhibitions. ✉ *121 Fontanka, No. 13, City Center* ☎ *812/314–4380* ⊕ *www.gisich.com* Ⓜ *Tekhnologichesky Institute.*

Matiss Club. Underground art is the main focus of this gallery, which represents a number of well-known local artists. ✉ *104 Kanal Griboedova, Admiralteisky* ☎ *812/310–6722* ⊕ *www.matissclub.com* Ⓜ *Sadovaya/Sennaya Ploshchad.*

> ### RUSSIAN BEATLEMANIA
>
> Pushkinskaya-10 is also known for housing one of Russia's most famous fans of the legendary Beatles, Kolya Vasin. Vasin, who is now in his early 60s, has never worked and never married because, as he says, he only had time for the Beatles. The little apartment he lives in at 10 ulitsa Pushkinskaya is called the "Office of John Lennon's Temple." Vasin dreams of building a temple to John Lennon in St. Petersburg, where thousands of people can worship the Liverpool Four.

★ **Mitki-VKhUTEMAS.** Occupying a spacious attic, the gallery exhibits works of the legendary nonconformist group Mitki, famous for their use of blue-and-white-stripe sailors shirts that they wear and often portray in their artworks. Call to make an appointment. ✉ *36–38 ul. Marata, Vladimirskaya* ☎ *812/764–6462* Ⓜ *Dostoyevskaya/Vladimirskaya.*

Pushkinskaya-10 Arts Center. Also known as the Free Arts Foundation, this musty maze of studios, galleries, yards, cafés, and performance spaces started life as a legendary squat for the pioneering artists of the nonconformist, unofficial, and Neo-Academy art movements that flowered here in the 1980s as the Soviet Union's grip on cultural life began to loosen. Today the foundation receives state funds but it has lost none of its thirst for exhibiting modern art that thumbs its nose at the establishment. Pushkinskaya-10 includes among others, the New Academy Fine Arts Museum, the Museum of Nonconformist Art, the St. Petersburg Archive and Library of Independent Art, FOTOImage, Navicula Artis Gallery, GEZ-21, and Kino-FOT-703. ✉ *10 Pushkinskaya ul., entrance at 53 Ligovsky pr., through the arch, Vladimirskaya* ☎ *812/764–5371* ⊕ *www.p10.nonmuseum.ru* Ⓜ *Ploschad Vosstaniya.*

The Russian Icon. This gallery exhibits and sells contemporary Russian Orthodox icons. It's possible to order customized icons. ✉ *15 Bolshaya Konyushennaya ul., City Center* ☎ *812/314–7040* Ⓜ *Nevsky Prospekt.*

★ **Sol-Art.** Next to the prestigious Mukhina Academy for Arts and Design and in the same building as the magnificent and crumbling Baron Stieglitz Museum, this wonderful gallery exhibits St. Petersburg's young artistic talents. The gallery showcases some of the big names in the local contemporary art scene as well. ✉ *15 Solyanoy per., Liteiny/Smolny* ☎ *812/327–3082* Ⓜ *Nevsky Prospekt.*

S.P.A.S. This spacious gallery exhibits a good collection of contemporary artists. ✉ *93 nab. Moiki, Admiralteisky* ☎ *812/571–4260* Ⓜ *Sadovaya.*

MUSIC

St. Petersburg oozes musical history, and there's a fascinating and thrilling concentration of the brightest names in classical music here. The spiritual presence of Tchaikovsky, Mussorgsky, Prokofiev, and Shostakovich is strong in their alma mater. But unlike Salzburg that made Mozart a successful, well-selling brand, or Bonn that organizes a rapidly expanding Beethoven Festival every year, the city hasn't ventured far into building an infrastructure or even a regular festival around any of its biggest classical names.

With its 18th-century heritage, St. Petersburg makes the perfect setting to hear Russia's sometimes-forgotten early music. The Early Music Festival spawned the Catherine the Great Orchestra, Russia's first baroque orchestra, which launched its own recording label and plays year-round at various venues.

Only the St. Petersburg Philharmonic is capable of programming its schedule well in advance, and other places are much more spontaneous. A detailed program of a festival at the Mariinsky is usually available three weeks before the event, while confirmed cast for premieres is normally announced a week prior to the performance. Last-minute changes and cancellations aren't uncommon at any venue. St. Petersburg's concert halls and theaters have been slow starters on the Web. Exceptions include the Philharmonic (⊕ *www.philharmonia.spb.ru*) and the Mariinsky (⊕ *www.mariinsky.ru*). You can find information on musical events around town at ⊕ *www.classicalmusic.spb.ru.*

MUSIC GROUPS

Fodor'sChoice ★

When scanning the listings, don't miss **Terem Quartet** (⊕ *www.terem-quartet.com*), the famous local four who have adapted "inviolable" classical jewels such as Oginsky's "Polonaise" or Schubert's "Ave Maria" for balalaika, bayan, domra, and alto domra to superb effect. Virtuosi in their instruments, and highly interactive in their performing style, which critics have branded "instrumental theater," they freely mix J.S. Bach's "Toccata and Fugue in D Minor" with Russian folk songs, and make every concert a fun experience.

★ Another must-see is the marvleous **St. Petersburg Male Choir** *(Peterburgsky Muzhskoi Khor)* led by artistic director Vadim Afanasiev. Their favorite venues are the Capella and Petropavlovsky Cathedral in Peter and Paul Fortress, where the choir performs Orthodox chants and choral works by Russian composers. The sound is mesmerizing, and their bottomless yet velvet profoundo basses make an extraordinary asset.

The **St. Petersburg Horn Capella** *(Rogovaya Kapella* ⊕ *www.horncapella.ru)* revives the traditions of 18th-century Russian horn music, and is the only ensemble of its kind in Russia. Apart from baroque pieces written specifically for horn, the musicians perform a wide repertoire of charming arrangements of well-known classical works.

CONCERT
HALLS

Academic Kapella. One of St. Petersburg's best-kept secrets is also its oldest concert hall, dating to the 1780s. It presents not only choral events but also symphonic, instrumental, and vocal concerts. Many famous musicians, including Glinka and Rimsky-Korsakov, have performed in this elegant space along the Moika, just near the Alexander Pushkin Apartment Museum and the Winter Palace. The main entrance and the surrounding courtyards have been beautifully restored. ✉ *20 nab. Moiki, City Center* ☎ *812/314–1153* Ⓜ *Nevsky Prospekt.*

Glinka Hall. For chamber and vocal music, head to this small hall, part of the Shostakovich Philharmonic (it's just around the corner from the Philharmonic). It's also known as the Maly Zal (Small Hall). ✉ *30 Nevsky pr., City Center* ☎ *812/571–8333* Ⓜ *Nevsky Prospekt.*

Hermitage Theater. This glorious and highly unusual theater in the Hermitage mainly hosts the St. Petersburg Camerata, a rather fine and often overlooked chamber ensemble. Note that the theater doesn't have a box office, so purchase tickets at a theater kiosk or via your concierge. ✉ *32 Dvortsovaya nab., City Center* ☎ *812/579–0226 or 812/966–3776* ⊕ *www.hermitagemuseum.org* Ⓜ *Nevsky Prospekt.*

House of Composers *(Dom Kompozitorov).* Lovers of contemporary classical music flock here for the concerts of music written by its members—look for names such as Sergei Slonimsky, Boris Tishchenko, and Andrey Petrov—and their students at the conservatory. ✉ *45 Bolshaya Morskaya ul., City Center* ☎ *812/571–3548* Ⓜ *Nevsky Prospekt.*

Shostakovich Philharmonic. Two excellent symphony orchestras perform in the Philharmonic's, newly refurbished grand concert hall (Bolshoy Zal): the St. Petersburg Philharmonic Orchestra and the Academic Philharmonic (a fine outfit, although it's officially the B-team). Both troupes have long, illustrious histories of collaboration with some of Russia's finest composers, and many famous works have premiered in this hall. ✉ *2 Mikhailovskaya ul., City Center* ☎ *812/710–4257 or 812/710–4290* Ⓜ *Nevsky Prospekt.*

Mariinsky Concert Hall. The Mariinsky Theatre's new $38 million concert hall opened in 2007 a few hundred meters from the theater itself at the site of its former warehouse. A fire in 2003 presented the chance to build a state-of-the-art classical music venue at the sight, and, with the help of Japanese acoustician Yasuhisa Toyota—also responsible for Los Angeles's Walt Disney concert hall—that dream has become a reality. Now Mariinsky soloists and stars of international classical music have a large-scale, world-class venue for their performances, something St. Petersburg hitherto lacked. ✉ *20 Pisareva ul., Admiralteisky* ☎ *812/714–4344* ⊕ *www.mariinsky.ru* Ⓜ *Sadovaya.*

OTHER
CLASSICAL
MUSIC VENUES

For a relaxing evening of classical music in a prerevolutionary setting, try the concert halls in some of St. Petersburg's museums, mansions, palaces, and churches. Performances are held regularly at the following venues:

Kochneva's House *(Dom Kochnevoi* ✉ *41 nab. Fontanki, City Center* Ⓜ *Nevsky Prospekt* ☎ *812/710–4062)* offers chamber music in an atmospheric palace. The **Palace of Prince Beloselsky-Belozersky** *(Beloselsky-Belozersky Dvorets* ✉ *41 Nevsky pr., City Center* ☎ *812/315-*

5236 or 812/319–9790 ⓂNevsky Prospekt) is a rose-color art nouveau palace with a large mirrored ball room. Popular with foreign worshippers, **St. Catherine Lutheran Church** (✉*1a Bolshoi pr., Vasilievsky Island* ☎*812/323–1852* Ⓜ*Vasileostrovskaya*) has an engaging classical concert program that mixes secular and religious music. Charming soirees are held in authentic surroundings at the **Samoilov Family Museum** (✉*8 Stremyannaya ul., entrance from back side of Nevsky Palace Hotel, City Center* ☎*812/764–1130* ⊕*www.theatremuseum. ru/eng/expo/sam.html* Ⓜ*Mayakovskaya*). The museum displays memorabilia related to Russia's greatest composers, musicians, conductors, and dancers. Chamber concerts are held in one of the grand rooms of the multifaceted **Sheremetev Palace** (*Sheremetev Dvorets* ✉*34 nab. Fontanki, City Center* ☎*812/272–4441* ⊕*www.theatremuseum.ru/ eng/expo/sher.html* Ⓜ*Mayakovskaya*). The museum also houses Russia's national collection of musical instruments. The **Smolny** cathedral (✉*3/1 Pl. Rastrelli, Liteiny/Smolny* ☎*812/271–9182* Ⓜ*Chernyshevskaya*) presents choral music in its beautiful, baroque confines. Many of the concerts organized at St. Petersburg's most historic venues are run by **Peterburg-Concert** (*In Kochneva's House* ✉*41 nab. Fontanki, City Center* ☎*812/710–4032* ⊕*www.petroconcert.spb.ru/* Ⓜ*Nevsky Prospekt*). These concerts are not of the highest standard found at other musical events in the city—although there are some exceptions—but they are a much better bet than most of the events organized especially for tourist groups. Tickets can be bought right at the Peterburg-Concert offices. The entrance is rather inconspicuous: look for a door on the right side in the passageway at 41 Fontanka.

OPERA & BALLET

Russian classical ballet was born in St. Petersburg. The Imperial Ballet School was founded here on May 4, 1738, by the order of Empress Anna Ioannovna, to be run by Frenchman Jean-Baptiste Lande. French and Italian masters taught the first class of 12 boys and 12 girls. Works of another Frenchman, Marius Petipa, who arrived at the academy in 1847 to shape up the Russian classical ballet together with his Russian counterpart Lev Ivanov, still dominate the repertoire of the Mariinsky Theatre. Today the school is called the Vaganova Ballet Academy in honor of Agrippina Vaganova, who radically changed the way ballet was taught in Russia. The best students traditionally appear on the venerable Mariinsky stage around Christmas in *The Nutcracker* and then in May and June in graduation performances.

During the high tourist season, *Swan Lake,* a signature production for the Russian classical ballet, appears by the dozen each day on various stages. If purity is important to you, go to either the Mariinsky or Mussorgsky theaters, and beware of the clones: not all stages are fit for such a grand ballet and there's a high risk of being served a brutally circumcised version, with difficult bits omitted, a few swans missing, and even no live orchestra.

Contemporary dance doesn't really flourish in the cradle of classical tradition but the dance company and school Kannon Dance

(⊕ *www.kannondance.ru*) organizes several modern dance festivals during the year.

Russian opera is much less known
and much less appreciated abroad.
Many potential spectators are
frightened merely by the sound
of them. There's always a peasant
riot, a doomed tsar, much chaos
and insanity, and a lack of tuneful,
languid, and tender belcanto hero-
ines. St. Petersburg opera singers,
who have long been complaining about a lobby against Russian

operas in the West, and who are all convinced that Tchaikovsky's *The
Queen of Spades* is the greatest-ever dramatic opera, are eager to make
you change your mind. The Mariinsky's artistic director, Valery Gergiev, has declared it the company's policy to reveal the obscure masterpieces of Russian operatic legacy to audiences. Opera in Russia is about
power, drama, depth, and philosophy. And among those most likely to
convert you are the philosophical and spiritual renditions of Rimsky-
Korsakov's *The Legend of the Invisible City of Kitezh* or Glinka's *A
Life for the Tsar*.

Fodor'sChoice ★ **Boris Eifman Ballet Theater** (☎812/232–0235). Psychological drama
reigns here. Most of the ballets in the repertoire of this internationally
acclaimed troupe—the only professional contemporary ballet company
in St. Petersburg—have been inspired by biographies of extraordinary
Russians with a tragic fate or are based on Russia's literary gems. A
must-see is *Red Giselle*, which tells the story of the great Russian ballerina Olga Spessivtseva, who fled Russia after the Bolshevik Revolution
and spent 20 years in a psychiatric ward in New York. Also highly recommended are *Anna Karenina, Tchaikovsky*, and *The Russian Hamlet*,
devoted to the doomed life of Russian tsar Paul I, who was murdered
by plotters in Mikhailovsky Castle. The troupe, founded in the late
1970s, has no permanent home, and spends most of its time abroad.
When here, the company usually performs at the Alexander Pushkin
Drama Theater, the Mariinsky, or the Mussorgsky.

The Rimsky-Korsakov Conservatory. The Conservatory is directly opposite
the Mariinsky, but the opera and ballet performances are nothing like
the level of its famous neighbor—partly because the Mariinsky is so
good at siphoning off the Conservatory's brightest talent. ⊠3 Teatralnaya Pl., Admiralteisky ☎812/312–2519 Ⓜ Sadovaya.

Fodor'sChoice ★ **Mariinsky Theatre of Opera and Ballet** (*Mariinsky Teatr Opery I Balleta*)
Formerly known as the Kirov and advertised internationally under tha
brand, the world-renowned Mariinsky is one of Russia's finest artistic
institutions, a definite must-see. The names Petipa, Pavlova, Nijinsky
and Nureyev—and countless others associated with the theater and
the birth of ballet in St. Petersburg—are enough to lure ballet lover

to an evening here. The Mariinsky is without doubt one of the best ballet companies in the world, with a seemingly inexhaustible supply of stars.

St. Petersburg maintains its reputation as a citadel of classical ballet, but the works of George Balanchine, Kenneth MacMillan, Michel Fokine, John Neumeier, and William Forsythe are winning greater prominence on the playbill. However, audiences are slow to change their expectations, and modern ballets almost always perform to a half-empty auditorium. Between February and March, the company runs the **Mariinsky International Ballet Festival,** an impressive and tantalizing one that features at least one premiere and an array of guest performers from other renowned companies such as London's Royal Ballet, Opera Bastille, and the American Ballet Theater.

The Mariinsky is also at the forefront of the world's opera companies, thanks largely to the achievements of the Mariinsky's artistic director Valery Gergiev (who now also masterminds many productions at New York City's Metropolitan Opera). The company's best operatic repertoire centers on Russian opera of all centuries: Tchaikovsky's *The Queen of Spades,* Prokofiev's *Semyon Kotko,* Shostakovich's *The Nose,* Rimsky-Korsakov's *The Legend of the Invisible City of Kitezh,* and *The Snow Maiden* are particularly recommended.

Wagner is sung in German, Puccini in Italian, and Saint-Saëns in French. Russian operas are all provided with English subtitles, while Russian subtitles are given for foreign operas. Verdi can be hit-or-miss, but Wagner is one of Gergiev's greatest passions, and the company now feels very much at home with the composer. Basses Yevgeny Nikitin and Viktor Chernomortsev have excellent Wagnerian voices and technique. The orchestra's rapport with the conductor is amazing, the sound is nuanced and powerful. Be sure to see *Parsifal* and *Tristan und Isolde,* and of course, if you have the stamina, the whole of Wagner's Ring Cycle.

Ballet and opera mix freely in the calendar schedule throughout the year; the opera and ballet companies both tour, but at any given time one of the companies is performing in St. Petersburg. ■ TIP→ **A two-year renovation is planned for the Mariinsky's main venue beginning sometime after the conclusion of the 2007/08 season.** The timing will depend on the completion of the Mariinsky's second stage in a controversial modern arts center known as "Mariinsky II." The project has been beset by delays and objections from St. Petersburg's preservationists, but Gergiev proved with the opening of the Mariinsky Concert Hall in 2007 that he has the will to push forward with bold projects. ⊠ *1/2 Teatralnaya Pl., Admiralteisky* ☎ *812/714–1211* ⊕ *www.mariinsky. ru/en* Ⓜ *Sadovaya.*

Mussorgsky Theater of Opera and Ballet. This lesser known venue, sometimes known as the Mikhailovsky Theater, was renovated in 2007 and new directors were hired to freshen up its repertoire. The best of the Mussorgsky's productions rival those at the Mariinsky. As far as opera is concerned, the Russian repertoire, now run by soprano

Yelena Obraztsova, is the theater's strong point, but it occasionally strikes gold with Italian works as well. Although the company hosted the world premieres of Shostakovich's *Lady Macbeth of Mtsensk* in 1934 and Prokofiev's *War and Peace* in 1946, the works of these composers are now absent from the repertoire, which focuses heavily on 19th-century classics. Highlights include Mussorgsky's *Boris Godunov*, Rimsky-Korsakov's *The Tsar's Bride*, Borodin's *Prince Igor*, and Tchaikovsky's *Iolanta*.

The company's strong dance division, now run by dancer Farukh Ruzimatov, is deservedly rated the second-best in town. The classical fare includes *Swan Lake, Giselle, La Esmeralda*, and *Don Quixote* as well as some jewels of Soviet-era choreography, like Rodion Schedrin's *The Little Humpbacked Horse* and Prokofiev's *Romeo and Juliet*.

The opera season usually opens in early September, traditionally with a gala performance of Mussorgsky's famous opera, *Boris Godunov*. Ballet and opera are both generally performed September through June or July. ✉*1 Pl. Iskusstv, City Center* ☎*812/595–4319* ⊕*www.mikhailovsky.ru* Ⓜ*Nevsky Prospekt.*

St. Petersburg Chamber Opera *(Opera Sankt Peterburg).* Until 2003 this company, founded in 1987 by former Mariinsky stage director Yuri Alexandrov as an "opera laboratory," had no permanent home. The company is now based in the former mansion of Baron Derviz, a place with a rich musical history. Vsevolod Meyerhold staged productions here at the end of the 19th century, before it was turned into a concert hall. The company's repertoire is small and dominated by Russian classics and light Italian operas, with occasional experimental performances. ✉*33 Galernaya ul., Admiralteisky* ☎*812/312–3982 or 812/312–6769* ⊕*www.spbopera.ru* Ⓜ*Sadovaya, Sennaya Ploshchad.*

THEATER

St. Petersburg has some excellent drama theaters with performances almost exclusively in Russian. Cutting-edge productions are a missing link in local repertoires due to a widespread escapist approach to theater. This means you have a choice of multiple productions of such classics as *Antigone*, Gogol's *Marriage*, and Chekhov's *Uncle Vanya*, among others.

There are a number of ways to get the most from St. Petersburg's theater scene if you don't speak Russian. First, stick to English-language authors whose plays you already know. Plays by Shakespeare, Oscar Wilde, and Tennessee Williams are popular and appear at many of the city's theaters. Broad comedies by the British farcist Ray Cooney are also regularly performed. Then there are Russian classics well-known outside Russia, usually by Chekhov, Dostoyevsky, Gogol, and Tolstoy. The Maly Drama Theater specializes in hosting foreign troupes and puts some effort into welcoming non-Russian-speaking audiences by means of playbills in English and occasionally headsets relaying a translation. The most useful Web site, ⊕*www.theart.ru*, which features listings and e-ticketing for all St. Petersburg theaters, unfortunately only appears in Russian.

Alexander Pushkin Drama Theater *(Alexandrinsky Teatr)*. Russia's oldest theater, opened in 1756, is also one of its most elegant. Its repertoire is dominated by 19th-century classics (and the productions can be as musty as the costumes). With prominent Moscow director Valery Fokin taking the helm in 2004, the company is enjoying a renaissance. Fokin's interpretations of Dostoyevsky's *The Double* and Gogol's *The Government Inspector* are thought-provoking and engaging. ⊠ *2 Pl. Ostrovskovo, City Center* ☎ *812/312–1545 or 812/710–4103* Ⓜ *Gostinny Dvor or Nevsky Prospekt.*

Baltiisky Dom Theater-Festival. An umbrella venue for a dozen experimental companies of various genres, Baltiisky Dom holds performances in its large hall and a variety of basements, attics, and backrooms. Once a full-fledged theater, it has turned into a modern art polyhedron, where aspiring directors play with material from Luigi Pirandello to Ivan Turgenev to the Presnyakov Brothers. This is the only venue in town staging plays written in the past five years. To get a sense of experimental Russian theater, look for the shows of "Farces" theater and productions directed by Andrei Moguchy as well as one-man shows by local actors. In October the theater hosts an impressive four-week Baltic Theater Festival, attracting the best talent from the Baltic Sea region. ⊠ *4 Alexandrovsky Park, Petrograd Side* ☎ *812/232–3539* Ⓜ *Gorkovskaya.*

Bolshoi Drama Theatre *(Bolshoi Dramatichesky Teatr)*. The legendary Bolshoi has some of the best-known names in Russian drama and film on its stage. The only problem is that most of its stars are well beyond retirement age. The company had its golden age between the 1960s and the 1980s under the directorship of Georgy Tovstonogov, who died in 1990. No adequate replacement was found, and it was decided to concentrate on "preserving the legacy" of the famous director. Now, the house that the director built is aged and rickety. Excellent actors Alisa Freindlikh and Oleg Basilashvili carry most of the repertoire on their shoulders, and any production with them on the list isn't going to be a disappointment. But after so many years of being denied any fresh influence and experimentation, the troupe is a shadow of what it once was.

In addition to Russian classics, the theater stages works by Shakespeare, Molière, Harwood, Miller, and Stoppard. Two productions—"The Pickwick Papers" and "Uncle Vanya"—have survived from Tovstonogov's day and miraculously even feature almost entirely the same cast as 30 years ago. An interesting theatrical phenomenon, it still leaves the viewer with a lingering feeling of sadness, as though looking at a pinned butterfly. ⊠ *65 nab. Fontanki, City Center* ☎ *812/310–0401* Ⓜ *Nevsky Prospekt.*

Fodor'sChoice ★ **Maly Drama Theater** *(Maly Dramatichesky Teatr)*. Even if you can't understand the dialogue, any performance at the MDT—home to one of the best theater companies in the city—is a must-see. The repertoire includes productions of Chekhov, Dostoyevsky, Shakespeare, and Oscar Wilde. Maly is also nearly the only company in town that continues to stage the finest plays from the Soviet era. Seeing their whole repertoire has been compared to living through the entire 20th-century history of Russia. If you have a whole day to spare and lots of stamina, the nine-hour performance of Dostoyevsky's *The Possessed* makes for an incredible theatrical experience, although it can be a bit hard on the posterior. It takes two consecutive evenings to sit through the company's veteran show, Fyodor Abramov's "Brothers and Sisters," but nobody is known to have regretted doing it. Order tickets well in advance, because it's rare that the Maly plays to a less than packed house. ✉ *18 ul. Rubinshteina, Vladimirskaya* ☎ *812/712–2078* ⊕ *www.mdt-dodin. ru* Ⓜ *Vladimirskaya.*

Molodezhny Theater. Although most troupes in town tend to work their most seasoned players to the bone, this theater is brave enough to have younger talent figure prominently in the troupe. Shows are bursting with youthful energy and romanticism, yet there's no amateur-student feel to them. Not really catering to intellectuals, the troupe appeals directly to one's heart, and this approach has found the company many admirers among the city's younger crowd. Most of the shows are expertly staged by artistic director Semyon Spivak, a professor at the renowned St. Petersburg Academy for Theatre Art. The company's signature show is Alexei Tolstoy's "The Swallow." Isaac Babel's "Cries From Odessa" and Alexander Ostrovsky's "Love Lace" are also among its hits. ✉ *2 Fontanka Embankment, Admiralteisky* ☎ *812/316–6870* Ⓜ *Tekhnologichesky Institute.*

☾ **Zazerkalye Theater** *(Through the Looking Glass Theater).* This is perhaps the best musical choice for children. Captivating shows masterfully blend dramatic and musical elements and are famous for daring direction experiments. The company is good at winning children over to opera with entertaining yet unabridged versions of serious repertoire such as Donizetti's *L'elisir d'amore*—during which Nemorino sings his famous aria while riding a bike—or Offenbach's *Les contes d'Hoffmann* and Puccini's *La Bohème.* It's open Friday through Sunday. ✉ *13 ul. Rubinshteina, Vladimirskaya* ☎ *812/764–1895 or 812/712–5000* Ⓜ *Vladimirskaya or Dostoevskaya.*

NIGHTLIFE

After the fall of Communism, St. Petersburg became the first Russian city to adopt club culture. The underground and rock scene here is thriving and a number of the first clubs and musical heavyweights are still around. Most of Russia's living rock patriarchs such as Boris Grebenshchikov of Akvarium and Sergei "Shnur" Shnurov, frontman for the ska-punk group, Leningrad, live here and make regular appearances at venues.

The city's nightclubs and discos don't compete with Moscow's glamorous establishments in terms of grand scale, pomp, exorbitant prices and attitude, but they do offer a more relaxed environment and laid-back feel. Even popular spots, however, are well hidden and you need to know where to look. At night, the town's quiet and serene historical center evokes associations with "Sleeping Beauty" so don't expect much of a seething street life—except during White Nights and public holidays (which seem to occur on a weekly basis).

It's also an ever-changing scene, so it's always best to consult current listings. The most reliable English-language sources are the Friday edition of the free *St. Petersburg Times* (⊕*www.sptimes.ru*) or the monthly English-language issue of *St. Petersburg In Your Pocket* (⊕*www.inyourpocket.com*). These publications include excellent unbiased club guides in addition to detailed listings. There are more comprehensive sources in Russian, such as the magazines *Afisha* (⊕*spb. afisha.ru*) and *Time Out/Kalendar*.

A good rule of thumb for tourists with little or no experience in Russia is to stick to the city center, where you have plenty of options: bohemian art clubs, trendy dance clubs, live-music venues, and simple pubs. Locals in the city center are friendly and more than a few speak English—and foreigners are not the novelty they once were. If you're seeking the company of expats, you'll find them in centrally located Irish and British pubs or at low-key artsy bars such as *Datscha*. The historical center is abundant with expensive strip clubs, but these are meant for deep-pocketed foreign tourists and ravenous Russian beauties hunting for them. The city's red-light district is the part of Nevsky prospekt farther north from Ploshchad Vosstaniya, where prostitutes stand at every other corner and can be rather aggressive. Beware that if you venture to a place beyond the historical center, the risk of being robbed or attacked by one of the city's many skinhead and hooligan gangs increases significantly. ⚠ **During the months when the rivers and canals are not frozen (generally April–November), watch the clock: bridges start to go up around 1:30 AM. If you get stuck on the wrong side, you'll have to wait until 5 AM or so to cross.**

BARS

The line separating bars, clubs, and restaurants in St. Petersburg is often not clear. For that reason, many establishments listed here could also be found under restaurants—though they may have the look and feel of bars, they also offer seating and a full menu. Bars and cafés regularly host live concerts, parties, and DJs, but prefer not to advertise themselves in the club section.

Achtung Baby. This large grungy bar and alternative music stage built in the former coaching house near the Imperial Stables at Konnyushenaya Ploshchad takes advantage of its high, vaulted brick ceilings to project surreal movies and provide a fancy light show, all timed to beats that include Britpop, '80s Retro, and Russian rock. Girls love to dance here and guys love to watch them at this hot pickup spot. Open daily from 5 PM to 6 AM. ⊠*2 Konnyushenaya Pl.* ☎*No phone* ⊕*www.achtung baby.ru* Ⓜ*Nevsky Prospekt.*

City Bar. One of the city's few true expat hangouts is opposite the U.S. consulate. The bar-restaurant draws a lively bunch of mostly foreign students and long-term expats who can't seem to leave the city—maybe American owner Ailene's "just-like-Mom-makes-it" daily specials (a bargain at around 150R) help them feel at home. It's also the only place

CLOSE UP

Getting Caught with Your Bridges Up

St. Petersburg's mighty Neva River creates some of its most picturesque views, making it easy to forget that it is a working river and transport route for the import and export of many goods and raw materials. A working river, yes, but not during winter when it freezes over. This means that during the navigation season (April–November), the Neva is crowded with ships making up for the winter months. However, since its bridges are too low to allow ships to pass and it would cripple the city to lift them frequently during the day, the city's bridges are raised at night from 1 AM to about 5 AM. There are published schedules for each bridge, some of which are lowered once during the night, but these are notoriously unreliable. If you don't want to get caught on the wrong side of the river from where you are staying and be stuck until morning, think about heading home before 1 AM. What at first sounds like a terrific inconvenience for a large, busy city has been turned into something positive by St. Petersburgers: during White Nights the raising of attractively illuminated bridges has become a crowd-pleasing ritual and "I missed the bridges" has become the perfect excuse to party until dawn.

in town where you'll find blueberry pancakes smothered in maple syrup for breakfast. More than a bar, this is the hub of the expat community, hosting meetings, screening films, and lending books. With Wi-Fi and a relaxed stay-as-long-as-you-like ethos, it's also a popular spot for teleworking. City Bar's Web site is a good place to post inquiries about St. Petersburg. ⊠ *20 Furshtatskaya ul., Liteiny/Smolny* ☎*812/448–5837* ⊕*www.citybar.ru* Ⓜ*Chernyshevskaya.*

Datscha. A tremendously popular haunt of expats, bohemians, students, and night owls, Datscha is influenced by the merry joints of the Reeperbahn in Hamburg (the owner is German). The galvanizing spirit of this friendly and eclectic art bar is hugely addictive—despite its claustrophobic size, low ceilings, shabby setting, horrific toilets, and no food service except for peanuts. The music, mainly rock and ska, is so loud that an intimate chat is out of the question. Reckless dance parties sometimes get out of hand and spill into the street, where neighborhood bars Fidel and Belgrad are also located. ⊠ *9 Dumskaya ul., City Center* ☎*No phone* Ⓜ*Nevsky Prospekt.*

Dickens. A stately slab of Olde Englande kitsch, Dickens is the second pub in a chain after the original opened in Riga, Latvia, in 1999. There's the best English breakfast in town for 350R. ⊠ *108 Nab, Reki Fontanki* ☎*812/380–7888* Ⓜ*Sennaya Ploshchad.*

Fodor'sChoice
★

Shamrock Irish Pub. A long-standing favorite of the local foreign community, this jolly inn with great pub food, cozy wooden furnishings, and two dozen types of beer stands across the street from the Mariinsky Theatre. The company's younger talent can be often spotted having a quick bite or beers here at any time of day. Live Irish music is played every night, except Tuesday and Friday. ⊠ *27 ul. Dekabristov, Admiralteisky* ☎*812/318–4625* Ⓜ*Sadovaya.*

The Other Side. An instant hit when it opened at the end of 2006, this comfortable two-hall "gastro pub" run by U.S. expat Douglas Pullar and his capable, informal team serves a good range of well-priced drinks and Thai, Mexican, and Middle Eastern food, as well as bagels and cream cheese (not often found in Russia) for 150R. It's understandably popular with foreigners, including Swedes from the nearby Swedish consulate. ✉*1 Bolshaya Konnushenaya, City Center* ☎*812/312–9554* ⊕*www.the otherside.ru* Ⓜ*Nevsky Prospekt.*

> ## BAR HOPPING
>
> A small street linking Nevsky prospekt and the Griboyedov canal has recently become the site of a cluster of hip and grungy bars that attract crowds of young people. Together with the presence of two of St. Petersburg's gay clubs, Dumskaya ulitsa, with its central location, disheveled colonnades, and dance-till-you-drop attitude has been dubbed the city's answer to London's Old Compton Street.

★ **Tschaika.** This legendary Russian-German establishment serving good beer, authentic bratwurst, sauerkraut, and other German specialties was one of the first foreign bars to open in town after the fall of communism. It has remained an unbeatable expat hangout since (President Vladimir Putin dined with former German chancellor Gerhard Schroeder here). Inspired by the pubs of Hamburg, Tschaika gets especially noisy on weekends. Live music gets started every night at 9 PM. ✉*14 nab. Kanala Griboyedova, City Center* ☎*812/312–4631* ⊕*www. tschaika.ru* Ⓜ*Nevsky Prospekt.*

CLUBS

Russia has adopted the concept of "face control" enthusiastically, but in schizophrenic St. Petersburg its rules can either fall to the whim of a zealous doorman or be ignored all together depending on the character of the place. Generally, dirty clothes or men going shirtless will be frowned upon, and in the more glamorous spots designer gear and shows of wealth are required. That said, St. Petersburg's nightclubs are often more like bars or music venues where anything goes. Women are expected to wear feminine clothes, nice shoes—preferably with heels—and makeup. Men can be more relaxed, but Russian men like to wear dark colors, sport coats, and dress shoes. Cover prices vary wildly from nothing at all to hundreds of dollars depending on the type of place, the day of the week, the time of night, and whether there is some sort of act on the bill. However, 500R is a fair average. Drink prices are generally double what they are in a regular bar. Reliable, if pricey, taxis swarm around clubs until chucking-out time.

St. Petersburg is hardly hip, but it's waking up to what hip really is. The city's vibrant and evolving club scene is diverse enough to incorporate funky theme clubs, bunker-style techno venues, cozy artsy basements, run-down discos, cool alternative spots, and elegant hedonist establishments to keep the clubbers up all night. There are still several chic nightclubs opened only to members, but more and more elitist venues are canceling memberships, so most of the places are generally accessible.

Havana. Welcoming and nonaggressive, this is the place to go if you have a craving for salsa, merengue, and other sensual Latin dances. A friendly and cosmopolitan crowd of diverse ages comes here. There are three dance floors at this bright and smart spacious club, plus a restaurant and pool tables. ⊠*21 Moskovsky pr., City Center* ☎*812/259–1155* ⊕*www.havanaclub.ru* Ⓜ*Tekhnologichesky Institute.*

Konyushenny Dvor. It's widely known that foreigners get in free here, and, well, you get what you pay for. Pop music and strip shows are the usual order, and there's no attitude. Also known as Marstall, it's a bit of an institution at this point. ⊠*5 Kanal Griboyedova, City Center* ☎*812/315–7607* Ⓜ*Nevsky Prospekt.*

> ### STRIPPED BARE
>
> St. Petersburg's "adult entertainment" sector promotes itself more vigorously and splashily than any other category of nightlife, particularly to foreign men who are usually offered discounted entry. These gaudy strip palaces feature shows that range from full-on sex shows to Moulin Rouge–style "erotic ballets"—often with real ballerinas who didn't quite make the grade. Vulgar, expensive, pushy, and sinister, St. Petersburg's strip clubs, increasingly seem like a relic from a different age: the fast and loose 1990s.

★ **Magrib.** Designed in ornate, Moroccan style, fashionable, and glamorous, small Magrib has dance parties every night, belly dancers, a hugely popular striptease show, and a very good but pricey restaurant with European and Middle Eastern dishes. DJs play a mixture of European disco, Latin, and Russian popular music. Dimly lit and relaxed, Magrib was initially aimed at the nouveau riches and "gilded youth" but eventually became much more democratic. ⊠*84 Nevsky pr., Liteiny/Smolny* ☎*812/275–1255* Ⓜ*Mayakovskaya.*

Metro. An old standard as far as dance clubs are concerned, Metro is frequented mostly by young teenagers from all over the city and the suburbs. Each of the three floors plays different music. Door policy is very strict. ⊠*174 Ligovsky pr., Vladimirskaya* ☎*812/766–0204* ⊕*www.metroclub.ru* Ⓜ*Ligovsky Prospect.*

Purga. They literally celebrate the New Year every night here, and it's still as engaging as ever. Whatever season and the weather outside, you get the full holiday package in Purga, complete with decorated Christmas tree, Father Frost, and Snow Maid, champagne, dance party, and festive atmosphere. It's archived an enviable collection of season's greetings recordings delivered by Soviet and Russian leaders, which is broadcast and mocked all through the night. This ritual has become one of St. Petersburg's most eccentric and memorable nights out. The food is good and inexpensive, the beer cheap, and the droll staff is dressed in white rabbit costumes. Each table has its own original design. Be sure to get there and fill your glass before midnight. Purga's clone next door throws wedding parties with the same regularity and similar comic bent. ⊠*11–13 nab. Reki Fontanki, City Center* ☎*812/313–4123* Ⓜ*Mayakovskaya.*

Tunnel. A cool military-theme spot in a former bunker and almost exclusively devoted to electronic dance music, Tunnel is one of the oldest and most popular techno clubs in town. In 2007, St. Petersburg's governor named Tunnel in a scathing attack on youth culture and drug misuse in published comments to her youth culture adviser, so its future is far from assured. ⊠*At Zverinskaya ul. and Lyubansky per., Petrograd Side* ☎*812/233–4015* ⊕*www.tunnelclub.ru* Ⓜ*Gorkovskaya.*

GAY & LESBIAN CLUBS

Unlike much of Europe and North America, Russia has not yet opened up to the idea of gay men and lesbians. The scene in St. Petersburg is in its embryonic stage and the few friendly and unpretentious venues that are available keep a relatively low profile, although St. Petersburg has not seen the levels of official homophobia and violence that have been seen in Moscow. One of the reasons the St. Petersburg gay scene seems so small is that just as places began to open and a community started to form around them, the Internet came along and everything moved online. The best starting point into St. Petersburg's scene then is ⊕*www.gay.ru*, which has some English content including a Traveler's Guide.

Central Station. Brought to you by the ruthlessly professional management of the insufferably glam Three Monkeys in Moscow, Central Station is its looser, more intimate St. Petersburg counterpart attracting a youthful, fashionable, mixed crowd. Three floors, each with its own character, are interlinked by a number of dark staircases. There are theme nights, drag shows, multiple lounge areas, and a restaurant. ⊠*1 Lomonosova ul.* ☎*812/312–3600* ⊕*www.centralstation.ru* Ⓜ*Nevsky Prospekt.*

Greshniki. No matter how much they complain about this crowded, central spot, people still come in droves to Sinners, even if it's their last stop of the night. There are go-go boys and a sometimes-amusing drag show. The third floor is for men only. Beware of hustlers. Also, note that the club uses a pay-as-you-leave system, so don't lose the card they give you on entry (you'll need it to buy drinks). ⊠*28 Kanal Griboyedova, City Center* ☎*812/318–4291* ⊕*www.greshniki. ru* Ⓜ*Nevsky Prospekt.*

Tri El. The only lesbian club in town, also known as LLL, this laid-back, smart venue with a big dance floor, is managed by a lesbian team with substantial experience in the clubbing field. The drinks are cheap, staff helpful, and there's a strip room and some pool tables. ⊠*45 ul. 5-ya Sovetskaya, Liteiny/Smolny* ☎*812/710–2016* ⊕*www.triel.spb.ru* Ⓜ*Ploshchad Vosstaniya.*

LIVE MUSIC CLUBS

Russia's rock movement was born in St. Petersburg and almost all key names in the country's rock culture come from the city. The first bands emerged in the 1970s, when rock and roll was branded alien music and rock culture was repressed by the Soviet culture bosses. Underground musicians and artists refrained from contacts with state-run music organizations. They worked as night guards, boiler-room operators, or street cleaners and expressed their protest in rock ballads, which reached a wider audience only with the arrival of perestroika.

Some of the most famous bands still play regular gigs—look for veteran bands like Akvarium, DDT, and Tequilajazzz. The strongest point of Russian rock ballads are the meaningful lyrics, but even without knowledge of the language, you can still feel the drive.

Achtung Baby. Nothing to do with the U2 album of the same name, this bar and live-music venue is at the center of a rapidly emerging hub of alternative nightspots on Konyushennaya Ploshchad that take advantage of the vaulted spaces of the former Imperial Stables. Achtung Baby's program is a bit of a mixed bag, but there's always something happening here. ⊠ *2 Konyushennaya Pl., City Center* ⊕*www. achtungbaby.ru* Ⓜ*Nevsky Prospekt.*

Fish Fabrique. A favorite haunt of locals and expats who enjoy drinking and listening to local alternative musicians, or who just want to play table football, Fish Fabrique is located in the Pushkinskaya-10 Arts Centre. ⊠ *10 Pushkinskaya ul., entrance through courtyard of 53 Ligovsky pr., Vladimirskaya* ☎*812/764–4857* Ⓜ*Ploshchad Vosstaniya.*

Griboyedov. The best underground (literally) club in the city, this small bomb shelter–turned–club is usually packed with friendly, down-to-earth hipsters. It's owned and operated by a local band. In addition to decent live music, there's a mix of talented DJs spinning house, techno, and funk; check listings for different nights. A new space has been added upstairs that operates as a sushi restaurant and stage for poppier music acts which is known as Griboyedov Hill, or GH. ⊠*2a Voronezhskaya ul., at intersection with ul. Konstantina Zaslonova, Vladimirskaya* ☎*812/164–4355* ⊕*www.griboedovclub.ru* Ⓜ*Ligovsky Prospekt.*

Jazz Philharmonic Hall. Russia's top jazz musicians, including the famous Leningrad Dixieland Band and the David Goloshchokin's Ensemble, regularly appear at this venue in a turn-of-the-20th-century building. ⊠*27 Zagorodny pr., Vladimirskaya* ☎*812/764–8565* ⊕*www.jazz-hall.spb. ru* Ⓜ*Dostoyevskaya.*

Jazz Time. The music starts at 9 PM nightly at this cozy, welcoming jazz club. It's in a neighborhood that is a dining hot spot; one of the best Italian restaurants in the city, Il Grappolo, is just around the corner on Belinskogo. ⊠*41 Mokhovaya ul., Liteiny/Smolny* ☎*812/273–5379* Ⓜ*Chernyshevskaya.*

JFC Jazz Club. They know good jazz here. The most popular jazz venue in town, the club attracts top musicians performing all styles of jazz from acid funk to swing and blues to avant-garde to mainstream jazz or improvisation. The only disadvantage is its modest size, so you may want to reserve a seat ahead of time. ⊠*33 ul. Shpalernaya, Liteiny/ Smolny* ☎*812/272–9850* ⊕*www.jfc.sp.ru* Ⓜ*Chernyshevskaya.*

Money Honey Saloon. If rockabilly is your thing, or if you simply want to see a country-western saloon in Russia, head to this always-crowded bar for dancing and lots of fun. The live music usually starts at 8 PM. The upstairs City Bar attracts a slightly older crew and often has live music, too. There's a 40R cover charge. ⊠*13 Apraksin Dvor, enter courtyard at 28–30 Sadovaya ul., City Center* ☎*812/310–0549* ⊕*www.moneyhoney.org* Ⓜ*Gostinny Dvor or Sadovaya.*

Red Club. Civilized and comfortable, this former warehouse close to Moscow station attracts the best local rock bands and some good international alternative acts, such as Marc Ribot and Solex. The downstairs level has a stage and dance floor; upstairs, there are tables, a bar, and billiards. ⊠*7 Poltavskaya ul., Vladimirskaya* ☎*812/277–1366* ⊕*www.clubred.ru* Ⓜ*Vladimirskaya.*

Sunduk. This is an intimate and quiet little art café in the colonial style offering live jazz, blues, or rock. The menu is varied and food commendable yet inexpensive, so Sunduk is a popular eatery during the day as well. The toilet, with its many large decorative but defunct locks, is designed to confuse the guests. ⊠*42 Furshtatskaya ul.Liteiny/Smolny* ☎*812/272–3100* Ⓜ*Chernyshevskaya.*

The Place. Cool and sophisticated, decked out in dark woods, chrome and steel fixtures, and clever lighting, it has a restaurant with a modern menu and a lively music program of international art rock, jazz, and experimental acts. The Place has it all. Well, almost; it's located in an anonymous industrial building in a wasteland far from the center, but it's still well worth seeking out. ⊠*47 ul. Marshala Govorova, Southern Suburbs* ☎*812/331–9631* ⊕*www.placeclub.ru* Ⓜ*Narvskaya or Baltiiskaya.*

SPORTS & THE OUTDOORS

Tickets for sporting events can be purchased at the sports arena immediately prior to the game or at one of the many teatralnaya kassa throughout the city, notably on Nevsky prospekt at Nos. 22–24, 39, 42, and 74. Alternatively, use ⊕*http://spb.kassir.ru* to order tickets online.

BANYAS

A word of warning: going to just any banya is not recommended. Many municipal banyas are free on certain days for the poorest and most deprived people. For the best experience, consider sticking to the places we recommend and opt for a private cabin, rather than the general section.

Kazachi Bani (⊠*11 Kazachii per.* ☎*812/315–0734* Ⓜ*Pushkinskaya*) is located in a somewhat dilapidated building, but is still a good place to try. It has a private banya for 10 people. **Yamskie Bani** (⊠*9 ul. Dostoyevskovo* ☎*812/713–3580* ⊕*www.yamskie.ru* Ⓜ*Vladimirskaya*) has individual rooms as well as a sauna, tanning, and a fitness center.

ICE HOCKEY & FIGURE SKATING

The **Ice Palace** (*Ledovy Dvorets* ⊠*1 pr. Pyatiletok, Southern Suburbs* ☎*812/718–2157 or 812/718–6620* ⊕*www.newarena.spb.ru* Ⓜ*Prospekt Bolshevikov*) hosts ice-hockey and figure-skating events.

SKA Sports Palace (⊠*2 Zhdanovskaya nab., Petrograd Side* ☎*812/230–7819 or 812/237–0073* ⊕*www.ska.spb.ru* Ⓜ*Sportivnaya*) is used for ice hockey. SKA, St. Petersburg's hockey team, plays at the **Yubilyeiny Sports Palace** (⊠*18 pr. Dobrolyubova, Petrograd Side* ☎*812/323–9315* Ⓜ*Sportivnaya*). Check any of the city's teatralnaya kassa for tickets.

RUNNING

In the center, a good option is **Tavrichesky Gardens**, about a five-minute walk east of the Chernyshevskaya metro station, in the direction of Smolny. For a more serious run, you should head outside the city center to **Primorsky Park Pobedy,** on Krestovsky Island. The park has both gravel and paved pathways, as well as a lake and beautiful views. To get here, take the metro to Krestovsky Ostrov or Staraya Derevnya station. **Kirovsky Park,** covering most of the island of Yelagin Ostrov, is one of the most beautiful parks in the city and a good option for running. To get here take the metro to Staraya Derevnya station; walk south along Lipovaya alleya. When you reach the embankment, you will see a bridge to the island. You might also stick to the Neva embankments or head for the Summer Garden or the Field of Mars.

SOCCER

Zenit, St. Petersburg's Premier League soccer team which has begun giving its better-known Moscow rivals a serious run for their money in recent years and won the Russian Championship in 2007, plays now at **Petrovsky Stadium** (⊠ *2g Petrovsky Ostrov, Petrograd Side* ☎*812/328– 8902* Ⓜ*Sportivnaya*). Check any of the city's teatralnaya kassa for tickets. A new stadium, dubbed "The Spaceship," is under construction on Kresovsky Ostov in place of the now-demolished Kirov Stadium.

SHOPPING

Pick up a copy of Russian *Vogue* and you may be surprised to see that it nearly outdoes its Parisian and American counterparts for sheer gloss, glitz, and elegant, trendy garb. And all those nifty threads that the models are wearing—Versace, Hugo Boss, Gucci, Kenzo, Prada, Armani—are fully stocked in the international boutiques around the city. The days of basic items being scarce are long gone. And to make room for all these new shoppers, stores stay open until 8 or 9 PM or later, and are open on Sunday.

"Western-style" shops taking credit-card payment long ago replaced the old Beriozka (Birch Tree) emporiums, which were stocked only for foreigners. Kiosks, street tables, and impromptu markets sell a colorful jumble of junk. You'll see women lined up selling socks, scarves, and who-knows-what near Sennaya Ploshchad, and if you're lucky you might pick up some great old books (watch in particular the corner of Nevsky and Fontanka, across the street from the Palace of Prince Beloselsky-Belozersky). But this mini-industry of individual entrepreneurs, which mushroomed wildly in the first years of glasnost, is on the wane. Everything is being tidied up and taken back inside. You may also be surprised to find a plethora of "24 chasa" stores (i.e., open 24 hours a day). They vary from smallish to big, but there will always be one near you, stocked with alcohol, cigarettes, and groceries.

Russian wrinkles in the way people shop occur haphazardly unless you seek them out by finding old-fashioned outlets in backstreets and away from the city center. There's nothing you can't buy and the biggest problem you are likely to encounter is unwillingness from sales assistants to count back large amounts of change.

SHOPPING DISTRICTS

The central shopping district is Nevsky prospekt and the streets running off it. Don't expect bargains beyond bootlegged CDs and videos (which could be confiscated at customs in the United States), however, because prices for items such as clothes and electronic goods are higher than in the West, particularly in the chic stores in hotels.

DEPARTMENT STORES

Outside the large department stores of Nevsky prospekt, you'll find some boutiques and lots of "variety shops"—part souvenir-oriented, part practical—which can be a bit bewildering. Check them out if you have time; you never know what you may find.

Gostiny Dvor. The city's oldest and largest shopping center, built in the mid-18th century, has upscale boutiques, but it's still a good place to find souvenirs, such as *matryoshka* (nesting dolls), at some of the best prices in the city (look upstairs). The second floor houses a string of multibrand designer boutiques selling women's and men's clothes from famous European designers. *Gostinka,* as Gostiny Dvor is also known, also has some stores with cheaper prices; it can be a good place to buy winter clothing, such as a fur hat. The store, open daily from 10 until 10, is smack in the center of town and easily reached by the metro—the metro station right outside its doors is named in its honor. ✉ *35 Nevsky pr., City Center* ☎ *812/710–5408* ⊕ *www.bgd. ru* Ⓜ *Gostiny Dvor.*

Grand Palace. Reigning at the top end of the boutique market and serving shoppers with the deepest pockets, this consumer temple carries Woolford lingerie, Escada dresses, and Trussardi suits as well as perfume and jewelry at knockout prices. The café on the ground floor offers irresistible desserts crafted by a sophisticated French chef who knows his art. ✉ *44 Nevsky pr., City Center* ☎ *812/449–9344* ⊕ *www. grand-palace.ru* Ⓜ *Gostiny Dvor.*

Passazh. Passage, a mid-19th-century shopping arcade across the street from Gostiny Dvor, caters primarily to locals. The souvenir sections, however, are worth visiting, as prices, in rubles, are a bit lower here than in the souvenir shops around hotels and in other areas frequented by tourists. You can also pick up fine table linens at bargain prices. The porcelain section at the far end of the ground floor is worth a look, too, and there's a large supermarket in the basement. ✉ *48 Nevsky pr., City Center* ☎ *812/312–2210* ⊕ *www.passage.spb.ru* Ⓜ *Gostiny Dvor.*

Stockmann. This branch of the Finnish company helped bring some Scandinavian efficiency and style to Russian commerce when it opened a decade ago. Now Stockmann, in partnership with St. Petersburg's government, is investing heavily in a new development at the Ploshchad Vosstaniya end of Nevsky prospekt. The seven-floor Nevsky Center, boasting more than 80 shops, a food court, and a rooftop restaurant, is due to open at the end of 2008. Meanwhile wares at the existing store include quality clothes, lingerie, toys, kitchen gadgets, linens, and bathroom goods, mainly by Finnish and Scandinavian producers. The Atrium café is a quiet place to take a break. ✉ *25 Nevsky pr., City Center www.stockmann.ru* ☎ *812/326–2637* Ⓜ *Nevsky Prospekt.*

Vladimirsky Passazh. This modern and spacious four-story store, just outside Dostoyevskaya metro station, has numerous small boutiques selling jewelry, clothes, shoes, bags, lingerie, and cosmetics at less than exorbitant prices. The basement houses a large, 24-hour supermarket, and there's a great bakery on the ground floor—an excellent budget choice for a quick refuel. ✉ *19 Vladimirsky pr., Vladimirskaya* ☎ *812/331–3232* ⊕ *www.vladimirskiy.ru* Ⓜ *Dostoyevskaya or Vladimirskaya.*

> **SECOND SKIN**
>
> Westerners are often surprised to see how many people in Russia really do wear fur, perhaps believing the Russian fur hat went the way of the fedora in New York. Although some young people hold anti-fur views, most Russians consider fur coats and hats not only chic but, in winter, eminently practical.

SPECIALTY STORES

CLOTHING

Defile. Devoted entirely to Russian designers, this boutique offers diverse and innovative collections from some of the biggest names in the country's fashion industry, including St. Petersburger Lilia Kissilenko. The boutique's owner is a co-organizer of the St. Petersburg's premier fashion event, the twice-yearly Defile on the Neva. ✉ *27 nab. Griboyedov Canal, City Center* ☎ *812/571–9010* ⊕ *www.defilenaneve.ru* Ⓜ *Nevsky Prospekt.*

Lena. A wide selection of furs is sold at this store across the street from Gostiny Dvor. Here's some help with the Russian: rabbit (*krolik*), sheep (*caracul*), raccoon (*yenot*), white fox (*pisets*), silver fox (*chernoburka*), sable (*sobol*), and, of course, mink (*norka*). Note that some furs from protected species, such as seals, cannot be brought into the United States. ✉ *50 Nevsky pr., at Malaya Sadovaya, City Center* ☎ *812/312–3234* Ⓜ *Gostiny Dvor.*

★ **Tatyana Kotegova Fashion House.** Kotegova creates stylish and romantic collections with a note of restraint. Her soaring classical silhouettes are believed to capture the essence of St. Petersburg. The designer uses only natural materials, with an emphasis on wool, silk, and cashmere. Kotegova's velvet evening dresses, simple yet exquisite, are the dream of a good half of the local female population. ✉ *44 Bolshoi pr., 2nd floor, Petrograd Side* ☎ *812/346–3467* ⊕ *www.kotegova.com* Ⓜ *Petrogradskaya.*

CRAFTS & SOUVENIRS

Angel. This embroidery fashion house produces stunning silk scarves, luxurious tablecloths, and bright-color blouses, all beautifully embroidered by hand. Visits are by appointment. ✉ *40-B1 11-ya Linia, Vasilievsky Island* ☎ *812/321–2199* Ⓜ *Vasileostrovskaya.*

★ **Armeisky Magazin.** All army surplus—belts, flasks, caps, pins, and marine shirts with Russian and Soviet army symbols—is a much better bargain here, at this state-run store, than in touristy markets. You'll find a huge variety. ✉ *24 Kirochnaya ul., Liteiny/Smolny* ☎ *812/579–2907* Ⓜ *Chernyshevskaya.*

Farfor. For china and porcelain made at the Lomonosov Porcelain Factory (LFZ), once a purveyor to the tsars, go to this noted porcelain resource. ✉ *32 Kondratyevsky pr., Vyborg Side* ☎ *812/542–3055* ⊕ *www.farfor.spb.ru/* ✉ *7 Vladimirsky pr., Vladimirskaya* ☎ *812/713–1513* Ⓜ *Vladimirskaya.*

Galereya Stekla. At this glass gallery, the city of St. Petersburg is reflected in carved Easter eggs, stained glass, vases, and candlesticks. Each work is handmade, and many are one-of-a-kind. ✉ *1/28 ul. Lomonosova, City Center* ☎ *812/312–2214* Ⓜ *Nevsky Prospekt.*

Guild of Masters. Jewelry, ceramics, and other types of Russian traditional art, all made by members of the Russian Union of Artists, are sold here. ✉ *82 Nevsky pr., City Center* ☎ *812/579–0979* Ⓜ *Mayakovskaya.*

Lomonosov Porcelain Factory. One of the most famous porcelain manufacturers in Russia, the factory was founded in 1744 to serve the imperial family. This is your source for the world-famous hand-painted cobalt-blue china. There is also a porcelain museum here which is part of the Hermitage's holdings. ✉ *151 Obukhovskoy Oboroni pr., Southern Suburbs* ☎ *812/ 326-1744* ⊕ *www.ipm.ru* Ⓜ *Lomonosovskaya.*

Slavyansky Style. This is a good source for linen goods created in the traditional Russian style of the 19th century. There are several branches throughout the city. ✉ *151 Nevsky pr., City Center* ☎ *812/717–5164* ⊕ *www.linorusso.ru* Ⓜ *Ploshchad Alexandra Nevskovo* ✉ *3 Pushkinskaya ul., City Center* ☎ *812/325–8599* Ⓜ *Mayakovskaya.*

Vernisazh. At this open-air market outside the Church of the Savior on Spilled Blood, more than 100 vendors sell nesting dolls, paintings, Soviet icons, and miscellaneous trinkets. It is probably the easiest and quickest to locate if your time in St. Petersburg is limited and there are sure to be items here that make good gifts and keepsakes. Most vendors speak several languages but the prices are far from fair. Don't accept the first price quoted. ✉ *1 Kanal Griboyedova, City Center* ☎ *No phone* Ⓜ *Nevsky Prospekt.*

FARMERS' MARKETS

The farmers' markets (*rynok*) in St. Petersburg are lively places in which a colorful collection of goods and foods are sold by individual farmers, often from out of town and sometimes from outside the Russian republic, although a recent government crackdown on illegal immigrants saw Interior Ministry troops rounding up traders for deportation and quotas imposed on numbers of non-Russian citizens allowed to work in markets. In addition to the fine cuts of fresh and cured meat, dairy products, and homemade jams and jellies, piles of fruits and vegetables are sold here, even in winter. Try some homemade pickles or pickled garlic, a tasty local favorite. You can also find many welcome surprises such as hand-knit scarves, hats, and mittens. The markets are much cleaner and better lit here than in Moscow, so it can be fun just to visit and browse. In general, the markets are open daily from 8 AM to 7 PM (5 PM on Sunday).

Apraksin Dvor. St. Petersburg's less wealthy citizens come to this seething bazaar to shop for cheap clothes, shoes, DVDs, household items, and whatever else you can think of. A chaotic relic of the Yeltsin years, and hardly befitting Russia's newfound love affair with Slavic glamour, the city's rulers have decreed that Apraksin Dvor must go, although its traders are a resourceful bunch who are fighting to remain in place. ✉28–30 Sadovaya ul., City Center Ⓜ Nevsky Prospekt.

Kuznechny Rynok. This is the best and most expensive of St. Petersburg's farmers' markets. It's just outside the metro station. ✉3 Kuznechny per., Vladimirskaya Ⓜ Vladimirskaya.

Polyustrovsky Rynok. On the weekend you can find a pet market, with puppies, kittens, chickens, and more. In a somewhat chilling twist, the market boasts an impressive fur department with some good bargains on things like rabbit winter hats. ✉45 Polyustrovsky pr., Vyborg Side Ⓜ Ploshchad Lenina.

Sennoi Rynok. Once a huge, sprawling flea market, this is now perhaps the cleanest and most organized farmers' market in the city; the entrance is just a short walk from Sennaya Ploshchad. However, like all St. Petersburg's farmers' markets, its existence is becoming increasingly decorative, since right next door there is now a cheaper and more convenient modern supermarket called Perekrostok. ✉4 Moskovsky pr., City Center Ⓜ Sadovaya or Sennaya Ploshchad.

FOOD

Where once babushkas legendarily carried a string bag at all times "just in case" they saw food for sale, now clean, freshly stocked modern supermarkets with smart-card loyalty schemes stand on every corner.

For cigarettes, snacks, drinks, and basic foodstuffs like bread, milk and tea, look for a *produkty* shop. You may have to ask at the checkout for your purchases but since produkty are increasingly becoming self-service, simply walk five minutes to the next one if you have any problems.

Among supermarket names to look for, with stores all over the city, are Pyatyorochka (there's a figure 5 in its logo), Perekrostok ("Crossroads," look for a cross), Lenta (featuring a daisy), Diksi (a red disc on a yellow square with "Diksi" written in black). French-style markets include Mega, O'Key, and Giant. If you see a red-and-white logo that reads Maksidom on what appears to be a superstore, don't go in looking for food—it's a home-improvement and furniture chain in competition with St. Petersburg's IKEAs. Apart from those mentioned below, Nevsky prospekt itself is not noted for its food shops, but a few steps along its cross streets will usually bring results.

Kalinka-Stockmann. If you're looking for a big Western-style supermarket that takes credit cards, try Kalinka-Stockmann. It's open daily 9 AM–10 PM. ✉ *1 Finlandsky pr., Vyborg Side* ☎ *812/542–2297* Ⓜ *Ploshchad Lenina.*

Supermarket. Within the Passage shopping arcade, Supermarket sells cheese and fresh fruits and vegetables. It opens daily at 10 (11 on Sunday) and closes at 9. ✉ *48 Nevsky pr., City Center* ☎ *812/312–4701* Ⓜ *Gostinny Dvor.*

Vladimirsky Supermarket. In the spacious basement of Vladimirsky Passazh, this good, well-stocked supermarket is conveniently open 24 hours a day. ✉ *19 Vladimirsky pr., Vladimirskaya* ☎ *812/331–3232* Ⓜ *Vladimirskaya.*

★ **Yeliseyevsky Food Emporium.** If for no other reason than to see its beautiful art nouveau interior, be sure to stop by Yeliseyevsky, across from Gostinny Dvor. The smaller shop on the right is a good place to buy caviar or a tasty fish snack. Otherwise, check out the local *dieta* (dairy-food store), *gastronom* (food store), and *produkty* (selling nonperishable products). It's open daily 10–10. ✉ *56 Nevksy pr., at Malaya Sadovaya, City Center* ☎ *812/312–1865* Ⓜ *Nevsky Prospekt.*

JEWELRY

Jewelry used to be an unlikely reason to come to St. Petersburg, but there are some good places to explore these days, particularly on Nevsky prospekt.

Ananov. Head and shoulders above the jewel meccas in town, this quiet, dim store is owned by former sailor and theater director Andrei Ananov, now internationally famous as a jeweler following in the traditions of the great Peter Fabergé. Ananov is as much a gallery as a shop, and no one here would ever be vulgar enough to list prices; if you have to ask, you probably can't afford it. ✉ *9 Michurinskaya ul., City Center* ☎ *812/235–4251* ⊕ *www.ananov.com/* Ⓜ *Gostinny Dvor.*

Etalon-Jenavi. The detour necessary to get here will be well rewarded: the best costume jewelry in town is fashionable, sophisticated, and original, embracing everything from fine replicas of museum artworks to children's collections of enameled pendants in the shapes of insects, toys, and balloons. It certainly won't empty your wallet. ✉ *172 Moskovsky pr., Southern Suburbs* ☎ *812/371–2722* Ⓜ *Elektrosila.*

Russian Jewelry House. This is a good bet for jewelry, particularly amber pieces. ✉ *27 Nevsky pr., City Center* ☎ *812/312–8501* Ⓜ *Nevsky Prospekt.*

★ **Russkie Samotsvety.** Many items in these collections were inspired by St. Petersburg's architecture, history, literature, and its immense artistic legacy. Jewelers play with well-familiar visual images, like ballet or shipbuilding, and incorporate city symbols in their designs. ✉ *1 ul. 1-ya Krasnoarmeiskaya, Admiralteisky* ☎ *812/316–7646* Ⓜ *Tekhnologichesky Institut.*

MUSIC STORES

Classica. This is the best shop for classical music. The oldest store of its kind in St. Petersburg, it sells a good choice of recordings as well as folk and religious music with an emphasis on Russian composers and performers. You can also find rare recordings on vinyl LPs here. ✉2 *Mikhailovskaya ul., City Center* ☎812/710–4428 Ⓜ*Nevsky Prospekt.*

Kailas. This shop obviously has someone on staff who pays attention to new and interesting music emerging around the world. You'll find the Flaming Lips or the White Stripes here before any other shop in the city, plus a vast selection of electronica, world music, jazz, and classical music. ✉*10 ul. Pushkinskaya, City Center* ☎812/320–9147 ⊕*www. kailas.sp.ru* Ⓜ*Mayakovskaya or Ploshchad Vosstaniya.*

Otkryty Mir. For classical music, the choice is surprisingly poor for a city that prides itself on its cultural legacy. Although no one could accuse this store of being overstocked, it does hold the occasional hidden classical delight, particularly when it comes to Russian composers and artists and recordings on the old Melodiya label. Hunt around. ✉*13 Malaya Morskaya ul., Admiralteisky* ☎812/715–8939 Ⓜ*Nevsky Prospekt.*

Titanik. The delights of megastores such as Virgin have yet to hit St. Petersburg, and even the best shops have a rather scruffy look about them, not to mention a cavalier attitude toward copyright law that has been one of the stumbling blocks in Russia's ascension to the World Trade Organization. But among the best sources is this chain, which sells a motley collection of Western and Russian rock and pop, plus DVDs and videos (the DVDs usually have an English track available, and many are without regional-zone coding). ✉*63 Nevsky pr., City Center* ☎812/336–5745 ⊕*www.titanik-spb.ru* Ⓜ*Mayakovskaya.*

ST. PETERSBURG ESSENTIALS

TRANSPORTATION

BY AIR

St. Petersburg is served by two airports, Pulkovo I (domestic) and Pulkovo II (international), just 2 km (1 mi) apart and 17 km (11 mi) south of central St. Petersburg. The runways of the two Pulkovos interconnect, so it's possible you could land at Pulkovo I and taxi over to Pulkovo II. Compared with Moscow's Sheremetyevo II, Pulkovo II is a breeze. It's compact and well lit, with signs in both Russian and English.

However, the airport's toy size—there are only eight gates and one landing line in Pulkovo II—prevents it from receiving more airlines and developing into a venue fit for a large European city. Remember that on departure you'll need to fill out a final customs declaration (available at all the long tables) before proceeding through the first checkpoint. If you have nothing to declare, just head through the "green channel" of the customs area. Try to arrive at the airport at least two hours in advance. Bear in mind that check-in stops 40 minutes before departure, so don't count on making the plane at the last minute without some frantic pleading.

St. Petersburg air carrier Rossiya, Russia's second-largest airline after Aeroflot, offers direct flights to more than 20 countries out of Pulkovo II. Aeroflot and its tough competitor Transaero fly from St. Petersburg only to Moscow, where the passengers have to get a connecting flight to other destinations.

Other international airlines with offices in St. Petersburg include Air France, Austrian, Alitalia, SN Brussels Airlines, Air Malta, Air Baltic, Korean Air Lines, Armenian Airlines, British Airways, CSA (Czech Airlines), Delta, El Al, Finnair, KLM, LOT, Lufthansa, Malev, and SAS. Note that there are no direct flights from the United States to St. Petersburg. Korean Air and Air Baltic don't have offices in town and sell tickets via tour operators, including Infinity Travel and Sindbad Travel (*see Travel Agencies*).

3

Airport Information **Pulkovo I Airport** (☎*812/704–3822* ⊕ *www.pulkovo.ru*). **Pulkovo II Airport** (☎*812/704–3444* ⊕ *www.pulkovo.ru*).

Contacts **Aeroflot** (☎*812/438–5583*). **Air Baltic** (⊕ *www.airbaltic.com*). **Air France** (☎*812/325–8252 or 812/336–2900*). **Air Malta** (☎*812/740–3820* ⊕ *www.airmalta.com*). **Alitalia** (☎*812/336–9131* ⊕ *www.alitalia.com*). **Armenian Airlines** (☎*812/388–3054*). **Austrian** (☎*812/331–2005* ⊕ *www.aua. com*). **British Airways** (☎*812/329–2565 or 812/380–0626* ⊕ *www.ba.com*). **CSA** (☎*812/315–5259* ⊕ *www.czechairlines.com*). **Delta** (☎*812/571–5820*). **El Al** (☎*812/380–6880*). **Finnair** (☎*812/303–9898* ⊕ *www.finnair.com*). **KLM** (☎*812/346–6868* ⊕ *www.klm.com*). **Korean Air Lines** (⊕ *www.koreanair.com*). **LOT** (☎*812/272–2982* ⊕ *www.lot.com*). **Lufthansa** (☎*812/320–1000* ⊕ *www. lufthansa.com*). **Malev** (☎*812/922–0662*). **Rossiya** (☎*812/331–4229*). **SAS** (☎*812/326–2600* ⊕ *www.scandinavian.net*). **SN Brussels Airlines** (☎*812/723–8691* ⊕ *www.flysn.com*). **Transaero** (☎*812/279–6463*).

TRANSFERS From Pulkovo I, Municipal Bus 39 (in Russian, the word to look for is "avtobus") will take you to the Moskovskaya metro stop on Moskovsky prospekt; the stop at the airport is right outside the terminal. Tickets are sold on the bus, which runs every 20 minutes during the day. From Pulkovo II, the service is less reliable and more inconvenient. If you have any luggage, the only realistic way to reach downtown St. Petersburg is by car. If you are traveling with a tour package, all transfers will have been arranged. If you're traveling alone, you're strongly advised to make advance arrangements with your hotel. There are plenty of taxis available, but you would be ill-advised to pick up a cab on your own if you don't speak Russian. Foreign tourists, especially passengers arriving at train stations and airports, are prime crime targets for scam artists, so be skeptical about offers. Cab fare from the airport will depend entirely on your negotiating skills; the range is $50 to $70 (1,250R to 1,750R) but should never approach three figures. Drivers will likely haggle in the dollar amount, or even in euros, but if you have rubles and have familiarized yourself with the exchange rate, you could get it down to half as much by offering rubles in cash. The airport is about a 40-minute ride from the city center. When you return to the airport, a regular cab that you order by phone will cost you between $30 and $50 (750R and 1,250R). The operator for Taxi Million tells you the fare in advance.

Public transportation to Pulkovo II is also more reliable than from it— take bus No. 13 from outside the Moskovskaya metro stop (you may have to buy an extra ticket for your luggage if it takes up what the conductor considers to be too much room). There are also *marshrutki* (taxi vans) outside the metro stop; these are clearly marked, but difficult to squeeze your suitcases into. Marshrutkas No. 213 and K-3 go along Moskovsky prospect down to Sennaya Ploshchad in the city center, and a single fare costs 18R–25R. Marshrutka No. 350 follows the same route until Sennaya Ploshchad, and then continues up to Primorskaya metro station via Teatralnaya Ploshchad. Full fare costs 30R.

Contacts **Central Taxi** (*Tsentralnoye Taksi* ☎ 812/312–0022). **Petersburg Taxi** (*Petersburgskoye Taxi* ☎ 068). **Taxi Million** (☎ 812/700–0000).

BY BOAT & FERRY

Traveling by boat between St. Petersburg and the Kotlin border is 1½ hours of sheer enjoyment: a pleasure cruise passes the island of Kotlin (Kronstadt), then travels along the coastline where Lomonosov, Peterhof, and Strelna can be seen with the aid of binoculars. Finally, it arrives into the huge city harbor, with St. Isaac's Cathedral as a constant focus. Make arrangements at the sea passenger terminal, which is on Vasilievsky Island at Ploshchad Morskoi Slavy. For inland trips to places such as Valaam Island, Kizhi Island, or even Moscow, boats depart from the river passenger terminal.

Contacts **Baltic Line** (☎ 812/322–1616 ⊕ www.balticline.ru). **River passenger terminal** (✉ 195 pr. Obukhovskoi Oborony, Vladimirskaya ☎ 812/262–0239 Ⓜ Proletarskaya). **Sea passenger terminal** (✉ Pl. Morskoi Slavy, Vasilievsky Island ☎ 812/322–6052).

BY BUS, TRAM & TROLLEY

Several firms operate bus routes between St. Petersburg and central Europe. A bus trip can be a reasonably comfortable way to connect with the Baltic states, Scandinavia, and Germany, although as with train travel in and out of the country, it entails a two- to three-hour wait at the border for everyone to clear customs. The Gorodskoi Avtobusny Vokzal (City Bus Station), open from 6:30 AM until 11:30 PM, sells tickets for international and domestic routes. It takes about 15 minutes to walk to the station from Ligovsky Prospect metro station, but you are better off targeting the representative offices of the company you wish to travel with or using a travel agent.

Among the most reliable of the bus companies is Eurolines, which runs coaches to Tallinn, Riga, Stuttgart, and destinations all over Europe. The Finnish bus company Finnord runs coaches between Helsinki and St. Petersburg via the border town of Vyborg. The service runs twice daily, leaving from Finnord's offices at 37 Italyanskaya ulitsa, and then at half a dozen Finnish towns before reaching Helsinki.

Although St. Petersburg is spread out over 650 square km (250 square mi), most of its historic sites are concentrated in the downtown section and are best explored on foot. These sites are often not well served by the extensive public transportation system, so be prepared to do a lot of walking. Bilingual city maps with bus routes marked on them are sold at the bookstore Dom Knigi (⊠ *62 Nevsky prospekt*), while *St. Petersburg In Your Pocket* prints valuable info about marshrutki routes in every issue.

When traveling by bus, tram, or trolley, you must purchase a ticket from the conductor. At this writing, a ticket valid for one ride costs 12R, regardless of the distance you intend to travel; if you change buses, you must pay another fare. Buses, trams, and trolleys operate from 5:30 AM to midnight, although service in the late evening hours and on Sunday tends to be unreliable.

Note that all public transportation vehicles tend to be extremely over-crowded during rush hours; people with claustrophobia should avoid them. It's very much the Russian philosophy that there's always room for one more passenger. Make sure you position yourself near the exits well before the point at which you want to disembark, or risk missing your stop. Buses tend to be newer and reasonably comfortable. Trol-leys and trams, on the other hand, sometimes give the impression that they're held together with Scotch tape and effort of will, and can be extremely drafty. In winter the windows tend to ice up to the point where it's impossible to see where you are, so ask the conductor to tell you if in doubt.

Contacts **The City Bus Station** (⊠ *36 Obvodnovo kanala nab., Vladimirskaya* ☎ *812/766–5777* Ⓜ *Ligovsky Prospekt*). **Eurolines** (☎ *812/380–5245* ⊕ *www. eurolines.ru*). **Finnord** (⊠ *37 Italyanskaya ul.* ☎ *812/314–8951* Ⓜ *Nevsky Prospekt*).

BY CAR

You can reach St. Petersburg from Finland via the Helsinki–St. Peters-burg Highway through the border town of Vyborg; the main street into and out of town for Finland is Kamennoostrovsky prospekt. To reach Moscow, take Moskovsky prospekt; at the hotel Pulkovskaya round-about, take Mosvoskoye shosse (M–10/E–95), slightly to the left of the road to the airport. Bear in mind that it will take at least two hours to clear customs and immigration at the border, and on occasions (e.g., Friday night and weekends) the lines can be lengthy, increasing your wait considerably.

BY METRO

Although St. Petersburg's metro does not have the elaborate design and decoration of Moscow's metro system, its good qualities are still substantial. Despite economic hardships, St. Petersburg has managed to maintain efficient, inexpensive service; the only drawback is that the stops tend to be far apart.

Stations are deep underground—the city's metro is the deepest in the world—necessitating long escalator rides. Some of them have encased landings so that entry is possible only after the train has pulled in and the secondary doors are opened.

A word of warning: avoid Sportivnaya station on Saturday, because it leads to the city's main soccer stadium and trains will likely be full of rowdy fans of the local club, Zenit. All central stations are infamous for theft and rank high in the city's list of pickpocket hot spots. Although the city police regularly trumpet successes and report arrests of more gangs, it doesn't seem to get any safer.

FARES &
SCHEDULES
To use the metro, you must purchase a token or a magnetic card (available at stations) and insert it, upon entering, into the slot at the turnstile. The fare (14R) is the same regardless of distance. Alternatively, you may purchase a pass valid for an entire month (600R) and good for transport on all modes of city transportation. You can also opt for a two-week all-inclusive pass (300R), well worth the convenience if you plan to use the metro often.

There's a monthly pass for the metro only (460R), and a choice of magnetic cards for 10 trips (82R) or 25 trips (194R). The price for tokens and passes has, in the last few years, been raised by a ruble or two each New Year, so if you are in St. Petersburg at around this time its best to check if there will be a fare hike. The metro operates from 5:30 AM to 12.30 AM, but is best avoided during rush hours. The nicer hotels often give out metro maps printed in English.

BY TAXI

Take the same precautions when using taxicabs in St. Petersburg as in Moscow. Although taxis roam the city quite frequently, it's far easier—and certainly safer—to order a cab through your hotel. Fares vary according to the driver's whim; you're expected to negotiate. Foreigners can often be charged much more than Russians, and oblivious tourists tend to be gouged. Make sure that you agree on a price before getting into the car, and try to have the correct money handy. If you speak Russian, you can order a cab by dialing one of the numbers listed below. There's sometimes a delay, but usually the cab arrives within 20–30 minutes; the company will phone you back when the driver is nearby. If you order a cab this way, you pay the official state fare, which turns out to be reasonable in dollars, plus a fee for the reservation. No tip is expected beyond rounding up the amount on the meter. If you hail a cab or a private car on the street, expect to pay the ruble equivalent of $5 for most usual trips.

Contacts **Central Taxi** (*Tsentralnoye Taksi* ☎ 812/312–0022). **Petersburg Taxi** (*Peterburgskoye Taxi* ☎ 068). **Taxi Million** (☎ 812/700–0000).

BY TRAIN

St. Petersburg has several train stations, the most important of which are Baltic station (Baltiysky Vokzal), for trains to the Baltic countries; Finland station (Finlandsky Vokzal), for trains to Finland; Moscow station (Moskovsky Vokzal), at Ploshchad Vosstania, off Nevsky prospekt, for trains to Moscow and points east; and Vitebsk station (Vitebsky Vokzal), for trains to Ukraine and points south. Trains for Karelia and points north depart from the Finland station (Finlandsky Vokzal). All the major train stations have a connecting metro stop, so they're easily reached by public transportation.

3

For information on train arrival and departure schedules, call the train-information number below. Train tickets may be purchased through the tourist bureau in your hotel or at the Central Railway Agency Office (Tsentralnoye Zheleznodorozhnoye Agenstvo) off Nevsky prospekt, adjacent to the Kazan Cathedral. The agency is open 8–8 Monday through Saturday and 8–4 on Sunday. The office has three information points that can point you in the direction of the correct desks. Even better is the Central Airline Ticket Agency on Nevsky, which has two train-ticket desks and is a far quieter option. It's possible to buy tickets at the stations themselves, but this is best attempted only by the brave or bilingual.

FARES & SCHEDULES
Several trains run daily between Moscow and St. Petersburg, the most popular of which is the *Krasnaya Strelka* (Red Arrow), a night train that departs from one end at 11:55 PM and arrives at the other at 8:25 AM the next day. Its Empire-style rival, *Nikolayevsky Express,* departs the city at 11:24 AM and gets to Moscow at 7:10 PM. Designed to resemble a typical early-20th-century train and named after Russia's last tsar, Nicholas II, this romantic train has staff dressed in turn-of-the-20th-century costumes, oak settings in its restaurant, and brass details in compartments. You pay less than 7,500R round-trip for a berth in a four-person compartment. The most sumptuous way to travel between the two cities is the *Grand Express*: the most luxurious cabin has an LCD TV, DVD player, air-conditioning, toilet and shower, and bathrobe and slippers. Check ⊕*www.trainsrussia.com* for availability and pricing with an easy-to-use, budget-airline style online booking system in English for all trains between St. Petersburg and Moscow.

During the day travelers can choose between the *Avrora,* which makes the trip in less than six hours, or the high-speed ER–200 trains, which leave twice a day and take a lightning-quick 4 hours and 45 minutes. There are two trains daily to and from Helsinki (the Repin and the Sibelius) from Finlandsky station; the trip takes 6½ hours.

Contacts **Central Airline Ticket Agency** (⊠ *7/9 Nevsky pr., City Center* ☎ *812/315–0072* Ⓜ *Nevsky Prospekt*). **Central Railway Agency Office** (⊠ *24 Kanal Griboyedova, City Center* ☎ *812/710–6616* Ⓜ *Nevsky prospekt*). **Train information** (☎ *812/768–3344* ⊕ *www.trainsrussia.com*).

CONTACTS & RESOURCES

EMERGENCIES

Most staff at police stations don't speak foreign languages, which makes it impossible or painstakingly long to report a crime. Travel agencies often arrange a translator and driver for their clients who have been victims. If you're on your own and need to report a theft or another crime committed against you, head to the central City Tourism Information Office. Staff there have been trained and can competently assist foreigners in preparing and filing a police report, which in case of theft of valuables is necessary for insurance claims. The center operates only during business hours and is closed on weekends.

A lost-and-found office operated by the police is available in English as well. The St. Petersburg chapter of the American Chamber of Commerce and the city police have developed a very helpful and detailed list of safety recommendations, which is available on the chamber's Web site at ⊕*www.amcham.ru* (click on AmCham St. Petersburg chapter and then go to Important Links section).

Emergency Services Ambulance (☎ *03 for Russian speakers only*). **City Tourism Information Center** (✉ *14 Sadovaya ul., City Center* ☎☎ *812/310–8286 or 812/310–2822* ⊕ *www.piter.ru* ☉ *Weekdays 10–6* Ⓜ *Sennaya Ploshchad*). **Fire** (☎ *01*). **Lost and Found** (☎ *812/578–3690 English speakers available*). **Police** (☎ *02 for Russian speakers only, 812/278–3018 foreigner hotline, 812/764–9798 task force for crimes against foreigners*).

DENTISTS In an emergency, you could ask your hotel for a referral, or try one of several private clinics in the city. Besides highly qualified doctors, the American Medical Center also has a dentist on staff, and even offers 24-hour emergency services; this place is not cheap, however. Another option is the chain of Medi clinics with 11 different locations; the clinics listed below are the most central ones. Other clinics that offer dental services include the Clinic Complex and Nordmed.

Contacts American Medical Center (✉ *78 nab. Moiki, City Center* ☎ *812/740–2090* ⊕ *www.amcenters.com* Ⓜ *Sennaya Ploshchad*). **Clinic Complex** (✉ *22 Moskovsky pr., Vladimirskaya* ☎ *812/316–6272* Ⓜ *Tekhnologichesky Institut*). **Medi** (✉ *82 Nevsky pr., Vladimirskaya* ☎ *812/324–0021* Ⓜ *Nevsky Prospect* ✉ *31 Italianskaya ul., City Center* ☎ *812/324–0006* Ⓜ *Nevsky Prospect* ✉ *13 10th Sovietskaya, Liteiny/Smolny* ☎ *812/324–0002* ⊕ *www.mam.ru* Ⓜ *Ploshchad Vosstania*). **Nordmed** (✉ *12/15 ul. Tverskaya, Liteiny/Smolny* ☎ *812/710–0401* Ⓜ *Chernyshevskaya*).

HOSPITALS & CLINICS Public medical facilities in St. Petersburg are poorly equipped. However, as with dentistry, private clinics, which offer a higher level of treatment, are proliferating. Several Russian clinics offer quality health services, but they rarely have English speakers available to assist you. In case of emergency, it's best to seek help from a Western-style clinic.

The American Medical Center is open weekdays 8:30 to 6, and offers 24-hour comprehensive care. The Clinic Complex has been around for years (formerly as the St. Petersburg Polyclinic No. 2); it's open weekdays 9–9, Saturday 9–3. The largest and most impressive clinic with an en-suite hospital is MEDEM, where multilingual staff can provide more than 2,000 medical tests and services. The clinic works 24 hours, and is certainly the best equipped in town. The central Euromed clinic provides high-quality medical services and is recognized by all major European insurance companies. Another possibility in the same neighborhood is Emergency Medical Consulting, a European medical center. If you're unfortunate enough to be hospitalized while in St. Petersburg, you'll probably be placed in Hospital No. 20.

Clinics American Medical Center (✉ *78 nab. Moiki, City Center* ☎ *812/740–2090* ⊕ *www.amcenters.com* Ⓜ *Sennaya Ploshchad*). **Clinic Complex** (✉ *22 Moskovsky pr., Vladimirskaya* ☎ *812/316–6272* Ⓜ *Tekhnologichesky Institut*). **Emergency**

Medical Consulting (✉ 78 Moskosvky pr., Vladimirskaya ☎ 812/325–0880 Ⓜ Frunzhenskaya). **Euromed** (✉ 60 Suvorovsky pr., Liteiny/Smolny ☎ 812/327–0301 Ⓜ Nevsky Prospect). **MEDEM International Clinic & Hospital** (✉ 6 ul. Marata, Liteiny/Smolny ☎ 812/336–3333 ⊕ www.medem.ru Ⓜ Mayakovskaya).

Hospital **Hospital No. 20** (✉ 21 ul. Gastello, Southern Suburbs ☎ 812/708–4808 or 812/708–4066 Ⓜ Moskovskaya).

PHARMACIES You can find pharmacies all over St. Petersburg, and, unlike in the West, just about everything is available without a prescription. Most pharmacies close by 8 or 9 PM, though there are several dozen places operating round the clock. Below are a choice of late-night pharmacies.

Late-Night Pharmacies **Natur Produkt** (✉ 19 Vossaniya ul., Admiralteisky Ⓜ Vasileostrovskaya ☎ 812/279–0830 Ⓜ Sennaya Ploshchad ✉ 47 Sredni pr., Vasilievsky Island ☎ 812/327–0990). **Pervaya Pomoshch** (First Aid ✉ 27 Moskovsky pr., Vladimirskaya ☎ 812/324–4400 Ⓜ Nevsky Prospekt). **PetroFarm** (✉ 22 Nevsky pr., City Center ☎ 812/314–5401 Ⓜ Nevsky Prospekt) **Pharmacy Doctor** (✉ 7 Liteiny pr., Liteiny/Smolny ☎ 812/273–6135 Ⓜ Chernyshevskaya ✉ 61 Lesnoi pr., Bldg. 3, Vyborg Side ☎ 812/245–7434 Ⓜ Lesnaya). **Pharmacy MEDEM** (✉ 6 ul. Marata, Liteiny/Smolny ☎ 812/336–3333 Ⓜ Mayakovskaya).

INTERNET, MAIL & SHIPPING

Internet cafés and other types of stores that provide Internet access, such as mobile phone shops, are widely available in central St. Petersburg. Many bars, restaurants, shops, and cafés also have Wi-Fi hot spots, although some less central places say they have it when they don't or don't yet. Free Internet access is rare.

Internet **A. S. Popov Postal and Telecommunication Museum's Internet Center** (✉ 4 Pochtammsky per., City Center ⊕ www.rustelecom-museum.ru). **CafeMax** (✉ 90–92 Nevsky pr., City Center ☎ 812/273–6655 ⊕ www.cafemax.ru). **Intelligent People** (✉ 32 Gorokhovaya ul., City Center ☎ 812/315–1223). **Kofein** (✉ 148 Nevsky pr., City Center ☎ 812/717–5793). **Quo Vadis?** (✉ 63 Liteiny pr., City Center ☎ 812/333–0708 ⊕ www.quovadis.ru). **Zebra** (✉ 85 Nevsky pr., City Center ☎ 812/336–3346 ⊕ www.zebra-ic.ru).

Mail & Shipping **DHL** (✉ 4 Ismailovsky pr., City Center ☎ 812/324–6400 ⊕ www.dhl.ru). **FedEx** (✉ 30 Nevsky pr., City Center ☎ 812/449–1878 ⊕ www.fedex.com). **WestPost** (✉ 86 Nevsky pr., City Center ☎ 812/336–6352 ⊕ www.westpost.ru).

MEDIA

ENGLISH-LANGUAGE BOOKSTORES Anglia is St. Petersburg's best-known English-language bookstore, with a large selection of Russian literature in translation, popular fiction, and classic English literature, as well as sections on photography, history, biography, and foreign languages. The friendly English-speaking staff is ready to assist you with all your literary needs. Though it doesn't have nearly the same selection, you could also try St. Petersburg's largest bookstore, Dom Knigi (House of Books). A limited selection of outdated English-language guidebooks on various parts of the former Soviet Union is available at Akademkniga. Iskusstvo, like Akademkniga, stocks English-language guidebooks.

Bookstores **Akademkniga** (✉ 57 Liteiny pr., Liteiny/Smolny ☎ 812/273–1398 Ⓜ Mayakovskaya). **Anglia** (✉ 38 nab. Fontanka, Vladimirskaya ☎ 812/279–8284

⊕ *www.anglophile.ru* Ⓜ *Dostoyevskaya, Vladimirskaya).* **Dom Knigi** (⊠ *62 Nevsky pr., City Center* ☎ *812/570–6546* Ⓜ *Nevsky Prospect* ⊠ *28 Nevsky pr., City Center* ☎ *812/448–2355* Ⓜ *Nevsky Prospekt).*

NEWSPAPERS & MAGAZINES

American and British paperbacks, newspapers, and magazines are on sale in hotel gift shops. The *St. Petersburg Times* (⊕ *www.sptimes.ru*), a free, local, English-language newspaper, is a good source for happenings around town. It's published Tuesday and Friday and is available at hotels, cafés, and clubs throughout St. Petersburg.

BANKS & EXCHANGE SERVICES

Exchange bureaus can be found throughout the city. ATMs are now as plentiful as in a typical North American or European city, and can be found on any of the main streets in the city center. ATMs and exchange offices work around the clock at both the Angleterre hotel (connected to the Astoria) and the Grand Hotel Europe.

TOUR OPTIONS

In addition to the private agencies, every major hotel has a tourist bureau through which individual and group tours can be booked. Explorer-Tour arranges city tours. The Modern travel agency offers incoming tour services for groups and individuals, arranges excursions around St. Petersburg and Moscow, and can also arrange wedding and business tours. Mir Travel Agency can custom-design tours.

Contacts **Explorer-Tour** (⊠ *50 ul. Marata, Office No. 9, Vladimirskaya* ☎ *812/320–0954* 🖨 *812/712–1967* ⊕ *www.explorer-tour.ru* Ⓜ *Mayakovskaya).* **Mir Travel Agency** (⊠ *11 ul. Marata, Liteiny/Smolny* ☎🖨 *812/325–7122* Ⓜ *Mayakovskaya).* **Modern** (⊠ *3 Torzhovskaya ul., Office 236, Vyborg Side* ☎ *812/246–9533* Ⓜ *Chernaya Rechka).*

BOAT TOURS

A float down the Neva or through the city's twisting canals—*Exkursii na katere po rekam i kanalam*—is always a pleasant way to spend a summer afternoon or a White Night. For trips through the canals, take one of the boats at the pier near Anichkov Bridge on Nevsky prospekt. Boats cruising the Neva leave from the pier outside the State Hermitage Museum. Both boat trips have departures early morning to late afternoon from mid-May through mid-September.

PRIVATE TOUR GUIDES

There are many private tour guides who can provide detailed tours in English on the many sights within and outside of St. Petersburg. They must go through a rigorous training process before becoming a licensed tour guide and can prove very helpful, especially in places like the Hermitage. Below is a sampling of a few trusted names.

Contacts **Ksenia Belous** (☎ *8905/229–1907* ✑ *bel-ksenia@yandex.ru).* **Taisisya Ivanova** (☎ *7904/644–5550* ✑ *encc.ru@gmail.com* ⊕ *www.enjoypetersburg. com).* **Natalia Velikaya** (☎ *8905/277–5394* ✑ *natour@mail.ru).* **Irina Yashenko** (☎ *8901/307–0341* ✑ *rina_yashl@mail.ru).*

WALKING TOURS

If you prefer to plunge into city life instead of observing it from the window of your tour bus, the best bet is to take an excursion (from 400R) with one of the city's best-known walking tour companies, Peter's Walking Tours. Founded by inveterate local backpacker Peter

Kozyrev, the company turns walks and pub crawls into a real experience. The guides masterfully interweave history, current affairs, mystery, and gossip. The most popular walk is the five-hour-long Original Walking Tour: express your wishes and the guide tailors the route. Check the schedule on the company's Web site at ⊕ *www.peterswalk. com*, choose a walk, and book it by e-mail. There's no telephone number for the company, and all private tours have to be made via e-mail.

Contact Information **Peter's Walking Tours** (⊕ *www.peterswalk.com* ✉ *info@ peterswalk.com*).

VISITOR INFORMATION

The staff members of the City Tourist Information Center (Gorodskoi Turistichesky Tsentr Informatsii ot Soveta po Turismu) are generally friendly, although they have a tendency to thrust maps and booklets at you in the absence of any great ideas themselves. The center has a database on cultural and sports events, hotels, major tourist attractions, and so on. You may also consult the St. Petersburg Tourism and Excursions Council (Soviet po Turismu i Ekskursiyam). You can also call the Infoline 24 hours a day; the operators may not have the answer to your question, but they will tell you so nicely.

Your best bet for information and assistance is your hotel, for virtually all of the hotels have established tourist offices for their guests. These offices, which provide many services, can help you book individual and group tours, make restaurant reservations, or purchase theater tickets. Even if you're not a hotel guest, you're usually welcome to use these facilities, provided you are willing to pay the hefty fees for their services.

If you plan on spending a great deal of time in the city, it might be worthwhile to invest about 125R in the *Traveller's Yellow Pages for Saint Petersburg* (⊕ *www.infoservices.com*), a compact telephone book and handbook written in English, with indexes in several languages, including English. You can pick one up at most of the bookstores that carry English-language books.

Tourist Information **City Tourist Information Center** (✉ *14 Sadovaya ul., City Center* ☎ *812/310–8286 or 812/310–2822* ⊙ *Weekdays 10–6* Ⓜ *Sennaya Ploshchad*). **Infoline** (☎ *812/325–9325*). **St. Petersburg Tourism and Excursions Council** (✉ *3 Italianskaya ul., City Center* ☎ *812/110–6739, 812/314–8786 office, 812/710–6690 foreign section* 🖷 *812/710–6824*).

Summer Palaces & Historic Islands

4

WORD OF MOUTH

"I was most impressed with Peterhof. the Palace is gorgeous and just the right size so you don't have to shuffle around in the little slippers they give you for too long. Catherine's Palace was beautiful, much larger—turquoise with gold baroque moldings. The Amber Room [was] unlike anything I have seen."

—mbt127

"Some of the palaces would probably best be done on a tour since they are outside of St. Petersburg. They are too wonderful to miss. Especially Peterhof and the fountains."

—Kristinelaine

Updated by
Irina Titova

IF ST. PETERSBURG IS THE star of the show, then its suburbs are the supporting cast without which the story could not be told. For every aspect of the city's past—the glamour and glory of its Imperial era, the pride and power of its military history, the splendor of its architecture, the beauty of its waterways—there's a park, a palace, a playground of the tsars somewhere outside the city limits with a corresponding tale to tell. From the dazzling fountains of Peterhof on the shores of the Gulf of Finland, to the tranquil estate of Pavlovsk to the south, to the naval stronghold of Kronshtadt—a quiet town with a turbulent history and a still-Soviet feel (and once completely closed to foreigners)—what surrounds St. Petersburg is as important to its existence and identity as anything on Nevsky prospekt. It might seem odd to exhort you to get out of the city almost as soon as you have arrived, but you'll understand why once you have seen the suburbs for yourself, wandered through the palaces imagining what it would be like to call them home, and strolled through the grounds in the footsteps of the aristocrats and officers who made Russia a world power.

Of all the palaces in Russia, the one that generally makes the most distinct and lasting impression on visitors is Peterhof, on the shore of the Baltic Sea, some 29 km (18 mi) west of St. Petersburg. More than a mere summer palace, it's an Imperial playground replete with lush parks, monumental cascades, and gilt fountains. In tsarist times, Tsarskoye Selo, now renamed Pushkin, was a fashionable haunt of members of the aristocracy who were eager to be near the Imperial family and to escape the noxious air and oppressive climate of the capital to the north. After the Revolution of 1905, Nicholas II and his family lived here, more or less permanently. Pavlovsk, the Imperial estate of Paul I, is some 30 km (19 mi) south of St. Petersburg and only 5 km (3 mi) from Pushkin and the magnificent Catherine Palace. Because of the proximity of the two towns, tours to Pavlovsk and Pushkin are often combined. However, it's difficult to do justice to each of these in a one-day visit. If you only have time to visit one of the two, pick Pushkin. The estate of Lomonosov, on the Gulf of Finland, some 40 km (25 mi) west of St. Petersburg and about 9 km (5½ mi) northwest of Peterhof, is perhaps the least commanding of the suburban Imperial palaces. It is, however, the only one to have survived World War II intact.

XPLORING SUMMER PALACES & ISTORIC ISLANDS

The area around St. Petersburg is one big monument to the city's history as Russia's Imperial capital, from the time of Peter the Great (1672–1725) to the ill-fated Nicholas II, whose execution in Ekaterinburg in 1918 brought the Romanov dynasty to an end. The palaces at Lomonosov, Peterhof, Pushkin, and Pavlovsk—the status symbols of the royal elite—are at the heart of any trip outside St. Petersburg. But even Russians who have already visited these tsarist residences in the suburbs find themselves returning time and time again, drawn by the acres of beautiful parks and gardens, which are wonderful places to

TOP REASONS TO GO

Peterhof Fountains: The grounds surrounding Peterhof palace (nicknamed the "Russian Versailles") are filled with whimsical fountains. Don't miss the beautiful Great Cascade fountains or the trick fountains in the Lower Park, where you're certain to hear children laughing in delight as they get caught by a burst of water.

The Amber Room: Visit Pushkin (Tsarskoye Selo) to see the famed Amber Room, located in Catherine Palace. The original carved amber panels that once filled this room went missing during World War II and their whereabouts remain a mystery. The panels have been painstakingly re-created and are still a wonder to behold.

Ekaterininsky Park: The landscaped park on the grounds of Pushkin (Tsarskoye Selo) contains mirror-effect lakes, vast lawns, and impressive views of Catherine Palace. Enjoy a picnic lunch here in the summer.

Kronshtadt: Experience a Russian navy town and learn about its history, taking in the Baltic Sea air as you tour.

Rostropovich-Vishnevskaya Collection: This once-private collection, now housed in Konstantine Palace in Strelna, took over 30 years to amass and includes works by some of Russia's most renowned painters, such as Ilya Repin and Boris Grigoryev.

wander through and relax. Unlike Moscow's Golden Ring, monasteries and churches are not much in evidence, with the exception of Valaam on Lake Ladoga, which is dominated by the 14th-century Transfiguration of the Savior Monastery.

Except for Kronshtadt and Valaam, all of the destinations in this section can be reached by commuter train (*elektrichka*), but the simplest way to see the palaces is to book an excursion (available through any tour company). The cost is reasonable and covers transportation, a guided tour, and admission fees. An organized excursion to any of the suburban palaces will take at least four hours; if you travel on your own, it's likely to take up the entire day. But whichever plan you opt for, you'll enjoy numerous sights filled with splendor and magic.

Note that the sights in this region do not make up one easy circuit. In a few cases—notably Gatchina—you have to return to St. Petersburg to find direct rail transport. Of all the places, the ones that make the most sense to do in tandem would be: Pushkin and Pavlovsk, Peterhof and Lomonosov, Peterhof and Kronshtadt, or Lomonosov and Kronshtadt.

Because this region is so close to St. Petersburg, hotels are few and far between, and are completely unnecessary for the typical day-tripper.

ABOUT THE RESTAURANTS

Because most of the suburbs involve only a short trip from St. Petersburg, there has not been any real demand for quality restaurants and cafés. There are some exceptions, notably in Pavlovsk and Pushkin but on the whole it's best to pack some sandwiches. You will, however find plenty of beer tents and ice-cream vendors, which at least offer temporary sustenance.

	¢	$	$$	$$$	$$$$
WHAT IT COSTS IN RUBLES					
RESTAURANTS	under 125R	125R–250R	251R–375R	376R–500R	over 500R

Prices are per person for a main course at dinner.

TIMING

To see the palaces and estates to their best advantage, you should try to time your visits to coincide with spring or summer. Peterhof in particular is best visited in summer, so you can fully appreciate the fountains, gilt statues, monumental cascades, and lush parks. A winter trip can be quite disappointing, as from late September to early June the fountains and cascades are closed down and take on the depressing look of drained pools. Autumn can also be a pleasant time for viewing the palaces. Note also that the waterway along the Neva River and Lake Ladoga to Valaam is only open from June through September.

If you're traveling in the extreme cold of winter or the hottest days of summer, dress carefully, as much of your time may well be spent outdoors.

THE SUMMER PALACES

A visit to this region takes you through a lavish trail of evidence of the Imperial spirit. These majestic old palaces, estates, and former nobles' residences—all set on lovingly tended grounds—are within easy reach of St. Petersburg.

LOMONOSOV (ORANIENBAUM) ЛОМОНОСОВ (ОРАНИЕНБАУМ)

39 km (24 mi) west of St. Petersburg's city center on the southern shore of the Gulf of Finland.

This was the property of Alexander Menshikov (circa 1672–1729), the first governor of St. Petersburg and Peter the Great's favorite, who, following Peter's example, in 1710 began building his own luxurious summer residence on the shores of the Baltic Sea. Before construction was complete, however, Peter died and Menshikov was stripped of his formidable political power and exiled, leaving his summer estate half finished. The palace reverted to the crown and was given to Peter III, the ill-fated husband of Catherine the Great. Most of the buildings on the grounds were erected during his six-month reign, in 1762, or completed later by Catherine.

This property was given the German name Oranienbaum after the orangery attached to its palace. A few years after the liberation of Leningrad, Oranienbaum was renamed for the 18th-century scientist Mikhail Lomonosov, who had conducted a number of experiments at

GREAT ITINERARIES

IF YOU HAVE 1 OR 2 DAYS
You can take your pick of the suburbs for any day trip, although your choice of destination will be influenced by the time of year. In summer, **Peterhof** is a must. At this time of year, **Pushkin** and **Pavlovsk** are at their most attractive, and can be seen in a single day or, better still, over two days. For a destination with a completely different historical feel, head for the naval town of **Kronshtadt**. If you have two days to see the summer palaces, you could also strike out for **Gatchina** or **Lomonosov** on the second day.

IF YOU HAVE 3 OR 4 DAYS
In summer head to **Peterhof** and **Pushkin** on your first two days. On your third day, take a break from the palaces and visit the unforgettable **Valaam Archipelago**. To get to Valaam, catch the boat on the evening of your second day down the Neva River and up into Lake Ladoga. Spend the third day admiring the secluded monasteries and natural beauty of the islands, and return to the city overnight. On your final day, head for **Gatchina, Lomonosov,** or the **Konstantine Palace**.

his nearby estate. Lomonosov was the only imperial residence to have survived World War II entirely intact. Unfortunately, it has been languishing in disrepair for some time now and much of it has been closed for long-term restoration work. Some sights are scheduled to reopen in the summer of 2008, but it's best to call ahead and find out what is open before you visit.

Menshikov's Great Palace (Bolshoi Menshikovskii Dvorets), the original palace on the property, is also Lomonosov's biggest. It stands on a terrace overlooking the sea. Built between 1710 and 1725, it was designed by the same architects who built Menshikov's grand mansion on St. Petersburg's Vasilievsky Island, Giovanni Fontana and Gottfried Schaedel. The palace hosts annually changing exhibits on everything from the Orthodox Church in St. Petersburg to Japanese artwork. Currently closed for restoration, the Great Palace should reopen its doors in the summer of 2008. Nearby is **Peterstadt Dvorets,** the modest palace that Peter III used, a two-story stone mansion built between 1756 and 1762 by Arnoldo Rinaldi. Its interior is decorated with handsome lacquered wood paintings. That it seems small, gloomy, and isolated is perhaps appropriate, as it was here, in 1762, that the tsar was arrested, then taken to Ropsha and murdered in the wake of the coup that placed his wife, Catherine the Great, on the throne.

The building that most proclaims the estate's Imperial beginnings, however, is unquestionably Catherine's **Chinese Palace** (Kitaisky Dvorets), also designed by Rinaldi. Intended as one of her private summer residences, it is quite an affair—rococo inside, baroque outside. Lavishly decorated, it has ceiling paintings created by Venetian artists, inlaid wood floors, and elaborate stucco walls. The small house outside served as the kitchen. Down the slope to the east of the Great Palace is the curious **Katalnaya Gorka.** All that remains of the slide, which was originally several stories high, is the pavilion that served as th

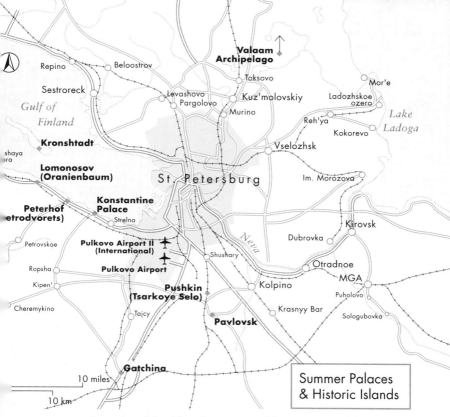

Summer Palaces
& Historic Islands

starting point of the ride, where guests of the empress could catch their breath before tobogganing down again. Painted soft blue with white trim, the fanciful, dazzling pavilion looks like a frosted birthday cake; it was, however, closed for extensive renovations at this writing. Also on the premises, near the pond, is a small amusement park offering carnival rides. When taking a commuter train here, be careful to exit at Oranienbaum-I (not II). ⊠48 ul. Yunovo Lenintsa ☎812/422–4796, 812/422–8016 for tours ⌧Exhibition at Menshikov's Great Palace 185R, Chinese Palace 370R, Peterstadt Dvorets 260R, Oriental exhibition at Japanese pavilion 185R ⊗Estate Wed.–Sun. 11–5, Mon. 11–4; Chinese Palace late May–late Sept., Wed.–Mon. 11–5. Some buildings are closed on Mon. Estate closed last Mon. of month.

'ERHOF (PETRODVORETS) ПЕТЕРГОФ (ПЕТРОДВОРЕЦ)

dor'sChoice
★

29 km (18 mi) west of St. Petersburg on the southern shores of the Gulf of Finland.

Visiting Peterhof and other Imperial palaces nearby, you may find it difficult to believe that when the Germans were finally driven out of the area toward the end of World War II, almost everything was in ruins. Many priceless objects had been removed to safety before the Germans advanced, but a great deal had to be left behind and was consequently looted by the invaders. Now, after decades of painstaking work, art historians and craftspeople, referring to photographs and records of descriptions, have returned the palaces to their former splendor. Peterhof and its neighboring palaces are so vast, however, that renovation work will be ongoing for many years to come.

The complex of gardens and residences at Peterhof was masterminded by Peter the Great, who personally drew up the original plans, starting around 1720. His motivation was twofold. First, he was proud of the capital city he was creating and wanted its evolving Imperial grandeur showcased with a proper summer palace. Second, he became attached to this spot while erecting the naval fortress of Kronshtadt on a nearby island across the Gulf of Finland; because it lay in easy view, he often stayed here during the fort's construction. When the fort was finished, by which time he had had a series of naval victories (including the Northern War against the Swedes), he threw himself into establishing many parts of the grounds that would be called Peterhof (Peter's Court), a German name that was changed to Petrodvorets after World War II.

If you travel by hydrofoil, you'll arrive at the pier of the Lower Park, from which you work your way up to the Great Palace. If you arrive by land, you'll simply go through the process in reverse. Either way, the perspective always emphasizes the mightiness of water. Half-encircled by the sea, filled with fountains and other water monuments, and with the Marine Canal running straight from the foot of the palace into the bay, Peter's palace was also intended as a loving tribute to the role of water in the life, and strength, of his city. The **Lower Park** was designed as a formal baroque garden in the French style, adorned with statues, fountains, and cascades. Peter's playful spirit is still very much in evidence here. The fun-loving tsar installed "trick fountains"—hidden water sprays built into trees and tiny plazas and brought to life by stepping on a certain stone or moving a lever, much to the surprise of the unsuspecting visitor and the delight of the squealing children who love to race through the resulting showers on hot summer days. Located in the eastern half of Lower Park is the oldest building at Peterhof **Monplaisir** (literally "My Pleasure"), completed in 1721. This is where Peter the Great lived while overseeing construction of the main Imperial residence. As was typical with Peter, he greatly preferred this modest Dutch-style villa to his later, more extravagant living quarters. The house is open to the public and makes for a pleasant tour. Some of its most interesting rooms are the Lacquered Study, decorated with replicas of panels painted in the Chinese style (the originals were destroyed during World War II); Peter's Naval Study; and his bedroom, where some personal effects, such as his nightcap and a quilt made by his wife, are on display. Attached to Peter's villa is the so-called Catherine Wing, built by Rastrelli in the mid-18th century in an utterly different style. The future Catherine the Great was staying here at the time of the coup that overthrew her husband and placed her on the throne; the space was later used mainly for balls.

In the western section of the Lower Park is another famous structure, the **Hermitage**, built in 1725. It claims to be the first of the great Imperial hermitages (the most famous, of course, still stands in St. Petersburg), or retreats, in Russia. This two-story pavilion gives new meaning to the concept of a movable feast. The building, which was used primarily as a banqueting hall for special guests, was at one time equipped with a device that would hoist the dining table area—diners and all—from the ground floor to the private dining room above. A slightly different system was put in place after Tsar Paul I's chair broke during one such exercise. The center part of the table could be lifted out, and guests would write down their dinner preferences and then signal for their notes to be lifted away. Shortly thereafter, the separated section would be lowered, complete with the meals everyone had ordered. The only way to the Hermitage was over a drawbridge, so privacy was ensured.

> ### TRICKSTER'S FOUNTAINS
>
> If you're traveling to Peterhof with small children in the summer, be sure to pack a bathing suit or an extra set of clothes for them and be prepared to get wet. The Lower Park's "trick fountains" are supposedly turned on by stomping on "magic" stones or pulling on levers and kids love to try and figure out which one makes the fountains work. You won't want to point out the person sitting nearby who secretly makes them spray at just the right moment.

Almost adjacent to the Hermitage is the **Marly Palace,** a modest Peter the Great construction that is more of a country retreat than a palace. As with Monplaisir, it's mostly Petrine memorabilia on display here. The four ponds around the back are where Catherine the Great used to stock fish.

A walk up the path through the center of the Lower Park (along the Marine Canal) leads you to the famous **Great Cascade** (Bolshoi Kaskad). Running down the steep ridge separating the Lower Park and the Great Palace towering above, the cascade comprises three waterfalls, 64 fountains, and 37 gilt statues. The system of waterworks has remained virtually unchanged since 1721. The ducts and pipes convey water over a distance of some 20 km (12 mi). The centerpiece of the waterfalls is a gilt Samson rending the jaws of a lion, out of which a jet of water spurts into the air. The statue represents the 1709 Russian victory over the Swedes at Poltava on St. Samson's day. The present figure is a meticulous replica of the original, which was carried away by the Germans during World War II. A small entrance halfway up the right-hand staircase (as you look at the palace above) leads to the grotto, where you can step out onto a terrace to get a bit closer to Samson before going inside to have a look under the waterworks.

Crowning the ridge above the cascade is the magnificent **Bolshoi Dvorets.** Little remains of Peter's original two-story house, built between 1714 and 1725 under the architects Leblond, Braunstein, and Machetti. The building was considerably altered and enlarged by Peter's daughter, Elizabeth. She entrusted the reconstruction to her

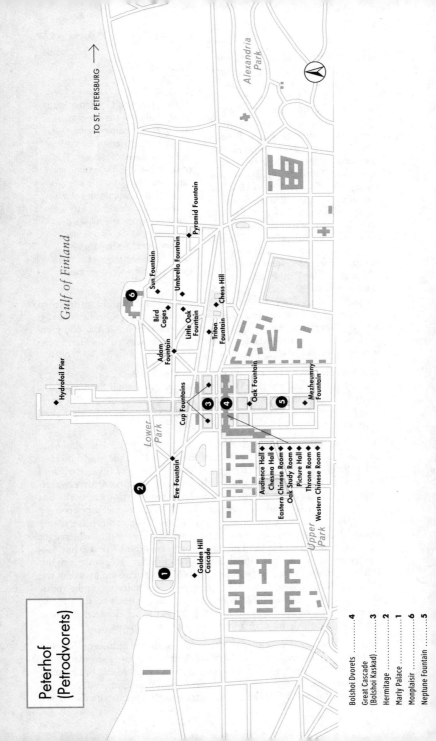

Peterhof
(Petrodvorets)

TO ST. PETERSBURG →

Gulf of Finland

Hydrofoil Pier

Lower Park

Alexandria Park

Sun Fountain

Umbrella Fountain

Pyramid Fountain

Bird Cages

Little Oak Fountain

Adam Fountain

Triton Fountain

Chess Hill

❻

Eve Fountain

Cup Fountains

❷

❸

❹

Oak Fountain

❺

Mezheumny Fountain

Golden Hill Cascade

❶

Upper Park

Audience Hall

Chesma Hall

Eastern Chinese Room

Oak Study Room

Picture Hall

Throne Room

Western Chinese Room

favorite architect, Bartolomeo Rastrelli, who transformed the modest residence into a sumptuous blend of medieval architecture and Russian baroque. Before you begin your tour of the palace interiors, pause for a moment to enjoy the breathtaking view from the marble terrace. From here a full view of the grounds below unfolds, stretching from the cascades to the Gulf of Finland and on to the city horizon on the shore beyond.

> ## FIRE FOR ART'S SAKE
>
> According to legend, when asked by Catherine the Great to depict the naval battles between the Russians and the Turks in 1770, painter Phillip Hackert explained that he could not paint a burning ship since he had never seen one. The solution: Catherine arranged to have ships blown up for him to use as models. Such were the privileges of divine right.

As for the main palace building, the lavish interiors are primarily the work of Rastrelli, although several of the rooms were redesigned during the reign of Catherine the Great to accord with classicism, the prevailing architectural style of her day. Of Peter's original design, only his **Oak Study Room** (Dubovy Kabinet) survived the numerous reconstructions. The fine oak panels (some are originals) lining the walls were designed by the French sculptor Pineau. The entire room and all its furnishings are of wood, with the exception of the white-marble fireplace, above whose mantel hangs a long mirror framed in carved oak.

One of the largest rooms in the palace is the **Throne Room** (Tronny Zal), which takes up the entire width of the building. Classically designed, this majestic room—once the scene of great receptions and official ceremonies—has exquisite parquet floors, elaborate stucco ceiling moldings, and dazzling chandeliers. The pale-green and dark-red decor is bathed in light, which pours in through two tiers of windows (28 in all) taking up the long sides of the room. Behind Peter the Great's throne at the eastern end of the room hangs a huge portrait of Catherine the Great. The empress, the epitome of confidence after her successful coup, is shown astride a horse, dressed in the uniform of the guard regiment that supported her bid for power.

Next to the Throne Room is the **Chesma Hall** (Chesmensky Zal), whose interior is dedicated entirely to the Russian naval victory over the Turks in 1770. The walls are covered with 12 huge canvases depicting the battles; they were created by the German painter Phillip Hackert at Empress Catherine's behest. Arguably the most dazzling of the rooms is the **Audience Hall** (Audients Zal). Rastrelli created the definitive baroque interior with this glittering room of white, red, and gold. Gilt baroque bas-reliefs adorn the stark white walls, along which tall mirrors hang, further reflecting the richness of the decor.

Other notable rooms include the **Chinese Study Rooms** (Kitaiskye Kabinety), designed by Vallin de la Mothe in the 1760s. Following the European fashion of the time, the rooms are ornately decorated with Chinese motifs. Finely carved black-lacquer panels depict various Chinese scenes. Between the two rooms of the study is the **Picture Hall**

(Kartinny Zal), whose walls are paneled with 368 oil paintings by the Italian artist Rotari. The artist used just eight models for these paintings depicting young women in national dress.

Following a tour of the palace interiors (they are offered regularly in English), a stroll through the Upper Park, on the south side of the palace, is in order. This symmetrical formal garden is far less imaginative than the Lower Park. Its focal point is the **Neptune Fountain,** made in Germany in the 17th century and bought by Paul I in 1782. During the war this three-tier group of bronze sculptures was carried away by the Germans, and eventually recovered and reinstalled in 1956.

You can reach the palace by commuter train from St. Petersburg but, minimal fog permitting, the best way to go is by hydrofoil (June–September only), from which your first view is the panorama of the grand palace overlooking the sea. The lines to get into the palace can be excruciatingly long in summer, and sometimes guided tours get preferential treatment. The ticket office for foreigners is inside the palace, which means admission is more expensive than it is for Russians, but the lines are significantly shorter. Some park pavilions are closed Wednesday and others on Thursday; visiting on the weekend is the best chance to see everything.

An integral part of visiting any museum-palace in Russia is encountering the autocratic *babushki* (a colloquial term for museum caretakers, often hearty grandmothers). In this, Peterhof is no exception. No matter how irksome, they deserve respect, for many survived the 900-day siege of Leningrad, witnessed the palaces' destruction, and saw them rise again, almost miraculously, from the ashes. As you enter the palace, you'll be given tattered shoe covers to wear, so as to protect the highly polished floors of the splendid halls. ■TIP➔**On most occasions, flash photography is not allowed, although for a fee, video may be used.** ⊠*2 ul. Razvodnaya* ☎*812/450–6527, 812/450–6513 kassa* ✉*Palace 500R, park 300R, separate admission fees (100R–150R) for park pavilions* ☉*Great Palace Tues.–Sun. 10:30–5; some park pavilions are closed Wed. and others on Thurs. Closed last Tues. of month.*

WHERE TO EAT

$$$–$$$$ ✕**Bolshaya Oranzhereya.** The best option on the grounds of the palace itself is in the palace's old *oranzhereya,* or garden house. A comfortable, quaint spot for a snack and cup of tea, it also serves prix-fixe meals of Continental cuisine featuring various kinds of fish and meat including venison and duck courses, or traditional Russian options such as borscht (beet soup) or solyanka (slightly spicy meat soup with pickles). The restaurant is open from 10 to 6. ⊠*Peterhof palace grounds, near Triton fountain* ☎*812/450–6106* ⊟*MC, V* ☉*Closed early Oct.–Apr.*

KONSTANTINE PALACE КОНСТАНТИНОВСКИЙ ДВОРЕЦ

19 km (12 mi) south of St. Petersburg on the southern shores of the Gulf of Finland.

Once one of the most neglected jewels in the dazzling necklace of St. Petersburg's historical suburbs, the Konstantine Palace (Konstantinovsky Dvorets), which was nearly destroyed in World War II, has been restored to its original splendor. After years of renovation, based on old photographs and plans, the Italian-baroque, coffee-color palace and grounds reopened in 2003. It's now officially the Palace of Congress, used to host government functions, such as the Russia-European Union Summit.

In 1720 Peter the Great commissioned work on this maritime country residence that was to be a "Russian Versailles." Italian architect Nicolo Micketti designed not only the palace, but also beautiful fountains and waterworks meant to draw water from the Gulf of Finland. However, the fountains never worked, and the palace itself underwent several fires, was redesigned, and had its name changed from Big Strelna Palace to Konstantine Palace.

The palace offers three different tours. One is a regular, 90-minute excursion to the eastern, historical part of the palace and includes narration about the tsar's family and its members who used to live here. The VIP tour covers the western part of the palace, which is used for official occasions and summits. You'll also see a part of the Russian president's apartments and the boudoir of the first lady. The third tour is a 90-minute amble through the vast park, which frankly doesn't have as many attractive sights as the parks of Peterhof and Pushkin.

Of the palace's 50-odd rooms, several are open to the public when no state functions are taking place. Both the VIP and historic tours visit the Marble Hall and Oval Hall. The central **Marble Hall,** used to host official events, lives up to its name with yellow marble pilasters framed by bluish marble walls. A balcony here affords a breathtaking view of the huge park and canals leading to the Gulf of Finland. Next door is the large, pink **Oval Hall,** also used for official meetings. The VIP tour goes on to visit the **Blue Hall,** opposite the Marble Hall, with blue walls, high mirrors, and gilt ornamentation. A **wine cellar** has been reconstructed; it holds Hungarian Tokay wines, as it did when this was a royal residence. The third-floor **belvedere** is a new addition. Styled as a ship's hold, it's made of oak, with a spiral staircase leading to an observation deck with lovely views of the grounds. In addition to the rooms themselves, you can see various permanent exhibits, such as Russian state symbols from the Hermitage, and naval memorabilia from St. Petersburg's Naval Museum. The grounds are worth exploring, particularly the Upper (English) Park, Big Pond, canals, drawbridges, and the monument to Peter the Great, which stands just in front of the palace.

Before visiting, be sure to call ahead to make sure the palace will not be closed for state functions. A great option is to join a special tourist bus (labeled "To Konstantine Palace") that leaves from Beloselsky-Belozersky Palace (located at Nevsky prospekt) in St. Petersburg. You can

Rostropovich-Vishnevskaya Collection

The much-discussed art collection of Rostropovich-Vishnevskaya will be on display in its entirety at Konstantine Palace in 2008. The collection of 850 items of Russian paintings, art, and crafts which took 30 years to acquire originally belonged to the famed Russian cellist Mstislav Rostropovich and his wife, opera star soprano Galina Vishnevskaya. The couple fled the Soviet Union in 1974 under fire for their support of dissident Alexander Solzhenitsyn. After Rostropovich's death, Vishnevskaya decided to auction the collection, saying she didn't have enough money to maintain it and keep it safe. Russian steel magnate Alisher Usmanov preempted a Sotheby's auction by buying the collection outright, reportedly for more than the $40 million it was expected to fetch at auction. He said he chose Konstantine Palace as the collection's home because: "I wanted to obey the will of Galina Vishnevskaya, who would like the collection to find its place in one of the palaces of St. Petersburg. I learned that one of the beautifully and recently rebuilt palaces, the Konstantine Palace, has no collection of its own." The collection includes works by some of Russia's most renowned painters, including Ilya Repin and Boris Grigoryev, as well as furniture, porcelain, silver, and other items.

purchase a ticket from any theater box office. The excursion departs weekdays at 2 PM and at 11 AM and 3 PM on weekends, and includes a visit to the eastern part of the palace and the return trip. ⊠ *3 Beryozovaya alleya, Strelna* ☎ *812/438–5360* 🖃 *Eastern palace tour and park: weekdays 170R, weekends 220R; VIP tour of western palace 280R; bus excursion from St. Petersburg 500R* ☉ *Thurs.–Tues. 10–5, ticket office open until 4. Closed for official events.*

PUSHKIN (TSARSKOYE SELO) ПУШКИН (ЦАРСКОЕ СЕЛО)

Fodor'sChoice
★ *24 km (15 mi) south of St. Petersburg's city center via commuter train from the Vitebsk station, 40 km (25 mi) southeast of Peterhof.*

The town of Pushkin was a summer residence of the Imperial family from the days of Peter the Great right up to the last years of the Romanov dynasty. Pushkin was initially known as Tsar's Village (Tsarskoye Selo), but the town's name was changed after the Revolution of 1917, first to Children's Village (Detskoye Selo) and then to Pushkin, in honor of the great Russian poet who studied at the lyceum here. During the 18th and 19th centuries, Tsarskoye Selo was a popular summer resort for St. Petersburg's aristocracy and well-to-do citizens. Not only was the royal family close by, but it was here, in 1837, that Russia's first railroad line was opened, running between Tsarskoye Selo and Pavlovsk, to be followed three years later by a line between here and St. Petersburg.

Fodor'sChoice
★ Pushkin's main attraction is the dazzling 18th-century **Catherine Palace** *(Ekaterininsky Dvorets)*, a perfect example of Russian baroque. The

Pushkin (Tsarskoye Selo)

Alexander Palace
(Aleksandrovsky Dvorets) ..**4**
Amber Room............**7**
Cameron Gallery **18**
Cameron's Pyramid **19**
Catherine Palace
(Ekaterininsky Dvorets)....**5**
Canal **16**

Chapel **1**
Chesma Column **11**
Chinese Theater **2**
Chinese Village **3**
Concert Hall **20**
English Garden **17**
Great Hall **6**

Great Pond **14**
Grotto **15**
Lyceum **9**
Marble Bridge **12**
Picture Gallery **8**
Pushkin Monument **10**
Ruined Tower **13**

bright-turquoise exterior has row after row of white columns and pilasters with gold baroque moldings running the entire length (985 feet) of the facade. Although much of the palace's history and its inner architectural design bears Catherine the Great's stamp, it's for Catherine I, Peter the Great's second wife, that the palace is named. Under Empress Elizabeth, their daughter, the original modest stone palace was completely rebuilt. The project was initially entrusted to the Russian architects Kvasov and Chevakinsky, but in 1752 Elizabeth brought in the Italian architect Bartolomeo Rastrelli. Although Catherine the Great had the interiors remodeled in the classical style, she left Rastrelli's stunning facade untouched.

You enter the palace grounds through the gilded black-iron gates designed by Rastrelli. The *E* mounted atop is for Catherine ("Ekaterina" in Russian). To your right, a visual feast unfolds as you walk the length of the long blue-and-gold facade toward the museum entrance. Sparkling above the palace at the northern end are the golden cupolas of the Palace Church. The interiors are just as spectacular, and many of the rooms are famous in their own right. Although little of Rastrelli's original design remains, the many additions and alterations made between 1760 and 1790 under Catherine the Great do; these were carried out by a pair of noted architects, the Scottish Charles Cameron and the Italian Giacomo Quarenghi.

Entering the palace by the main staircase, which was not added until 1861, you will see displays depicting the extent of the wartime damage and of the subsequent restoration work. Like Peterhof, the palace was almost completely destroyed during World War II. It was used by occupying Nazi forces as an army barracks, and as the Germans retreated, they blew up what remained of the former Imperial residence. Today the exterior of the palace again stands in all its glory, and work on the interior is ongoing.

The largest and arguably most impressive room is the **Great Hall** (Bolshoi Zal), which was used for receptions and balls. The longer sides of the hall are taken up by two tiers of gilt-framed windows. Tall, elaborately carved, gilded mirrors have been placed between them. Light pouring in through the windows bounces off the mirrors and sparkles on the gilt, amplifying the impression of spaciousness and brilliance. The huge ceiling painting, depicting Russian military victories and accomplishments in the sciences and arts, makes the room seem even larger. Here it's easy to imagine the extravagant lifestyle of St. Petersburg's prerevolutionary elite.

On the north side of the State Staircase is one of the palace's most famous rooms, the **Amber Room** (Yantarnaya Komnata), so named for the engraved amber panels that line its walls (*See Close Up: The Story of the Amber Room*). The room owes much of its fame to the mysterious disappearance of its amber panels in World War II. In 1979 the Soviet government finally gave up hope of ever retrieving the panels and began the costly work of restoring the room. After 25 years of restoration a nearly exact replica of the room opened in June 2003.

CLOSE UP

The Story of the Amber Room

The original Amber Room panels, a unique masterpiece of amber carving once referred to as the "Eighth Wonder of the World," were presented to Peter the Great in 1716 by Prussian king Friedrich Wilhelm I in exchange for 55 "very tall" Russian soldiers (that was Friedrich's request). The panels were eventually incorporated in one of the numerous halls of Ekaterininsky Dvorets (Catherine Palace) in Tsarskoye Selo. After the Revolution of 1917, Catherine Palace was turned into a museum, and the public had its first chance to see the Amber Room. The Nazis looted the palace in 1941 and moved the contents of the Amber Room to what was then the German town of Königsberg. That town (soon to become the Russian town of Kaliningrad) was captured by the Soviets in 1945, but by the time the Soviet troops entered the city, the amber panels had disappeared.

There are two major theories on the fate of the amber: the panels were either destroyed by Allied bombing or were somehow hidden by the Nazis. For obvious reasons, the second theory has held the most appeal, and over the years it has given hope to eager treasure seekers. Some postulated that the amber could have been buried in a silver mine near Berlin, hidden on the shores of the Baltic Sea, or secreted as far away as South America. Explorers have searched caves, jails, churches, salt mines, tunnels, bunkers, and ice cellars. For some, the quest was an obsession: Georg Stein, a former German soldier, searched for more than two decades, spent almost all his fortune, and in the end was found mysteriously murdered in a Bavarian forest in 1987. In 1991 the German magazine *Der*

Spiegel organized its own ultimately unsuccessful archaeological expedition to search for the amber in the ruins of Lochstedt Castle in the Kaliningrad region.

In 1979 the Soviet government gave up all hope of relocating the panels and initiated the reconstruction of the Amber Room, allocating about $8 million for the project. It would take another $3.5 million donation from the German company Ruhrgas AG in 1999 to complete the restoration work. More than 30 craftspeople worked tirelessly, some dedicating up to 20 years of their lives to the project. Using microscopes to make the tiniest engravings in the amber, many lost their vision over the years or suffered illness from inhaling amber dust. Ironically, most of the amber came from the world's largest deposit of the fossil resin, in Kaliningrad—the very place where the original amber panels had disappeared. After 25 years of work and 6 tons of amber (though 80% of this amber was waste product), the replica of the Amber Room was unveiled in 2003 in time for St. Petersburg's 300th-anniversary celebrations.

Covered with more than a ton of amber, the room embraces you with the warm glow of more than 13 hues of this stone, ranging from butter yellow to dark red. One panel, *Smell and Touch,* is an original, found in Bremen, Germany, in 1997; a German pensioner whose father had fought in the Soviet Union was caught trying to sell the panel. The rest remain a mystery.

4

Leaving the Amber Room, you'll come to the large **Picture Gallery** (Kartinny Zal), which runs the full width of the palace. The paintings are all from Western Europe and date from the 17th to the early 18th century.

Highlights among the other splendid rooms on the north side include the Blue Drawing Room, the Blue Chinese Room, and the Choir Anteroom, all of which face the courtyard. Each has pure-silk wall coverings. The Blue Chinese Room, originally designed by Cameron, has been restored on the basis of the architect's drawings. Despite its name, it's a purely classical interior, and the only thing even remotely Chinese is the Asian motif on the silk fabric covering the walls. The fine golden-yellow silk now on the walls of the Choir Anteroom is from the same bolt used to decorate the room in the 18th century. When the postwar restoration began, this extra supply of the original silk was discovered tucked away in a storage room of the Hermitage.

Having savored the treasures inside the palace, you can now begin exploring the beautiful **Catherine Park** outside, with its marble statues, waterfalls, garden alleys, boating ponds, pavilions, bridges, and quays. The park is split into two sections. The inner, formal section, known as the French Garden, runs down the terraces in front of the palace's eastern facade. The outer section encloses the Great Pond and is in the less-rigid style of an English garden. If you follow the main path through the French Garden and down the terrace, you'll eventually reach Rastrelli's Hermitage, which he completed just before turning his attention to the palace itself. The hermitage was closed at this writing for extensive renovation. Other highlights of the French Garden include the Upper and Lower Bath pavilions (1777–79) and Rastrelli's elaborate blue-dome Grotto.

There is much to be seen in the English-style garden, too. A good starting point is the **Cameron Gallery** (Galereya Kamerona), which actually forms a continuation of the palace's park-side frontage. It's off to the right (with your back to the palace). Open only in summer, it contains a museum of 18th- and 19th-century costumes. From its portico you get the best views of the park and its lakes—which is exactly what Cameron had in mind when he designed it in the 1780s. The double-sided staircase leading majestically down to the Great Pond is flanked by two bronze sculptures of Hercules and Flora. From here, descend the stairs to begin your exploration of the park. Just beyond the island in the middle of the Great Pond, actually an artificial lake, stands the Chesma Column, commemorating the Russian naval victory in the Aegean in 1770. At the far end of the pond is Cameron's Pyramid, where Catherine the Great reportedly buried her beloved greyhounds. If you walk around the pond's right side, you'll come to the pretty blue-and-white Marble Bridge, which connects the Great Pond with a series of other ponds and small canals. At this end, you can rent rowboats Farther along, up to the right, you come to the Ruined Tower. It's neither authentic nor ancient, having been built in the late 18th century merely to enhance the romantic ambience of these grounds.

Outside the park, just north of the Catherine Palace, stands yet another palace, the **Alexander Palace** (Alexandrovsky Dvorets), a present from Catherine to her favorite grandson, the future Tsar Alexander I, on the occasion of his marriage. Built by Giacomo Quarenghi between 1792 and 1796, the serene and restrained classical structure was the favorite residence of Russia's last tsar, Nicholas II. The left wing of the building is open to the public and hosts topical exhibits. Most of the interior was lost, with the notable exception of Nicholas's cabinet, a fine example of art nouveau furniture and design. A visit is most interesting in the context of the ongoing rehabilitation of Nicholas II's reputation in Russia.

> ## WORD OF MOUTH
>
> "As for the Tsarskoye Selo [Push-kin] and Pavlovsk the best way is to book a private tour. Yes you can get there by train or minibus but usually there are lines in Catherine's palace (Tsarskoe Selo) and no chance to get in without a guide. Besides that, an advantage of having a guide for that trip is an opportunity to listen to all interesting stories about two palaces and ask all your questions about St.Pete and Russia on the way."
>
> —Zhenya

Built in 1791 and originally intended for the education of Catherine the Great's grandchildren, the **Lyceum** later became a school for the nobility. Its most famous student, enrolled the first year it opened, was the beloved poet Alexander Pushkin. The building now serves as a museum; the classroom, library, and Pushkin's bedroom have been restored to their appearance at the time he studied here. In the school's garden is a statue of the poet as a young man, seated on a bench, presumably deep in creative meditation. The building is attached to the Catherine Palace. ✉7 ul. Sadovaya ☎812/465–2024 or 812/466–6669 ☞Park 160R, Catherine Palace 720R, Alexander Palace 300R, Lyceum 200R ☉Park and palaces Wed.–Mon. 10–5. Catherine Palace closed last Mon. of month, Alexander Palace closed last Wed. of month.

WHERE TO EAT

$$$$ ╳**Admiralteistvo.** This charming land-friendly little restaurant is on the second floor of an old redbrick pavilion just across the lake from the Catherine Palace. Its nostalgic, retro-style interiors are furnished with antique furniture and a number of partially enclosed seating areas give you some isolation for a private dinner. The restaurant specializes in European and excellent Russian cuisine. For a genuine Russian delight, go for fish such as baked sturgeon or sterlet, which was very popular at the tsars' tables. You can also try traditional Russian homemade pelmeni or different kinds of *kotleta*, a stuffed and breaded meat dish (also known as Kiev). ✉7 Sadovaya ul., in Ekaterininsky Park ☎812/465–3549 ▭MC, V.

$$$–$$$$ ╳**Staraya Bashnya.** Tucked away in a clutch of buildings known as the Fyodorovsky Gorodok (a short walk north of Alexander Palace) is the Old Tower, a tiny restaurant that serves Russian and European cuisine. The European dishes are perhaps more expensive than they

should be, so stick to Russian items such as the *pelmeni* (meat dumplings) with garlic or beef Stroganoff. The portions are very generous. ✉*14 Akademichesky per.* ☎*812/466–6698* ⌕*Reservations essential* ▱*MC, V.*

PAVLOVSK ПАВЛОВСК

★ 30 km (19 mi) south of St. Petersburg's city center, a 5-min train journey from Tsarskoye Selo, 6 km (4 mi) south of Pushkin.

The estate grounds of Pavlovsk had always been the royal hunting grounds, but in 1777 Catherine the Great awarded them to her son, Paul I (Pavlovsk comes from "Pavel," the Russian word for Paul), upon the birth of his first son, the future tsar Alexander I. Construction of the first wooden buildings started immediately, and in 1782 Catherine's Scottish architect Charles Cameron began work on the Great Palace and the landscaped park. In contrast to the dramatically baroque palaces of Pushkin and Peterhof, Pavlovsk is a tribute to the reserved beauty of classicism. Paul's intense dislike of his mother apparently manifested itself in determinedly doing exactly what she would *not*—with, most visitors agree, gratifying results. The place is popular with St. Petersburg residents, who come to stroll through its beautiful 1,500-acre park, full of woods, ponds, tree-lined alleys, and pavilions.

Begin a tour of Pavlovsk with the golden yellow **Great Palace** (Bolshoi Dvorets), which stands on a high bluff overlooking the river and dominates the surrounding park. (If you walk the grandious park first, you risk being too tired or too late for touring the palace, whose rooms begin closing after 4 PM.) Built between 1782 and 1786 as the summer residence of Paul and his wife, Maria Fyodorovna, the stone palace was designed in imitation of a Roman villa. The architect Vincenzo Brenna enlarged the palace between 1796 and 1799 with the addition of a second story to the galleries and side pavilions. Despite a devastating fire in 1803 and further reconstruction by Andrei Voronikhin in the early 19th century, Cameron's basic design survives. The building is crowned with a green dome supported by 64 small white columns. Its facade is currently under renovation. In front of the palace stands a statue of the snub-nosed Paul I, a copy of the statue at Gatchina, Paul's other summer residence.

Many rooms are open for viewing, and you may start on either the first or the second floor. The splendid interiors, with their parquet floors, marble pillars, and gilt ceilings, were created by some of Russia's most outstanding architects. Besides Cameron, Brenna, and Voronikhin, the roll call includes Quarenghi, who designed the interiors of five rooms on the first floor, and Carlo Rossi, who was responsible for the library, built in 1824. The state apartments on the first floor include the pink-and-blue **Ballroom;** the formal **Dining Hall,** where the full dinner service for special occasions is set out; and the lovely **Corner Room,** with walls of lilac marble and doors of Karelian birch. On the first floor, on the way from the central part of the palace to the southern section, are the **Dowager Empress Rooms** (Komnaty Vdovstvuyuschei Imperatritsy), six rooms that were designed for Maria Fyodorovna after the death of Paul I. The most impressive of these is the Small Lamp Study (Kabinet Fonarik), a light-green room that overlooks Tsar's Little Garden. The empress's library and other belongings are on display here.

Among the lavishly decorated state rooms on the second floor is the famous **Greek Hall,** with a layout like that of an ancient temple. Its rich green Corinthian columns stand out against the white of the faux-marble walls. The hall, which also served as a small ballroom, linked the state chambers of Paul I to those of his wife, Maria. The last room on his side, leading to the Greek Hall, was the **Hall of War.** Maria's **Hall of Peace,** was designed to correspond to it. The gilt stucco wall moldings of her suite are decorated with flowers, baskets of fruit, musical instruments, and other symbols of peace. Beyond Maria's apartments is the light-filled **Picture Gallery,** with floor-length windows and an eclectic collection of paintings. From the gallery, via a small, pink, marble waiting room, you reach the palace's largest chamber, **Throne Hall.** It once held the throne of Paul I, which was removed for a victory party after Napoléon's defeat and somehow never returned.

Like the palace, the design of the park was shared by the leading architects of the day—Brenna, Cameron, Voronikhin, and Rossi. The park differs greatly from park designs of other Imperial palaces, where the strict rules of geometrical design were followed; at Pavlovsk nature was left unfettered, with simple beauty the splendid result.

The combined length of the park's paths and lanes is said to equal the distance between St. Petersburg and Moscow (656 km [407 mi]). Because you can't possibly cover the entire territory in one day anyway, you might just want to follow your whim. If you walk down the slope just behind the palace to the **Tsar's Little Garden** (Sobstvenny Sadik), you can see the Three Graces Pavilion, created by Cameron. The 16-column pavilion encloses a statue of Joy, Flowering, and Brilliance. Directly behind the palace, a stone staircase, decorated with lions, will take you to the Slavyanka Canal. On the canal's other side, down to the left, is the graceful **Apollo Colonnade,** built in 1783, whose air of ruin was not entirely human-made: it was struck by lightning in 1817 and never restored. If you bear right at the end of the stairs, you come to the **Temple of Friendship,** meant to betoken the friendship between Empress Maria and her mother-in-law, Catherine the Great. Beyond it is a monument from Maria to her own parents; the center urn's medallion bears their likenesses. Of the other noteworthy pavilions and memorials dotting the park, the farthest one up the bank is the **Mausoleum of Paul I,** set apart on a remote and overgrown hillside toward the center of the park. Maria had the mausoleum built for her husband after he was murdered in a palace coup. Paul was never interred here, however, and though Maria is portrayed as inconsolable in a statue here, historical evidence indicates that she was well aware of the plot to kill her husband. ✉ *20 ul. Revolutsii* ☎ *812/470–2156* ✎ *Palace and grounds 370R, park 60R, additional 30R for Dowager Empress Rooms, Sobstvennyi Sadik 60R* ☉ *Sat.–Thurs. 10–5. Closed 1st Mon. of month.*

WHERE TO EAT

$$$$ ✕**Podvoriye.** Past guests at this wooden restaurant built in the *terem*
★ (folk- or fairy-tale) style include the presidents of France and Russia.
Inside, a stuffed bear greets you with samplings of vodka. Traditional
Russian fare includes pickled garlic and mushrooms, excellent sturgeon
dishes, and cutlets of wild boar, bear, or elk. Among the less expensive
mains are pelmeni and *golubtsy* (a mixture of rice and meat wrapped
in cabbage or grape leaves). Drinks to try are *kvas* (a sweet, lightly
fermented drink made from bread or grains) and *mors* (a sour-sweet
cranberry juice). It's best to make a reservation. ✉16 Filtrovskoye
shosse ☎812/465–1399 ▭AE, DC, MC, V.

$$–$$$ ✕**Great Column Hall.** The former servants' quarters inside Pavlovsk
house this Russian restaurant with both cafeteria-style and full-menu
service. The European offerings include different kinds of salads and
well-prepared trout and pike-perch. If you want to try Russian cuisine
you can order traditional national dishes, such as pancakes with caviar,
or fish or meat in aspic, by phone beforehand. You can also order picnic
items here to eat on the palace's extensive grounds. Keep in mind that
the restaurant closes by 6 PM. ✉*Pavlovsk Palace* ☎812/470–9809
▭MC, V.

GATCHINA ГАТЧИНА

45 km (28 mi) southwest of St. Petersburg's city center.

The main attractions of Gatchina, the most distant of St. Petersburg's
palace suburbs, are an expansive park with a network of bridges for
island-hopping, and a grim-looking palace—actually more like a feudal
English castle—that has unfortunately been allowed to deteriorate over
the years. Perhaps because Gatchina doesn't hold the Imperial splendor
that's available in excess at the other suburbs, it's usually not included
in prearranged excursions, and thus is rarely visited by foreign tourists.
Because it does offer a chance to escape from the crowds for a while,
however, it's worth a visit. Keep in mind that fine dining is not widely
available, so be sure to bring along a lunch that you can enjoy on the
shores of Silver Lake.

The name Gatchina itself is of questionable origin. One popular sug-
gestion is that it comes from the Russian expression *gat chinit,* meaning
"to repair the road." Others believe it comes from the German phrase
hat schöne, meaning "it is beautiful." In its current state, both expres-
sions could apply. Gatchina, which is the name of both the city and the
park-palace complex, dates to the 15th century, when it was a small
Russian village. In 1712, following the final conquest of the area by
Russia, Peter I gave Gatchina to his sister, the tsarevna Natalya Alex-
eyevna. The land changed hands several times over the years, eventually ending up as a possession of Catherine the Great. She gave it to
one of her favorites, Count Grigory Orlov, in 1765. Orlov maintained
possession of the complex until 1783. It was during this period that the
architect Antonio Rinaldi designed and built the palace and laid out the

park, which was eventually decorated with obelisks and monuments in honor of the Orlovs.

In 1783 Orlov died, and Gatchina passed to Catherine's son, Paul I, and his wife. While Gatchina was in Paul's possession, the architect Vincenzo Brenna produced plans for the construction of the Eagle and Venus pavilions, the Birch House, and the Constable Column, which are scattered throughout the park. But at various times, Gatchina Palace was a residence of Nicholas I, Alexander II, and Alexander III, and it bears witness to many important historic events, as well as the political and personal secrets of the Romanov dynasty.

COUNT ORLOV

Count Grigory Orlov, the young, handsome, and kindhearted favorite of Catherine the Great, was also in love with his empress. Ready and willing to do anything for her, he headed the coup against Catherine's husband, Peter III, in 1762, which allowed Catherine to take the thrown. Orlov was also supposedly the father of Catherine's illegitimate son Alexei.

In contrast to the pastel colors and flashiness of the palaces of Pushkin and Peterhof, Gatchina Palace has the austere look of a military institution, with a restrained limestone facade and a blocklike structure almost completely bereft of ornamentation. The palace, which is built on a ridge, is also surrounded by a deep moat, which emphasizes the castle design of the facade. Its northern side faces a green forest tract stretching for some distance. The southern facade opens up to the main parade grounds, which were once used for military displays. Along the outer edge of the parade grounds runs a short bastion with parapets cut out with embrasures for firing weapons. The palace is also accentuated by two five-sided, five-story towers, the Clock Tower, and the Signal Tower.

Construction on the palace was carried out in three main phases. The first period began in 1766 under the guidance of Rinaldi. He built the three-story central part of the palace, as well as the service wings and the inner courtyards, known as the Kitchen Block and the Stable Block (later called the Arsenal Block). The second stage of construction began in 1783, when Brenna made the side blocks level with the galleries and installed cannons, adding to the palace's image as a feudal castle. Brenna also integrated new palatial halls, thus turning Rinaldi's chamberlike interiors into ceremonial rooms.

The third stage took place under the watchful eye of Nicholas I. He hired the architect Roman Kuzmin to reconstruct both side blocks between 1845 and 1856. He also built a new chapel, and living rooms were arranged in the Arsenal Block. Kuzmin's work also eventually led to the restoration of the 18th-century rooms, the construction of a new main staircase in the central section, and the reshaping of the bastion wall in front of the palace.

The palace was badly damaged during World War II, and restoration is still in progress (though you can still visit the palace). Fortunately, a collection of watercolors by the artists Luigi Premazzi and Edward

Hau survived. Painted during the 1870s, these watercolors are accurate depictions of the state- and private-room interiors, and have provided the information necessary for workers to restore the palace to its prewar condition. Within the palace you can see some partially restored rooms and exhibits of 19th-century arms and clothing.

A 10-minute walk from Gatchina Palace will bring you to Black Lake and the white **Prioratsky Palace,** a unique construction made of rammed earth. It was built at the end of the 18th century by architect Nikolai Lvov, the first person in Russia to introduce cheap, fireproof, rammed-earth construction. The palace was meant for the great French prior Prince Condé (though he never lived here). The southern part of the palace resembles a Gothic chapel, but the rest resembles a fortification. On the first floor are exposed samples of the rammed earth; the second floor has displays on the palace's construction.

After touring the palaces, you may want to consider heading down to the lakes for a little relaxation. Rowboats and catamarans are available at a cost of 100R for 30 minutes—just look for the bare-chested, tattooed men standing along the lake (you may also be asked to provide your passport as a deposit, just to make sure you actually return the boat instead of fleeing to Finland). The Gatchina park is laid out around a series of lakes occupying about one-third of its entire area. One of the largest sections of the park is called the **English Landscape Gardens** (Angliiskiye Sady), built around the White and Silver lakes. On a clear day the mirrorlike water reflects the palace facade and pavilions. The park is dotted with little bridges, gates, and pavilions, among which several are dedicated to the state and military deeds of the Orlov brothers. These include the Eagle (Orliny) Pavilion, built in 1792 on the shores of the Long Island, and the so-called Chesma Column, built by Rinaldi in honor of the Orlovs' military deeds. Keep in mind that the signs in the park are in Russian and point to eventual destinations, such as Berlin, but if you keep to the lakeshore at all times, you shouldn't have any trouble. ⊠ *1 Krasnoarmeisky pr.* ☎ *81371/93492 Gatchina Palace, 81371/76467 Prioratsky Palace* ✆ *Gatchina Palace and park 380R, Prioratsky Palace 120R* ☉ *Park, Gatchina Palace, and Prioratsky Palace Tues.–Sun. 10–5. Closed 1st Tues. of month.*

KRONSHTADT & VALAAM

Two islands, one to the west and one to the northeast of St. Petersburg, set a different tone than the palace suburbs but are still of historic significance. The town of Kronshtadt, on Kotlin Island, has a long and proud naval tradition, while the monasteries of Valaam Archipelago hark back to the earliest days of Christianity, more than a millennium ago, in the land of Rus'.

KRONSHTADT КРОНШТАДТ

30 km (19 mi) west of St. Petersburg.

CLOSE UP

Hydrofoils: Ships on Wings

Hydrofoils, or *meteory*, are a popular mode of transport in St. Petersburg, especially for visiting the city suburbs of Peterhof and Kronshtadt near the Gulf of Finland. A hydrofoil is essentially a ship that works on underwater wings, or hydrofoils, below the hull. As the ship picks up speed, the hull lifts off the water and the boat becomes "foilborne," creating less drag and allowing for even greater speed—they can go as fast as 80 kph (about 43 knots). Travel by hydrofoil from St. Petersburg to Peterhof takes only about half an hour. By car, the same trip may take up to an hour and a half to two hours with traffic. Aside from providing speed, the foil helps to stabilize the ship, making it more comfortable for passengers. As with any boat, however, they may not operate in bad weather. Hydrofoils are only available in the summer months, between June and September, as the Neva River freezes in winter.

4

Kronshtadt, on Kotlin Island to the west of St. Petersburg, was built between 1703 and 1704 by Peter the Great as a base from which to defend St. Petersburg or to attack the long-standing enemy of the Russian empire, the Swedish navy. For a long time it was the only military harbor of the empire, which is why it was off-limits to all but its permanent residents; visitors were stopped at special checkpoints as late as 1996. Today anyone can visit, either by boarding Bus 510 or the hydrofoil *Meteor* (both depart from St. Petersburg), or by taking an excursion from one of the agencies on St. Petersburg's Nevsky prospekt (between Gostinny Dvor and the old City Duma). If you take the bus you'll be traveling on a huge dike erected in 1979 where the Finnish border was until 1939.

In the first half of the 20th century the Kronshtadt "Commune" aimed to break the monopoly of the Communist Party and to give back to peasants the right to use their land freely; the revolt lasted two weeks, seriously jeopardizing Lenin's hold on power, but was finally bloodily repressed. Tellingly, the streets of Kronshtadt are still named after Marx and Lenin, and the town still seems to live in the past, as if to hold on to the mighty era of the Soviet military machine. Despite being in dire condition, Kronshtadt is proud of its naval pedigree. Its significance was gradually diminished by the development of St. Petersburg throughout the 19th century, but there are still military and scientific vessels using its harbors. Off the shore of Kotlin Island are several forts that were constructed during the Crimean War (1853–56). The most interesting of these is **Fort Aleksandr,** which in the 19th century was turned into a laboratory to research the bubonic plague. These days it's a favorite stop-off point for yachters sailing either from Kotlin Island or St. Petersburg; it also hosts the occasional evening dance in summer. One of Kronshtadt's highlights is its **Church of Seamen** (Morskoi Sobor), built between 1902 and 1913 by Vassili Kosyakov—the finest example of neo-Byzantine architecture in Russia. Other sights include the Gostinny Dvor (one of Kronshtadt's first buildings and now a department store in need of renovation), the Summer Garden, and the Menshikov Palace, now a club for the island's sailors.

VALAAM ARCHIPELAGO ВАЛААМСКИЙ АРХИПЕЛАГ

★ 170 km (105 mi) north of St. Petersburg, east along the Neva River, and up into Lake Ladoga.

An overnight trip by boat from St. Petersburg delivers you out of the bustle of the city and into the Republic of Karelia. The republic is one of the 88 federal subjects of the Russian Federation and though its language is Russian, it has close cultural ties to its neighbor, Finland. One of its most tranquil and beautiful settings is Valaam, a cluster of island jewels in the northwestern part of Lake Ladoga, Europe's largest freshwater lake, which is completely frozen over in winter. The southern part of the lake borders Russia. The archipelago consists of Valaam Island and about 50 other isles.

Valaam Island is the site of an ancient monastery said to have been started by Saints Sergey and German, missionaries who came to the region (probably from Greece) sometime in the second half of the 10th century—perhaps even before the "official" conversion of the land of the Rus' to Christianity. The next 1,000 years are a sorry story of Valaam and its monks battling to survive a regular series of catastrophes—including plague, fire, invasion, and pillage—only to bounce back and build (and rebuild) Valaam's religious buildings and way of life. In 1611 the monastery was attacked and razed by the Swedes; it languished for a century until Peter the Great ordered it rebuilt in 1715. Valaam was also to pass into the hands of Finland on more than one occasion, the longest period being from the end of World War I to 1940. After World War II, during which the islands were evacuated and then occupied by Finnish and German troops, the monasteries fell into almost total disrepair, and it was only in 1989 that monks returned to Valaam.

A guided tour of Valaam takes about six hours, although with a break for lunch this is not at all as arduous as it might sound. You can also buy a map of the island (easy to find at any of the many tourist shops here) and strike out on your own. But the tour guides, most of whom live on the island throughout the summer, have an enormous amount of interesting information to impart about Valaam (most, however, don't speak English). The guides also know where the best shady spots to sit and relax are, and while you catch your breath they will tell you everything about Valaam's history, prehistory, wildlife, geology and geography, religious life, and gradual renaissance as a monastic center. The island's beauty has also inspired the work of many Russian and foreign artists, composers, and writers; the second movement of Tchaikovsky's First Symphony is said to be a musical portrait of the island, and you will hear it played over loudspeakers as your ferry departs.

Most tours to Valaam spend the first half day on a small selection of the *skity,* a monastery in seclusion. Only four *skity* are currently used as places of worship, and some of them are in the archipelago's most remote areas. Closest to where the ferries dock is the **Voskresensky (Resurrection) Monastery,** consecrated in 1906. In the upper church, you can hear a performance of Russian liturgical music (for an extra 20R) performed by a rather good male quartet. Another monastery within easy walking distance is the **Getsemanskii (Gethsemene) monastyr** consisting of a wooden chapel and church built in a typically Russian style, and monastic cells, which are inaccessible to the public. The squat construction next door is a hostel for pilgrims, some of whom you may see draped in long robes on your walk.

After lunch, buy a ticket (100R for a round-trip ticket) for the ferry that will take you to the 14th-century **Spaso-Preobrazhensky Valaamskii (Transfiguration of the Savior) Monastyr,** the heart of the island's religious life. You can walk the 6 km (4 mi) from the harbor in either direction, but if you choose to walk back from the monastery, make sure you give yourself enough time to catch the ferry back to St. Petersburg (about 1¼ hours should be enough time to walk back). As you reach the monastery, you'll see tourist stands and beer kiosks—something about which the monks themselves have mixed feelings. The walk up the hill past the bric-a-brac, however, is well worth it, as you reach the splendid Valaamskii Monastyr cathedral (under ongoing restoration). The cathedral's lower floor is the **Church of St. Sergius and St. German,** finished in 1892, and is in the best condition. It's a living place of worship, as you'll see from the reverence of visitors before the large icon depicting Sergey and German kneeling before Christ. The upper **Church of the Transfiguration of the Savior,** consecrated in 1896, is still in a terrible state, although the cavernous interior, crumbling iconostasis, and remaining frescoes are still impressive in their own right.

■TIP➜ Although drinking and smoking are freely permitted in most areas of the island, you'll be asked to refrain while on the territory of the monasteries. Visitors are also required to observe the dress code on the grounds of the cathedral: women must wear a long skirt and cover their heads (scarves and inelegant black aprons are provided at the entrance for those who need appropriate garb), and men must leave their heads uncovered and wear long trousers—shorts are strictly forbidden.

You can only visit Valaam from June through September, when the waterway along the Neva River and Lake Ladoga is open. Note that the level of luxury on the 10-hour ferry journey to Valaam is not high. Nevertheless, you'll be witnessing a real throwback to the Soviet era. The rooms are clean, if spartan, and are perfectly manageable for two nights' sleep. In any case, you can spend much of the journey sitting on the sundeck; watch the industrial south of St. Petersburg give way to the rural setting of the lower Neva, before the ancient fort of Petrakrepost ghosts past on your right as the ferry sails into Lake Ladoga. The return journey is just as magical, as the golden spires and cupolas of the monasteries poke out of the tree line and glint in the setting sun.

■TIP➜ One crucial piece of advice is to take some food with you for your trip to Valaam. Although three meals are included in the price of most tours, they are best avoided. Instead, pack some sandwiches, fresh fruit, and perhaps some wine. You might want to poke your head into the incredibly Soviet bar on the island, but you are unlikely to want to linger. ⊕ *www. valaam.ru.*

SUMMER PALACES & HISTORIC ISLANDS ESSENTIALS

TRANSPORTATION

BY BUS

Though not as convenient and comfortable as train travel, travel by bus from St. Petersburg can be a good way to go as long as it's not the height of summer, when buses can be exceedingly stuffy. Buses or minibuses run on direct routes to almost all of the suburbs, as well as to Kronshtadt. Tour companies also operate their own, rather scruffy coaches, to Kronshtadt.

Although all the palaces are theoretically within walking distance from their respective train stations, there are often buses linking the two. Bus 1, 5, 7, 431, or 525 will take you to Gatchina from the station for 20R. You can also get to Gatchina Palace taking Bus 18 or 100 from the city's Moskovsky metro station for 50R. For Pavlovsk, should you for some reason not want to walk from the station through the lovely park to the palace, Bus 370 or 383 will take you directly there for 20R.

Minibuses (called *marshrutka*) from the city to the suburbs are more convenient than commuter trains (called *elektrichka*) because they usually take you directly to the sights. Minibuses 299, 286, and 545 will take you from St. Petersburg's Moskovskaya metro station to Pavlovsk for 30R. The same buses can take you to Pushkin for 30R. Bus 287 leaves Moskovskaya for Pushkin as well. Yellow double-decker buses marked "Peterhof" and minibuses 340 and 404 leave from outside St. Petersburg's Baltic station (Baltiisky Vokzal) for Peterhof, charging 40R. From Avtovo metro station you get to Peterhof train station by minibuses 424, 420, 300, 224 (for 30R); then take Bus 350, 351, 351a, 352, 353, 354, or 356 to the palace park for 20R. The ride lasts 10 minutes. Minibus 300 will take you to Lomonosov/Oranienbaum from Avtovo metro station as will Bus 340 from Baltic station (also Baltiyskaya metro station) for 30R.

To catch a bus to Kronshtadt, take the subway to St. Petersburg's Chernaya Rechka metro station; walk across ulitsa Savushkina to the embankment of the River Chernaya Rechka and catch Bus 405 or 406 for 40R to the very end. Buses leave every 3–5 minutes from 5:40 AM through midnight and take about an hour.

BY HYDROFOIL

June–September, the *Meteor* hydrofoil is the best way of getting from St. Petersburg to Peterhof, and it's also one of the options for traveling to Kronshtadt. It's possible to buy a ticket on the embankment the day that you would like to travel.

For Kronshtadt and Lomonosov, boats depart from St. Petersburg's naberezhnaya Makarova (Makarova Embankment), near the Tuchkov Bridge joining the Petrograd Side with Vasilievsky Island. For Peterhof, hydrofoils depart from the pier just outside the State Hermitage Museum in summer; they leave approximately every 30–40 minutes, and the journey time is about a half hour and costs about 200R for a one-way ticket. June–September, ferries to the Valaam Archipelago leave from 195 prospekt Obukhovskoy Oborony, not far from Proletarskaya metro station in the south of St. Petersburg. The journey takes around 10 hours.

BY TAXI

You'll usually have no trouble getting a taxi at a train or bus station in these towns. Most of the towns are small enough to be navigated easily on foot, but a taxi is an alternative to short bus or train trips (e.g., from Pushkin to Pavlovsk). In an emergency, it's also possible to take a taxi all the way back to St. Petersburg from most of these towns (about 900R–1,000R), if you speak Russian.

BY TRAIN

Do not be discouraged by the chaos of St. Petersburg's train stations, for traveling by *elektrichka* (commuter train) is not only to a certain extent a convenient way to get to the suburbs, it also provides a slice of authentic Russian life all on its own. Given the astonishingly low fares, the less than 45-minute journey time to most suburbs, and infrequent delays, train travel is well worth the minor discomforts of the press of humanity and hard wooden seats.

Check with a local travel agent or at the station for schedules. With the exception of traveling by elektrichka at busy times (Friday evening and weekends), you should not have trouble getting a ticket on the same day you wish to travel. For the most part, ticket booths are easy to find; if you don't speak Russian, just say the name of your destination and hold up as many fingers as there are passengers. Bear in mind that there's a lull in departures between 10 AM and noon.

The elektrichka to Gatchina leaves from Baltic station (42R); the trip lasts around 45 minutes. For Lomonosov, catch the elektrichka from Baltic station to Oranienbaum-I (not II), approximately one hour from St. Petersburg (60R). For Pavlovsk (28R) and Pushkin (36R), take the elektrichka from Vitebsk station to Detskoye Selo; the trip to Pavlovsk lasts approximately 30 minutes, and it's another 5 minutes to Pushkin (from which you'll have to walk 15–20 minutes to the palace). For Peterhof, take the elektrichka from Baltic station to Novy Peterhof (48R) station, approximately 40 minutes from St. Petersburg; from the station take one of the many buses (number 350, 351, 351a, 352, 353, 354, or 356) to the palace.

CONTACTS & RESOURCES

TOUR OPTIONS

There are several local tour groups congregated on St. Petersburg's Nevsky prospekt, and although they operate out of somewhat flea-bitten kiosks, they are good enough to get you to where you want to go in the suburbs. Usually, it's enough simply to step up and buy a ticket, the price of which includes coach seating and a guided tour in English, but you can also book in advance by visiting or phoning the tour-company offices.

Two of the most reliable excursion companies are Mir and Davranov-Travel. Mir, which specializes in serving foreign tourists, offers excursions to the whole list of St. Petersburg suburbs. For groups of less than six people Mir organizes a minivan (for more than six people, a microbus) that will take you to a suburb you choose. The company can also take you to Valaam and even to the old Russian town of Novgorod, known for its fascinating kremlin, and located 200 km (124 mi) from St. Petersburg (for 4,585R). Everything can be organized by phone. Davranov-Travel also offers excursions to all suburbs. You can buy tickets to their travel bus at their kiosk at the corner of Nevsky prospekt and ulitsa Sadovaya (it's outside Gostinni Dvor metro station). Usually they take you on the bus with Russian tourists but provide you with a guide who speaks English. It's less expensive if you're not alone. Buses of Davranov-Travel leave four times a day to each suburb from 10 AM through 2 PM. There are no buses to Pushkin on Tuesday, to Peterhof and Gatchina on Monday, and to Pavlovsk on Friday because the museums are closed these days.

Contacts **Mir** (✉ Office 1, 11 Nevsky prospekt, City Center ☎ 812/325–7122 or 812/380–6867 ⊕ www.mirtc.ru). **Davranov-Travel** (✉ 17 Italianskaya ul., City Center ☎ 812/571–8694 or 812/312–4662).

VISITOR INFORMATION

Any questions about the suburbs should be directed to officials at St. Petersburg's City Tourism Information Center (where operators are very helpful and speak English, French, and German) or private travel agencies and guided-tour companies. St. Petersburg's City Tourism Information Center also has an information kiosk at Palace Square.

Contact **City Tourist Information Center** (✉ 14/52 ul. Sadovaya, at Nevsky prospekt and ul. Sadovaya, City Center ☎ 812/310–2822, 812/310–2231 for information in English Ⓜ Nevsky Prospekt).